STRAPPED FOR CASH

M A C K   F R I E D M A N

STRAPPED FOR CASH

A HISTORY OF AMERICAN HUSTLER CULTURE

alyson books
los angeles

MANUFACTURED IN THE UNITED STATES OF AMERICA.

THIS TRADE PAPERBACK ORIGINAL IS PUBLISHED BY ALYSON PUBLICATIONS,
P.O. BOX 4371, LOS ANGELES, CALIFORNIA 90078-4371.
DISTRIBUTION IN THE UNITED KINGDOM BY TURNAROUND PUBLISHER SERVICES LTD.,
UNIT 3, OLYMPIA TRADING ESTATE, COBURG ROAD, WOOD GREEN, LONDON N22 6TZ ENGLAND.

FIRST EDITION: MAY 2003

03 04 05 06 07 a 10 9 8 7 6 5 4 3 2 1

ISBN 1-55583-731-X

LIBRARY OF CONGRESS CATALOGING-IN-PUBLICATION DATA
FRIEDMAN, MACK.
    STRAPPED FOR CASH : A HISTORY OF AMERICAN HUSTLER
CULTURE / MACK FRIEDMAN.—1ST ED.
    INCLUDES BIBLIOGRAPHICAL REFERENCES.
    ISBN 1-55583-731-X (PBK.)
    1. MALE PROSTITUTION—UNITED STATES—HISTORY.
2. MALE PROSTITUTION—HISTORY. I. TITLE.
HQ144.F66 2003
306.74'3—DC21   2003041842

CREDITS
• TEXT FROM THE ARCHIVAL COLLECTIONS OF THOMAS PAINTER AND DR. HARRY BENJAMIN AND FROM THE MANUSCRIPT DOM IN EXILE BY GUY STRAIT REPRINTED BY PERMISSION OF THE KINSEY INSTITUTE FOR RESEARCH IN SEX, GENDER, AND REPRODUCTION.
• AUTHOR PHOTOGRAPH COURTESY OF LESLEY FOSTER.
• COVER DESIGN BY MATT SAMS.

For my parents

And in memory of Benny, Hal, Michael, and Shawn

CONTENTS

ACKNOWLEDGMENTS

Many thanks to my family: Carol, Dan, George, Kate, Fay, Isaac, Matt, Michelle, Mika, and Nicky.

For initial encouragement, thanks to Lesley Foster, Brian Broome, Frederique Delacoste, Margo St. James, Priscilla Alexander, Michael Lowenthal, Raphael Kadushin, Alisa Dix, Greg Pierce, Justin Chin, Matt Bernstein Sycamore, Adrienne Walnoha, Sharon Bernstein, and Scott Brassart.

For gracious archival assistance, many thanks to staff at the following research centers: Brown University Library (Mark Brown), The Kinsey Institute for Research in Sex, Gender, and Reproduction (Shawn C. Wilson, Liana Zhou, and Catherine Johnson), the ONE Institute (Mischa Schutt and Pat Allen), the Northern California Gay, Lesbian, Bisexual, and Transgender Historical Society (Willy Walker and Susan Stryker), the HIV Center for Clinical and Behavioral Research (Lucia O'Sullivan and Charles Klein), the University of Pittsburgh Health Sciences Library (Ammon Ripple), the Swarthmore College Peace Collection (Wendy Chmielewski), the New York Public Library, the New-York Historical Society, the Lilly Library at Indiana University, the Andy Warhol Museum, and the Canadian Lesbian and Gay Archives.

For careful readings of draft chapters, thanks to Henry L. Minton, Joanne Meyerowitz, D. Michael Quinn, P. Jayne Bopp, Thomas Waugh, John Encandela, Caroline Acker, Scott Sandage, Brian Funk, and Nick Street.

For their time and insight, thanks to Karen Trondson, Connie Sponsler-Garcia, Don LeTorneau, Michael Kaplan, Shannon Smith, G. Cajetan Luna, John Rechy, J.T. LeRoy, Bruce Benderson, Shira Hassan, Stuart Fisk, Joyce Hunter, April Weiss, and Win Smith.

For inspiration and candor, thanks to Aaron, Jazmine, Juan, Kristen, Todd, Rob, Shafrika, Ray, Antonio, Doc, Wes, Ryan, Al, Candy, Lisa, Jeremy, Selece, Jonathan, Newcomer, Shane, Dev, Edwin, Angel, Jason, and Dimitri.

INTRODUCTION
A POPULAR HISTORY OF AN UNPOPULAR SUBJECT

When I was 13, and in 8th grade, one of my best friends was a kid named Eric. He had alopecia—premature, uneven balding—which he wore as a punk cut: the back half shaved off and long blond hair flopping over his forehead. We were in an air band called the Imposters. Our tennis rackets were guitars. Eric lived with his mom in a ramshackle apartment close to some railroad tracks, in a sketchy part of town on the "bad side" of the Milwaukee River. He sat next to me during assemblies. The lump crawling down a leg of his corduroys riveted me. One day before school, Eric asked me if I knew what a blow job was. I said, Yeah, I thought so. Wasn't it when someone blew on your dick? He just glanced at me sidelong and cracked a crooked smile. "It's when someone sucks you," he clarified. "And I just got one on my paper route."

"You did?" I asked, stunned. I looked around the playground to make sure nobody had heard.

"Yeah," he said. "At this one house. The guy always gives me a blow job when it's time to collect. You should come with me sometime."

Back then I demurred. But I knew I was hooked. That summer, we hung out, smoked pot, and walked along the railroad tracks to a paper plant, where we freed surplus porn from hog-tied bales.

I didn't see Eric much after that summer. He got shipped off to military school. After school and on weekends, I flirted with guys at health clubs and received propositions to model. "You'd have to come to my house," one man said. "You'd be a great model. How much would you charge?" I smiled, walked away. A boy on my soccer team reported that a guy had approached him in the second-floor restroom at the college union and offered him a blow job plus ten bucks. I memorized the rumored nooks where these things happened. Soon I graduated to jerking off freely with men in park bathrooms. It was 1986 and AIDS was making headlines. I didn't do much more because I was scared and didn't need extra money. As a Midwestern kid in the 1980s, my basic context for "gay" enjoined prostitution, intergenerational public sex, and HIV.

The library books I read furtively during high school and college shared these associations. Putting off homework, I'd canvas sexuality sections for *The Boys of Boise*, an account of teenage hustlers in the 1950s, or *The Sexual Offender and His Offenses*, a compendium of deviant sexual behavior that contained a section on boy prostitutes of the 1930s. My searches were motivated by lust more than learning. Still, they gave me ideas.

Back on campus, a queer group had formed. They were mostly identifiable by SILENCE=DEATH T-shirts. Instead of joining them, I moved off-campus and found a job cleaning apartments in a jockstrap with an organization called the Hot Jock Cleaning Service. The owners had placed a help-wanted ad in *Au Courant*, the first gay newspaper I had ever read. To supplement this sporadic income, I joined an escort agency also listed in the classifieds.

I was broke, impetuous, and horny. I wanted to be independent. I wanted to find out what having sex with men was like. I wanted to *be* those narratives I had found so sleekly dangerous in high school. In the hours leading up to my first appointment, I saw myself as Ganymede—the shepherd who became a demigod after Zeus abducted him. I imagined it was April 25, 100 C.E., and I was a Roman servant celebrating the national holiday for male prostitutes.[1] I pretended I was a street urchin hired as a model-catamite by Caravaggio, who would gently encircle his crimson oils around the arrows glued to my chest.[2] In my cramped bathroom, I was Keanu Reeves, fresh from *My Own Private Idaho*. I practiced my notion of a Boise accent. But I was only a sexed-up, naive kid from Wisconsin, still in the closet, and strapped for cash. I shook my jeans halfway down my ass. The mirror liked what it saw, wanted more.

My first appointment turned out to be a threesome. The other young escort smelled acrid, like subway steam. The client reeked sweetly of poppers. The pimp and his administrative assistant watched us coalesce from the balcony. I felt like a deer in track lighting. The client commanded me to take down the escort's pants and give him a blow job. Reality sunk in, that nothing was going to happen the way I wanted it to, that I was not in control of events, or even myself. I was naked on a convertible couch with two strangers, one arm over my eyes as if I was on a nude beach and just shading my face from the sun. It was tacky and unpleasant, but I was sure it could get better. I didn't think about it getting worse.

My next appointment was an in-call. A boisterous, self-loathing, obese businessman came over to my apartment, blew the joints off my loft, called me names, and tried to pinion me to my mattress. My neighbors looked at me funny after that. To avoid shared hallways, I started to come and go by the rear fire escape. This led into a parking lot filled with transgender street workers at night and crushed crack vials by morning. I remember hoping I was better than they were because I didn't work the streets. But they were nicer to me than anyone else around my building. I'd fall asleep to their hoots and catcalls.

The stripper-cleaning agency was no great shakes, but clients were nicer and I felt more legit. (Andy, a cute, young eye doctor from Manila, kept his apartment spotless. "You don't have anything I can clean!" I said, looking confusedly at my supply bucket. "That's OK," he said, "we can do other things." And we did—though I refused to charge him after that.) The only thing was, it was a new business, and there weren't many gigs.

A few weeks later I joined another escort agency, run by a man who bred Persian cats. That was better: He treated his boys like prize felines. He understood my rules and assigned me appropriate clients. I also did sensual massages at his place: hard work, good fun. I got to know a few regulars over the next several months. Many were openly gay, but even married, closeted ones with kids were generally sweet and friendly. They wanted to talk while someone in skimpy briefs listened to them and rubbed them down. I made $60 an hour for those massages. I was wiser by then, and that helped. More importantly, the guy who ran the outfit didn't take any crap from his clients. Plus, I loved his kittens.

I made few friends in sex work, and no lasting ones. I took to hanging out with Edwin, a street hustler who worked around my building at Sixteenth and Lombard in Philadelphia. I met him one night as I walked home from a massage call. Once, screaming and bloodied, Edwin rang my bell, claiming that a trick had beaten him up and insisting that I take photographs. I helped him out, but he never wound up reporting the incident. The last time I saw him, he told me he had gotten evicted. He was crying. I told my school I was dropping out, left Edwin my television, and went on a road trip. I never moved back.

I came out to my family and moved to Minneapolis, where I finished college. I found employment as an outreach worker for homeless and runaway youth with a consortium called StreetWorks. My focus was on male and transgender youth in prostitution. In Loring Park, I met dozens of adolescent sex workers. I was still working out my own issues, and was probably of limited assistance to my clients. Still, they helped me understand our common motivations and experiences, and I helped them find access to condoms, clean works, education, employment services, counseling, housing, food, health care, drug treatment, and legal representation.

I understood that hustling could be dismal and terrifying, but I didn't believe it had to be. Was that just the American way? I reread the accounts I'd romanticized in high school, and began to research the working conditions hustlers have historically faced. It can always get worse: In 3rd century Rome, under an edict from Theodosius I, male prostitutes were pulled from brothels and burned alive before cheering mobs.[3]

I feel ambivalent about sex work. On the one hand, sexual commerce is necessary and useful, an inevitable byproduct of capitalism. Hustling strolls can be sexy, thrilling, and socially vital; they are historical sites of Americana, holding legacies that often go back 50 years or more. On the other hand, sex work is often exploitative, and the streets are incredibly dangerous.

Throughout Western European and American history, male and transgender prostitutes have traditionally been slaves, servants, and menial laborers, members of the underclass. These workers' social conditions have been subject to widely varying cultural restrictions that chafed most during periods of binding dogma. For the last 400 years, the dominant conservative Protestant culture has reviled sexual relations between American men, thereby exacerbating danger and distorting pleasure. In one of the curious paradoxes typical of religious orthodoxy, this pattern of social repression has both nurtured and sought to eradicate male and transgender sex work. Since the early 1800s, male and trans sex work has been popularly represented as a trade only for the terribly decadent or the innocently victimized. But there are multiple dimensions to the phenomenon. Hustling has meant freedom, sexual exploration and expression, and community; yet it has also meant restriction, sexual risk and violence, and isolation.

The subject has not been easy to research. Because of the scarcity of source material, and because of the charged nature of many of the remaining documents, it seemed pointless to write about cultural representation without also providing a more comprehensive history. This patchwork study covers the ways in which male and transgender sex work has been impressed upon the masses, an impression that has become a sort of folklore. As references to male and transgender sex work become more common in the 20th century, I have used different methods of investigation, including anthropology and sociology, media analysis, gender and gay studies, medical history, photographic and literary criticism, and public health review.

The Western tradition of sexual repression and the concomitant need for secrecy have occluded much of gay history. Accordingly, I have tried to avoid simple explanations for cultural phenomena that occur for complex and often hidden reasons. To give ample space to the personal histories I uncovered during my research, I chose to elaborate on some of the most compelling themes in the notes that accompany each chapter.

From the more than 50 oral histories I conducted for this project I have chosen to include only a dozen or so. I believed every word my interview subjects told me, even when I knew they were lying. Sometimes the truth is too painful to reveal or too elusive to pin down with words. The essence of experience, rather than abstract truth, is what I worked to capture in these pages.

The most comprehensive archive for research into male sex work in the United States is housed in the library at the Kinsey Institute for Sex, Gender, and Reproduction. I was especially grateful for the Kinsey library's collection of correspondence, books, essays, and photos donated by Thomas Painter, a researcher of American male prostitution from the 1930s to the 1970s. If I have sometimes relied too heavily on the Painter Papers, I offer my apologies: I was entranced by Painter's wit, honesty, and robust sexuality, as well as his unmatched insight.

I hope you find all of the material contained in this book as absorbing as I do and that you might learn some things along the way.

---

[1] SEE GARY DEVORE, "ECHOES OF GANYMEDE: MALE PROSTITUTION IN ANCIENT ROME." *BLACK SWAN REVIEW*, 1997.

[2] SEE JOHN BOSWELL, *THE KINDNESS OF STRANGERS*. UNIVERSITY OF CHICAGO PRESS, 1998.

[3] DAUPHIN, CLAUDINE. "BROTHELS, BATHS, AND BABES: PROSTITUTION IN THE BYZANTINE HOLY LAND." *CLASSICS IRELAND*, VOL. 3; UNIVERSITY COLLEGE (DUBLIN), 1996.

one

In ancient and premodern Western Europe, sex between men was primarily sanctioned between upper-class adults and underclass youth, and it often took the form of prostitution. Abandoned boys and desperate young men prostituted in public spaces such as parks, amphitheaters, brothels, bathhouses, and city streets from classical Athens to premodern Paris.[1] In precolonial North America, Native Americans developed various roles that integrated puberty rites, gender transgression, and sexual provision. The *mujerado,* the *berdache,* and the *coniurer* were spiritually revered and offered a noncommercial, nonspousal sexual outlet for men in their tribes. But in the early 1600s, puritanical sexual taboos invaded Virginia. Colonial sodomy codes (in which sexual contact between males was punishable by death) were established as early as 1610.[2] Evidence of male and transgender sex work in the days of American colonists and pioneers survives in judicial documents, prison lore, early newspapers, medical journals, and social reform reports. The Puritans' fear and hatred of homosexuality is preserved in these documents as well.

Scandalous Imputations: Unsettled Puritans, 1607-1677

John Smith settled in Jamestown in June 1607. The journey had been rough from the get-go. "On the 19 of December, we set sail," wrote Smith, "but by unprosperous winds, were kept six weeks in the sight of England."[3] On the ship were more than 100 men and boys (sailors, settlers, and servants), but no women. There was a strong European legacy of intimacy between men at sea; all-male crews commonly spent years away from home ports. In 17th-century England, boys were expected to leave home at the age of 10 to serve as apprentices. These apprenticeships were often seasonal, and boys were subject to their masters' whims. Fleeing abusive masters, many relied on their wits and bodies to secure steady employment on ships.[4]

On the streets of Stuart England, runaway boys joined beggar bands.[5] These wandering teenage vagabonds were well versed in homosexual practice, using it as an initiation rite. Most bands traveled southeasterly, toward Atlantic ports, where they might be conscripted for service or find employment on merchant vessels.[6]

From Britain's poorest classes, these destitute boys often rejected their sovereign flag to become pirates and buccaneers in the New World. Once on the pirate ship, English runaway boys discovered sexual conditions similar to their beggar band experiences. Caribbean buccaneers engaged in a practice called *matelotage,* a commonplace and often coercive form of male prostitution. Young *matelots* were expected to perform sexual favors for buccaneers, who in turn taught their apprentices the ropes.[7]

It is not surprising that Puritan colonists should have found these young sailors so highly suggestive. John Smith ruefully recalled that neither "the storm's weather nor the *scandalous imputations...*could rejuvenate the ship's sole preacher."[8] The journey had taken seven months, and the colonists had depleted their provisions. Once ashore, America's first English settlers scrounged what they could from mercenary sailors, who were happy to trade goods for sex. Detailing "the sailers' abuses" from the time the colonists disembarked to the day the ships left again for England, Smith wrote:

> *Being thus left to our fortunes, it fortuned that within tenn da[y]s scarse ten amongst us coulde...stand, such extreame weaknes and sicknes oppressed us. And thereat none need mar[vel], if they consider the cause and reason, which was this; whilest the ships sta[y]ed, our allowance was somewhat bettered, by a daily proportion of bisket which the sailers would pilfer to sell, give or exchange with us, for money, saxefras, furs, or love.[9]*

Jonathan Ned Katz confirms that "'love,' seemingly meaning sexual favors, was something that colonists first exchanged...to keep themselves alive."[10] Katz asserts that "love" referred to sacrificing one's body, and linguistically carried classical pederastic connotations.[11]

While acknowledging their impoverishment (their only remaining food was worm-addled barley and wheat), and their endless toil, the Jamestown colonists had (irrationally) linked sex trading and sickness.[12] The indelible notion that male sex work causes disease has been part of America's collective unconscious since the arrival of the first English settlers. We will see this notion roll through this history, collecting derogatory metaphors like sticks as it snowballs.

Mindful of the earliest settlers' experiences, generations of colonists set down sodomy laws that punished the act by execution. Between 1610 and 1740, colonial courts executed a total of four men for committing sodomy; only 19 were prosecuted.[13] Courts rarely prosecuted cases involving sexual contacts between masters and their male slaves and indentured servants, implicitly sanctioning *matelotage* and its onshore equivalent.[14] But two relevant cases did go to court. The first case, whereby ship's master Richard Cornish was executed for screwing his steward, was very much a byproduct of the Jamestown's colonists' shipboard fears.

In late August 1624 (or 1625), the good ship Ambrose was anchored in the James River. Cornish had been drinking, and he called his steward, 29-year-old William Cowse, to "lay a clean pair of sheet into his bed." Cowse did this, and prepared to leave. Cornish asked his steward whether he would join him in bed, but was refused. Cornish got up suddenly and approached William Cowse. He grabbed and cut Cowse's codpiece. Then the ship's master "made Cowse go into the bed, and then Cornish went into the bed with him, and there lay upon him, and kissed him and hugged him, saying that he would love Cowse if he would now and then come and lay with him, and so by force he turned Cowse upon his belly, and so did put Cowse to pain in the fundament, and did wet him, and after did call for a napkin which Cowse did bring unto him."[15]

On another occasion, Cornish suggested that Cowse might be a good seafarer if he allowed interactions like this with captain and crew, and thrust his hands into his steward's codpiece.[16] When the young man stopped heeding his master's requests, Cornish ordered Cowse to cook the crew's meals, and then exiled him from the dining area. The General Court sentenced Cornish to death for sodomy, and he was hanged at the town gallows.

In a similar case, some 50 years later, Windsor aristocrat Nicholas Sension faced a Connecticut court pursuant to complaints made by his indentured servant, Nathaniel Pond. In 1677, Nathaniel's older brother Isaac explained that his teenage brother initially fought his master's "grossly lascivious carriages towards him." Sension's "unseemly manner" and his "attempts tending to sodomy" had required Nathaniel to either submit or to fight off his master.[17] Samuel Barboe, a man from the town, remembered that Sension "proffered me a bushel of corn if I would put down my breeches."[18] Another witness, Peter Buoll, was offered gunpowder:

> [Sension] told me if I would let him have one bloo at my breech he would give me a charge of powder.

And when my breeches were down he threw me upon my belly and would have committed the Sin of Sodom with me; but when I perceived what he was about I resisted him out of shame, not knowing the use of the thing.[19]

Removing his pants, Buoll curiously agreed to the exchange, only reneging when Sension changed the sexual terms.

Following an intervention arranged by a leading Windsor aristocrat, Nathaniel Pond was given a year off and 40 shillings as recompense "for his abuse."[20] He decided to stay on with his master, who had raised the boy since he was an orphaned infant. Nathaniel Pond received an education and became more intimately involved with his master, according to several of Mr. Sension's servants.

Daniel Saxton, the primary witness, "saw Nicholas Sension come to bed with Nathaniel Pond and make the bed shake." John Moses, who reported being fondled by Sension while sharing a bed with Nathaniel, said that Sension "returned back again to the other side of the bed where Nathaniel Pond lay, and called softly to [him]."[21] There is no direct testimony from Nathaniel Pond in this trial, as he was killed in 1676, fighting in King Philip's War.

Nicholas Sension was found guilty of sodomy. His assets were placed into escrow for the remainder of his life, under the proviso that his wealth would return to his family unless he further tarnished his legal record by "infecting the rising generation."[22] Although he was married, Sension fathered no children. Katz argues that "his relatively lenient sentence...may be due to his wealth, high status, and personal favor in the community."[23]

The Sension case is indicative of colonial sex work, commissioned by wealthy landowners in exchange for food, goods, and shelter. "Servants were vulnerable to sexual abuse by their masters, although their rights as free men and women offered at least the possibility of legal recourse against such abuse," wrote historian Richard Godbeer about the 1700s.[24] (Of course, Southern slaves were not offered any recourse at all.)[25] Sex work was, in many cases, a condition of employment for servants. Slavery, indentured servitude, and *matelotage* gave sanction to male sex work in the British North American colonies throughout the 17th and 18th centuries.

Evil Name and Fame: Harbored Boys, 1816-1817

European immigrants flocked to New York in the 18th and 19th centuries, arriving on Ellis Island and settling on Manhattan Island. In such a large urban center, commercial prostitution flourished and soon lost the relative formality of master-servant coupling. Entrepreneurs opened their houses to women, and sometimes boys, willing to engage in sex for money. These proprietors were, however, subject to state laws against whoring. On February 20, 1816, a woman named Lettice Matthews filed a complaint against her neighbor, Mary Hassan, for allowing Matthews' young son in Hassan's bawdy house. It appears that Mary held some power over young John, which makes the case compelling. Matthews' complaint follows:

> *City of New York for Lettice Matthews wife of Robert Matthews of No. 53 Banoker St. Being duly sworn says that a woman calling herself Mary Hassan...now keeps and for some time last past has kept a House for the resort of womans generally called and denoted Common Prostitutes and also for the reception of young men and apprentice boys that they frequently remain in her House at all hours of the night drinking tipling quarrelling and disturbing the peace, deponent further says that she has frequently taken her son a boy aged about 17 years named John Matthews from the House of said Mary Hassan and has likewise requested the said Mary not to harbour deponents son, but the said* **Mary continues to harbour him and declares that she will keep him in her place whenever she pleases.** *Wherefore deponent prays that Mary may be contrained to answer the charges.[26]*

We can read Matthews' account in two ways. Lettice may have been worried about young John hanging around a disorderly house, drinking with the boys and paying the girls for sex. But she may have been more concerned about the possibility of

Mary Hassan's pandering John, for she made no complaint about her son's spending any money at the bawdy house. It is likely that Hassan kept John Matthews, against his mother's wishes, as a resident boy. Given her declaration that "she will keep him in her place whenever she pleases," Hassan's authority over the teenager had the ring of a madam's dictum.

Since the language of New York's disorderly house statute did not distinguish between male and female prostitution, we cannot know for sure whether young John Matthews was prostituting. A year later, two men—one named James Pessinger, and one identified only as "Smith"—were charged with the same crime as Mary Hassan: keeping and maintaining "a certain common, ill-governed and disorderly house." Pessinger and Smith were formally charged with maintaining houses "for their own lucre and gain," where "certain persons, as well men as women, of evil name and fame, and of dishonest conversations" were compelled "[to] come together."[27] This confusing phraseology encompassed a variety of social vices. The words suggest that males as well as females were generally present in disorderly houses (though of course the males were usually customers rather than employees or "inmates"). Authorities could cite a house as disorderly as long as guests were "drinking, tippling, gambling, whoring, and misbehaving themselves."

Pessinger's and Smith's young guests might not have misbehaved in the summer of 1817; their hosts were ultimately acquitted of this charge. Still, the story is intriguing, for Smith was identified as a mulatto, and his guests were a commingling of male, female, black, and white. The court document from June 10, 1817, reads:

> City of New York p.[resents] Walter McDonald ...being duly sworn deposeth and saith that Smith a Mulatto man now keeps and for some time past has kept and maintained a disorderly House commonly called a Bawdy House where the said Smith causes to come together members of men and women of evil name and fame and Dishonest conversations...both black and white men and women and among [them] quite young boys whom the said Smith permits to be there tippling cursing and swearing and as Deponent believes whoring.[28]

The deponent obviously believed the "quite young boys" joined the crowd in whoring. But in this case, "whoring" could only clearly connote promiscuity; it's unclear whether the term also included paying for sex, getting paid for sex, or having free sex with nonspousal partners.

Despite their ambiguities, these two cases offer tantalizing evidence of mixed-race and mixed-gender brothels in New York City in the early 1800s. Historian Timothy Gilfoyle asserts that several female brothels in mid 1800s New York City were prosecuted for "'harboring' young boys (in contrast to 'abducting'), possibly for the purposes of letting them prostitute with male clients."[29] In the unusual event that a resident boy was prosecuted and sent to the reformatory, chances were he would have learned a few new tricks.

Kinshon and Punks: Pens and Goths, 1824-1892

Louis Dwight's 1826 missive to a legislator about postcolonial penal conditions underscored the larger society's social intolerance for intimacies between men:

> Since October, 1824, I have visited most of the prisons on two routes, between Massachusetts and Georgia, and large number of Prisons besides, in the New England States and New York. Juvenile Delinquents have been subjects of particular consideration, in all these visits; and I have found melancholy testimony to establish one general fact, viz. THAT BOYS ARE PROSTITUTED TO THE LUST OF OLD CONVICTS.
>
> I am aware that the mere suggestion of this subject, is so revolting, that we should gladly omit the further consideration of it; but if we would meet the evil and remove it, we must give our attention to the facts.
>
> I have seen boys in Prison, of a very tender age, who had no natural deformity, who were among the most unnatural and deformed objects, which I ever saw. The peculiar skin, the strained and sunken eye, the distorted mouth and head, and the general expression of the countenance; as if God had impressed the mark of the beast upon them, for unnatural crime; were things, which I did not understand, till I learned, that the SIN OF SODOM IS THE VICE OF PRISONERS, AND BOYS ARE THE FAVORITE PROSTITUTES....
>
> Another witness, who is a respectable man...writes in answer to my question as follows.... "Boys are said to be kept and rewarded; and I have frequently heard [men] say, they were forced to give up their **Kinshon,** (which is the name given to a boy thus prostituted,) for want of funds."[30]

Apparently, sexual conduct in the American penal system hasn't changed much in the last 200 years.

If Dwight's letter offers an accurate portrayal of American jails in 1824, we may reasonably conclude that intergenerational sex exchange between men was a common feature of prison life from the earliest days of the Republic. How did these conditions arise? Prisoners were segregated by gender, but not by age or class affiliation. The only outlets for conjugal activity were with other male inmates. In addition, patriarchal social conventions imposed a distinction between what Katz calls the *emissive* and the *passive,* a boundary that promoted "feminine" affectations and contrived hypermasculinities.[31]

While economic and class differences were irrelevant to prison life, there remained a dramatic disparity in the degree of safety, respect, and (relative) freedom each prisoner could expect during his incarceration. Older, more experienced convicts could offer these intangibles to juveniles in exchange for a sexual relationship structured to resemble heterosexual conduct. Male sex work enjoined the elder partner with the duties of warder and rewarder. The youth's job description was simpler. He was expected to be loyal and compliant. As we learned in Louis Dwight's correspondence, prison youth were called *kinshon,* an interesting descriptor. Etymologically, the word derives from *kinchin,* itself a corruption of the German *kindchen,* a word analogous to the ancient Greek *pais*: children of the community who do favors for adults.[32] The word's evolution into convict slang emphasizes the variably parental, affectionate, sleazy, and idly protective role older convicts took when with the *young'ns.*

Dwight himself used several notable descriptors. The boys were not naturally (or congenitally) deformed; they were *un*naturally deformed, apparently as a result of their nonprocreative sexual activities. These kids were strained, sunken, tender, distorted, peculiar, and, above all, unnatural. It is unfortunate that Dwight, who ostensibly wrote his letter to rescue imprisoned youths from sexual servitude, treated them, at least semantically, more contemptuously than did their cellmates. The sex-exchanging young delinquents to whom Dwight devoted his letter had been bitten by werewolves, bore the mark of the beast, and threatened to pass their disease to others. Gothic tenets still hold strong today, forging an implicit cultural link between behavior and illness—a link the mainstream media often uses to justify its depiction of sex workers as vectors of infection.

Of course, sex workers *could* be vectors of sexually transmitted infections. An unusually objective account of this kind of transmission examined a Baltimore reform school where, in 1886, Dr.

Randolph Winslow administered treatment to boys between 9 and 21 years of age:

> For a long time sodomy had been practiced to some extent in the institution, but without any especially ill results in regard to health. The younger boys were generally selected to take the part of the female, usually for some substantial benefit, as a piece of tobacco, candy, or other delicacy, or a reciprocation of the favor.[33]

One unfortunate Baltimore boy was infected with gonorrhea while on leave. He effectively transmitted it to others before the boys were prohibited from having sex with one another, a measure that stopped the mini-epidemic. Ironically, Gothic opprobrium rang true in this case, neatly fitting the boys' beliefs about the effects of anal sex. When they reluctantly confessed to "buggery," they readily "attributed the disease to it."[34]

Similar Gothic metaphors pervaded American sexual mores in the 1800s. The *Whip,* a popular New York tabloid, referred to men who had sex with men as "beasts who follow that unhallowed practice."[35] In the latter half of the 1800s, penal and hobo culture spawned the primally charged terms *wolf,* for an active partner, and *punk,* which referred to the younger, presumably passive sexual recipient.

Alexander Berkman, an anarchist serving time in a Pittsburgh prison for attempting to assassinate steel baron Henry Clay Frick in 1892, talked congenially with "George," a convict wise to the ways of pederasty and onanism. George told Berkman that "those kids [sent to the penitentiary directly] from the reformatories...they are terrible. You can spot them by looking at them. They are worse than street prostitutes."[36] Referring to transgender sex work in the prison, Berkman wrote that George, who preferred unsullied youths, was "very bitter against the prison element variously known as 'girls,' 'Sallies,' and 'punks,' who *for gain* traffic in sexual gratification."[37]

In this case, the language used to describe transgender sex work was related to business interests rather than to physical or emotional needs, and it correlated to the passive role prostitute boys played in prison society. Like Roman slaves on the auction block, American prison boys learned the rewards of prettifying themselves in order to appeal to older inmates.[38] (In the late 1800s, Pittsburgh's penitentiary economy provided "de weed," and if you had "de dough," you could "buy anything 'cept booze.")[39]

Berkman couldn't believe the America described by his cellmates. Another convict, known as "Red," claimed that the nation was "chuckful of punks. It's done in every prison, an' on th' road, everywhere. Lord," the hobo told Berkman, "if I had a plunk for every time I got th' best of a kid, I'd rival Rockefeller, sir." The same incarcerated hobo traced this use of *punk* to Shakespeare. "Ever read Billy Shakespeare? Know the place, 'He's neither man nor woman; he's punk.' Well, Billy knew. A punk's a boy that'll...Give himself to a man." This disturbed even the staunch anarchist. "The panegyrics of boy-love are deeply offensive to my instincts," Berkman wrote.[40]

The Man-Monster: Trannies and Metaphors, 1836-1842

Monstrous and demonic representations of prostitutes can be traced back to Europe in the Middle Ages, when female sex workers were often considered succubi or vampires. In the 14th century, "demon streetwalkers were said to have been everywhere, painted, jeweled, seductively attired, and doing a thriving business among the clergy."[41] The American Gothic version crawled out of its medieval coffin as early as the 1830s, when African-American, transgender prostitute Peter Sewally (using the aliases Mary Jones and Eliza Smith) was arrested, in full drag, in connection with grand larceny. This charge stemmed from an incident on June 14, 1836, when Jones had sex in an alleyway with a stranger, Robert Haslem. During their tryst, she allegedly lifted Haslem's wallet from his pocket. She hit the jackpot with that heist: Haslem claimed that his wallet had contained "99 dollars in Bank Bills" (equal to a few thousand of today's dollars) and "Omnibus Stage Tickets, worth about Two Dollars."[42] And as a coup de grâce, Mary smartly replaced Haslem's pocketbook with another man's wallet.[43]

When Haslem discovered the theft, he notified a beat cop, Constable Bowyer. Later that evening, Bowyer tracked Mary Jones down on her Bowery stroll. He pretended to go along with her suggestions, acting the part of the trick. The constable followed Jones into the same alleyway near her Green Street lodgings, then arrested her. When he frisked her, he realized she was actually a man. She appeared for testimony in full drag, which was probably ordered by a highly amused court, as masquerade laws would ordinarily have prohibited such a display.[44]

As evidence mounted, Jones found herself labeled "The Man-Monster" by the tabloids.[45] The court learned she lived in a female brothel on Green Street, where she served as cook, cleaner, and hostess, among other duties. The Man-Monster sensation revealed the limits of 19th-century American tolerance for male and transgendered sex workers. The public tolerated female prostitution much more readily than sodomy or cross-dressing. The Sewally-Jones-Smith case is an example of the fluid world of antebellum sex work, where boys, trans folk, and women were often employed by the same houses and worked the same streets. Never mind that Peter/Mary/Eliza had "always attended parties of the people of [her] own color dressed in this way." This gender-bending was, according to the media, monstrous.

New York tabloids reported the case to an eagerly appalled public. The *Herald* asserted that "Sewally has for a long time past been doing a fair business, both in money making and *practical* amalgamation, under the cognomen of *Mary Jones*."[46] The *Sun*, another tabloid, went on to claim that

> [Peter Sewally] generally promenades the street, dressed in a dashing suit of male apparel, and at night prowls about the five points and other similar parts of the city, in the disguise of a female, for the purpose of enticing men into the dens of prostitution, where he picks their pockets if practical, an art in which he is a great

THE MAN-MONSTER,

Peter Sewally, alias Mary Jones &c&c.

Sentenced 18th June 1836. to 5 years imprisonment at hard labor at Sing Sing for Grand Larceny

Published by H R Robinson. 48. Courtlandt St. N Y

fig. 1.1 "The Man Monster—Peter Sewally, Alias Mary Jones," Collection of the New-York Historical Society, negative #40697.

adept.... Owing to the scruples of the complainants against exposing themselves in the Court...they have generally abandoned their complaints, and their stolen money, watches, etc. On this occasion, however, the complainant, to recover his money, mustered courage enough to stand the brunt of the trial.[47]

The public's avidity for the case had more to do with the element of sexual deception than with prostitution. The media's sensational coverage of the case focused on Sewally's subversion of rigid social and economic hierarchies. As Katz puts it, Sewally as Mary Jones was "working the race, class, sexuality, and gender systems to appropriate...a little of the wealth of white men."[48] Sewally was ultimately sentenced to five years in a federal prison for stealing Haslem's thick pocketbook.

Gilfoyle infers from this case that "certain forms of homosexuality, even male prostitution, were probably tolerated and linked to the brothel subculture during these years."[49] We might also conclude that while a culture of transgender sex work pervaded street life in New York City—and quite probably in other metropolises, like New Orleans—the nature of media attention to cases such as Sewally's suggests gender and sexual transgression met with outrage as often as they met with tolerance.

Titillating reportage in the *Whip* and the *Rake* occasionally referred to male and transgender prostitution in brothel exposés. The *Whip,* for instance, followed up on the Sewally sensation with an 1842 profile of Sally Binns. Binns was "a nondescript victim of a morbid appetite...usually to be seen on the 'four-shilling' side of Broadway... He puts on feminine attire and enacts feminine parts in the Thespian Association... He has lost all sense and feeling of manhood."[50] The naming and scandalizing of Mary Jones and Sally Binns served as warnings against the dark, magnetic, emasculating evil of sodomy.

Katz traces the origins of the *Whip* and the *Rake* to the 1820s. Marketed for "sporting men," these tabloids "openly encourag[ed] men's sexual intercourse with female prostitutes."[51] Gilfoyle mentions that "the term 'male prostitute' was ambiguous and sometimes synonymous with 'sporting men' during the antebellum years."[52] However, the *Whip* and the *Rake* had no tolerance for male prostitution. Like Louis Dwight, the authors of pieces that ran in these papers made sex between men sound monstrous.

Clients of male prostitutes, termed "beasts" and "fiends," were taken to task for their responsibility in emaciating and crippling young boys. The New York sporting press was particularly concerned by the recruitment of boys into sodomitical sex work. One alleged sodomite, known as Captain Collins, kept a Reade Street residence called the Star House. Wrote the *Whip* in 1842:

*There is no language...to expose the fiendish enormity of this brute, who has been the instrumental cause of the death of a young man, who was employed by the monster as a barkeeper; **who was forced to nightly lie with beasts in the shape of men, by the order of his employer.** Though horrid as this may seem, we can prove it by a number of young men*

*who are now in the city, and who have also felt the
inhuman embrace of this monster.*[53]

One wonders about this: Did the young barkeeper get additional pay for these trysts? Couldn't he have dashed out as soon as he realized what was going on? The use of such words as *force, beasts,* and *monster* imputed a supernatural, primal strength to Captain Collins, the "King of the Sodomites." Collins was charged, in turn, with sapping the youth's life force by emasculating him—forcing him into a submissive role during sex, and draining him of his life force by causing him frequent orgasms. Collins's financial control over the boy was his initial advantage; as the *Whip* would have it, he used this power to enslave the boy sexually, thereby killing him slowly.[54]

Another alleged customer, Johnny L'Epine, was also stung by the flailing *Whip.* L'Epine was known to "perambulate the west side of Broadway and, whenever he can meet a youth of prepossessing appearance, to accost and entice him with proffers of employment."[55] L'Epine was accused of luring these boys into his dark den. Then, "after Johnny has kept a boy a week he may be known in the street by his pallid countenance, his effeminate lip and his mincing gait."[56] Be careful, the *Whip* warned: Male prostitution saps vigor, induces a mincing gait, and causes one to waste away.

The King of the Sodomites and the tale of Johnny L'Epine are cautionary fables, with different moral meanings than the Jones and Binns legends. While the Jones and Binns reports were a warning to white men prowling for African-American women, the Collins and L'Epine stories admonished would-be rakes who might consider sex work to make some quick cash. Proffering these urban legends as antimiscegenation and antisodomy lessons, the New York City sporting press created a consumer's guide to the streets. At the same time, the sporting press portrayed male and transgender sex work as the ultimate degradation. In this way the popular press attempted to keep the sexual street culture of New York City from blending, as it was naturally doing throughout the 19th century; the tabloids both nurtured sexual street culture and isolated it from the wider Protestant culture that had come to dominate American society.

He-Harlots and Chickenship: Whitman and Buskirk, 1840-1865

From 1841 to 1859, when he was working on *Leaves of Grass,* native New Yorker Walt Whitman wrote for legitimate Manhattan- and Brooklyn-based newspapers. He was also cruising the streets, the trains, and the gymnasiums, looking for "that perfect and Divine lover." He was fascinated by male and female prostitution, though his sensibilities were vastly different from the editorializing of the *Whip* and the *Rake.* A beautifully sexual call-to-arms, Whitman's "Poem of the Proposition of Nakedness" appeared in the 1856 edition of *Leaves of Grass:*

Respondez! Respondez!
Let every one answer! Let those who sleep be waked!
Let none evade—not you, any more than others!

Let that which stood in front go behind! and let that
  which was behind
advance to the front and speak!...[lines 1-3]
Let none but infidels be countenanced!...[line 21]
Let death be inaugurated!...[line 24]
Let there be no God!...[line 42]
Let shadows be furnished with genitals! Let substances
  be deprived
of their genitals!...[line 45]
Let the she-harlots and the he-harlots be prudent! Let
  them dance on,
while seeming lasts! (O seeming! seeming! seeming!)
[line 47] [57]

Whitman was at his best when trying his hardest to wake us up. He called on us to celebrate death, to renounce God, and to embrace the promiscuous. If in a world of illusory freedom we must appear seemly, let our prudent prostitutes dance on!

Whitman praised the sexually ambiguous sex worker in the touching poem, "To a Common Prostitute," which appeared in the 1860 *Leaves of Grass*. The published version looked like this:

Be composed—be at ease with me—I am Walt
Whitman, liberal
and lusty as nature
Not till the Sun excludes you, do I exclude you,
Not till the waters refuse to glisten for you, and the leaves

to rustle for you, do my words refuse to glisten
  and rustle for you.
My girl, *I appoint you with an appointment—and I*
  charge you
that you make preparation to be worthy to meet me,
And I charge you that you be patient and perfect till I
  come.
Till then, I salute you with a significant look,
that you do not forget me.[58]

But the manuscript version had "My love" in place of "My girl," according to Whitman scholar Gary Schmidgall. And, where a "significant look" was placed, Walt had first placed "a kiss."[59] This second revision is especially important because it is code for an already encrypted exchange. Whitman replaced the action of kissing a prostitute (an image connoting sex) with a "significant look," a gesture with two hidden meanings: a recognition of homosexuality and an expression of interest in sex with a male prostitute. The latter was the originally intended meaning. His deletion of "love" and insertion of "girl" can also be read as double entendre, acknowledging the presence of fairy prostitutes on the streets of New York. By 1860, *my love* had become a gender-neutral term, but it may have too closely resembled the precolonial term *love-boy*, leaving too much open to interpretation for Whitman's comfort. He performed his deletions before publication.

Still, Whitman would continue "singing the song of prostitutes / Renascent with grossest Nature," for the prostitutes "who detained me when I went to the city."[60] This poem,

"Enfans d'Adam 2," is another lovely, gender-neutral expression of support for the enlivening services of the street prostitute, whether male, female, or in-between. Yet Whitman's diaries strongly suggest he was only prowling for men. His fleeting mention of "he-harlots" is interesting, for it was used in place of any better vernacular. His friend Horace Traubel wrote that Whitman asked him mirthfully one day what the word "hustler" meant. "'Hustler' is a new vulgarism for a busy man," Traubel innocently replied.[61] No doubt it meant more than that, and was being used in America to denote males who were sexually available for money. Historian D. Michael Quinn finds that "*little hustlers* and *kept boys* have been slang phrases in vernacular English for male prostitute since at least the twelfth century."[62]

And where did Whitman find his he-harlots? Everywhere, seemingly: the streets, parks, public baths, piers, the theater, the bushes, and the decks of ships. "Locating prostitutes was scarcely a problem in his day," wrote Gary Schmidgall.[63] The diary of aristocrat George Templeton Strong confirms that in 1840 "the street [was] always crowded, and whores and blackguards [made] up about two-thirds of the throng."[64] Bohemian saloons thrived in the Village, where Pfaff's, on Broadway between Houston and Bleecker, was especially popular.

The first references to American military prostitution come from the diaries of Philip Van Buskirk, a sailor in the mid 1800s. His entries hint that Whitman's maritime friends had been schooled in remunerative sex by the time they took leave on land. Van Buskirk, who joined the Marines at age 12, quickly discovered the "boom cover trade," a reciprocation of sexual favors performed under the boom cover, a shelter for masts that weren't in use.[65] While "trade" did not necessarily indicate a monetary exchange, the subsuming practice of "chickenship" did entail remuneration. Shipyard and cabin boys were generally referred to as *chickens*; their relations with older partners acquired the term *chickenship*.[66]

Chickenship was similar to *matelotage*, though without the possibility of enslavement. Chickens were rewarded with protection and affection when they participated in chickenship with the senior crew. These congresses drew congressional attention: An 1890 congressional record deplored chickenship, there defined as "the Affection which a sailor will lavish on a ship's boy to whom he takes a fancy, and makes his 'chicken.'"[67] One popular song memorialized chickenship, showcasing the vengeful cabin boy:

> *The cabin boy, the cabin boy,*
> *The dirty little nipper.*
> *He filled his ass with broken glass,*
> *And circumcised the skipper.*
>
> *There'll be a frigging in the rigging,*
> *There'll be a frigging in the rigging,*
> *There'll be a frigging in the rigging,*
> *When there's fuck all else to do.*[68]

Shipyards were by no means the only places where Whitman sought inspiring encounters. On Fifth Avenue in 1857, he met Charly, who was "hurt, diseased, deprived." On Fourth Avenue, there was a man with a "thin face superb sonorous voice." Traverce Hedgemann was "young slight fair feminine." Arthur was "big round sandy hair coarse, open." John Kiernan typified the he-harlot: Whitman found him to be a "loafer saucy looking pretty goodlooking."[69] On a Broadway streetcar, Whitman met a young man named Philip, who was "black-eyed brownish sharp-faced, with a suspicion of a squint in his eyes—reckless."[70] On December 28, 1861, Whitman found Mike Ellis on Lexington Avenue and 34th Street, and "took him home to 150 37th Street, fourth story back room." And in Washington, D.C., in 1862, Whitman met Union soldier Jerry Taylor, who "slept with me last night weather soft, cool enough, warm enough, heavenly."[71] In none of these accounts does Whitman directly mention a monetary transaction. Nonetheless, some of the street boys he talked up were likely among the prostitutes to whom these selected poems were dedicated.

Mormons and *Mujerados*: Frontier America, 1850-1899

We have, so far, focused on the Eastern seaboard. But the Western frontier towns were notorious for their bawdy side. Female brothels in the Wild West were storied and, in places where men usually outnumbered women, indispensable. In the 1870s, the population of Jackson County, Mo. (home to Kansas City), was 55% male and largely transitory, young, and unmarried. By the end of the 1800s, Kansas City had more than 40 houses of prostitution, employing at least 250 women.[72] Similar figures were reported in Salt Lake City at the end of the 19th century, when officials discovered that they presided over 500 public female prostitutes and 35 houses of female prostitution.[73]

There is evidence that, in the 1800s, male prostitutes in Kansas City and Salt Lake City were serving the same clientele as females; both worked the same streets and even the same houses. The first reference to male prostitution in Utah was in 1877, when William Wright was fined $50 for "prostituting at the Great Western on evidence of Mrs. Smith."[74] Wright's nickname, "Dick," was probably an early instance of the word's current colloquial usage. If so, this might have been a way for William to advertise his availability. Utah police did not routinely jail prostitutes between 1870 and 1900, but the enormous fines for prostitution (equivalent to thousands of dollars today) given to unfortunates like Wright usually guaranteed lifelong penance.[75]

The *Kansas City Evening Star* noted the existence of female impersonators as early as 1880. These "strange men" were not just found in female brothels, but performed (and perhaps advertised) in the theaters. At the Theatre Comique, one performer particularly disgusted a reporter. "As a female impersonator, he draws a large salary and is a most remarkable success," the newsman editorialized, "but as a man he is a gigantic failure and not worth the powder that would blow his effeminate soul to purgatory."[76] The Civil War transformed Kansas City, which in the postwar years became a hub for newly free men, drifting youth, and outlaws on the run. By the early 1880s, rampant crime and prostitution inspired the *Evening Star* to plead for better police intervention. Sarah Coates and other civic-minded women formed a volunteer organization, the Humane Society, to ease the suffering of the "thirty or forty bootblacks and newsboys [who] slept nightly in the board of trade building, huddling about the steam heater to keep from freezing."[77] These boys were sure candidates for sex work, needing money, food, and shelter.

Male sex work was not just a sideshow to urban America's circus, as the 1878 case *Montana Territory v. Mahaffey* reveals. Mr. Mahaffey, having been convicted of unnatural acts ("the infamous crime against nature"), appealed and was allowed to plead his case in front of a Montana tribunal.

> The appellant [Mahaffey] has been convicted of the offense which is described in the statutes as "the infamous crime against nature either with man or beast"... The indictment alleges that the offense was committed "on or about the 9th day of November, A.D. 1877," at Deer Lodge, with B.
>
> B., a boy fourteen years of age, testified that the appellant **committed the offense with his consent,** at the Scott House, in Deer Lodge.... Against the objection of the appellant, the witness then testified that the appellant had, on various occasions, committed this offense with him at the appellant's ranch, about seven miles from Deer Lodge before said date; and that **the appellant called him a boy prostitute and threatened to put him in the penitentiary.**[78]

Why did young B. file a complaint when he and Mahaffey apparently had consensual sex? A close reading of the appeal suggests that Mahaffey scared B. when he "called him a boy prostitute and threatened to put him in the penitentiary," causing B. to fear for his own safety and make a report to the police.

And in San Francisco's Presidio district, according to Edward Prime-Stevenson (using the pseudonym Xavier Mayne), garrisoned Spanish-American War soldiers were known for their sex work. In 1898, he wrote, "a garrison noted for its homosexual contingent...was so active that the 'Presidio' quarter was the regular goal of the philostrats." In fact, "amiable young soldiers were to be 'had' so plentifully that their tariffs fell to nominal prices, and the lodgings of popular amateurs were fairly invaded."[79]

A case explored by Dennis Drew, from his 1969 *Boys for Sale,* vividly illustrates San Francisco during the Gold Rush. Drew presents the story of Mike:

> Mike was a 12-year-old Irish boy who worked as a bootblack in the San Francisco of the 1890's. He was always hanging around outside saloons, hustling for business.... Mike was one of the many boy-bootblacks who were much more "polished" at mas-

turbating or fellating a customer than at waxing his boots. In darkened outhouses and alleyways, a small kneeling bootblack could easily fellate a customer. If anyone approached, the man could cover himself with his hat while the boy returned to giving the shoes a lick and a promise—resuming their more exciting activity after the intruder had gone on.[80]

This vignette shows how important the Western sex worker mythos was to the culture of gay liberation. Lacking much documented history, writers began to create a larger story from their own folklore.

Drew describes the culture of frontier America's male brothels, or "peg-houses," which took their name from the Mediterranean brothel tradition of displaying available boys on a long rack. The boys were anally impaled on pegs of various sizes abutting the rack, to help customers choose an appropriately capacious catamite. Drew's description of the American version is as follows:

> Most of the boys in coastal peg-houses were poor runaways who had gone West in search of adventure. They were easily preyed on and seduced by wily agents who received anywhere from $100 to $500 for each boy they delivered to the brothel syndicate. At first, the boys were sent to a farm or "camp" where they were fattened up, beautified

> and trained.... Boys were not sent to the regular $1.00 houses until they were twelve or quite large for their ages at 10 or 11. They usually stayed in the peg-houses until they were 16 or 17. Upper class, or "$10 houses"...had boys from 6 to 16.... Opium was sometimes available too. The boys in these houses were usually narcotics addicts and therefore easy to keep under control (through drugs) for as long a time as they remained desirable for sexual purposes.
>
> In the common "$1.00 houses," the boys served dozens of customers a day. These boys were kept in line with a whip...but most of them seemed content.[81]

It is ironic that Drew, having vividly described a litany of abuse, drew only one interpretation of the peg-boys' emotional state: one of contentment. By presenting peg-boys as eager masochists, Drew's sociological study does little more than update old Roman notions of boy sex workers' disposability. But he does refer to the intensely male culture of the Gold Rush days, which presented ample opportunity for sexual exchanges between men. In this respect, the West was no different than the rest of the country in the in the Gay '90s, when many cities had male houses of prostitution. Boston, Philadelphia, New York City, Chicago, New Orleans, St. Louis, and San Francisco all had boy brothels, houses of prostitution manned by cash-strapped teenagers and young men. Supplementing these were traditional female whorehouses, many of which offered at least one male for those customers desiring male-male sex.[82] Not surprisingly, these latter houses, also called "benny houses," seem to have been more common.

In Utah, as in New York City, 19th-century male prostitutes were usually arrested for being inmates of traditionally female houses of prostitution. One Utah brothel in the mining town of Eureka was apparently geared just for sex between men. In an 1897 raid, police arrested the owner (whose wife also ran a female brothel in the same town) as well as three men "Resideing in a House of Prostitution," Thomas Paramore, William Holmes, and a 15-year-old Mormon youth named David Baum.[83] In Park City, a former mining town now known for its downhill skiing, Fred Stephenson and Ray Osborne were arrested (in Osborne's case, repeatedly) during brothel raids and fined for being inmates of houses of ill fame. Osborne, then 20 years old, was arrested in 1901 along with 14 female prostitutes. These raids were usually conducted during the day to protect more influential clients who usually took their pleasures in the evenings. Utah state historian John McCormick concludes that the regular police raids were conducted "not so much to suppress prostitution as to produce revenue for the city."[84]

Western sexual tourist zones featured lively street commerce in addition to brothels. In this respect, Salt Lake City was no exception. Commercial Street was an area where young men could work alongside women. In the 1890s, street-based sex workers and their clients made their introductions on the street and conducted further negotiations in rented, streetside rooms.

Louisville physician George Monroe placed little distinction between male and female sex workers practicing fellatio in Kentucky. In an 1899 article, Monroe recorded that "males and females in every large city were said to devote themselves to oral/genital acts for profit." In Louisville, "a number of instances have become public where young men, middle-aged men, and the aged even, have made a regular business of using their mouths for this purpose."[85]

Dr. Monroe's observation of multigenerational male sex workers is unusual. Louisville's fluid sex work scene may have been more inclusive of older workers than were similar zones in other cities. This could be due to the novelty of oral sex, which carried the stigma of sodomy. In Louisville, clients eager to experience this sensation perhaps cared less about gender and youthful good looks.

In many Western cities, messenger boys could also be contacted for the purposes of prostitution. Seventeen-year-old George Raymond, alias George Conley, was arrested in Salt Lake City for vagrancy in January 1892. Described as a brown-haired, brown-eyed "card cutter" and "call boy," George was a little over 5 feet tall and weighed 104 pounds. He had been jailed most likely for petty larceny unrelated to his prostitution. Police captured him again only after he was injured by a moving train when he tried to escape. By 1900, the phrase "call boy" was used synonymously with "messenger boy" and "male prostitute," sharing the slang meaning of "call girl."

Call girls passing as call boys created more gender confusion in the Wild West's sexual economy. Calamity Jane both worked in brothels (as a woman) and patronized them (as a man). "One of Calamity's claims," wrote Cy Martin, "was that, in male garb and with the aid of a dildo, she could deceive any prostitute she wanted."[86] The custom of having intercourse in the dark aided Jane in her efforts at disguise. The practice of removing only the clothing that hindered intercourse also helped matters. Jane's mother had been the madam of a house called the Bird Cage, in Blackfoot, Montana, Jane was 13 when she herself became a prostitute. At 17, in men's attire, she sold sex to railroad section hands in Wyoming.[87]

Calamity Jane's facility with varied gender and sexual roles underscores the pliability of these categories. Her cross-dressing allowed her to explore and learn what were then exclusively male activities—shooting and railway work, for example—and to make money from sex work no matter which gender she chose.[88]

New Mexico was equally fertile ground for sex exchange around this time—and had been long before that. Dr. William Hammond chronicled his visits to Pueblo villages in New Mexico, beginning in 1850. There he discovered *mujerados* (literally, women who had been men). Hammond went from Laguna to Acoma, examining genitals and testes. He reported that the breasts of one *mujerado* were enlarged (she said she had "nursed several infants whose mothers had died"), and each of her testicles was "the size of a small filbert."[89]

Hammond described the process by which this transgenderism occurred. Like religious practices among East Indian *sadhu,* the Pueblo's *mujerado* technique was arduous, painful, and ecstatic:

> A ***mujerado*** is an essential person in the saturnalia or orgies, in which these Indians, like the ancient Greeks, Egyptians and other nations, indulge. He is the chief passive agent in the pederastic ceremonies, which form so important a part in the performances. They take place in the Spring of every year.... For the making of the ***mujerado,*** one of the most virile men is selected, and the act of masturbation is performed on him many times every day. At the same time he is made to ride continuously on horseback. The genital organs are thus brought to a state of extreme erethism, so that the motion of the horse is sufficient to produce a discharge of seminal fluid.... It eventually happens that though an orgasm may be caused, emissions can no longer be effected, even upon the most intense degree of excitation. Finally the accomplishment of an orgasm becomes impossible. In the meantime the penis and testicles begin to shrink, and in time reach their lowest plane of degradation. Erections then altogether cease.[90]

Blending the spiritual and the transcendent, *mujerados* were, in a way, living sacrifices to Native American matriarchy and its distinctive standards of masculinity. Hammond also suggests that *mujerados* were available for sex with unmarried men, a function shared by the *berdache*.[91] Transcending their original manliness and athleticism, *mujerados* became sexually appealing to other males and were honored as surrogate females. By contriving this third sex, and then enlisting these third-sexers to provide non-procreative sexual release for bachelors and young men, Pueblo cultures were able to develop a healthy and sustaining pansexual culture.

Big-City Degenerates: Resorts and Reports, 1890-1899

There is a sharp contrast between Euro-American and Native American attitudes toward transgendered people. While Native tribes deferred to their transgendered members as highly spiritual people, European immigrants labeled them "degenerates." In Native American cultures, where transgenderism was part of a larger worldview, people developed terms such as *berdache* and *mujerado* to place themselves and others within this cosmology. In European America, value-neutral transgender categorizations were employed only by trans folk and their friends.[92] By contrast, court and medical reports from the 1890s insistently blended the terms "fairy," "degenerate," and "male prostitute" in such a way that a person identified by one of these names was often assumed to represent all three. Similarly, New Orleans newspapers used the pluralisms "its" and "jennie-men" to describe transgendered sex workers.[93]

In 1894, a medical report described the New York streets as crazed with transgendered prostitutes:

> In many large cities the subjects of contrary sexual impulse form a class by themselves and are recognized by the police.... They adopt the names of women, and affect a feminine speech and manner, "falling in love" with each other, and writing amatory and obscene letters. In New York City alone there are no less than one hundred of these, who make a profession of male prostitution, soliciting upon the streets and in parks when they get the opportunity. Physically, many of these men whom I have examined present the stigmata of degenerative insanity....[94]

In the 1890s, journalists and missionaries descended on New York City's brothels. One house that received undue attention was the Slide, located at 157 Bleecker Street, on Manhattan's Lower East Side. Medical student Charles Nesbitt described the scene in 1890 as if he were writing a gay guidebook:

> There were several resorts called beer gardens in those days on the Bowery and lower east side in which male perverts, dressed in elaborate evening costumes, "sat for company" and received a commission on all the drinks served by the house to them and their customers. The only place of assemblage that I remember for male perverts was a place called "The Slide." Here

a great number of those queer creatures assembled each night, dressed in male costume and sitting for company on the same basis as the others (the female prostitutes).[95]

Nesbitt quoted Princess Toto, "the social queen of the group," in his report:

"My kind finds out early in life that he desires above all things sexual gratification and that he cannot secure satisfaction with the opposite sex in a normal way. It is but a short step to the adoption of our kind of life. We, quite naturally, consider ourselves superior to the perverts in artistic, professional, and other circles who practice perversion surreptitiously. Believe me there are plenty of them and they are good customers of ours."[96]

With these few words, Princess Toto offered an incisive portrait of sexuality and sex work in late-1800s urban America. The Princess theorized that it was a "short step" from heterosexual frustration to same-sex prostitution. She spoke for her fellow queens when describing her clients, for whom she felt both sympathy and disdain. Fearful of openly pursuing relationships with the objects of their desire, Toto's clients were forced to buy love in secret, on an installment plan.

There were other houses in New York that offered transgendered sex workers a place to ply their trade. The campy Golden Rule Pleasure Club (depicted in 1894 by Detective Charles Gardner in *The Doctor and the Devil*) was one of these. Gardner recalls his visit:

I led the way to the "Golden Rule Pleasure Club." This dive was situated on West Third Street, in a four-story brick house. We entered the resort through the basement door, and as we did so a "buzzer," or automatic alarm, gave the proprietors of the house information that we were in the place. The proprietress, a woman known as "Scotch Ann," greeted us....

The basement was fitted up into little rooms, by means of cheap partition, which ran to the top of the ceiling from the floor. Each room contained a table and a couple of chairs, for the use of customers of the vile den. In each room sat a youth, whose face was painted, eye-brows blackened, and whose airs were those of a young girl. Each person talked in a falsetto voice, and called the others by women's names.[97]

The periodic intrusions of vice cops, religious reformers, and opinionated physicians effectively served to close these brothels down. The Slide was the first to go, in 1894. No later records exist to tell us of the fate of the mysterious Princess Toto. The owner was found guilty of running a disorderly house.

Luckily, brothels were not the only places where transgendered people could socialize. The case of Peter Sewally/Mary Jones documented that informal parties were common among trans folk in antebellum America. Formal drag balls also thrived in urban centers like New York and Washington, D.C., in the 1890s, allowing queens the opportunity to mingle with butch lesbians and feminine-identified trannies. On his visit to Walhalla Hall, at the invitation of Princess Toto, Nesbitt unearthed "quite a few" participants who "were masculine-looking women in male evening dress."[98] And Dr. Charles Hughes, investigating "erotopathia," wrote:

> There is, in the city of Washington, D.C., an annual convocation of negro men called the drag dance....
>
> In this sable performance of sexual perversion all of these men are lasciviously dressed in womanly attire, short sleeves, low-necked dresses and the usual ballroom decorations and ornaments of women, feathered and ribboned head-dresses, garters, frills, flowers, ruffles, etc., and deport themselves as women.[99]

These convocations sparked heated political battles. In New York, a row erupted between state Republicans who positioned themselves as reformers, and city Democrats who styled themselves as realists. This simmering social war heated up in 1899 over an alleged disorderly house known variously as Paresis Hall or Columbia Hall. *Paresis,* a paralysis thought to be caused by venereal disease, was an epithet used here against fairy prostitutes.

Located in the back of a saloon on Bowery and Fifth Street in Manhattan, Columbia Hall was investigated repeatedly by the Reverend Charles Parkhurt's City Vigilance League. Testimony from this war for control of the streets of New York reflects the turbulence that preceded the turn of the century. Upstate reformers used charged moralizing language in an attempt to berate city politicians. The Republican Mazet Committee grilled New York City mayor Robert A. Van Wyck, who held firm in his belief that New York was no different from any other big city:

> Q: Do you know that we now have **male harlots** thronging the streets, who have their peculiar places of resort, which can be found as easily as any saloon can be? Did you know that?
> A: No, I do not.
> Q: You have never heard of that?
> A: No. I know there are **whores** in every big city in the world.[100]

From the testimony of Columbia Hall witness John R. Wood:

> Last night I was at 392 Bowery...that is a place where **fancy gentlemen** go; it is near Fifth Street. It is...a place where **male prostitutes** resort.... There were such persons present. They were soliciting men at the tables—that is, men were soliciting men at the tables...I have always observed these **degenerate**

men there in large number, quite large numbers from 25 to 50 [people]....[101]

From the testimony of Wood's friend, Joel Harris:

I was with Mr. Wood last night at Paresis Hall....
*That is a well-known resort for **male prostitutes**; a*
place having a reputation far and wide, to the best of
my knowledge. I have heard of it constantly. I have
never had any trouble getting in there. You go in off the
*streets with perfect ease. These **men** that conduct*
themselves—well, they act effeminately; most of them
are painted and powdered; they are called Princess this
and Lady So and So and the Duchess of Marlboro, and
*get up and sing as **women,** and dance; ape the female*
*character; call each other **sisters** and take people out*
for immoral purposes.[102]

From the testimony of witness George Hammond, Jr.:

*They have one **woman** who goes there they call a*
***hermaphrodite.** These **male degenerates** solicit*
men at the tables, and I believe they get a commission
on all drinks that are purchased there; they get
checks.... They go from there across the street to a
place called Little Bucks.... They have a piano there,
*and these **fairies** or **male degenerates,** as you call*
them, they sing some songs.[103]

Later in 1899 Hammond was subject to further questioning:

Q: [There are] places that are well known as being
resorts for male prostitutes. Has that unmentionable
crime, so far as it is open to the people, been on the
increase?
A: It has increased wonderfully within the last six
months.
Q: How many of those places do you know of that are
open from the street, where boys go in freely, and
where they have attached to it as a feature of the
place, a male degenerate?
A: On the Bowery alone there is to my knowledge cer-
tainly six places. There are other places where they
have them.
*Q: Do these **poor, miserable creatures** make them-*
selves public? Do they show themselves?
A: They do. They exhibit themselves and solicit. I have
seen them solicit openly, and they have solicited
me.[104]

The intermingling of clinical, Victorian, and implicitly bibli-cal language brilliantly illuminates the confusion of the times, even as it sheds light on portions of queer history previously shrouded by centuries of taboo.

Meanwhile, transgendered sex workers had developed a tidy lexicon to describe their culture. They referred to them-selves as "sister," "princess," "lady," and "woman," terms that were both glittering and mundane, but always apposite.

The Female Impersonators provides a true insider's guide to Columbia Hall. Written by Jennie June (real name Ralph Werther, pseudonym Earl Lind), a female impersonator and Hall habitué, the book traces the history of the Hall as "the headquarters for avocational female impersonators of the upper and middle classes." Columbia Hall was located on Fourth Avenue, south of 14th Street, and contained a modest bar and lounge and a small beer garden in the back. The top floors were divided into small rooms for tenants.[105] The rooms directly above Columbia Hall provided hassle-free housing for the female-impersonating sex workers who performed below. June recalls the Hall's notoriety:

> *Paresis Hall bore almost the worst reputation of any resort in New York's Underworld. Preachers in New York pulpits of the decade would thunder Philippics against the "Hall," referring to it in bated breath as "Sodom!" They were laboring under a fundamental misapprehension. But even while I was an habitué, the church and the press carried on such a war against the resort that the "not-care-a-damn" politicians who ruled little old New York had finally to stage a spectacular raid. After this, the resort, though continuing in business (because of political influence), turned the cold shoulder on androgynes and tolerated the presence of none in feminine garb....*
>
> *Androgynes had only "the Hall" with the exception of three of four slum resorts frequented by only the lowest class of bisexuals who had never known anything better than slum life....[106]*

In *Autobiography of an Androgyne,* June was more forthcoming with stories of sexual exchange. In the 1890s, as a teenager, June learned that "fairies are maintained in some public houses of the better class." She "met several of these refined professionals." Oddly, she noted that transgendered prostitutes "commonly have plates substituted for their front teeth." This body modification may have allowed sex workers greater ease during fellatio. Or they may have lost teeth to violence; June recounts two cases in which upper-class fairies were murdered by their dates.[107]

As Americans in the late 19th century began to catch their first glimpse of the underground sexual economy that flourished in all parts of the new nation, the tendencies toward various forms of oppression that lay beneath the dominant Protestant culture also became more apparent. The goings-on in male and transgender brothels may have been shocking. But the violence that characterized mainstream responses to sexual variation was an affront to the conscience. No matter how vice committees would try to "eradicate the evil," commercialized queer sex would continue. Only the conditions would change.

[1] FOR ANCIENT GREECE AND ROME, SEE DEVORE AND DAUPHIN; FOR PREMODERN PARIS, SEE BOSWELL.

[2] SEE KATZ, JONATHAN NED. *GAY AMERICAN HISTORY.* THOMAS Y. CROWELL (NYC), 1976.

[3] SMITH, JOHN ET AL. *A MAP OF VIRGINIA.* OXFORD, 1612; SECTION II, CHAPTER 1, P.2.

[4] SEE BURG, B.R. *SODOMY AND THE PIRATE TRADITION.* NEW YORK UNIVERSITY PRESS, 1984, P. 46.

[5] IBID., P. 51.

[6] IBID., PP. 49-50.

[7] SEE BURG, PP. 128-129. *MATELOTAGE* OCCASIONALLY WARRANTED PUNISHMENT IN COLONIAL COURTS. PROSECUTIONS OF BUGGERY WOULD REVEAL A GREATER FEAR OF INTERRACIAL, RATHER THAN INTERGENERATIONAL, MALE COUPLING. (SEE BURG'S SYNOPSIS OF A CASE BROUGHT AGAINST 16-YEAR-OLD JOHN DURRANT AND THE ADULT "HINDOSTAN PEON," ABDUL RHYME, PP. 146-147).

[8] SMITH, SECTION II, P. 2 (EMPHASIS MINE).

[9] SMITH, SECTION II, CHAPTER 2, P. 9.

[10] KATZ, JONATHAN NED. *GAY/LESBIAN ALMANAC,* HARPER & ROW, 1983; PP. 66-67. "THE CASUALNESS OF THE REFERENCE TO THE EXCHANGE OF 'LOVE' FOR BISCUIT SUGGESTS THAT SUCH LIFE AND DEATH BARTERS WERE COMMON KNOWLEDGE AMONG SOME 17TH-CENTURY ENGLISHMEN," KATZ WRITES.

[11] SEE KATZ, *GLA,* P. 672, DOCUMENT 1, FOR AN ANALYSIS OF THE "LOVE-BOY" AND THE PRECOLONIAL MEANINGS OF "LOVE."

[12] TO BE FAIR, THE JAMESTOWN SETTLERS ALSO OFFERED OTHER RATIONALE FOR THEIR ILL HEALTH: "SOME AFFIRMED IT WAS ILL DONE OF THE COUNCEL TO SEND FORTH MEN SO BADLY PROVIDED," WROTE SMITH; SECTION II, CHAPTER 2, P. 10.

[13] SEE KATZ, *GLA.*

[14] THIS DOUBLE STANDARD WAS ALSO A BRITISH TRADITION, WHICH BRUCE SMITH CALLS THE MYTH OF MASTER AND MINION. SEE SMITH, *HOMOSEXUAL DESIRE IN SHAKESPEARE'S ENGLAND: A CULTURAL POETICS.* UNIVERSITY OF CHICAGO PRESS, 1991; PP. 191-223. AN ANCIENT CONSTRUCT DISTINGUISHED SEXUAL RELATIONSHIPS MARKED BY DEPENDENCY OR COMMERCIALIZATION. IN GREEK PEDERASTY, FREE BOYS OF THE ARISTOCRACY WHO HAD SEXUAL RELATIONSHIPS WITH THEIR MENTORS WERE DELINEATED AS *EROMENOS,* OR BELOVED. BUT WHAT IF A SENIOR PARTNER EXPLOITED HIS CHARGE, USING THE BOY SOLELY FOR SEXUAL RELEASE AND NEGLECTING HIS EDUCATION? IN CLASSICAL GREECE, THIS WAS NO LONGER *PAEDERASTIA,* BUT *PORNEIA*": STRICTLY PROSTITUTION, NO BETTER THAN SLAVE TRADE. (SEE THOMAS MARTIN, *ANCIENT GREECE.* YALE UNIVERSITY PRESS, 1996, P. 141.) ATHENIAN BROTHELS, *PORNOBOSKOI,* WERE USUALLY STAFFED BY SLAVES. (SEE WAYNE DYNES, *HOMOLEXIS.* GAI SABER MONOGRAPH NO. 4, 1985; P. 23.) EVENTUALLY, *PORNEIA* CAME TO TAKE ON A NASTY, MERCENARY QUALITY AND WAS USED TO DESCRIBE MANY KINDS OF SEXUAL BEHAVIOR TOWARD WHICH ITS WRITER WAS CONTEMPTUOUS. (SEE KENNETH J. DOVER, *GREEK HOMOSEXUALITY.* HARVARD UNIVERSITY PRESS. CAMBRIDGE (MA), 1978, 1989; P. 16.) IN THE LATER DAYS OF THE ROMAN REPUBLIC, WROTE HISTORIAN JOHN BOSWELL, "NONCITIZEN ADULTS (E.G. FOREIGNERS, SLAVES) COULD ENGAGE IN [PASSIVE HOMOSEXUAL] BEHAVIOR WITHOUT A LOSS OF STATUS, AS COULD ROMAN YOUTHS, *PROVIDED THE RELATIONSHIP WAS VOLUNTARY AND NONMERCENARY.* SUCH PERSONS MIGHT IN FACT CONSIDERABLY IMPROVE THEIR POSITION IN LIFE THROUGH LIAISONS OF THIS TYPE.... THOSE WHO COMMONLY PLAYED THE PASSIVE ROLE IN INTERCOURSE WERE BOYS, WOMEN, AND SLAVES—ALL PERSONS EXCLUDED FROM THE POWER STRUCTURE. OFTEN THEY DID SO UNDER DURESS, ECONOMIC OR PHYSICAL." (SEE BOSWELL, *CHRISTIANITY, HOMSEXUALITY, AND SOCIAL TOLERANCE,* P. 74.) IN OTHER WORDS, MALE PROSTITUTION HAD BEEN INTIMATELY LINKED WITH SLAVERY IN THE WESTERN WORLD FOR 1,500 YEARS BEFORE *MATELOTAGE* PRESENTED ITSELF ON AMERICA'S EASTERN SEABOARD AND THE EARLIEST EUROPEAN COLONISTS ARRIVED IN VIRGINIA.

[15] SEE MCILWAINE, H.R. (ED.). *MINUTES OF THE COUNCIL AND GENERAL COURT OF COLONIAL VIRGINIA, 1622-1632, 1670-1676.* COLONIAL PRESS, RICHMOND (VA), 1924; PP. 42-47. ALSO SEE KATZ, *GAH,* PP. 16-19, 568. IN THESE QUOTATIONS, "COWSE" HAS BEEN INSERTED IN PLACE OF "THE EXAMINEE," FOR READABILITY.

[16] THIS MIGHT BE AN INTERPRETIVE STRETCH, BUT IT BEARS WITH THE TIMES. THE RECORD IS INCOMPLETE: CORNISH WOULD "PUT HIS HANDS IN THIS EXAMINEE'S COD PIECE AND PLAYED AND KISSED HIM, SAYING TO THE EXAMINEE THAT HE WOULD HAVE BROUGHT THEM TO SEA WITH HIM, IF HE HAD [PASSAGE INCOMPLETE] HIM, THAT WOULD HAVE PLAYED WITH HIM." SEE MCILWAINE, P. 47.

[17] *CONNECTICUT ARCHIVES, CRIMES AND MISDEMEANORS, 1662/63-1789.* IN "CRIMES AND MISDEMEANORS," VOL. 1, DOCUMENT NUMBERS 87-103.

CONNECTICUT STATE ARCHIVES, CONNECTICUT STATE LIBRARY, HARTFORD. REPRINTED IN KATZ, *GLA*, PP. 111-118, 678.

[18] IBID. P. 116.

[19] IBID, IDEM.

[20] IBID., P. 114.

[21] IBID., P. 116.

[22] IBID., P. 113. THIS CITATION RELIES ON THE TESTIMONY OF WILLIAM PHELPS, AN ACQUAINTANCE OF SENSION'S FOR 30 YEARS AND AN ORIGINAL COMPLAINANT. I INCLUDE IT HERE TO FRAME THE PERSPECTIVE THAT MALES MUST BE PROTECTED AGAINST "INFECTION," WHERE INFECTION IS A METAPHOR FOR SUCCUMBING TO HOMOSEXUAL TEMPTATION AND THEN BEING POTENTIALLY INFECTIOUS TO OTHERS, E.G. RECKLESSLY ENDANGERING OTHERS WITH ONE'S DESIRES. IT IS ALSO AN EXAMPLE OF PURITAN DENIAL OF SEX BETWEEN MEN—AND SURVIVAL SEX—AS *INSTINCTIVE.* IT WAS SEEN, INSTEAD, AS *INFECTIVE,* AN ILLNESS THAT CARRIERS COULD PASS ON TO NORMAL MEN.

[23] IBID., P. 118.

[24] GODBEER, RICHARD. "WILLIAM BYRD'S 'FLOURISH.'" IN *SEX AND SEXUALITY IN EARLY AMERICA* (EDITED BY MERRIL D. SMITH). NEW YORK UNIVERSITY PRESS, 1998; P. 143.

[25] SEE BLOCK, SHARON. "COERCED SEX IN BRITISH NORTH AMERICA, 1700-1820." PH.D. DISSERTATION, PRINCETON UNIVERSITY; 1995.

[26] DISTRICT ATTORNEY PAPERS OF NEW YORK CITY, *MATTHEWS V. HASSAN,* FEBRUARY 20, 1816 (ITALICS MINE).

[27] FROM CITY AND COUNTY OF NEW YORK DISTRICT ATTORNEY PAPERS, CASES UNDER DISTRICT ATTORNEY RODMAN, HERE 1816-1817 (ITALICS MINE).

[28] FROM CITY AND COUNTY OF NEW YORK DISTRICT ATTORNEY PAPERS, JULY 12, 1817.

[29] GILFOYLE, TIMOTHY J. *CITY OF EROS.* W.W. NORTON, 1992; P. 137. ALSO SEE NOTES, P. 370. SEE CHAPTER 3 IN THIS TEXT FOR A DISCUSSION OF THE "BENNY HOUSES" IN THE EARLY 20TH CENTURY.

[30] DWIGHT, LOUIS. "SODOMY AMONG JUVENILE DELINQUENTS." LETTER DATED APRIL 25, 1826. HELD IN UNION THEOLOGICAL SEMINARY LIBRARY. ALSO REPRINTED IN KATZ, *GAH*; PP. 27-28, 572.

[31] FOR HISTORICAL DELINEATION BETWEEN THE EMISSIVE AND THE PASSIVE, SEE KATZ, *GLA* (THROUGHOUT).

[32] *COMPACT OXFORD ENGLISH DICTIONARY,* 2ND EDITION. CLARENDEN PRESS; 1996. FOR THE ANCIENT GRECIAN USAGE OF *PAIS* TO DENOTE "ONE WHO IS PASSIVE" (INCLUDING WOMEN, GIRLS, BOYS, AND SLAVES OF EITHER SEX) SEE DOVER, P. 16. FOR FURTHER NOTES ON THE ETYMOLOGY OF *KINSHON* IN GERMAN CONVICT SLANG (AS "A THIEF'S APPRENTICE") SEE KATZ, *GAH*, P. 572.

[33] WINSLOW, RANDOLPH. "REPORT OF AN EPIDEMIC OF GONORRHEA CONTRACTED FROM RECTAL COITION." *MEDICAL NEWS* (PHILADELPHIA), NOVEMBER 1886; VOL. 40, PP. 712-713. REPRINTED IN KATZ, *GLA,* PP. 202, 204, 690.

[34] IBID., P. 202.

[35] GILFOYLE, P. 136.

[36] BERKMAN, ALEXANDER. *PRISON MEMOIRS OF AN ANARCHIST.* MOTHER EARTH PUBLISHING ASSOCIATION, 1912. (REPRINTED BY SCHOCKEN, 1970; P. 433 IN REPRINTED EDITION.) ALSO SEE CHAUNCEY, GEORGE. *GAY NEW YORK.* HARPERCOLLINS, 1994; P. 88.

[37] IBID., P. 433 (ITALICS MINE).

[38] CLEMENT OF ALEXANDRIA DOCUMENTED THAT YOUNG MALE SLAVES WERE SHAVED, PLUCKED, AND OTHERWISE PRETTIFIED ON THE ROMAN REPUBLIC'S AUCTION BLOCKS. SEE BOSWELL, *THE KINDNESS OF STRANGERS,* P. 113.

[39] BERKMAN, P. 47. "DE WEED" REFERRED TO TOBACCO.

[40] IBID., PP. 170-173.

[41] SEE BENJAMIN, HARRY AND MASTER, R.E.L. *PROSTITUTION AND MORALITY.* THE JULIAN PRESS, 1964; P. 169.

[42] CITY AND COUNTY OF NEW YORK DISTRICT ATTORNEY PAPERS, JUNE 16, 1836.

[43] KATZ, "COMING TO TERMS: CONCEPTUALIZING MEN'S EROTIC AND AFFECTIONAL RELATIONS WITH MEN IN THE UNITED STATES, 1820-1892." IN *A QUEER WORLD* (MARTIN DUBERMAN, EDITOR). NEW YORK UNIVERSITY PRESS, 1997; PP. 227-8.

[44] IBID., PP. 228-9.

[45] GILFOYLE, PP. 136-7.

[46] THE *HERALD*, JUNE 17, 1836. ALSO SEE KATZ, "COMING TO TERMS," P. 229. KATZ ADDS HERE THAT "'AMALGAMATION' WAS USED OFTEN IN THE 19TH CENTURY TO REFER TO SEXUAL CONTACTS BETWEEN WHITES AND AFRICAN-AMERICANS."

[47] THE *SUN*, JUNE 17, 1836. ALSO SEE KATZ, "COMING TO TERMS," P. 229.

[48] KATZ, "COMING TO TERMS," P. 230.

[49] GILFOYLE, P. 137.

[50] *WHIP*, FEBRUARY 26, 1842. ALSO SEE KATZ, "COMING TO TERMS," P. 224.

[51] SEE KATZ, "COMING TO TERMS," PP. 222-227.

[52] GILFOYLE, P. 370.

[53] FROM THE *WHIP*, FEBRUARY 12, 1842. ALSO SEE KATZ, "COMING TO TERMS," P. 223. (ITALICS MINE.)

[54] FOR A REFERENCE TO THE NOTION OF "VITALISM," THE BELIEF THAT SPERM WAS A PURE AND DISTILLED ELEMENT SYMBOLIZING ONE'S LIFE FORCE, AND THE "METAPHOR OF LIQUIDITY" THAT CONFLATES NONPROCREATIVE MALE ORGASM WITH DRAINING VITALITY, SEE BARKER-BENFIELD, G.J. *THE HORRORS OF THE HALF-KNOWN LIFE*. HARPER AND ROW, 1976; PP. 176-181 IN THE CHAPTER "THE SPERMATIC ECONOMY." THANKS TO D. MICHAEL QUINN FOR SUGGESTING THIS REFERENCE.

[55] FROM THE *WHIP*, FEBRUARY 26, 1842. ALSO SEE KATZ, "COMING TO TERMS," P. 224.

[56] IBID, IDEM.

[57] WHITMAN, WALT. "POEM OF THE PROPOSITION OF NAKEDNESS." *LEAVES OF GRASS*, 1856. ALSO SEE GARY SCHMIDGALL, *WALT WHITMAN: SELECTED POEMS, 1855-1892*. ST. MARTIN'S, 1999; PP. 157-160.

[58] WHITMAN, "TO A COMMON PROSTITUTE," *LEAVES OF GRASS*, 1860. REPRINTED IN SCHMIDGALL, *WALT WHITMAN: SELECTED POEMS*, PP. 254-5. (ITALICS MINE.)

[59] SCHMIDGALL, GARY. *WALT WHITMAN: A GAY LIFE*. PLUME, 1997; P. 147.

[60] WHITMAN, "ENFANS D' ADAM 2," *LEAVES OF GRASS*, 1860.

[61] SEE SCHMIDGALL, *A GAY LIFE*, P. 121

[62] QUINN, P. 187, FOOTNOTE 62. ACCORDING TO MERRIAM-WEBSTER, THE ENGLISH USE OF *HUSTLER* ULTIMATELY DERIVES FROM THE DUTCH VERB *HUSSELEN*, DEFINED AS TURNING SOMEONE OVER AND SHAKING THE CHANGE FROM HIS POCKETS. *HUSTLER* IS ALSO A HOMONYM FOR *HOSTLER*, A TRUNCATED FORM OF *HOSTELER*. *HOSTLER*, AS USED IN AMERICA IN THE 1800S, MEANT ONE WHO PROVIDED LODGING. WHEN CONFUSED WITH *HUSTLER*, *HOSTLER* MAY HAVE ALSO CARRIED A SEXUAL DOUBLE ENTENDRE, THE LOOSE EVOCATION OF BEDDING SOMEONE FOR A FEE. CUSTOMERS FREQUENTLY CALLED UPON HUSTLERS TO NEGOTIATE THE RENTAL OF SAFE ROOMS. WE SEE THIS USAGE IN AN 1842 LETTER TO THE NEW YORK-BASED *SPORTING WHIP*, IN WHICH THE CORRESPONDENT, IDENTIFIED AS "STIR 'EM UP," CAUTIONED "JARED S......G, THE COCKNEY HOSTLER," WHO "HAD BETTER LOOK AHEAD, OR HE MAY GET INTO A SCRAPE. 'TWONT DO FOR YOU, MY LAD, TO THROW YOUR HEELS TOO HIGH AMONG 'YANKEES.' YOU ARE A PRETTY BOY, BUT YOU CAN'T COME IT." FROM THE *NEW YORK SPORTING WHIP*, FEBRUARY 11, 1843. LETTER DATED JANUARY 31, 1842, FROM HACKENSACH, NEW JERSEY.

[63] SEE SCHMIDGALL, *A GAY LIFE*, P. 111.

[64] IBID., P. 99.

[65] BURG, B.R. *AN AMERICAN SEAFARER IN THE AGE OF SOIL*. YALE UNIVERSITY PRESS, 1994; P. 75. SEE ALSO KATZ, "COMING TO TERMS," P. 219. KATZ NOTES THAT THE USE OF THE WORD "TRADE" HERE IS AN EARLY ONE; MY FEELING IS THAT IT CONNOTED MUTUAL MASTURBATION AND/OR RECIPROCAL ORAL SEX RATHER THAN A MONETARY EXCHANGE. OTHER EROTIC SLANG INCLUDED "YANKUM," FOR MASTURBATION; AND "GOING CHAW FOR CHAW," FOR MUTUAL MASTURBATION.

[66] BURG, 1994, P. 79.

[67] *CONGRESSIONAL RECORD*, APRIL 21, 1890. ALSO SEE DYNES, P. 29, FOR AN ETYMOLOGY OF "CHICKEN."

[68] LYRICS ACCORDING TO HISTORIAN THOMAS LOWRY, PERSONAL COMMUNICATION. THANKS TO SCOTT SANDAGE FOR THIS REFERENCE.

[69] SEE SCHMIDGALL, *A GAY LIFE*, P. 121 (QUOTED FROM WHITMAN'S DIARIES).

[70] IBID., P. 124.

[71] IBID., P. 129.

[72] MONTGOMERY, RICK. *KANSAS CITY EVENING STAR*. OCTOBER 31, 1997.

[73] QUINN, D. MICHAEL. *SAME-SEX DYNAMICS AMONG NINETEENTH-CENTURY AMERICANS: A MORMON EXAMPLE*. UNIVERSITY OF ILLINOIS PRESS, 1996; P. 317.

[74] SALT LAKE CITY POLICE RECORDS, JANUARY 5, 1877. SEE QUINN, PP. 275 AND 298.

[75] SEE QUINN, P. 344: "THE TAX REVENUE PURPOSE OF THESE PROSTITUTE ROUND-UPS IS EVIDENT FROM THE FACT THAT THOSE ARRESTED WERE FINED BUT NEITHER BOOKED NOR PHOTOGRAPHED."

[76] *KANSAS CITY EVENING STAR*, 1880, "STRANGE MEN." SEE MONTGOMERY, 1997.

[77] *KANSAS CITY EVENING STAR*, 1882. SEE MONTGOMERY, 1997.

[78] *TERRITORY V. MAHAFFEY*, 3 MONT. 112. ALSO SEE KATZ, *GAH*, PP. 35-6. (EMPHASIS MINE). IN POINT OF FACT, MAHAFFEY HAD OFFERED B. SEX RATHER THAN MONEY AS PAYMENT FOR HIS RANCH HELP; IF ANYONE WAS A PROSTITUTE IN THIS CASE, IT WAS THEN MR. MAHAFFEY HIMSELF. IT SHOULD ALSO BE NOTED THAT B.'S OLDER BROTHER, C., MADE THE INITIAL COMPLAINT WHEN B. WAS TRUANT FROM SCHOOL AND HIS WHEREABOUTS UNACCOUNTED FOR. (HE WAS, AT THE TIME, SPENDING THE DAY IN MAHAFFEY'S BED.)

[79] MAYNE, XAVIER. *THE INTERSEXES*. PRIVATELY PRINTED IN SWITZERLAND, 1909; PP. 221-222. MAYNE DEVOTED A LARGE SECTION TO EUROPEAN SOLDIER-PROSTITUTION; IN BRITAIN OF THE 1880S, MAYNE WROTE, SOLDIER-PROSTITUTES COULD EARN AS MUCH IN A HALF-HOUR'S SEX WORK AS THEY COULD IN A WEEK OF SOLDIERING. HIRING BRITISH SOLDIER-PROSTITUTES WAS TERMED "FEASTING WITH PANTHERS" AND, REFERENCING THEIR VIVID UNIFORMS, HAVING A "TOUCH OF SCARLET." SEE JAMES GARDENER, *A CLASS APART*. SERPENT'S TAIL (LONDON), 1995.

[80] DREW, DENNIS. *BOYS FOR SALE*. BROWN BOOK PUBLISHING, 1969; P. 151.

[81] IBID., P. 143.

[82] SEE QUINN, P. 316. IN THE 1890S, IN CHICAGO, GAY "CATHOUSES," OR BROTHELS, EXISTED ALONGSIDE STRAIGHT CATHOUSES. SEE ARNO KARLEN, *SEXUALITY AND HOMOSEXUALITY, A NEW VIEW*. W.W. NORTON (NYC), 1971. "GEYCAT," AN EARLY 20TH-CENTURY REGIONAL HOBO TERM (ANALOGOUS TO "SEXUALLY AVAILABLE MALE YOUTH") NO DOUBT DERIVES FROM CHICAGO'S GENDER-BLENDED CATHOUSE CULTURE OF THE LATE 1800S.

[83] SEE QUINN, PP. 317 AND 343.

[84] SEE QUINN, PP. 318 AND 345-346, FOR MCCORMICK'S "RED LIGHTS IN ZION."

[85] MONROE, GEORGE. "SODOMY-PEDERASTY," *SAINT LOUIS MEDICAL ERA*, VOL. 9 (1899); PP. 431-434. ALSO SEE KATZ, *GLA*, P. 302.

[86] MARTIN, CY. *WHISKEY AND WILD WOMEN*. HART PUBLISHING COMPANY, 1974; P. 111.

[87] IBID., P. 113.

[88] IN THE LATE 1800S, FEMALE PROSTITUTES IN NEW ORLEANS' RED-LIGHT DISTRICT (THEN KNOWN, AS MANY AMERICAN RED-LIGHT DISTRICTS WERE, AS THE TENDERLOIN) SOMETIMES TOOK ON MALE NICKNAMES IN ADVERTISEMENTS. (AN 1895 *BLUE BOOK* AD PLUGS OLLIE AND COUNTESS WILLIE ALONG WITH MAY, CLARA, ETTA, ET AL; AND AN EARLY 1900S *SPORTING GUIDE* LISTED EARL WESLEY ALONG WITH 110 OTHER WOMEN.) WAS THIS TO DENOTE THEY WERE JUST "ONE OF THE BOYS"? SOURCE MATERIAL COURTESY THE COLLECTION OF THE NEW-YORK HISTORICAL SOCIETY.

[89] HAMMOND, WILLIAM A. *SEXUAL IMPOTENCE IN THE MALE AND FEMALE*. GEORGE S. DAVIS (DETROIT), 1887; PP. 1557-1573. AS REPRINTED IN HENRY HAY'S "THE HAMMOND REPORT," *ONE INSTITUTE QUARTERLY*, VOL. VI, NOS. 1, 2 (WINTER, SPRING 1963), PP. 6-20. ALSO SEE KATZ, *GLA*, P. 181.

[90] IBID., IDEM.

[91] FOR THE *BERDACHE*, SEE CALIFIA, PAT. *SEX CHANGES*. CLEIS PRESS, 1997. HAMMOND'S USE OF "PEDERASTIC" REFLECTED AN AMERICAN USAGE FOR MALE-MALE SEX RATHER THAN A YOUTH-ADULT RELATIONSHIP.

[92] *ANDROGYNE*, FOR INSTANCE, AND *FAIRIE* WERE USED BY JENNIE JUNE IN PLACE OF MORE DEROGATORY TERMS IN HER *AUTOBIOGRAPHY OF AN ANDROGYNE*.

[93] SEE THE *NEW ORLEANS DAILY HERALD*, JUNE 2, 1901, SOCIETY PAGES.

[94] HAMILTON, ALLAN. "INSANITY IN ITS MEDICO-LEGAL BEARINGS," FROM *A SYSTEM OF LEGAL MEDICINE*, 1894.

[95] NESBITT, CHARLES TORRENCE. SEE HIS PAPERS, DUKE UNIVERSITY LIBRARY. ALSO REPRINTED IN KATZ, *GLA*, P. 219.

[96] IBID., IDEM.

[97] GARDNER, CHARLES. *THE DOCTOR AND THE DEVIL.* GARDNER, 1894.
(VANGUARD REPRINT, 1931; P. 57.) ALSO SEE KATZ, *GAH*, P. 40.

[98] SEE KATZ, *GLA*, P. 219.

[99] HUGHES, CHARLES. "POSTSCRIPT TO PAPER ON 'EROTOPATHIA,'—AN
ORGANIZATION OF COLORED EROTOPATHS." *ALIENIST AND NEUROLOGIST*, VOL. 14,
NO. 4 (OCTOBER 1893). ALSO SEE KATZ, *GAH*, PP. 42-43, 575.

[100] NEW YORK STATE, *REPORT OF THE SPECIAL COMMITTEE OF THE ASSEMBLY
APPOINTED TO INVESTIGATE THE PUBLIC OFFICES AND DEPARTMENTS OF THE CITY OF
NEW YORK*. JAMES B. LYON (ALBANY, NY), 1900; PP. 940-941. ALSO REPRINTED IN
KATZ, *GAH*, PP. 44-45. (EMPHASIS MINE.)

[101] IBID, P. 46 (EMPHASIS MINE).

[102] IBID., PP. 46-7 (EMPHASIS MINE).

[103] IBID., P. 47 (EMPHASIS MINE).

[104] TRIAL PROCEEDING FOR THE CITY VIGILANCE LEAGUE, REPRINTED IN
KATZ, *GLA*, P. 299 (EMPHASIS MINE).

[105] LIND, EARL. *THE FEMALE IMPERSONATORS.* THE MEDICO-LEGAL JOURNAL
(NYC), 1918. REPRINTED BY ARNO PRESS (NYC), 1975; P. 146.

[106] IBID., P. 147. JUNE USED "BISEXUAL" AS "TWO-GENDERED."

[107] LIND, *AUTOBIOGRAPHY OF AN ANDROGYNE,* THE MEDICO-LEGAL JOURNAL,
NYC, 1918; P. 125. I AM UNAWARE OF ANY FURTHER CORROBORATION FOR THE
UNUSUAL PRACTICE OF PORCELAIN TEETH PLATES. THOUGH JUNE WAS ASKED TO
"BECOME AN INMATE OF SUCH A HOUSE," SHE DECLINED. "MY SISTER COURTESANS,
BOTH MALE AND FEMALE," SHE WROTE, "THOUGHT ONLY OF THE SENSUAL, AND
HAD ADOPTED THEIR OCCUPATION AS A GAINFUL ONE, WHEREAS I SOUGHT MERE-
LY THE SATISFACTION OF STRONG INSTINCTS."

two

We have visited the early days of American hustler culture by exploring legal cases, hobo and frontier folklore, journalistic and medical reportage, Native American traditions, and personal anecdotes. These varied research methods have also revealed many variations in hustler representation. The sex workers themselves have generally fallen into three categories: transgendered workers, teenage boys, and young military men. We will now follow these narrative threads into the early 20th century, as we examine the evolution of military hustling, street drag culture, and the sexual commercialization of destitute youth from the period just before World War I until the period just before World War II.

On the Waterfront: Ports, Forts, and Resorts, 1900-1917

There are no records of male prostitution during the Civil War. The historian Tom Lowry has examined 60,000 court-martials from that period, and has found that males were having sex with each other more for lust than for money.[1] But many adolescents were enlisted, which may have given rise to new forms of chickenship; "powder monkeys," for example, were boys whose function it was to carry shipboard gunpowder to Union vessels. This famous photo of a powder monkey on the Union ship *Monitor* shows how young these boys could be.

Military wages presumably had something to do with this; in the Civil War, Union soldiers were induced to enlist with the promise of substantial financial reward. The Depression of the 1890s meant that most World War I enlistees were in fairly difficult circumstances. Magnus Hirschfeld recorded an example of American military prostitution in his 1914 book, *Homosexuality in American Cities*. Sharing a letter he received from a man in Denver, Hirschfeld presented this piece in his correspondent's voice:

> I know quite a number of homosexuals in Denver... Male prostitutes can sometimes be met in the Capitol Gardens, but not a large number of them....
>
> In the vicinity of Denver there is a military fort with a force of a few hundred men. Last summer a soldier from there propositioned me on the street in Denver. I've heard that this happens quite frequently in San Francisco and Chicago. I recall meeting a soldier who was a prostitute long ago in San Antonio, Texas, and last summer I met a young sailor from Massachusetts. The latter was on leave and looking

42

fig. 2.1 *"Powder Monkey," courtesy of the Library of Congress.*

for homosexual intercourse out on the street late at night. **In all of these cases it was difficult to tell whether the soldiers were really homosexual or just prostitutes, or whether they went with men for lack of anything better.** *It's never easy to draw the line, and things are so expensive nowadays that someone could easily be moved to earn a little pocket money one way or the other.[2]*

As soldiers and sailors were called to garrison forts and coastal ports during World War I, the influx of sexually available young men drew not only young women looking for romance, but also older men, fairies, and other teenage boys.

In 1916, E.S. Shepherd reported on these developments in the *American Journal of Urology and Sexology,* claiming that "our streets and beaches are overrun by male prostitutes."[3] The same journal published a piece two years later about juvenile delinquents in Seattle. Dr. Lilburn Merrill, of the Seattle Juvenile Court, studied the sexual habits of 100 boys. This diagnostician concluded that:

> *A fact of social significance was shown in the histories of five twelve to fourteen-year old boys of the fellatio group who, after a year and more of association with playmates, voluntarily frequented low-grade amusement resorts and the water front to solicit men with whom they consorted for financial considerations.[4]*

There was an established hustling scene in Seattle during World War I, along the waterfront and at amusement parks, where two boys in Merrill's study had been "taken by the police for fellationous association with men. The boys had personally sought adult companionship, and their selection of consorts older than themselves was a choice based on other experiences they had had with both boys and men."[5] The two pennywise boys had realized they were more likely to get paid for having sex with older men than with boys their age.

Unfortunately, concomitant with these "financial considerations" was a higher risk of arrest. It is unclear here whether the men were also arrested and charged, or whether the men were sailors or civilians. Describing the history of one 14-year-old, Merrill traces the boy's thievery to

> *...an inceptive act of stealing from the hotel room of a man directly after they had mutually induced orgasms. Notwithstanding the fact that the subject stated he encouraged the sedulous interest of the man during more than an hour of erotic desire, he impulsively purloined his gold watch and did not fully comprehend the nature of the theft until he was on the way home.... He expressed no consciousness of guilt nor dislike of the man during the analysis though he recalled some feeling of disgust at the close of his orgasm which the man had coercively prolonged.[6]*

Merrill, anxious to infuse the unknown adult partner with culpability, and faced with the unpleasantness of having described a consensual affair, was left blaming the adult for the youth's "coercively prolonged" orgasm—and the "feeling of disgust" it excited.

The force that Dr. Merrill attributed to the boy's orgasmic prolongation can be seen as connective tissue in the tract of hustler representation from the 19th century to the 20th. It hearkens back to the *Whip*'s depiction of the vampiristic strength of Captain Collins, earlier seen sucking the lifeblood out of his young charges. Even Edward Prime-Stevenson, a homosexual activist, doomed his sailor-prostitute subjects. "As a rule," he wrote, "those who begin with health and robustness of body and pretensions to good-looks become feeble, pallid wrecks." But he gave context to the metaphor of the spermatic economy, explaining that "sexual debilities, the precarious, nerve-shattering life, misery, late hours, weather, careless habits of person, drink—all sap away physical attractiveness."[7]

Some young hustlers told a different story. Jimmy Harrington, who wrote a pornographic book about his alleged indoctrination, recounts that he got his first hotel job at the age of 13, when he was hired as a bellman in a 200-room hotel in Pittsburgh. "I knew the hustlers, the pimps, and most of the fags," Harrington writes, and "also the dope peddlers." He describes his homosexual initiation, which took place in 1906, and for which he claims to have made today's equivalent of at least $60.

My next meeting with sex came in the form of a male shoe salesman, and was also, I must assure you, quite a surprise to me.

He checked in one night about nine o'clock, and when I had roomed him he asked me to get him two Manhattan Cocktails.

When I returned to his room he was completely stripped. After being told to charge the drinks to his room, I started to leave, but he called me back, saying, "That one drink is for you. What's your hurry?"

I told him I was in no hurry, but that I had never drank anything before. For some reason this seemed to please him, but he insisted that a cocktail would not intoxicate me and insisted that I take the drink.

Then when I had drank that one, he sent me for two more. When we drank them he began to question me about how old I was and if I liked girls and if I had ever been fucked or sucked. All the time, while he was talking to me, he kept caressing my thighs and each rub I noticed, he went a little higher.

After we had talked about twenty or thirty minutes he told me to go in the bathroom while he called another bellman to bring us more drinks, and he didn't want the other boy to see me in his room. Having received the drinks he came into the bathroom, put his arm around me and kissed me. Then, dropping his hands to my trousers he started to take them off me.

I asked him what he was going to do. He laughed and said, "Go ahead and take them off and don't be afraid. I am not going to hurt you, and if you don't like what I am going to do to you, just tell me so and I shall stop. And on top of that, here's five dollars for yourself, and never mention this to anyone."

After that he turned off the lights and sat me on the bed, then he dropped to his knees in front of me between my legs and started to lick all over my thighs,

balls, and then slowly he licked towards the head of my prick, and when he reached that, he engulfed that in his mouth and started to suck softly.

His was the softest mouth I have ever experienced, a velvet mouth would have been a very good name for it.

He sure knew his business. Not once did I feel a tooth or the slightest roughness or hurt. Slowly and surely he brought on the expected culmination.

He came to the hotel about once every month, and each time we went through this same procedure.[8]

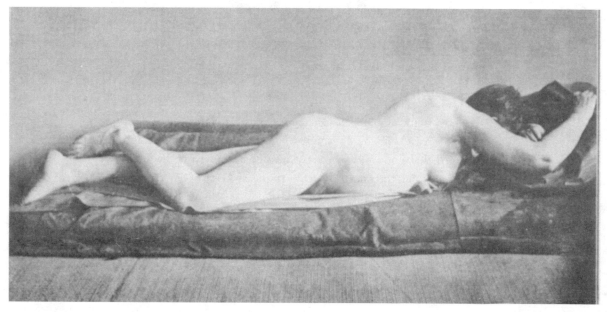

fig. 2.2 "Jennie June," reprinted from *The Autobiography of Jennie June.*

Loop-the-Loop: Fairy Sophisticates, 1903-1933

A more feminine alternative to young hustlers like Harrington, fairies enticed sailors looking for blow jobs by selling themselves both as clients and as substitutes for female prostitutes. In her youth, Jennie June claimed to have paid hundreds of young soldiers and sailors for sex, usually eschewing opportunities to charge for her services, as many fairies did. "In my fairie apprenticeship and during my career around the military posts," she wrote, "I was the financier."[9] Fairies like June made Greenwich Village below 14th Street a sexually electric sector.

The most notorious fairy prostitute of the era, Loop-the-loop, was arrested one night in 1906 and charged with solicitation, at the age of 23. Deriving her nickname from a Coney Island ride, Loop loped the streets of Brooklyn and the trails of Prospect Park.[10] Loop bribed beat cops so that she wouldn't be arrested under masquerade laws. She reported that she strolled "chiefly for the money in it" and did not shave her legs only because "most of the boys don't mind it."[11] One man, a musician interviewed after Loop's arrest, said he considered himself Loop's husband, and bragged that Loop was "the most passionate mortal he had ever heard of, and the most difficult to satisfy."[12] (Loop herself reported that she had once serviced "no fewer than 23 men...one immediately after another...in a room in Brooklyn.")[13]

Dr. R.W. Shufeldt, who had taken photographs of Jennie June, also photographed Loop and interviewed her for a medical article. Shufeldt noted that Loop-the-loop "believed his anus to

fig. 2.3 "Loop-the-loop," reprinted from *The American Journal of Sexology and Urology*, 1919.

be an 'aborted vagina' and claimed to menstruate."[14] Loop's confidence in her feminine qualities factored into her success as a fairy prostitute. Like Calamity Jane, Loop-the-loop's free-floating between genders fortuitously complemented her desire to make money.

Jennie June attributed the modern usage of *fairy* to maritime trade. "The term 'fairie'...probably originated on sailing vessels of olden times when voyages lasted for months," June asserted. "While the crew was either actually or prospectively suffering acutely from the absence of the female of the species, one of their number would unexpectedly betray an inclination to supply her place. Looked upon as a fairy gift or a godsend, such individual would be referred to as 'the fairy.'"[15] If June was right about this etymology, then the colloquial usage of *chicken, trade,* and *fairy* in America's contemporary queer culture can all be traced to 19th-century seafarers.

There are various reasons for America's WWI-era fascination with oral sex, one being suppressive church doctrine. Oral sex was still considered sodomy, not something a man might expect from his wife, or a young man from a good girl. But he could get head when he patronized prostitutes of any gender, or if he became a prostitute himself. It is no coincidence that blow jobs for money have for the last hundred years been the most common transaction for male and transgendered American sex workers (and even, arguably, for women in the sex industry). Oral sex is fast, intimate, sufficiently pleasurable, not particularly messy, and less exposed than most other acts. If that is what

the majority of customers still want today, then people who knew "the French way" were in great demand 100 years ago. As Jennie June, who claimed to have satisfied 800 young soldiers and sailors in her day, concluded: "The fairie's success is inversely proportional to unmarried adolescents' opportunities with the gentle sex."[16] If the vice squads had anything to do with it, this success rate would precipitously decline.

During and just after World War I, the New York City vice squad (acting under pressure from the federal government) cracked down on female and transgendered prostitutes. To that end, the chief of the vice squad told his officers that "one prostitute was more dangerous than five degenerates" (his use of "degenerates," in this case, referred to men who had sex with men but did not charge for it, and were not noticeably effete).[17] This logic was indicative of the popular misogynist belief that female—and feminized—sex workers were likely to be carriers of disease, and it denied that supposedly "normal" men would involve themselves in prostitution.[18] Also implicit here is the assumption that gender-queer individuals were always prostitutes.

Using these rationales, the NYPD stepped up its efforts to repress fairy sex workers working Riverside Drive, Bryant Park (on 42nd Street), and 14th Street.[19] Perry Lichtenstein, a prison physician, recorded this account in 1921 at New York's City Prison (also known as the Tombs and Riker's Island).

One of these individuals was arrested, charged
with soliciting...he was searched, and on him were

found a set of artificial busts, a wig and a box containing powder and rouge.... He lisped and in speech closely approached a bashful female. When interviewed his answers were usually prefixed by "my dear."

...He ran away from home and met some boys whom he considered good company. These young men were of the same type as he. It was not long before he began pervert practices, and in this way made enough money to live....

One finds many of these unfortunates among negroes. Several years ago a negro was shot and killed by a detective. This negro's practice was to dress up as a female, solicit men and then go thru their pockets while having intercourse in some hallway. He had...gotten possession of a rubber arrangement which in every way resembled the female external genitals.[20]

We can thus add murder to the list of dangers facing trans street folk in the 1920s, along with arrest, rape, and beatings.

Whether the detective responsible for the preceding murder was investigated is unclear. Judging from Lichtenstein's chilling description, and recalling the invective of the chief of the vice squad, we may assume the authorities considered the shooting to be an acceptable discharge of the detective's duty. Following this precedent, the *San Francisco Examiner* reported on another police killing.

Blonde Turns Brunette And She Ain't No Lady
Female Impersonator Jailed After Fight

When a blonde lady—in fifteen minutes—suddenly becomes a brunette lady—she ain't no lady. No lady was Alfred Ames, 35, who early yesterday battled two police officers, was beaten in the melee, taken to Central Emergency Hospital, and there stripped of his feminine disguise.

SKULL FRACTURED

After being charged with impersonating a woman, resisting an officer, and vagrancy, he was taken to San Francisco Hospital, suffering from a fractured skull. Attaches said he may die.

Officers Ed Schultz and Robert Williams, investigating a parked car at Fifth and Natoma Streets, found a man and a "blonde" in the car. The "blonde" was excused, disappeared. When the companion, whose name was not divulged, began a search for his wallet he discovered two one-dollar bills missing.

BATTLES OFFICERS

At Fifth and Harrison Streets, the officers saw the "blonde" again—now a brunette. A battle followed, in which officers were forced to use a nightstick to complete the arrest.

Taken to Central Emergency, Ames' feminine ruse was uncovered in a heap of silk stocking, a pink slip, high heeled shoes, two wigs. Later, at San Francisco

Hospital, he lapsed into unconsciousness. He gave his
address as 712 Eleventh Street, Oakland.[21]

As transgendered sex workers became more visible in American urban centers, police sweeps intensified. Trans girls were not, however, consigned only to dangerous streets. Drag revues flourished from Harlem to Florida's Coconut Grove and San Francisco's Barbary Coast. Backstage dates with patrons were common, filling starving artists' pocketbooks. In Chicago, the vice squads reported in 1911 that:

> *Some [men] impersonate women on the cheap*
> *vaudeville stage, in connection with the disorderly*
> *saloons. Their disguise is so perfect, they are enabled*
> *to sit at tables with men between the acts, and solicit*
> *for drinks the same as prostitutes.*
>
> *Two of these "female impersonators" were recently*
> *seen in one of the most notorious saloons.... These*
> *"supposed" women solicited for drinks, and afterwards*
> *invited the men to rooms over the saloon for pervert*
> *practices.[22]*

In response, Chicago vice urged that language in the 1845 crimes-against-nature law be "altered and made specific, under the guidance of scientific men...to make it clearly understood that society regards these abhorrent deeds as crimes."[23] They held that statutes should especially criminalize cross-dressing and other "pervert methods." In this way, trans folk might be more easily jailed, for "better definition would probably make it more possible to readily obtain conviction when desirable."[24]

Intensified law enforcement action against male and transgender sex work encouraged cooperation between the masculine and feminine factions of the male sex work world. For protection and with an eye toward a new clientele, fairy solicitors often linked up with sailor hustlers. In the 1920s and 1930s, Chicago's brothel scene was dominated by peg-houses, informal spaces "where a queen used personal contacts to put customers in touch with prostitutes and, for a split of the fee, provided the use of an apartment."[25] Thomas Painter, a sex client and researcher, provides evidence that New York brothels functioned similarly. Painter frequented several Manhattan brothels, which he also called peg-houses, one of which opened in 1928. That house was run by "Danny R. (prostitute-name Molly King)...[She] began with her husband, a seaman."[26] Molly King's house exemplified the post-WWI confluence of fairy prostitutes, their sailor husbands, and their sex-working sailor friends.

The busiest waterfront brothel in Manhattan between the World Wars was a floating house. This brothel was "never more than six months in the same place—Third Ave. at 27th, at 32nd, at 52nd, at 44th, at 42nd, at 67th. Always Third Avenue."[27] The vice committee's stance on fairies compelled this brothel's continual migration. The resort was "Matty Costello's (prostitute-name Dolores Costello)," who in 1930 initially "ran it with her 'husband'...then another 'husband,' a merchant seaman."[28] Costello reputedly had a dozen boys at the house at any given time.

Both Molly King's and Dolores Costello's male brothels were established as joint ventures with their seafaring husbands. Their husbands offered protection and were instrumental in recruiting other sailors into sex work. It is no coincidence that two transgendered sex workers were at the helms of the largest male brothels in New York City between 1920 and 1940. Both Molly and Dolores had previous experiences with sexual exchange that gave them the necessary training to manage their respective resorts. While local police were brutalizing fairy prostitutes, Molly and Dolores were able to elude capture and become madams of their own establishments.

Dolores grew up surrounded by sex workers. In a letter to Alfred Kinsey, Tom Painter related her history, using her boyname:

> *Matty is 57 years old, was brought up in a whore house by his grandmother, who was its madam. At 12 he was penetrated by his brother, at 13 his cousin taught him to fellate him. He is now the estimable gentleman my yesterday's report referred to as a "stitch bitch." He is older looking, thin and gray, limps, is toothless, and lisps, for some reason. He also is on the deaf side....*

In 1908, at age 21, Dolores moved to New York and quickly discovered the "homosexual underworld":

> *He snuffed cocaine, as was the fashion with the group then. He frequented Bowery dives where icemen,*

> *teamsters and longshoremen came to get fellated. He then became an expert dressmaker for the great female impersonators of the period.... He knew Julian Elting[e]....[29]*

Famous drag performer Julian Eltinge was only one nugget from Costello's "mine of contacts," as Painter described it. "Incidentally," Painter wrote in 1944, Costello "knows Gypsy Rose Lee very well."[30] Costello's peg-house was a sort of a gay prototype for the Playboy Mansion, where Painter met David Mir, Taliakhan, Ed Stearns, Mary Rupert, Monty Wooley, Cole Porter, and Ramon Novarro.[31] Costello's progression from a boy prostitute to fairy prostitute and then to madam is not unusual, and charts an informal, hierarchical form of promotion within transgender sex work.

Transgendered hustlers had a hand in Times Square's transformation into a sex work zone before male hustlers claimed it as their turf in the late 1930s. A 1931 *New Broadway Brevities* article lamented Bryant Park's reputation for "boys and men with painted faces and dyed hair" who were "camping and whoopsing for hours each night."[32] The novel *Goldie*, written by Kennilworth Bruce in 1933, pairs a "mincing" Southern boy on the run, Goldie, with his hotel porter, the streetwise Skinner, who introduces Goldie to sex and the square. "The fairies pull down the big dough, too," Skinner tells Goldie. "Say, I could wise you up plenty!"[33] It is not long before Goldie flips his pretty locks from a darkened subway entrance on 42nd Street.

Inside the walls of the military bases that attracted the sex trade, soldiers and sailors re-created this culture by transposing familiar American heterosexual conventions into all-male communities. Sailors held drag shows, developed crushes, went steady, and had lovers' spats. This behavior unsettled military brass, though many varied forms of male bonding—from homoerotic activity to simple friendships—have been features of military life throughout recorded history. Responding to voracious demand, port towns became centers of commercialized vice, prompting quick retribution from politicians and military police under the anti-vice laws of the Draft Act of 1917.[34] According to transgender historian Susan Stryker, in San Francisco "the old Barbary Coast, the nighttime vice district, was shut down by 1917...as part of the war effort: Navy MPs [Military Police] coming in, saying, 'We don't want our boys butt-fucking each other on the ships, spreading venereal disease.'"[35] Wartime conscription drew thousands of recruits to America's port cities and filled their streets with randy young men.

Coy Decoy Boys: Newport Naval Academy, 1918-1921

The U.S. Navy established a training station in Newport, R.I., at the beginning of World War I. This station quickly grew to accommodate as many as 20,000 boys and young men, who lived in "cheap lodging houses," according to the *New York Times*.[36] One of those houses was, naturally, the local YMCA.

The Young Men's Christian Association ran a campaign in 1918 to raise funds for more lodging facilities. Posters featuring wounded boys with older men at their sides, or with their buddies carrying them on stretchers back to the hearth of the YMCA, served to advertise the Y's mission. Beneath the image of a distinguished general draped over the body of a young recruit, one caption read FOR YOUR BOY.

Recruits who stayed at the Newport Y quickly learned the local customs. One seaman recalled, "the Army and Navy YMCA was the headquarters of all cocksuckers the early part of the evening."[37] Another described a YMCA common room party held by two rouged, powdered sailors wearing women's clothing, one of whom, "Beckie" Goldstein, kept leaving the room with other sailors.[38] "Us girls need our pennies," a Navy fairy reportedly told newcomers.[39]

After the end of World War I, in the spring of 1919, the Navy reacted to these and similar reports. The Y was not affiliated directly with the Navy, so military investigators sent out spies to investigate the indiscretions of sailors and civilians. These spies or decoys were—to the horror of *The New York Times* and to the chagrin of Assistant Secretary of the Navy, Franklin D. Roosevelt—young men, some only 16 years old.[40] Decoy boys were ordered to ingratiate themselves to suspected homosexuals, and many eagerly carried out their targets' subsequent suggestions—either they were very patriotic, or simply glad to have the government's help in finding sexual partners. The Navy gave their operatives a great incentive in return for prostituting them: an additional $3 per diem, equivalent to $50 in 2000.[41]

fig. 2.4 "For Your Boy," Committee of Public Information,
Division of Pictorial Publicity, ca. 1918.

A casual form of military prostitution already existed in Newport:

> ...a gay man might take a sailor to a show or to dinner, offer him small gifts, or provide him with a place to stay when he was on overnight leave; in exchange, the sailor allowed his host to have sex with him that night, within whatever limits the sailor cared to set.... Men who were "trade" normally did not expect or demand direct payment for their services, although gay men did sometimes lend their partners small amounts of money without expecting it to be returned, and they used "trade" to refer to some civilians who, in contrast to the sailors, paid **them** for sexual services.[42]

This arrangement was curiously heteronormative, imitating dating patterns in the straight world. One wonders how difficult it was for sailors to meet single women in newly sailor-heavy Newport; they certainly had no problem meeting guys.[43] Historians who study the period play down the transfer of money during same-sex liaisons, while emphasizing the components of physical contact and companionship. But some clients were incredibly generous: One man told the sailors that "[Chaplain Samuel] Kent and [Arthur] Green paid 'well for their pleasure,' having given enlisted men up to five dollars 'to let him go down and suck them off.'"[44]

Trainees came from all over the country, and were often strapped for cash to begin with. In Newport they were underpaid, lived on institutional food, and got lonesome and homesick. For teenage boys far from home, offers of money, dinner, and some company would all meet their most immediate needs, and were certainly sufficient compensation for sex. And sailors could use some of that money to have sex with others—a local girl, a punk, a female prostitute, or a fairy prostitute—thus repeating the cycle, as sex work merged into sex play.

Government hustlers reacted very differently to their assignments. Some men were excited by the prospect of meeting other men. Others plainly relished the prospect of contributing to a fairy's discharge. And some were simply confused when the government changed its mind about the wisdom of the effort midway through the operation.

Newport elites were outraged after both a local minister and a YMCA volunteer were arrested for trying to pick up decoys. John Rathom, editor of the *Providence Journal,* wrote several editorials condemning the methods of the Navy's decoy operation. "Many boys wearing the uniform of the United States Navy," wrote Rathom, "have been forced into the position of moral perverts by specific orders of officers of the Navy Department."[45] It is doubtful the matter would have come to light if decoys had lured only other seamen and ignored the civilians. This would have averted a situation in which Newport's elite felt compelled to shelter their own from what Rathom termed the Navy's "vicious practices."[46]

In defense of Samuel Kent, the compromised chaplain who was eventually acquitted of all charges, the local Reverend J.

Howard Deming testified before a naval board of inquiry that "at first [I] did not believe that the Navy Department would sanction such methods...[but I] believe it now."[47] Bishop James Perry lambasted the Navy for allowing its charges to "prostitute themselves and corrupt others."[48] And John Rathom wrote Franklin D. Roosevelt personally: "[The minister's case] is sufficient to illustrate the rotten system inaugurated by you."[49] In response, Roosevelt sued Rathom for libel (for suggesting that Roosevelt was a governmental pimp and cover-up artist). But FDR could not proceed against Rathom because the alleged libel had not been sent through the mails; in other words, Rathom's speeches and editorials constituted a form of protected free speech.[50]

Meanwhile, the citizens of Newport responded to their city's scandalized reputation. "Newport is the cleanest city in America," Chief of Police John Tobin told the naval court of inquiry. "Newport was as clean as any city in the United States, North, South, East, or West."[51] Tobin clearly meant here that Newport *was* clean, at least before the Navy got there. The similarity of these comments to the 1899 testimony of New York City Mayor Robert Van Wyck is striking. Both men stood up for their cities, male prostitution and all. Their argument was that prostitution simply exists in all cities. The influx of thousands of teenage boys made such efflorescence all but inevitable. The realism of these men was a bright spot in a very dark time.

The Newport uproar sparked further congressional and naval inquiries. FDR's superior, Josephus Daniels, said he was "shocked" when the decoy operation came to light (thanks to Rathom's perseverance). Daniels told the press that when he learned of the fiasco he immediately ordered a stop to the operation. "Such base methods," said Daniels, "were unspeakable and would not be tolerated for a moment."[52] Pure deceit: Daniels had known all along what Navy boys were doing. Perhaps some very straight-identified decoys were able to wrangle promotions from this mess. But not at Newport: The Naval Training Station closed down abruptly, after only four years of operation.[53]

Truly vile was the Navy's treatment of its operatives after the fiasco came to light. Naval intelligence reports suggest that some decoy boys were not immune from court-martialing.[54] Luckily, FDR's later recommendations let Newport operatives off the hook.

A Senate committee, convened two years later, found that their task was "practically forced upon [these] boys, who, because of their patriotism...had responded to the call of the country to defend their flag and their homes."[55] The committee concluded: "To send into Newport young men, some of them mere boys...to use their own 'discretion and judgment' whether they should or should not actually permit to be performed upon them immoral acts, is in the opinion of the committee utterly shocking to the American standard of morality."[56]

Finally, a happy ending. The decoy boys were spared prison time (although the unfortunate sailors they ferreted out received court-martials and jail time). And with the rise of FDR's political star, progressivism and better economic opportunities were on the way.

Benny Boys, Cadets, and Defectives: City Kids, 1900-1935

We have explored how many American boys growing up in the first third of the 20th century happened into sex work, how they negotiated sexual exchange with men, and how they have been historically represented. One point of entry was, of course, the way of Dolores Costello, who learned sexual exchange at home.

This phenomenon attracted the attention of historian Al Rose, whose interviews with female sex workers from 1920s New Orleans suggest that the practice was both a novelty (for the customer) and a puberty rite (for the daughter of the sex worker).[57] Thomas Painter commented on the availability of boys in predominantly female houses of prostitution, writing that in cities with flourishing underworlds, like New Orleans, female brothels commonly accommodated a client's desire for boys. The street slang "benny house" described these inclusive brothels.[58] But there were other means for boys to enter sex work.

Boys were an important component of brothel subcultures in early 20th-century America. Progressive Era social reformers established the Committees of Fourteen and Fifteen, which consistently reported on New York City disorderly houses staffed by boy "runners," who would meet the client at the door and negotiate his price and tastes before introducing him to a sporting girl. A 1911 report from the Vice Commission of Chicago terms these boys "cadets," going on to say that "in some houses the keepers insist on the inmates having cadets of their own choosing, [and] in one house of white inmates the 'cadets' are all colored young men."[59]

Messenger boys employed by a Telegraph Company branch office often witnessed shady business at houses in restricted districts. Many of these boys were recruited as drug runners, bringing cocaine and hypodermics to their secondary employers.[60] One messenger boy started with cocaine running and soon became a virtual tour guide to Chicago's sexual underground:

> He knows the name of nearly every prostitute in the restricted district and can recognize them at sight. Whenever he comes into a house of prostitution the girls fondle him and nearly always kiss him. At different times he has had sores on his lips.[61]

Chicago's newsboys and street vendors were available for many odd jobs. Originally called Hull-House, the Juvenile Protective Association was the first agency to provide services directly to male prostitutes. Its inspiring founder, Jane Addams, wrote about child labor in a style at once circumspect, controversial, and folksy. She had a knack for combining grim street realism with fairy-tale language, and her Depression-era Progressivism set the tone for the coming New Deal. Addams described a hierarchy of sexual commerce, in which "there is almost a system of apprenticeship." Addams stated that "boys when very small act as 'look-outs' and are later utilized to make acquaintances with girls in order to introduce them to professionals. From this they gradually learn the method of procuring girls and at last do an independent business."[62] The apprentice pimps were "merely out-of-work boys idle upon the streets, who readily len[t] themselves to these base demands because nothing else [was] presented to them."[63]

Late-night newspaper hawking sometimes served as a front, allowing many young vendors to meet potential sexual clients. In 1906, as a youth, Nels Andersen began selling newspapers on Chicago's Madison Street. He partnered with his friend Steve, who had been warned by his mother to "beware of men who acted too friendly."[64] Not long after getting started, Steve rushed to his partner's side when young Nels finished a sale to "a man who had given me a dime for the [one-cent] paper and told me to keep the change." Steve warned Andersen, "That's the kind I said to watch out for. They talk soft and sweet." Andersen recalled: "I learned something and was nine cents to the good."[65] Young Nels and Steve discovered that newspaper clients could "trick" them into sexual relations by overpaying for papers.

A report conducted by Addams's Hull-House Association termed semi-employed newsboys as "hustlers" and "bootjackers." "These boys hanging out in the delivery room are not properly newsboys at all," a Hull-House reviewer surmised. "They hang around the newspaper offices in the hope of getting jobs as 'hustlers' if at any time a newspaper desires to strengthen its selling organization.... These bootjackers frequently go into [hustling] as a matter of private speculation."[66] The term "hustler" would, within 40 years, evolve into the most common descriptor for men purveying street-based sex.

By 1903, in an arrangement called the hustler system, Chicago's streets had been mapped into delivery territories.

Wagons carrying current editions would circle regular points set up in each boundary and drop off papers to the news dealers who owned each particular route. Most news dealers hired young male assistants to help them with house-to-house delivery. These boys had to prove themselves with their selling power. "The competition for the employment is so keen," wrote Hull-House investigator Myron Adams, "that the boy must 'hustle' or another will be given the coveted position."[67] The hustler system developed rapidly and spread to many American cities.

In the years just before and just after World War I, states passed new child labor laws that left the impoverished young boys who were formerly news hustlers at the mercy of the wagon men. By 1924, Chicago's news alleys were full of homeless boys whenever the police did not kick them out. When the heat was on, these "small boys...[would] ride with the men on the wagons of a later edition and make dates to go home with them and sleep."[68] Within 20 years, strict outside regulation of a formerly organic social system *forced* new boys to work on the sly, propelling them to find shelter and trade sex with their older former colleagues.

Of course, the old system had already incorporated sex-for-money exchanges into its informal structure. A previous study that had reported on Chicago newsboys between 1903 and 1905 indicated that it was not unusual for newsboys to have sex with customers. One key informant, a former school superintendent, asserted that "one-third of the newsboys who come to the John Worthy School have venereal disease, and that 10% of the remaining newsboys...are, according to the physician's diagnosis,

fig. 2.5 "Newsboys," courtesy of the Library of Congress.

suffering diseases due to unnatural relations with men."[69]

Vice Commissions from various cities tapped into this medical metaphor. Chicago vice asserted that "male prostitutes [were] principally perverts" who "spread infection of the eyes," used drugs, begot "defective and deformed" children, got sick, and died.[70] Opium, cocaine, and marijuana were the drugs of the day.[71] As for disease, syphilis (which causes blindness) and gonorrhea were prevalent. With little in the way of medical knowledge, curatives, and prevention information, social leaders familiarly used the Gothic metaphor as folk wisdom. "Men given to great sexual excesses die from conditions due to those excesses," Chicago's commission declaimed.[72] Estimations of transmissibility were masked as tracts of morality and virtue. Missing a real chance to open a dialogue on risks, benefits, and social conditions associated with prostitution, the Chicago report closed by dispassionately proposing "a study of eugenics" to help control sexually transmitted infections among the wayward young.

A 1913 report by the Philadelphia Vice Commission fell in with this trend, conflating "infection" with "perversion" and entwining disease with sexual preference. After describing a vast residential Tenderloin, the authors noted the panoply of pliant boys in knickers:

> Numbers of boys with kneepants are commercializing themselves openly on our streets for the practice of perversion. This use of boys from eight to fourteen has developed in the past five years to an appalling extent.

> Centers of infection, both places and individuals, are found scattered in various parts of the city. It is hard to see how this can be effectively dealt with. The Child Labor Laws contain some provisions intended to effect improvement. Even the name and character of this unnatural form of vice are probably outside the knowledge of the city's people. Yet it has grown to such proportions as to be a present risk to every boy in street trades and to many others throughout the city.[73]

This Philadelphia report goes on to cite the use of alcohol, tobacco, opium, and cocaine among street youth, as well as the resourceful practice of huffing gasoline "from rags dampened in the street lamps," or gaslights.[74] The authors concluded that commercial sex and drug use among street youth had created a situation by which their great-grandchildren would pay dearly for their progenitors' transgressions:

> The venereal morbidity among children cannot be presented statistically, but it has many victims, both by direct infection and inherited defect—blindness, paralysis, feeblemindedness, imbecility, congenital malformation, and syphilis, organic diseases transmissible to the third and fourth generations.[75]

What their descendants would inherit was a street hustling niche carved out by these low-income, adolescent street vendors at the turn of the century.

One 21-year-old Philly boy explained to the Philadelphia Vice Commission that male sex work was initiated by voracious customers who tarried from the streets to the bathhouses in their search for willing youngsters. He told a cautionary tale of his own:

> Since this town is tight, I notice that there are a lot of "faries" (sexual perverts) hanging around the tenderloin. They usually go after messengers first. Most of the boys are on to them and fight shy of them. They hang around the bath-houses. They will creep up to a man who is fast asleep and go for him. They are in with the watchman in the baths. I know one messenger whom we all dared to stay with one of these men. He did, and instead of giving the messenger five dollars, as he had promised, the man chased the messenger out. Since then I think this messenger has been going with such men. He is off the force a long time. The last I heard from him was Pittsburgh. He's not working. He's being kept by some women there.[76]

The 1913 report suggested that the "victims of the perverts" constituted "a high percentage of criminals and vagrants. Among working-class boy delinquents," it averred, "75 percent are in the age group 13 to 15 years."[77]

In the rest of the country, destitute and runaway boys composed the youngest male sex work market in the 1920s. Nels Andersen, who became a sociologist, wrote that "homosexual practices among homeless men" were "widespread," giving rise to travel "partnerships" between hobo youths and adults crossing the country.[78] "It does not seem probable that force is so extensively employed," Andersen remarked of these partnerships, noting that boys "often become reconciled to the practice and continue it." He did observe hobo youth making short-term financial partnerships with older men. "Often they become promiscuous in their relations," wrote Andersen, "and many of them even commercialize themselves."[79] In 1922, Andersen related the case of a runaway boy named C.J. who willingly joined an older hobo in Michigan:

> This man worked on a boat plying between Michigan ports and Chicago. He persuaded a Michigan boy whose home was near Lansing but who had run away and was loafing about the docks on the lake front, to come with him to Chicago. He promised to help the boy get a job, etc. He took him to a room on South State Street where he held him for three days and had improper relations with him. Prior to his apprehension he had turned the boy over to another man for the same purpose.[80]

This trademark admixture of adventurism and kidnapping suggests that an informal, underground sex work network existed between boys and their clients. Runaway boys could find a way to escape their hometowns, if they were willing to sacrifice their bodies in return.

The relative openness of these activities, where young men

encoded their sex work into their surroundings, discouraged police from arresting the very young on obvious morals violations. In Ogden, Utah, in 1921, Nels Andersen reported that a boy of 14 made himself available in the middle of a crowded park. The boy struck Andersen as unapologetic, funny, and pragmatic, "strong, active and mentally alert." He happily announced to a group of older male hobos that "he would 'do business' with anyone in the crowd for 50 cents," the price of a fine night's lodging in downtown Salt Lake City.[81] Andersen interviewed the chatty teen, who philosophized that prostitution was "an easy way to get by." Concluded Andersen: "He didn't hurt anyone. He minded his own business and paid his way. He didn't steal or beg. It wasn't any worse than many other things people did. No, he didn't work; he didn't have to."[82]

By the 1920s, the term "punk" was still used by hobos, but was "beginning to have a milder and more general use and the term 'lamb' [was] taking its place."[83] Andersen noted that "a Punk is a boy who travels about the country with a man known as a jocker" (synonymous with "wolf"), and that a jocker was "a man who exploits boys; that is, he either exploits their sex or has them steal or beg for him or both." Less at liberty was the "Road Kid" or "Preshun" (similar to *kinshon,* and a truncation of "precious one"), a "boy held in bondage by [a] jocker." Finally, to distinguish urban prostitution from mentor-protégé traveling partnerships, American hobo culture employed the terms "fairie" and "fag" to refer to "men or boys who exploit sex for profit." Neophytes—those boys waiting to be adopted by jockers—were called "gonsils."[84]

Afraid that "runaway boys were drifting into the Madison [Street] area and were being 'snared by the wolves,'" the Juvenile Protective Association hired Nels Andersen to research the problem. He learned that Chicago's Grant Park was a spot for *homos,* if not hobos:

> ...boys were much more exposed to homosexual contact in downtown movies and along the lakefront park than in Hobohemia [the Madison Street area]. In the midtown area was a homosexual community. Their loafing and meeting area was on the benches of Grant Park. Most of these homos were young men, most of them better dressed and most of them cherished a professional image of themselves.[85]

Andersen found that a male prostitution scene, replete with its own newspaper, code words, and other trappings of culture thrived in Grant Park, where business was conducted in a more "professional" manner than it was in darkened West Side movie houses, like the Haymarket, that catered to impoverished, and very young, boys.[86]

Instead of targeting older hustlers in Grant Park, the JPA concentrated on risqué theaters for outreach. "The willful exploitation of the sex instinct in youth are found in the movies, the theatres," wrote JPA director Jessie Binford in 1926. Taking in a burlesque show in a West Side theater, JPA staff discovered "the almost unbelievable situation of little boys, as young even as ten years of age, frequenting certain theatres for the purpose of soliciting men for homosexual practices; and many of these boys have been brought to us by a volunteer worker. We found them to be truants, runaways, defectives—and thus they live. We have been able to be of great assistance to them."[87]

For the next five years (until its funding ran dry), the JPA worked dually with these young hustlers, providing direct service—and disturbing their work environment. Binford wrote, "One of our men continually visits the cheaper theaters where men congregate for the obvious purpose of finding runaway boys who need money."[88] Over the next five years, JPA reports dramatically proclaimed small successes. Movie house managers were enlisted to protect defenseless youth, and seven men were arrested in one theater during Spring 1931.[89]

The Hull-House and JPA were enormously effective in advocating for the enactment and enforcement of Child Labor Laws. The immediate effect of these laws on destitute youth was clear: For a lack of legitimate opportunities, underclass kids were driven to prostitution. For all its progressive social action, the JPA's reform politics were decidedly old-fashioned. Citing a case where a runaway boy had lost his glasses (and thus, in an allusion to syphilis, his eyesight) after being subjected to perverted practices, Jessie Binford announced an increasing number of "small boys who are victims of homosexual practices. They are picked up on the streets and in certain theatres," she went on. "Where a colony of sex perverts live, no child is really safe."[90]

Still, the JPA left Chicago parks alone. Male and transgender sex work would continue to grow in Grant Park, Chicago's principal downtown park. By 1932, Chicago's Washington Square Park was also a popular cruising ground. In the 1910s, the mansions surrounding Washington Square were converted into inexpensive rooming houses, and the park attracted bohemians. These flophouses, also called bughouses, gave Washington Square Park the nickname Bughouse Square. "Nothing in town has been so aptly named," wrote one observer. "An evening at Bughouse Square is like a three-ring circus, like a carnival.... You have a feeling, as you leave the square that you'd go bughouse if you stayed there any longer."[91] The Bughouse would continue to be a prime hustling spot for the next 50 years.

Parks were being used all over the country for male sex work. Even Omaha had a park where boys would go to make money. In describing the Iowa sex panic of the 1950s, Neil Miller traces the history of Ernie Triplett, who would have been 19 years old in 1924:

At 16, he began living on his own in Council Bluffs, Iowa, and Omaha, where he worked as an apprentice painter. After someone gave him a shot of morphine, he woke up in the army trading post at Fort Mead, South Dakota. He went AWOL, spent four months in a military stockade, and returned to Omaha where he married a prostitute named Doris Spencer. There he worked at a carnival, a pool hall, and as a poker shill in a saloon. Doris continued to carry on her trade, sometimes giving the proceeds to her husband, sometimes keeping them for herself.

Triplett didn't seem to mind. In fact, he was doing some of the same, hanging around an Omaha park where "fairies" would give you a dollar if you let them "suck your peter," as he later told an interviewer. A dollar would buy "10 sticks of hay (marijuana)," he said, which could "really knock you out."[92]

Both Ernie's story and the JPA reports evidence the hardscrabble prospects youth engaged in sex work faced as the Great Depression approached.

In New York City, the Depression caused youth sex work to escalate and become structurally solidified into gang doctrine. Juvenile gangs incorporated prostitution into their modus operandi. In a study of 256 boy sex offenders convicted between 1928 and 1934, New York City Children's Court psychiatrist Lewis Doshay found that the "intimidation and seduction of junior members of a gang by their leaders, the urge in young boys to gain the friendship and protection of older members of a gang, and the lure of money and favors from adult degenerates" facilitated juvenile prostitution.[93]

The Seamen's Church Institute and nearby Battery Park were prime places for punk and gang boys to meet seamen—and for seamen to sell themselves to one another and to civilians. In 1931, the Committee of Fourteen sent an investigator to spend his spring and summer "anchored within the vail" in Greenwich Village, on Sixteenth Street between Ninth and Tenth Avenues. The investigator quickly learned that female prostitutes "charge $3 for a short time," representing a $2.50 increase since the Committee of Fifteen's 1901 notes.[94] Perhaps the women did a brisk business, but at the height of the Depression, SCI men were not so flush with cash. According to the investigator,

Ray, a wireless operator unemployed, informed me that most of the men who congregate here are not seamen at all.... He informed me that many male perverts hang around and solicit men.... Four men approached me and asked for cigarettes and tobacco. Two asked for money. Three asked me to buy them food. One stated he had no place to sleep and when questioned where he spent the previous night he said, "In the subway and on Staten Island ferry."[95]

The Institute was a legitimate enterprise, offering social services and inexpensive lodging to hundreds of out-of-work sailors, either mercantile or military, and of many nationalities. It was situated in a perfect area for sex work: between waterfronts, banked by Battery Park to the southeast and flanked by the East Village, where a pint of grappa could be purchased for $1.50, a gallon of dry red wine for $3.50. At Village speakeasies, "liquor was openly served."[96] Sailors down on their luck commonly smoked opium on the banks of the East River. Tommy Dixon, a regular at the SCI and one of the Committee's favorite sources, asked:

Have you heard the other day about a man's body being dragged out of the river right in front of the

Institute? He was one of the smokies. There are many
seamen consuming that "smoke," and sit down at the
edge of the water and doze off, and fall in and drown.
Some of the bodies are never recovered.[97]

The interior of the Seamen's Church Institute was laid out like the Newport Y, and bathroom sex was rampant. The government investigator discovered that the hard way in the cafeteria "gents' room," where he had a desperate encounter with a Swedish seaman, who (cheekily?) claimed to work on the United Fruit Line. Asked whether he charged anything, the seaman asked for "a little present...50 cents."[98] The investigator fled the situation, but not before making an unrealized observation. In an area so saturated with single men living in poverty, male sex work paid only 17% of the going rate for female sex work, even as males, females, and fairies worked the same park.

Sex work also flourished in Battery Park. Along with Riverside Drive and Fifth Avenue, it was a major center of homosexual prostitution around 1925.[99] Six years later, the Committee of Fourteen found the park teeming with sex workers:

> *Tommy asked me to go with him to Battery Park....*
> *He pointed out to me in Battery Park about 15 men*
> *whom he said were fairies. I had seen them on many*
> *occasions in the Institute. They sat on separate*
> *benches, always leaving room for a casual [a male*
> *passerby] to sit down. Tommy also told me there are*

many girls scouting around in this park trying to pick
up men.[100]

The thicket of sailors, fairies, and female sex workers on the Hudson provided an ideal environment for sexual exchange. Of course, where there were sailors and fairies, there were usually punks.

In the park and outside the SCI, shoeshine boys sold pornographic cards for 35 cents apiece.[101] One park guide asked the Committee's investigator whether he was interested in punks. The investigator asked his guide whether he knew of "a house where there are young boys who are punks," but his guide demurred. "I know [that] all the punks in the park and in the Institute are about 16 or 17 years old and of all nationalities. They haven't a house where they congregate, but they'll go with you any place you take them."[102] In the early 1930s, keeping with earlier historical patterns, American boys were more likely to work as independent sexual entrepreneurs in open public spaces than as brothel assignees or street trade under pimp control.

Julius was a 16-year-old moonlighting punk who frequented Battery Park and the SCI. He was 5-foot-4 and weighed 110 pounds, with black hair and eyes. He had a fair complexion, and wore a white shirt, no tie, and gray trousers on a mid-July night in 1931. Apparently Julius sensed the investigator's nervousness, for he asked,

> *"Are you here for the first time?"*
> *I [the investigator] said "No but I never saw you*
> *before."*

He said "Have you met any of the others?"
I said "No."
He said "It is just the same. Have you a room?"
I said "I have a room at the Institute."
He said "That's no good. Come with me, I'll show
you where to go."
I said "Have you a room?"
He said "I'll get a room for you."
I said "Where and how much?"
He said "Around Chatham Square in a lodging
house. It will be $1 for the room."
I said "How much do you want?"
He said "50 cents for ____ (perversion) [in other
words, oral sex], and 75 cents for ____ (in the anus)...."
I said "Where do you live?"
He said "Why do you want to know that?"
I said "I wouldn't go with you now because my friend
is here. I prefer to meet you alone some other time."
He said "After 7 you can always find me here. And
during the day and late in the evening, you could find
me at the Institute."[103]

In 1931, 75 cents would buy what $8.50 would today. These rates were consistent with those in other cities. Pioneering gay filmmaker Otis Wade described a similarly buyer-friendly price scale among Los Angeles sailors in the late 1920s. "They're so easy to pick up—just 50 cents for breakfast and he's yours," he wrote.[104] Julius must have been able to make some money,

devoting as much of his time as he did to his profession. His street-savvy was also impressive, apparent by how deftly he deflected the investigator when he asked for the boy's address.

Happy Campers:
Civilian Conservation Corps Camps, 1933

Franklin Delano Roosevelt had a knack for fostering the ideal male sex work ecology. During the Great Depression, when scores of men were out of work, Roosevelt—elected president in 1932—established the Civilian Conservation Corps, a set of camps that provided forest conservation work for unemployed young men, mostly from urban centers. FDR called an emergency session during the 73rd Congress to promote his Emergency Conservation Work Act. On March 31, 1933, three months after taking office, Roosevelt signed a bill ordering the implementation of the CCC, to be run by the government with help from the Army.

The ECWA provided for hundreds of camps set up across the country to accommodate destitute young men. During the first calendar year of their existence, CCC camps created housing and employment for 800,000 boys and veterans.[105] According to the National Association of Civilian Conservation Corps Alumni (NACCCA), the government quickly realized that

Logistics was an immediate problem. The bulk of
young unemployed youth was concentrated in the East,
while most of the work projects were in the western

parts of the country. The Army was the only agency with the slightest capability of merging the two and was in the program from the beginning. Although not totally unprepared, the Army nevertheless devised new plans and methods to meet the challenge. Mobilizing the nation's transportation system, it moved thousands of enrollees from induction centers to working camps. It used its own regular and reserve officers, together with regulars of the Coast Guard, Marine Corps and Navy to temporarily command camps and companies.[106]

Many enlistees traveled far away from their homes to remote locations, where they camped out with hundreds of other young men. It is not surprising that male prostitution flourished in this context. Money, of course, was the primary consideration for campers. Men in positions of power at the CCC camps were able to grant their youthful charges certain privileges. Mining the archives of the Kinsey Institute for Research in Sex, Gender, and Reproduction, gay historian Martin Duberman has unearthed three accounts of sexual exchange in the CCC camps, all of which are worth noting here.

One camp was set up for 200 boys, who ranged in age from 15 to 22. The boys were not recruited from big cities, in this case, but from towns and farms. Most of them were from Texas. Kinsey's correspondent seems to have benefited from an odd, unspecified arrangement that recalls the Newport decoys:

Camp 1: Record kept by BA [code name]. BA was a man of 47 who was known to have had considerable experience in sex relations with men and boys. He was intentionally planted in the camp under an agreement with him that he would make all the sex contacts he could and learn all he could and keep a record which he would turn over from time to time.... He had sufficient influence with camp authorities that he could often obtain better or easier work assignments for the boys and favor ones in issuing supplies, etc. etc.... His pay was small but he had a small private income and he made some money from men for arranging dates with the boys.[107]

Of the 104 boys that BA hit on, 39 demurred. Of the 65 young men who allowed him to masturbate and fellate them, 20 "openly and frankly asked for it." In return, they received easier assignments and better supplies. Some were pimped out, either to other officers or to men from the nearby town. Whether they received money from these engagements is not discussed, but we can assume that if their dates were paying BA, they were probably paying the boys too. But the sexual availability of these boys was not solely related to their need for money or desire for favors. Being masturbated and fellated was likely reward enough in these times of deprivation.

Though this report to Kinsey does not mention any peer sexual relations, another does: Thomas Painter recorded in 1941 that a casual hustler named Nick had, at age 16, "sampled three different boys on a number of occasions" in two different CCC camps.[108] Another unnamed source portrays the easy, flirty environment of a camp located near a saloon town. There, sexual relations between CCC boys were common and friendly: In the report, two young men describe having sex in the woods and picking up men "in a camp latrine."[109] Sexual exchange served as an initiation into gay life for two youths:

> [A] boy who was contacted in a saloon town said he had coitus with girls before enrolling but no relations with males. He was seduced by a man he had met in a saloon after enrolling. There had been subsequent relations with the same man and others.... He had always been well paid by the men....
>
> Another [boy] of 19...had had female coitus but no homosexual contacts. He was seduced in camp by the boy who introduced him [to the unnamed source]. He had had 5 experiences with men in town and was willing to have more. He expected to be paid.[110]

The source observed that about 40% of boys in the CCC camp had sex with other boys. Their intimacies included advice about how to make extra money, as in the example above.

This opportunity for entrepreneurship mobilized the happy campers, and a hustling scene developed in the saloon town, where

> ...several of the boys were known to have "regulars"...men whom they met frequently and secretly. One would stand out in front of the camp quite openly every few evenings and be picked up by the same man in a good car and not return until late at night. There was a good deal of joking about him but he kept by himself and ignored it. Quite a number had plenty of spending money the source of which was a mystery. Several foremen and officers commented on it.[111]

This scene does not sound secretive at all—quite the contrary. The casual joking and official indifference, in combination with such open solicitation, hint that sex for pay between CCC boys and civilians was considered an inconsequential matter.

The Camp 2 source cites one foreman and one superintendent who kept favorite boys. The superintendent

> ...observed the boys carefully and when he saw one who appealed to him and who he thought would be susceptible he assigned him as his clerk. If the boy did not respond to his careful approaches he found an excuse for replacing him with another.... Relations consisted of almost nightly fellatio on the boy by the Supt. with swallowing of the ejaculate. He thought it kept him vigorous and acted as a tonic. Orgasm by the Supt. once or twice a week preferably by fellatio but he was not very particular. Generally a boy became tired of it in a month of two and quit and was replaced by another. He paid them well.[112]

The advantage of submitting to the superintendent was office duty rather than outdoor labor. The clerks also received their own room assignment (albeit a room right next to the superintendent's) rather than a tent. Welcome as they were, these privileges did not prevent the boys from quickly moving on; the hassles of sex work could outweigh the benefits.

Camp officials also had a hand in extending sexual exchange beyond the CCC posts and into the surrounding community. The sheer isolation of another Texas camp, located "over 100 miles from a railroad and town," left its workmen craven in their search for off-camp connections and confections:

> *Near the camp was a small store with 6 or 8 cabins which were rented to summer campers.... The owner was about 50 and had been running the place for at least 10 years.... One of the camp foremen who was about 40, married and a former Boy Scout Executive, used to rent one of the cabins.... One night the owner noticed a boy go into the foreman's cabin and not come out. Next time the foreman took a cabin the owner watched and a boy entered. The owner listened outside and heard them having sex relations. The foreman continued the practice all summer.*
>
> *The owner had had male sex relations in his younger days but had given them up when he married. The foreman's action gave him the idea and he had no difficulty in establishing relations with—all told—9 boys—ages 17-21. Boys frequently visited the store to buy candy, soda pop etc. so it was easy to arrange contacts. The boys involved were given unlimited credit at the store so they considered the liaison a good bargain. The act was consummated usually in a cabin but sometimes in an outbuilding and consisted mostly of fellatio with more or less petting and some anal coitus. When possible they stripped and went to bed. Sometimes [two] of the boys slept together in a cabin with relations.... On one occasion a visiting man, the owner, and 3 boys spent about 3 hrs. in a cabin in the act. On another a man spent a night with a boy and the owner was with them for over 2 hrs. The boy had 7 orgasms. A man, fisherman who rented a cabin for a few nights threw out some hints to the owner who responded in kind and an agreement was reached whereby the owner arranged to have a boy visit the man. The man remained a month with almost daily or nightly visits by various boys.[113]*

It is a testament to the persistent appeal of male sex work that an efficient male brothel blossomed in the middle of the American wilderness.

On the whole, the hustlers in these three CCC camps appear to have faced little danger. They were not evicted from the CCC, transferred, raped, beaten, or arrested. In one instance, the most brazen hustler was gently mocked, and kept boys eventually found their Super tiresome. But that's as tough as it got, according to these sources.

Kenneth Marlowe, who lived near one of the camps, remembers that when he was 13, he would have liked to have had sex with the

CCC boys if he could have. "There was a CCC camp outside of Tipton [Iowa]," Marlowe recalls. "I would have liked to 'comfort' the dull evenings for many of the CCC boys. But in a small town only window-shopping [was] permitted."[114]

CCC backers lauded the program for dramatically reducing crime. One Chicago judge attributed to the CCC a 55% reduction in local crimes committed by young men.[115] The official report was that "the news from the camps was welcome and good. The enrollees were working hard, eating hearty and gaining weight, while they improved millions of acres of federal and state lands, and parks. New roads were built, telephone lines strung and the first of millions of trees that would be planted had gone into the soil."[116] FDR had learned his lesson well, and was not eager to have any more publicity about government-funded hustlers.

Street Fleet:
Hustlers in Paul Cadmus's Paintings, 1934-1935

The painter Paul Cadmus got a career boost from the FDR administration's denunciation of his painting "The Fleet's In!" This funny, garish work, executed in egg tempera, depicts several sailors carousing on a New York City sidewalk. On the right side of the painting, two Navy boys approach three female sex workers: One of the women wears a red dress and a world-weary expression, her right hand suggestively propped on her hip as she saunters up. A well-proportioned woman in the middle blocks our view of the third woman; we can see only her face, which is strikingly masculine. Perhaps a transgendered prostitute?

On the left side of the painting, a sailor seated on a park or waterfront ledge accepts a cigarette from a markedly primped and genteel male civilian. The civilian is wearing a red tie.

Even the Committee of Fourteen would have picked up on the thinly veiled meaning: The genteel civilian prefers sex with other men. George Chauncey, analyzing this painting, comments that:

> *The man offering the cigarette to the sailor has the typical markers of a fairy: bleached hair, tweezed eyebrows, rouged cheeks, and red tie. The sailor's eyes suggest he knows exactly what is being offered along with the smoke.*[117]

Unlike the female and transgendered sex workers, who would extract money from the fleet, the man in the red tie no doubt

2.6 Paul Cadmus, The Fleet's In! (detail), 1934; oil on canvas, 30 x 60 inches; from the collection of the Navy Museum, Washington, D.C.

fig. 2.7 Paul Cadmus, *Shore Leave*, 1935; etching, original edition of 50, 10 3/8 x 11 1/2 inches; courtesy of the DC Moore Gallery, NYC.

fig. 2.8 Paul Cadmus, *YMCA Locker Room*, 1934; etching, original edition of 50, 6 1/2 x 12 5/8 inches; courtesy of the DC Moore Gallery, NYC.

intends to pay his sailor for a sexual encounter; he has already given him a cigarette, as a harbinger of things to come. By the 1930s, sailors were no longer expected to pay for blow jobs by effete civilian men, as they were in the late 1800s. Sailors now expected to get paid when older men got them off.

"The Fleet's In!" demonstrates the easy flow of information and desire between client and worker. The sailors have it three ways: getting sucked off, getting paid, and retaining their masculine identity to boot. It is also marvelously illustrative of the cooperative aspect of sex work in 1930s New York City, where fairy prostitutes, punk youths, sailor hustlers, and female sex workers could be seen together as a community. "The Fleet's In!" and "Shore Leave," a companion piece that depicts sailors interacting with fairies and female prostitutes, are memories of Riverside Park of the 1920s and 1930s. Bordering the Hudson River at 95th Street, Riverside Park was then, according to Cadmus's friend Lincoln Kirstien, "a fast and happy hunting ground for sailors on summer liberty with their casual pickups, male or female."[118]

These implications were not anything with which FDR's Navy wanted to be associated. Cadmus had been receiving public money for his painting, under a New Deal program called the Works Progress Administration. When "The Fleet's In!" was included in a Washington, D.C., exhibit of WPA artists, the Navy hit the cabin roof. Recently, the Naval Historical Center published an official history of this painting's fate:

1934: The painting is selected by the WPA for inclusion in a show of PWAP (Public Works of Art Project) *art at the Corcoran Gallery of Art. The exhibition opens with the painting included. Following the publication of an adverse letter to the editor in the **Evening Star** (Washington, D.C.) and subsequent outcry, Secretary of the Navy Claude A. Swanson orders Assistant Secretary of the Navy Henry Latrobe Roosevelt to remove the painting from the show. It is either confined to H. L. Roosevelt's home, the "Navy Department brig," or the Secretary of the Navy's bathroom (depending on which story you believe).[119]*

"The Fleet's In!" was hidden from the public for the next 50 years, until the Navy succumbed to the pleas of the organizers of a Cadmus retrospective and released the painting. It now hangs on public display at the Navy Art Gallery at the Washington Navy Yard, an ironic and fitting home.

While Cadmus would go on to paint hustlerama through the years, two other 1930s paintings of his are worth mentioning here. Both "YMCA Locker Room," painted in 1934, and "Horseplay," painted in 1935, explore the sexual realm of the locker room. While not as explicit in their depictions of male sex work as "The Fleet's In," these two paintings are suffused with a free-for-all energy, where men in varied states of undress interact with one another. Cadmus used age and clothing differences to impart a sex work component into these images. "Horseplay" depicts a naked youth, standing beside a leering older man, fully dressed, seated strategically next to him. The stripling seems to be ignoring the man, who's set to whip him with a towel.

In "YMCA Locker Room," and a pen-and-ink sketch titled "YMCA Locker Room II," Cadmus depicts two couples making what might be seen as sex work arrangements amid a crowd of about 20 other men. In the foreground, a half-dressed older man gestures to a younger man, who is naked save for a hat, socks, and shoes. In the background, a plump man wearing black leather chaps and a vest looms over a skinny youth squatting on a locker room bench in his underwear. In the corner (the left corner in the sketch, the right corner in the painting), a man who resembles the fairy from "The Fleet's In!" is getting dressed. While male sex work is not as apparent in these works as it is in "The Fleet's In!" it is similarly encoded. And from what we know of the history of the YMCA as an early pick-up spot for male sex workers and their clients, an insider's portrait of the milieu is likely to include male sex work.

The beginning of an American artistic examination of male sex workers leads us into the astonishing military prostitution scene at the onset of World War II, when the Navy's last great mobilization flooded the streets of American port cities with single young men.

[1] PERSONAL COMMUNICATION, FEBRUARY 2002.

[2] FROM HIRSCHFELD, MAGNUS. *DIE HOMOSEXUALITAT DES MANNES UND DES WEIBE.* LOUIS MARCUS, BERLIN, 1914, PP. 550-554. TRANSLATION BY JAMES STEAKLEY FOR KATZ, *GAH,* PP. 50-51. (EMPHASIS MINE.)

[3] SHEPHERD, E.S. "CONTRIBUTION TO THE STUDY OF INDETERMINACY," *AMERICAN JOURNAL OF UROLOGY AND SEXOLOGY,* VOL. 14, NO. 6, PP. 241-252. ALSO SEE KATZ, *GLA,* P. 380.

[4] MERRILL, LILBURN. "A SUMMARY OF FINDINGS IN A STUDY OF SEXUALISM AMONG A GROUP OF ONE HUNDRED DELINQUENT BOYS," FROM THE *AMERICAN*

JOURNAL OF UROLOGY AND SEXOLOGY, VOL. 15 (1919), PP. 259-269. REPRINTED IN KATZ, *GLA,* P.381. THE "FELLATIO GROUP" REFERS TO A GROUP OF BOYS IN THIS REFORM SCHOOL WHO PRACTICED FELLATIO WITH OTHER JUVENILE DELINQUENTS.

[5] IBID, IDEM.

[6] IBID, IDEM.

[7] MAYNE, P. 428.

[8] HARRINGTON, JIMMY. *MEMORIES OF A HOTEL MAN.* ART-GUILD PRESS, 1935; PP. 3, 4, 7, AND 31-33. STATISTICS FROM NEWSENGINE'S CONSUMER PRICE INDEX COMPARISONS (WWW.NEWSENGINE.COM). BASED ON 1917 AND 1997 STATISTICS ($5 IN 1917 WAS EQUAL TO $58.15 IN 1997, THE EARLIEST AND LATEST YEARS IN THE PITTSBURGH RECORDS).

[9] LIND, *AUTOBIOGRAPHY,* P. 128.

[10] SHUFELDT, R.W. "BIOGRAPHY OF A PASSIVE PEDERAST." *AMERICAN JOURNAL OF UROLOGY AND SEXOLOGY,* NO. 13 (1917); PP. 451-460. ALSO SEE CHAUNCEY, *GNY,* P. 68.

[11] IBID., IDEM.

[12] IBID., IDEM.

[13] IBID., IDEM.

[14] IBID., IDEM. ALSO SEE KATZ, *GLA,* P. 320.

[15] LIND, *AUTOBIOGRAPHY,* P. 7.

[16] IBID., P. 124.

[17] FROM COMMITTEE OF FOURTEEN PAPERS, NYC: MARCH 24, 1922.

[18] SEE CHAUNCEY, *GNY,* P. 86.

[19] IBID., P. 68.

[20] LICHTENSTEIN, PERRY. *MEDICAL REVIEW OF REVIEWS,* 1921. REPRINTED IN KATZ, *GLA,* P. 401.

[21] *SAN FRANCISCO EXAMINER,* JULY 27, 1927. TWO DOLLARS WAS A STANDARD PRICE FOR FEMALE PROSTITUTES IN THE 1920S, SO IT SEEMS AN EVEN EXCHANGE.

[22] THE VICE COMMISSION OF CHICAGO, *THE SOCIAL EVIL IN CHICAGO: A STUDY OF EXISTING CONDITIONS AND RECOMMENDATIONS.* CHICAGO, 1911; P. 297.

[23] IBID., P. 298.

[24] IBID., IDEM.

[25] NICOSIA, GERALD AND RICHARD RAFF. *BUGHOUSE BLUES.* VANTAGE PRESS (NYC), 1977; P. 85.

[26] FROM A 1945 LETTER WRITTEN BY THOMAS PAINTER TO ALFRED KINSEY THAT PREFACES PAINTER'S BOOK *MALE HOMOSEXUALS AND THEIR PROSTITUTES.* TRACING THE NEW YORK CITY SAILOR PEG-HOUSE CULTURE IN THE MID 1920S, PAINTER REPORTS THAT GEORGE BEEKMAN OPENED UP THE FIRST LONG-STANDING AMERICAN SAILOR BROTHEL. "BEEKMAN RAN EXCLUSIVELY TO UNIFORMS, MOSTLY SAILORS," PAINTER WROTE. "RAN ON WEST 43RD ST[REET] FOR YEARS, THEN RETIRED TO BROOKLYN." KINSEY INSTITUTE LIBRARY FOR RESEARCH IN SEX, GENDER, AND REPRODUCTION (KIL): THOMAS PAINTER PAPERS.

[27] IBID., IDEM.

[28] IBID., IDEM.

[29] FROM A LETTER WRITTEN BY PAINTER TO KINSEY, DATED AUGUST 1, 1944. HOUSED IN PAINTER PAPERS (KIL). "PEDICATED" MEANS "FUCKED."

[30] FROM A LETTER BY PAINTER TO KINSEY, AUGUST 2, 1944.

[31] FROM PAINTER'S NAME BOOK, KIL.

[32] SEE *NEW BROADWAY BREVITIES,* 1931, AS QUOTED IN *CITIZENS NEWS,* JANUARY 1966.

[33] BRUCE, KENNILWORTH. *GOLDIE.* WILLIAM GODWIN, 1933; P. 105. THIS MAY BE THE FIRST AMERICAN COMING-OF-AGE MALE PROSTITUTION NOVEL, AND IT IS WORTHY OF FURTHER ANALYSIS AND RESEARCH. GOLDIE HAILS FROM NEW ORLEANS; HIS TIME IN MANHATTAN IS AN ESCAPE FROM A SON HE HAS HAD OUT OF WEDLOCK. WHILE IN NEW YORK, HE HAS HIS GOOD AND BAD TRICKS AND IS EVENTUALLY SAVED BY A FAIRY WHO HOSTS HOUSE PARTIES, AT WHICH GOLDIE IS MUCH IN DEMAND. WHEN GOLDIE RETURNS HOME, HE WALKS TO THE HUSTLER STROLL AND PROMISES HE WILL MAKE THE STREETS BETTER FOR THE BOYS WHO ARE OUT THERE (PERHAPS, HE WONDERS, HIS SON?).

[34] SEE SECTION 17, U.S. DRAFT ACT OF 1817.

[35] INTERVIEW WITH SUSAN STRYKER, CONDUCTED BY THE AUTHOR, 11/16/01.

[36] *THE NEW YORK TIMES,* JULY 20, 1921.

[37] FROM NEWPORT NAVAL ACADEMY TESTIMONY, 1920. REPRINTED IN CHAUNCEY, "CHRISTIAN BROTHERHOOD OR SOCIAL PERVERSION?" IN

DUBERMAN'S *A QUEER WORLD,* P. 296. FOR A RICH AND DETAILED ACCOUNT OF THE NEWPORT SCANDAL, SEE LAWRENCE R. MURPHY, *PERVERTS BY OFFICIAL ORDER.* HARRINGTON PARK PRESS (NY), 1988.

[38] SEE CHAUNCEY, "CHRISTIAN BROTHERHOOD," P. 297.

[39] MURPHY, P. 13. MURPHY SUPPOSES THAT "PENNIES" WAS ALSO A DOUBLE ENTENDRE FOR "PENES" (PENISES), ALTHOUGH IT ALSO REFERS TO THE TYPICAL WARTIME 10- TO 50-CENT RATE SAILOR-PROSTITUTES RECEIVED.

[40] SEE MURPHY, P. 264

[41] SEE MURPHY, P. 106; COMPARATIVE RATES FROM NEWSENGINE ($52.46 IN 2000 EQUALED $3 IN 1919, ACCORDING TO NEWSENGINE'S NEW ENGLAND DATABASE).

[42] CHAUNCEY, "CHRISTIAN BROTHERHOOD," P. 303.

[43] MURPHY ARGUES THAT THE CITY OF NEWPORT, URGED ON BY NAVAL AUTHORITIES, BEGAN A SUCCESSFUL SOCIAL MARKETING CAMPAIGN TO KEEP YOUNG SINGLE WOMEN FROM TEMPTING NAVAL TRAINEES.

[44] MURPHY, P. 26.

[45] FROM *THE NEW YORK TIMES,* JANUARY 27, 1920.

[46] FROM *THE NEW YORK TIMES,* JANUARY 20, 1920.

[47] FROM *THE NEW YORK TIMES,* JANUARY 25, 1920.

[48] SEE MURPHY, P. 158.

[49] FROM *THE NEW YORK TIMES,* OCTOBER 25, 1920.

[50] FROM *THE NEW YORK TIMES,* OCTOBER 28, 1920.

[51] FROM *THE NEW YORK TIMES,* MARCH 5, 1920.

[52] FROM *THE NEW YORK TIMES,* MAY 23, 1920.

[53] SEE *THE NEW YORK TIMES,* JANUARY 20, 1919.

[54] FROM *THE NEW YORK TIMES,* MAY 29, 1920, QUOTING NAVAL INTELLIGENCE RECOMMENDATIONS: "'THE SERVICE RECORDS OF FOURTEEN MEN [SHOULD] BE GIVEN NOTATION, *FOR THEIR INTEREST AND ZEAL* IN ASSISTING THE JUDGES OF THE COURT.'" (EMPHASIS MINE.)

[55] FROM *THE NEW YORK TIMES,* JULY 20, 1921. ALSO IN KATZ, *GLA,* P. 399.

[56] IBID., IDEM.

[57] SEE ROSE, AL. *STORYVILLE.* UNIVERSITY OF ALABAMA PRESS, 1974.

[58] PAINTER, *MHP,* P. 13. COURTESY OF THE THOMAS PAINTER PAPERS (KIL).

[59] THE VICE COMMISSION OF CHICAGO. *THE SOCIAL EVIL IN CHICAGO,* P. 73.

[60] IBID., P. 243.

[61] IBID., P. 244.

[62] ADDAMS, JANE. *A NEW CONSCIENCE AND AN ANCIENT EVIL.* MACMILLAN, NYC, 1912. REPRINTED IN 1972 BY ARNO PRESS; PP. 107-8 OF THE ARNO EDITION.

[63] ADDAMS, P. 52.

[64] ANDERSEN, NELS. *THE AMERICAN HOBO.* E.J. BRILL (NETHERLANDS), 1975; P. XII OF PREFACE, FOR DATES, AND P. 170, FOR STEVE'S MOTHER'S WARNING. ANDERSEN ALSO REMEMBERED RUNNING ERRANDS FOR PROSTITUTE GIRLS IN THE SAME TIME PERIOD, ACTIVITIES FOR WHICH HE MADE "A NICKEL TIP, EQUAL TO THE PROFIT ON TEN PAPERS."

[65] ANDERSEN, *THE AMERICAN HOBO,* PP. 25-26. WHAT ANDERSEN CONSIDERED DECEPTION MAY REALLY HAVE BEEN AN INTRODUCTORY AND SCRIPTED CODE THAT RELIED UPON A NEWSBOY'S COMPREHENSION, AND PARTICIPATORY RESPONSE, FOR A NEWSPAPER SALE TO ESCALATE INTO SEX WORK.

[66] FROM AN UNTITLED INTERNAL DRAFT, IN "NEWSBOY CONDITIONS IN CHICAGO." JANE ADDAMS PAPERS, SWARTHMORE COLLEGE PEACE COLLECTION.

[67] ADAMS, MYRON. "CHILDREN IN AMERICAN STREET TRADES," CONDUCTED FOR AND PUBLISHED BY THE HULL-HOUSE ASSOCIATION, 1903; P. 5.

[68] F. ZETA YOUMANS, REPORTING IN THE 1924 JUVENILE PROTECTIVE ASSOCIATION ANNUAL REPORT, P. 28.

[69] FROM *NEWSBOY CONDITIONS IN CHICAGO,* JUVENILE PROTECTIVE ASSOCIATION REPORT, 1903-1905; P. 17. WHETHER THESE DISEASES WERE REAL (SUCH AS GONORRHEA, SYPHILIS, OR HERPES) OR IMAGINARY (THOSE "INFECTED" WITH HOMOSEXUAL DESIRE) IS UNCLEAR.

[70] VICE COMMISSION OF CHICAGO, P. 290. THE REPORT GOES ON TO DISTINGUISH IN TYPE THE "OCCASIONAL AND CLANDESTINE MALE PROSTITUTE" FROM THE PROFESSIONAL. THE AUTHORS ALSO CLAIMED THAT PERVERTS WERE NOT AS INFECTIOUS AS FEMALE PROSTITUTES AND OTHER PROMISCUOUS FALLEN WOMEN; HOWEVER, THEY WERE MORE LIKELY TO INFECT "VIRTUOUS" PARTNERS (I.E., THEIR WIVES AND CHILDREN). EVEN MARRIED MEN, THEY SUGGESTED, WERE "PRACTIC-

ING PERVERT METHODS" (AT GREAT RISK TO THEIR WIVES AND CHILDREN, WHO
MIGHT SUDDENLY BE COMPELLED TO PROSTITUTE THEMSELVES, HAVING
ACQUIRED—EITHER CONGENITALLY OR THROUGH "PHYSICAL" CONTACT—THEIR
SICKNESS).

[71] SEE ACKER, CAROLINE. *CREATING THE AMERICAN JUNKIE.* JOHNS HOPKINS
UNIVERSITY PRESS, PREPUBLICATION COPY, 2001.

[72] VICE COMMISSION OF CHICAGO, *THE SOCIAL EVIL IN CHICAGO,* PP. 290-1.

[73] PHILADELPHIA VICE COMMISSION. "A REPORT ON THE EXISTING
CONDITIONS WITH RECOMMENDATIONS TO THE HONORABLE RUDOLPH
BLANKENBURG, MAYOR OF PHILADELPHIA." PHILADELPHIA, 1913; P. 23.

[74] IBID., P. 23, 34.

[75] IBID., P. 24.

[76] IBID., P. 81. INTERVIEW CONDUCTED MAY 17, 1912, DURING THE 10 P.M. TO 6
A.M. SHIFT.

[7]IBID., P. 25.

[78] ANDERSEN, NELS. *THE HOBO: THE SOCIOLOGY OF THE HOMELESS MAN.*
UNIVERSITY OF CHICAGO, 1923; PP. 144-147.

[79] IBID., P. 146.

[80] IBID., IDEM.

[81] ANDERSEN, "THE JUVENILE AND THE TRAMP." *JOURNAL OF THE AMERICAN
INSTITUTE OF CRIMINAL LAW AND CRIMINOLOGY.* NO. 14, 1923-1924; P. 307. ALSO
SEE QUINN, PP. 322, 348-9, FOR PRICES ON SALT LAKE CITY ROOMS.

[82] ANDERSEN, "THE JUVENILE AND THE TRAMP."

[83] ANDERSEN, *THE HOBO,* P. 99, FOOTNOTE 1.

[84] IBID., PP. 101-103. ANDERSEN ALSO MENTIONED THE "JACK ROLLER," CALLING
HIM "A TRAMP WHO ROBS A FELLOW-TRAMP WHILE HE IS DRUNK OR ASLEEP. THERE
IS A TYPE OF 'JACK'," HE REPORTED, "WHO OPERATED AMONG THE MEN GOING TO
AND FROM THE HARVESTS. HE MAY HOLD THEM UP IN A BOXCAR WITH A GUN OR
IN SOME DARK ALLEY. HE IS USUALLY CALLED A HI-JACK" (P. 103). IN 1940, OR
ABOUT 20 YEARS LATER, THE TERM *JACKROLLER* WOULD BE USED TO REFER TO HUS-
TLERS WHO ROBBED THEIR CLIENTS INSTEAD OF SLEEPING WITH THEM. (SEE
PAINTER, *MHP.*) AND HI-JACK WOULD, OF COURSE, EVENTUALLY BE RESTRICTED

TO AIRLINE *HIJACKINGS.* ALSO SEE BERKMAN FOR AN EARLY REFERENCE TO
PRESHUN (THERE SPELLED *PRUSHUN*), P. 173.

[85] ANDERSEN, *THE AMERICAN HOBO,* P. 172.

[86] SEE "THIS YEAR'S WORK—1925," JPA. A MORE DETAILED REPORT OF GRANT
PARK WOULD BE FASCINATING TO EXAMINE, BUT IT IS HARD TO COME BY. IT'S
NOT AVAILABLE IN EITHER THE SWARTHMORE COLLEGE PEACE COLLECTION'S
JANE ADDAMS PAPERS OR THE UNIVERSITY OF CHICAGO HULL-HOUSE ARCHIVE.
FOR A REFERENCE TO THE HAYMARKET THEATER, SEE JUVENILE PROTECTIVE
ASSOCIATION BOARD OF DIRECTORS NOTES, DECEMBER 1926. FOR A QUINTESSEN-
TIAL NEWSBOY-CUM-MOVIE-HOUSE-AND-AMUSEMENT-PARK HUSTLER IN THE EARLY
1900S, SEE ARTHUR FOXE, "PSYCHOANALYSIS OF A SODOMIST." *AMERICAN
JOURNAL OF ORTHOPSYCHIATRY,* 1941; PP. 137-138. FOXE PRESENTED HIS PATIENT'S
SEXUAL HISTORY FROM 1914, FOLLOWING 515 HOURS OF ANALYSIS CONDUCTED IN
PRISON, WHERE JERRY WAS SERVING TIME FOR SODOMY. "AT A NEWSSTAND HE LET
HIS EMPLOYER PLAY WITH HIS PENIS. HE WAS TOLD EVERYONE DID IT. HOWEVER,
WHEN THIS MAN TOOK DOWN HIS PANTS AND ATTEMPTED TO PENETRATE HIS REC-
TUM, JERRY FOUND IT SOMEWHAT PAINFUL, QUIT HIS JOB AND TOLD HIS SISTER.
HE WAS IN PANIC AND CRIED.... FROM ONE FRIEND HE LEARNED HOW TO GET
INTO THE MOVIES BY LETTING A MAN PLAY WITH HIS PENIS. HE JOINED AN
AGGRESSIVE GROUP WHO MADE IT A PRACTICE TO MEET IN AN EMPTY LOT AT
NIGHT, OFTEN WITH GIRLS PRESENT, WHERE HE INDULGED IN MUTUAL MASTURBA-
TION, FELLATIO, AND ANAL INTERCOURSE."

[87] BINFORD, JESSIE. "THE YEAR'S WORK—1925," JUVENILE PROTECTIVE
ASSOCIATION OF CHICAGO (CHICAGO: 1926). MICROFICHE REEL 113.53, JANE
ADDAMS PAPERS, SWARTHMORE COLLEGE PEACE COLLECTION.

[88] BINFORD, JESSIE. "THIS YEAR'S WORK—1928."

[89] SEE JUVENILE PROTECTIVE ASSOCIATION, "THIS YEAR'S WORK—1931." IN
THIS IS A REGRETFUL PASSAGE ABOUT THE FUNDING RESTRICTIONS THAT HAD
FORCED THE JPA TO FOREGO ITS MOVIE HOUSE OUTREACH. IT PREFIGURES THE
FINANCIAL DIFFICULTIES THAT HUSTLER-FOCUSED PROGRAMS HAVE FACED IN THE
CONTEMPORARY WORLD OF NONPROFIT SOCIAL SERVICES.

[90] JESSE BINFORD, "THIS YEAR'S WORK—1926," PP. 6-7 (EMPHASIS MINE}.

[91] FROM *CHICAGO HUSH,* SEPTEMBER 18, 1932. "STREETWALKER AND ELITE MEET IN BUGHOUSE SQUARE." LIKE NEW YORK CITY'S BRYANT PARK, THE BUGHOUSE WAS (AND STILL IS) DIRECTLY ACROSS FROM A LIBRARY, IN THIS CASE NEWBERRY LIBRARY, ON THE NEAR NORTH SIDE.

[92] MILLER, NEIL. *SEX CRIME PANIC.* ALYSON BOOKS (LOS ANGELES, CA): 2002; P. 14, PREPRODUCTION MANUSCRIPT.

[93] DOSHAY, LEWIS. *THE BOY SEX OFFENDER AND HIS LATER CAREER.* GRUNE AND STRATTON: 1943. REPRINTED IN 1969, PATTERSON SMITH REPRINT SERIES IN CRIMINOLOGY, LAW ENFORCEMENT, AND SOCIAL PROBLEMS, PP. 80-81. ONE BOY, AN 11-YEAR-OLD WEST INDIAN, WAS "A MEMBER OF AN AGGRESSIVE GANG." ANOTHER, A 15-YEAR-OLD "WHITE NATIVE CATHOLIC" HAD "ACQUIRED A TASTE FOR STREET LIFE" AND HAD "PROSTITUTED HIMSELF FOR THE ADVENTURE AND PROFIT DERIVED." FROM PP. 80-81, 96-97.

[94] INVESTIGATOR'S REPORT, SEAMEN'S CHURCH INSTITUTE FOLDER, COMMITTEE OF FOURTEEN; APRIL 14, 1931. COURTESY NEW YORK PUBLIC LIBRARY SPECIAL COLLECTIONS (NYPLSC).

[95] IBID., APRIL 27, 1931.

[96] IBID., JUNE 6, 1931.

[97] IBID., JUNE 11, 1931.

[98] IBID., JUNE 19, 1931.

[99] PAINTER, *MHP,* P. 29.

[100] INVESTIGATOR'S REPORT, COMMITTEE OF FOURTEEN, SEAMEN'S CHURCH INSTITUTE FOLDER, JUNE 22, 1931. ALSO SEE CHAUNCEY, *GNY.*

[101] INVESTIGATOR'S REPORT, COMMITTEE OF FOURTEEN, SEAMEN'S CHURCH INSTITUTE FOLDER, JUNE 23, 1931.

[102] IBID., JUNE 15, 1931.

[103] IBID., JUNE 16, 1931.

[104] SEE WAUGH, THOMAS. *HARD TO IMAGINE.* COLUMBIA UNIVERSITY PRESS, 1998; P. 352.

[105] SEE JUDD, CHARLES. "EDUCATIONAL PROGRAM OF CCC CAMPS," 1935.

[106] FROM NATIONAL ASSOCIATION OF CIVILIAN CONSERVATION CORPS ALUMNI (NACCCA) PROMOTIONAL MATERIALS, 1998. SEE WWW.CCCALUMNI.ORG/ABOUT.HTML.

[107] FROM DUBERMAN, "1933: THE NEW DEAL: SEX IN THE CCC CAMPS." *NEW YORK NATIVE,* NOVEMBER 16-29, 1981; P. 15.

[108] PAINTER, THOMAS. *MALE HOMOSEXUALS AND THEIR PROSTITUTES.* UNPUBLISHED MANUSCRIPT, 1941; P. 114. COURTESY KINSEY INSTITUTE FOR RESEARCH IN SEX, GENDER, AND REPRODUCTION.

[109] DUBERMAN, "1933," P. 16.

[110] IBID., IDEM.

[111] IBID., IDEM.

[112] IBID., IDEM.

[113] IBID., IDEM.

[114] MARLOWE, KENNETH. *MR. MADAM.* SHERBOURNE PRESS, 1964; P. 32 IN SWAN (TORONTO) EDITION, 1965.

[115] FROM NACCCA MATERIALS, 1995.

[116] IBID., IDEM.

[117] CHAUNCEY, *GNY,* P. 64.

[118] KIRSTIEN, LINCOLN. *PAUL CADMUS.* CHAMELEON (NYC), 1992; P. 21. TOM PAINTER VERIFIES THIS SETTING WHEN DESCRIBING POPULAR NEW YORK HUSTLER STROLLS OF THE 1920S AND 1930S IN *MHP,* P. 21.

[119] NAVAL HISTORICAL CENTER. SEE WWW.HISTORY.NAVY.MIL/AC/CADMUS/CADMUS.HTM.

three   Much of what we know about America's hustlers in the World War II era comes from the work of sex researchers. Orbiting around Alfred C. Kinsey, these researchers ranged from aloof criminologists to closely engaged participant-observers. Their opinions and descriptions differed according to their biases, but they all captured the growth of hustler culture at the end of the Great Depression. They observed that military hustling predominated from 1935 to 1945 and diminished after World War II was settled. As the war ended and older sailors returned to their homes, younger toughs and femmes took over the street. Of the sex researchers who documented the era, few knew more about street trade than Thomas Painter.

Born in 1905 in New York City, Painter attended Yale and Oxford Universities, and spent two years studying at New York City's Union Theological Seminary. While passing through Austria on academic travel, Painter had a homosexual experience with a prostitute in a bathhouse. Full of faith, he felt compelled to report this to his seminary instructors. They were not pleased. In 1934, when he was just about to graduate, Painter suddenly found himself without employment prospects: His professors weren't willing to recommend him for a teaching position. As historian Henry L. Minton concludes, "his academic career was over before it ever got started."[1]

In an effort to understand and affirm his sexual identity, Painter soon became a participant-observer in Manhattan's male sex work milieu. An old Yale friend started sending him money to carry out field research about homosexuality. "I persuaded Luther Tucker," Painter wrote, "to get his father [millionaire Carl Tucker] to grant me some money for that purpose—$500 I believe."[2] That was a considerable sum in an era when working men made $20 a month, and apartments could be rented monthly for a few dollars on 42nd Street. [3] Painter soon began taking notes and writing essays on what he saw and experienced.

Through his friendship with sex research pioneer Robert L. Dickinson, Painter began a correspondence with Alfred C. Kinsey. Painter tried valiantly to publish his own account, but met with constant rejection: Trade publishers were simply not ready to take a risk on an honest look at the subject matter, and Painter lacked the scientific credentials that made academic publishing easier for Drs. Henry and Kinsey.[4]

In 1936, with the grant of $500 from the Tuckers, Painter rented an Upper West Side apartment, sharing the tenement with a hustler named Blackie. "He was a member of a group of hustlers on 42nd Street," wrote Painter. "They were always hungry and seldom had a place to sleep—so my place became an open house to them. With the result that I was sleeping with a different one most every night." Painter found Blackie's crew to be "victims of the Depression, hustling as a modus vivendi (in lieu of work unobtainable), most of whom would never have done so otherwise."[5] Blackie and his friends were straight-identified street toughs, heroin users (and injectors), and petty criminals. But many were honest and gentle in bed. One of these, Willie O'Rourke, prompted Painter's tenderness: "He had never been loved by anyone."[6] O'Rourke and Painter soon moved in together on West 55th Street, closer to the action of Times Square.

Sex researcher George Henry, who was compiling a case-studies-in-homosexuality project for the ad hoc Committee for the Study of Sex Variants, interviewed Painter and his circle. "He is striving to improve the lot of the underprivileged sex variant," Henry wrote of Painter.[7] Henry documented his subjects' personal histories faithfully, taking care to accurately preserve their experiences. Daniel met paying customers in Central Park and on Riverside Drive. Victor, who was transgendered, "saw a lot of effeminate boys" who taught her the ropes in Bryant Park. She later opened a male brothel and claimed to clear "about a hundred fifty a month" by splitting her boys' $2 to $5 rates. And Antonio was introduced to sex work at the age of 9 by "Dirty Bill," an old skipper who gave him a pair of shoes. "Since then I have liked old men," Antonio told Henry. "I like them because they admire my body and because they give me presents and pay me well."[8]

Painter did not generally agree with Henry's conclusions (which he would characterize as "distorted"), although there were basic categorizations that neither researcher could escape. Just as the 1911 Vice Commission of Chicago differentiated between the male prostitute and the *occasional and clandestine* male prostitute, Painter saw a difference between the *professional* hustler and the *casual* or *temporary* hustler. In addition, Painter added two other categories: that of the "private circulation" kept boy and the "fish-queen," or gigolo.[9]

When the Cat's Away: Fish-Queens and Studs, 1932-1941

Before the Depression Era there is scant evidence of female demand for the services of male sex workers. In the early 1930s, the tabloid presses began to pick up on this industry. *Broadway Brevities,* a New York City antecedent to the *Sporting Whip,* issued new warnings. The following article written by Harold Stanning appeared on December 26, 1932:

> GALS NIP HARD NUTS!
> *Society Dames Make Menial Workers*
> **Park Avenue Pretties Play Working Class**
> *Delivery Boys Do Double Duty with Jaded Jennies*
>
> *...While there are plenty of playful papas, many meandering mamas go for it on their own. If the old gent is on the loose, his frau needs somebody to take her places and do things with her. That's where the handsome sheiks with the trained seal hair get their luxurious roadsters. But it is not always done as obvi-*

ously as this. Take a dame with plenty of jack. She is feeling lonely and beginning to realize what she has missed in life. So she grabs the bankroll and hikes down to the Curb, or the Big Board. There she finds a nice young guy, fresh from football, who is ready to take her plenty. She plays the market and he plays her, and they both get their money's worth. The customer's man-on-the-make sees that her account is active for he makes his money on a commission basis and the more she buys and sells, the nearer he is to having a bankroll big enough so that he can afford to ditch the dame. If his attentions aren't ardent enough to keep her coming, she'll quit his firm and go some place where there is a good man who appreciates her and is perfectly willing to take her places in her limousine, with, perhaps, a bit of necking on the side.

These people are accepted by the best of Society, which merely smiles at their foibles....[10]

The article concludes with a passionate argument for higher moral standards and social salvation and a comparison between New York City and ancient Rome. Did society women really "hike it down to the Curb," pursuing men as publicly as men pursued one another?

Indeed they did. Accounts of Times Square street life describe the excursions of numerous unaccompanied, well-dressed women. There were also a few houses that catered to women interested in procuring a male escort. But it was easier for lonely society women to give the eye to working men within their circle: drivers, riding trainers, waiters, bellhops, even the "colored elevator boy."[11] Stanning's *Broadway Brevities* articles titillated, to be sure. They also served as a warning to wealthy men to mind their wives and to be wary of lower-class men in their employ. (Stanning's elevator boy received five years for dallying with a Park Avenue matron.)

Guy Strait, the homophile activist, gay media pioneer, and pornographer, recalled that his childhood grocery-delivery job brought him sex work offers from wealthy men and women. He grew up in Texas, and would have been 14 in the mid 1930s.

At 14 I had a job, although it was making me only $3.60 a week carrying packages every evening after school and working all day Saturday, from 7 A.M. till midnight.

But pretty soon I met this guy who would come in every Monday afternoon and buy $25-$35 worth of groceries. That was a hell of a lot of food. A big bag, about three times as big as the biggest now in the grocery stores could only hold about $5 worth of groceries. He claimed he needed someone to help him unload the groceries at his house and then he would bring them back. Now doing a thing like that was good for a 10 cent tip and I was all for it, so I went with him and helped him unload and he gave me twenty five cents—man, that would buy five loaves of bread, fresh bread. And if we bought week old bread it would buy ten loaves. The second time he came I went *to his house with him and he gave me a blow job and $3. I was in heaven, got my rocks and $3. He never did want me to take off my clothes, just lay back in a big easy chair he had and he would unbutton my pants, take it out and start eating it.*

And then there was the army officer's wife—He later was a general, prominent in the Pearl Harbor investigation. She would call in and order and have it delivered and I was the delivery boy. When I had put down the groceries and she had paid me, the first time, she said, "I love little red-headed boys."

And, "Do you have red hair anywhere except on your head?"

"Yes, Ma'am, a little."

"Down there?"

"Yes, Ma'am."

"Let me see!"

And I took down my pants and let her see and she took me into the bedroom and asked me if I had ever had a woman and I told her never a woman but a girl, yes.

Well, she taught me a lot about sex in that year and she paid me $5 each week.[12]

Painter paid little attention to gigolos. But he took a special interest in "fish-queens," male sex workers who specialized in performing cunnilingus. Fish-queens, whom Painter described as "phallically impotent," met society women in certain bars, acting on the assignations of a certain "escort agency" that specialized in "the sexy Latin."[13] Painter's reference to the Latin lover is probably a nod to Hollywood's Latin lovers of the 1920s and 1930s, like Rudolph Valentino, the legendary dance-hall gigolo turned movie star.

In the 1940s, Porfirio Rubirosa inherited Valentino's mantle. Rubirosa was born in the Dominican Republic in 1909 to a farmer and his wife. His father joined the Dominican military during World War I, and Porfirio accompanied him to France, remaining there until his 20th birthday. Upon his return to the Caribbean in 1929, the young Rubirosa was introduced to, and eventually married, President Rafael Trujillo's teenage daughter, Flora del Oro. An enterprising young man could do no better than to marry the president's daughter.[14] Trujillo made his son-in-law a diplomat, and sent him to Berlin in 1935, where his affairs with German girls sufficiently riled Flora to prompt her to file for divorce. For a time, Trujillo revoked Rubirosa's post, but the president relented in 1939, making Porfirio a *charge d'affaires* in Paris. Three years later, Rubi married French film starlet Danielle Barrieux. Five years after that, he married American tobacco heiress Doris Duke. Though this last marriage lasted only a year, Rubirosa came out of it with Duke's Paris home and a generous financial settlement. Rubirosa soon acquired the nickname "Rubi of great price."[15]

What did Rubirosa possess that so attracted wealthy women? Historian Lynn Ramsey quotes one society matron: "Rubi made any woman, young or old, feel that she was the most divine creature alive. He made you feel that if you weren't at that party, it just wouldn't be worth being there."[16] Rubi's combination of toughness and beauty were only part of his charm though.

> *The Italians, who are preoccupied with physical endowment, paid a special tribute to Rubi. It became common when ordering ground pepper in a restaurant in Italy to ask the waiter for the "Rubirosa." If you have ever seen a 15-inch carved pepper mill, you will understand one of the reasons why this man had women of five countries fighting for his attention.[17]*

Diplomats, ambassadors, and well-heeled matrons welcomed handsome strangers like Rubi to their gala events. Society women were also slumming at bohemian parties where hustlers happily switched between male and female clients. In one instance, a young man named Rudy met Peggy Guggenheim at a small party in Manhattan. Wrote Painter:

> *Rudy...came with Marty—and informed Edward that he wanted to "fuck a woman—without preliminaries." So he was introduced to Peg Guggenheim (of **the** Guggenheims, you know) who is no chicken, being about ten years older than I, and she took him home with her, along with a male of uncertain sex[uality] from the party—where Rudy's story is that practically everything occurred which can occur with three people for which he was paid "only $15."[18]*

This evidence suggests that male prostitution to women began to resemble male prostitution to men in World War II-era America. As women slowly gained independence and tentatively asserted their sexual freedom, men already catering to other men proved eager to grant their wishes.

Best Kept Boys:
James Dean, Marlon Brando, Denham Fouts

The premier hustler was, in Painter's account, the kept boy. But differentiating between the kept boy and the underemployed, younger boyfriend posed a peculiar set of problems for the researcher. Marco's, on West 52nd between Fifth and Sixth Avenues, exemplified these challenges. Painter wryly noted that while Marco's was an "exclusive" club, the only rules were to pay their high prices, wear a jacket, and "keep one's voice...below a scream."[19] At Marco's,

> *the properly select group...consists of some few rich homosexuals, many more homosexuals who wish they were rich and like to feel "exclusive" anyhow, a few kept boys, and many other boys who are gambling their few spare dollars on the evening's drinks, hoping to catch some "homo's" fancy and become kept-boys too.[20]*

For Painter, a greater ambition to climb up the class and career ladder was all that distinguished kept boys from hustlers.

In Times Square, Hollywood, and other American theatrical

districts, young actors hustled well-connected patrons for roles. MGM aide Richard Gulley remarked that "homosexuality for many stars was an opportunistic thing, a passing phase to get their careers off the launching pad."[21] Painter believed Marlon Brando was a kept boy.[22] James Dean's romantic status with Rogers Brackett has been well documented, and Dean's persona was a hustler image, masculine and pretty, cigarette dangling suggestively from his lips.[23] Where did young actors meet their benefactors? The most exclusive places were reputed to be "past the city limits, into the 'glens.'"[24]

Biscayne Bay and Miami were also known for their kept-boy culture in the years just before World War II. On the sun-baked streets of Jacksonville in the early 1930s, street hustler Denny Fouts was readying himself for royalty. Gore Vidal's version of the legend goes something like this:

> Denham [had] been picked up by a German baron [in Florida] when he was about 16. He looked like an American Indian—with an asymmetrical face. Good-looking in a cadaverous way. Like many drug addicts he had a medicinal, acrid odor. He looked like a boy with straight black Indian hair, black eyes. Fouts's own sexual taste was for small boys. But he put up with older gentlemen as that was his occupation. He fell out with the German baron and hitchhiked from Berlin to Venice. A Greek shipping magnate stopped and picked him up. They drove on to Venice and the magnate's yacht. At Capri, he and a sailor skipped ship, taking as much of the Greek's money as they could find in a strongbox.... When the money started to run out, the sailor vanished. Denham dressed every night for dinner in his beautiful evening clothes, sitting at smaller and smaller tables as he was not paying his bills. Finally, when it became apparent to everybody that he had no means of support, the police came. He was being led across the lobby of the Quisiana when Evan Morgan, the Lord Tredegar, entered and called out, "Unhand that handsome youth, he is mine."
>
> For a time Denham moved in the glamorous Mountbatten world.... In that world, Denham was extremely popular. In due course, he was passed from Tredegar to Prince Paul, later King Paul of Greece, who had not yet married Frederika....
>
> Denham [later] lived in the Rue du Bac with only a bed and six Venetian chairs. He was on opium. He was being kept by Peter Watson, the oleomargarine king of England.[25]

At some point during World War II, Fouts wound up in Los Angeles, where he stayed for a time with Christopher Isherwood. (Isherwood wrote a short story about their liaison, titled "Down There on a Visit.") After the war, Tom Painter met Fouts at Edward Melcarth's apartment. Painter's 1945 addition to the Fouts legend whimsically includes the Earl of Whatsit. He describes a night of carousing, and Denham finally scoring with a peg-house boy.[26]

How long Denny spent in New York is uncertain. Painter's portion of the legend does jibe with Vidal's, though it is less archly Gothic. In both accounts, Denham is almost exclusively nocturnal, keenly interested in young men, and sexually indentured to a margarine magnate. "He was at his best with pubescent boys," wrote Vidal, "but then he was one himself, I should think, a southern Penrod who still spoke with a North Florida accent."[27] Painter confirmed Fouts's whereabouts in a letter to Kinsey, writing, "Denny Fouts is now in Paris, living with his financial provider. Reports things very good there, from his angle."[28]

On the Rue du Bac, Fouts corresponded with wealthy British merchants, Yugoslavian princes, and flamboyant young writers. George Plimpton writes that Fouts was "so entranced by the famous book jacket photograph of Truman [Capote] reclining on the sofa that he had sent him a blank check with the single word on it: 'Come.'"[29] Vidal reports that Denham kept Capote's picture in a safe place: "There," he writes, "under the opium pipe, was Truman's picture, as posed for *Life* magazine."[30] And come Truman did, only to find Denham rendered impotent by opium. (Or perhaps Truman's prized photo was outdated?)

"Denham stayed in bed all day, smoking his opium," recalled Vidal. "At sundown, like Dracula, Denham would appear in the streets leading his dog down St.-Germain-des-Pres."[31] Fouts moved to Rome. He died shortly thereafter, in 1948. His death occurred under mysterious circumstances, fulfilling the neo-Gothic destiny of a street cub raised by wolves and taught to hunt by princes.[32]

Camping for Jam:
Extraordinary Perverts, 1936-1943

All the margarine in the world couldn't save Denham Fouts. If only he'd have had more jam. In 1936, in a self-service cafeteria in the heart of Greenwich Village,

> *Boys, usually known as "pansies," are seen with make-up; heavy mascara, rouge, and lipstick. In high-pitched voices, these exhibitionists smirk indecent suggestions at each other.*
>
> *Wide-eyed school girls and boys from neighboring parts of the city gape at the unbelievable sight—boys with rouge on!—and drunken parties end their carousing here. An occasional brawl started indoors is ended outside.*
>
> *There is wide-spread use of slang among some of these human misfits. Once I heard one say: "That queen over there is camping for jam." I was puzzled...The statement meant that a ringleader (queen) of a group of homosexuals was making a play (exhibiting-camping) for a young boy (jam-virgin).*
>
> *The use of drugs is fairly common among these people. Marijuana is a favorite....[33]*

As some trannies bucked the system, the system bucked back. Their increased visibility and safety-in-numbers strategy discouraged general harassment, but didn't prevent their arrest in public places. The cafeteria described above was raided just before the article's publication. In the 1930s and 1940s, it was safer to don drag at established clubs and party circuits, which often paid their impersonators. Where could one witness this form of performance art?

One place to start would have been the Keg on 42nd Street. Run by former bootleggers, the Keg was a quirky mélange during the mid 1930s, its "heyday of male prostitution."[34] Painter describes it as a place filled with "homosexuals, male prostitutes, pick-pockets, strong-arm gangsters, thieves, soldiers, sailors, and marines, dope-peddlers...some women of extremely questionable character (including out-and-out two buck whores—prices subject to reduction on request)."[35] And, yes, it was a space for "painted young effeminates to 'camp.'" Still, a first-time camper might have found sweeter jam at the Gold Fleece, in the Bowery, where the clientele really let their hair down. On a given night, guests might see "a strong-looking seaman...an old 'wolf' stroking a boy tramp's plump buttocks...a fat, painted young homosexual male whore 'swishing' and posing...[and an] old bum who seems to have some money tonight."[36] The crowd would sway to jazz bursting from the coin Victrola jukebox.

Way up in Harlem, there was the Cosmopolitan Club, with a ballroom, tables, and room for 400 people. Here,

Homosexuals and Lesbians, white and colored, all mingle together and dance with one another—women with women, and men with men, which is illegal and seldom tolerated in the United States—in the most amorous, close-hugging, and ecstatic manner. Negro hustlers, normal and flamboyantly homosexual, respond easily to suggestions to "dance" or to visit the men's toilet. The noise, the smoke-filled, foul air, the reek of beer and whiskey, the monosexual dancing couples, and the heavy fog of sexuality drawn over the leering, sensual faces, and the miscegenational nature of the place render it amazing, alluring, exciting, or repulsive as one may feel it to be.[37]

The Cosmopolitan Club, Cotton Club, and Savoy Ballroom were also known for their drag balls, contests that were the inspiration for the drag ball revival of the 1980s.[38] By the early 1930s, Harlem drag balls had "surpassed those of Chicago and New Orleans in size and opulence."[39] The main event in the biggest drags was the "parade of the fairies," which was followed by a costume contest that offered cash prizes and was often judged by famous actors and writers.[40]

But there was only one big winner, and in the 1930s and 1940s drag ball performers faced harsh economic circumstances. Female impersonators from impoverished areas had little free cash and seldom found employers who would tolerate them in makeup and heels. Many performers supplemented their meager salaries by catering to amorous patrons in the audience.

During the speakeasy days of the 1920s, drag balls became ever more hip and popular, but increased police "protection" rackets in the 1930s forced some establishments to close.[41] In the early

1930s, New York City police often raided clubs and arrested patrons and performers for same-sex dancing or appearing in public in disguise or masquerade. The only way to avoid harassment was to ask police to license the event. Once promoters and owners paid a licensing fee, a drag ball could resume openly.

Sadly, even police presence at the licensed affairs turned out to be a big drag. When the ballgoers traded their privacy for increased security, they lost some of the freedoms they had been enjoying. In 1936, an observer of the Hamilton Lodge balls described a mix of "effeminate men, 'sissies,' 'wolves,' 'fairies,' 'faggots,' the third sex, 'ladies of the night,' and male prostitutes."[42] But a 1938 advertisement in the *Amsterdam News* cautioned that "scant clothing will not be permitted" at the venerated Harlem ball. That year, in fact, "plainclothesmen kept dancers under closer surveillance than usual and arrested seventeen for homosexual solicitation."[43] This increased police activity in the later 1930s can be attributed to two things: Mayor Fiorello LaGuardia's conservative administration, which barred transgendered people from midtown Manhattan, and the city government's inclination toward civic housekeeping that preceded the World's Fair of 1939.[44]

By 1938 the New York State Liquor Authority began to clamp down on the queerer bars around Times Square. Armed with a favorable appellate court decision, the SLA could close down bars where "lewd and dissolute" people congregated. Among the bars the SLA had closed by World War II were the Keg and the Gold Fleece. When the drag community transplanted itself to legitimate establishments, the SLA struck again, closing down Alvin's, the Times Square Garden and Grill, and Gloria's.

In keeping with this authoritative quelling of sex work, trans folk were still getting arrested on the streets. In one example, a 29-year-old syphilitic had been living and working as a woman in an unspecified American city, passing so successfully that clients were "visibly affected and incredulous" when they were informed of their partner's biological gender by staff at the United States Public Health Service.[45]

Described as a "very tall" individual with "long, dark-brown hair, coarse features, and a husky voice," the subject solicited streetside and took clients to a nearby rooming house. "She denied being a prostitute," wrote Army surgeons A.J. Jones and Lee Janis, "and gave as one of the reasons for not wanting to be examined, the fact that she was a 'hermaphrodite.'"[46] But doctors found their patient to be a full-fledged male whose "anal orifice...was bathed in a thick, creamy, foul-smelling discharge." Jones and Janis placed this trans prostitute under quarantine and began treatment. Upon further examination, they were astounded to find that her "sphincter [was] practically devoid of tone. Two fingers were freely admitted and manipulated with no complaint of pain from the patient." All this finger-fucking was too much for the authorities. "This was no ordinary pervert," wrote Jones and Janis. The patient was diagnosed with a syphilitic anal chancre and rectal gonorrhea, and charged with "perverted sexual practices." For her gender deception, she was sentenced to 20 years in a penitentiary, then the maximum term established for sexual misconduct.[47]

By the start of American involvement in World War II, there was no safe haven in New York City for a transgendered sex worker. Her balls were closed, her bars were barred, her streets no longer hers. With the July 1941 passage of the antiprostitution May Act, female sex workers were scarcer than ever, leaving the trans girl highly exposed. She could only starve, pass as a guy, or join the armed forces. For the moment, sailors had again overtaken the streets.

Where to Sin:
A Cruising Guide to the USA, 1935-1941

In the pre-World War II years, transgendered sex workers were only safe in female brothels. Driving from Manhattan, one could stop at Hudson, N.Y., where, on Diamond Street, one might encounter "a tall blonde called Foxy." Historian Bruce Hall reports that slender Foxy was "different than the others," sitting fully dressed rather than in a negligee. Foxy "would provide ecstasies that the other girls couldn't even dream of, ecstasies that drove other male customers wild.... While [madam] Esther Curtis wore pants and walked like a man, Foxy *was* a man."[48]

In Kansas City, one could adjourn to a similar house, one that also included masculine workers. According to a former patron:

This "house" existed in a well-to-do residential section of Kansas City. It consisted mainly of a large, circular room, elegantly furnished with a bar, couches and lounge chairs, tables, etc. The male prostitutes were both masculine and effeminate types, some of the latter dressed as girls. Opening off of this large, circular room were nine or ten small alcoves, containing beds. The alcoves could be cut off from the main room by means of drapes; or exhibitionistic customers could leave the drapes open, so that other customers could walk around the room and observe what was going on in the alcoves.

Fees in this establishment ranged from $10.00 for a single contact up through $50.00 and even more for an all-night session.[49]

The price scale is consistent with peg-boy rates of the day. While Painter's Times Square boys sold themselves for a fin (a fiver), they charged twice (or more) as much when working out of peg-houses, where the usual split with the madam was 50-50.[50]

The focus of homosexual prostitution in WWII-era Chicago was Michigan Boulevard, between the bridge crossing the Chicago River and Oak Street.[51] Still popular was Bughouse Square, where as many as 100 hustlers hung out at night.

In Detroit, psychiatrists uncovered widespread juvenile male prostitution in 1941. One 16-year-old was arrested "on the complaint of accosting and soliciting a man, who happened to be a detective." The boy was described as "affectionate, warm, generous, active, alert, and full of fun." He "wished to be a girl and envied their clothing, jewelry, and opportunities."[52] An 11-year-old Syrian-American youth was turned in by his mother, who feared her son was "becoming morally depraved." This "friendly, cooperative boy, who was very anxious to make a good impression," had been raped by three men when he was only 9.

> Since then he has been approached constantly by men who offered him money for this privilege and [the] patient usually submitted. One of the men was a boarder in the home. Police officers stated that the boy was known as a male prostitute and solicited men. It was their impression that [his] mother made the complaint because she had quarreled with the boarder over money and saw an opportunity to get him into trouble and also get rid of the boy....
>
> ...He freely admitted indulging in this type of sexual relation, largely driven by fear of the men, but also attracted by the money offered. He stated he was very unhappy at home because [his] mother beat him severely and "she doesn't want me. She says she wants to get rid of me until I am 21. She says she wishes I would die." However, patient liked her better than [his] father because "he beat me even worse." Boy was anxious to leave home and find a place offering security and affection.[53]

Another Detroit boy, "resented" and "disregarded" by his parents, had been rewarded for sex by neighborhood youths since the age of 8. He had a big penis ("conspicuous genital over-development"), but "was uncooperative in the treatment of syphilitic and gonorrheal infections." Although he expressed no shame about his sexual behavior, he admitted he had "the desire to murder someone." Other boys suffering parental abuse and neglect sought affection and companionship in the gang-dominated Detroit underworld, where older youths and adults enjoyed their sexual favors.[54]

Toilet inscriptions as sex work advertisements were especially common in Portland and Seattle.[55] Glory holes were well established (some intrepid cruisers had even drilled through marble!) by the 1930s. But tea room customers had to be wary of jackrolling, for "the unwise homosexual very often appear[ed] in the obituary columns."[56] There was an established hustler bar scene as well: Edward Melcarth, who moved to Seattle in 1950, frequented the Olympia Hotel bar, the Totem Bar soda counter, the Sander and Unique cafeterias, the Anchor Inn, and a drag-friendly club, the Garden of Allah. "There is also a very ripe *bain-turque* [the South Street baths] and a collection of juvenile faggots," wrote Melcarth. "Bars cannot serve under twenty-one so there is a great malted-milk belt of hang-outs."[57]

Bar hustling was quite common in San Francisco's Tenderloin district, where impoverished sex workers poured into the bars to meet their customers from all over town.[58] San Francisco's sexual economy during the World War II era was as libertine and eclectic as any other city's. There is even some indication that Tenderloin hustlers paid other hustlers for sex.[59] Hustler bars clustered along the 900 block of Market, and by the mid 1930s Tenderloin hustlers were mingling with transgendered sex workers and a sizable female teenage runaway population.[60]

Although District Attorney Mat Brady had instigated a vice crackdown in 1935, by 1939 the Tenderloin was again going nonstop.[61] Turk Street, which runs almost parallel to Market Street, housed the Blue and Gold Saloon and the Old Crow bar, both of which attracted transgendered girls, male hustlers, women, and a tremendous influx of servicemen brought by the impending war.[62] Up Powell Street toward Union Square, the Prince Edward Hotel was, according to one old-timer, "the best place to cruise." Serviceman saturation had brought free sex to the Tenderloin, but street sex prices jumped to $5 after the war was resolved.[63]

Streets of Paris, located at 54 Mason St., was one of the most notorious bawdy houses in San Francisco. It boasted a strikingly mixed crowd, with a lot of rough trade, straight tourists, people from the sexual underground, and trannies.[64] A guidebook entitled "Where to Sin in San Francisco" offers this peek into Streets of Paris:

> "I've got the lousiest floor show in town and I know it" [says manager Frank de Goff]. "There's a hag who does a striptease and a fag who does a female impersonation and an MC and all the usual baloney. But the pay-off is the customers. The biggest collection of sailors, soldiers, crooks, gamblers, jitterbugs, streetwalkers, madams, dikes, and fruit in California. About midnight they're all here, tearin' up the joint. Boy, does it stink!"
>
> ...Naked women sprawl on every wall, bedeck every pillar above tear-sheets with French jokes on them. There are two bars, lots of nooks with sofas. And a model of a cylindrical French street structure in the lobby.
>
> What strangely struck us funny was that the food seemed good and the liquor **there**.
>
> VITAL SINTISTICS Open: six to morning. Dancing starts at nine. Show: starts at 10, continuous; one set between every dance. Host: Frank de Goff. Barchief: Gene. Hats to: Eva. SINTAX: All drinks, 25 cents at the bar, 35 cents at table.[65]

The guidebook offers advice to sex tourists, suggesting that district experts were "taxi-drivers, bell-boys, bar-tenders, shoe-shine boys," and, of course, newsboys. "Especially the [news]boys down around Jones and Turk," who impressed the book's authors as especially helpful.[66]

In downtown Los Angeles circa 1940, cozy Pershing Square held at least 50 hustlers a day at any given time.[67] Driving down Hollywood Boulevard, one could find boys "facing the street as they lounge along the curb, not facing inward toward the buildings as is done elsewhere."[68] Police intervention had not yet compelled Hollywood hustlers to avert their faces. Because of the general sprawl of the great Western city, and its lack of a subway system, automobile cruising—rather than cruising by foot—was de rigueur in Hollywood. On the way out of any of these cities, one could find men hitchhiking on the side of the road—another popular form of cruising. All across the country, queers were beginning to enjoy a new celebration of sexuality, and street-based sex workers went along for the ride.

Female prostitutes congregated along the gasoline alley of northeastern roadway rest stops and stations during the trucking industry's boom of the 1920s and 1930s.[69] Traveling hustlers and runaways began to populate American roads by the 1930s, and young men who accepted a lift from strangers were introduced to sex work as a means of "payment."[70] In the 1940s, the side of the road had become an established commercial sex venue. One driver recalled:

> *Being very poor one year I drove my rich old aunt to Florida for the vacation and my keep.... When we got there, though, she obligingly gave me the afternoon off with the car while she rested. I made a bee-line for Miami, closely watching hitchhikers who were coming out from there on the main road. Finally I saw one boy who was rather cute—a handsome body in one of those polo shirts that show more than they hide, and a mop of curly blond hair. About 18... So I turned around a mile down and picked him up coming back. He told me right away... that he was one of a number who had been expelled by the police that morning—taken to the city line and told not to come back. Vagrants. I immediately mentioned some of the queer joints in town and asked if he had hung around there. He caught on and said Yes, he had. Well, would he like to make two dollars right now to help him*

> *along his way[?] Sure he would, you bet. Well, I liked to do so and so, and if it was all right with him for a deuce, we would. O.K. with him. So we went [down] to a lonely stretch of beach—there were some in those days not too far from Miami, just north of Fort Lauderdale—and put a blanket out of the car on the sand, and stripped naked. I came in about thirty seconds flat, once I got started, and I didn't wait long. He was a very nice boy, well built and affectionate. Then I took him back to a good spot for hitchhiking on the road, gave him his money, and we both went more happily on our way.[71]*

Once on the road, casual hustlers with limited resources could make their way across the country, in the process becoming paraprofessional. "Hustlers will go back and forth," wrote Painter, "New York to Miami to New Orleans, to Los Angeles, to Denver, to Chicago, and back again to New York; all with the turn of the seasons."[72]

Back in Manhattan, where to go? We have noted that Lexington Avenue was one of Walt Whitman's favorite cruising spots in the 1850s. Painter noted a short-lived revival of male sex work along Lexington in the early 1930s. The Bowery was passé by the 1930s, although 14th Street was still campy. Battery Park, Riverside Drive, and Fifth Avenue were out of fashion by 1940.

During World War II, Columbus Circle, Central Park, and Times Square were the places to be. A number of factors prompted this shift, including changing patterns of police activity, workers' concerns for their physical safety, the availability of clientele, and the degree of anonymity afforded by different parts of the city. But the overriding factor was economic. As the entertainment district—and the people with money—moved uptown, so did male sex workers.[73] Times Square was ideal for multiple reasons. The corner of Broadway and 42nd was the perfect spot to catch the eyes of patrons at elite theaters as well as inexpensive "grind" movie houses. Pornography had hit Times Square during the Depression, when cinematic competition was fierce.[74] In 1940, there were four subway lines serving the area, and millions of pedestrians passed through the square each year. Painter described the carnival atmosphere as the world's busiest male prostitution market.

> There are amusement places with pinball machines, sharp-shooting ranges...medicine men, and peep-show machines, all for pennies, nickels, and dimes. There are pool-parlors, dime-a-dance halls...a myriad of cheap eateries, drug-stores, haberdashery....
>
> Princes and financiers rub elbows with truck-drivers, would-be poets, sailors, saboteurs, pick-pockets, and Brooklyn kids up to see the flashy life.
>
> All these people have come with a little money to spend on a good time—that is why they come. And that is why another type comes too—the rapacious and the criminal: pick-pockets, small-time gangsters, confidence men, pimps, prostitutes, petty racketeers, drug-addicts and sellers, fake beggars, "lush-rollers," "clip-artists," "steerers," "boosters," and all the sorry array.[75]

Male prostitution was concentrated on the intersection of 42nd Street and Eighth Avenue, but hustlers floated through different parts of the square to avoid police harassment. Bryant Park, across from Bryant Hall and behind the New York Public Library, had been a transgender sex work haven since the early 1930s. Demand for male prostitutes proved so high in Times Square that it supported several satellite sex work sites. Intermittent police roundups kept the points of contact between workers and their clients widely dispersed, encouraging hustler culture to spread across a broad swath of midtown Manhattan.

Street hustlers were experts at camouflage. Hustlers wore coats, hats, ties, trousers, and sailor uniforms, to present "as complete and well-appearing an ensemble of civilian clothes as possible."[76] A hustler with some skill in his trade looked like *any other working man:* a sailor, a construction worker, or day laborer. The constant human traffic conspired with the hustlers' inconspicuous dress to thwart the efforts of the police to extinguish—or even to distinguish—male sex work in the square.

The road, the street, the bar, the toilets, the parks, the movie house, and the peg-house were all meeting points for male sex workers and clients in the 1930s and 1940s. Peg-houses offered protection from the elements and assured workers a steady client stream; hustlers did not have to seek out johns when they spent time in the brothel. There was more security too. With other people around, clients were less inclined to physical violence and workers seldom had to resort to extortion to ensure fair payment. But male brothels were still easy targets for the police—and, in one infamous case, for the U.S. government.

FDR Avenges: The Senator Walsh Scandal, 1942

At the beginning of America's involvement in World War II, President Franklin Delano Roosevelt's administration ordered the closing of every American brothel, a giveaway to conservatives disguised as a precaution against espionage. Female brothels from Butte to Baltimore were forced to close, and the increase in police pressure popped New York's ballooning peg-house scene. For years, Gustave "George" Beekman had run one of the most popular peg-houses in the city. Beekman shifted frequently from 1925 to 1939, working out of a West 43rd Street apartment before winding up at 329 Pacific St., near the Brooklyn Navy Yard, just before World War II. This auspicious location guaranteed him a steady clientele and eager staff but soon attracted police attention. While other peg-houses demanded a policy of admission by recognition or introduction only, thereby reducing but not eliminating their chances of getting raided, Beekman simply required that his clients purchase a bottle of his "Swedish punch" to gain entry. The punch was "home-brewed and violent," but the sailors must have liked it.[77]

The flow of businessmen and sailors streaming in and out of Beekman's place did not go unnoticed by his neighbors. Responding to their complaints, Brooklyn police began a surveillance operation in February 1942. Local forces soon had the help of officers from the Bureau of Naval Intelligence and the Federal Bureau of Investigation, who were panicked by the proximity of Beekman's residence to the Brooklyn Navy Yard. These three agencies mounted a joint stakeout, recording the movements of the young recruits and older gentlemen who gained entrance. Through license-plate checks, the authorities identified among the clientele a Philadelphia surgeon, an esteemed New York doctor, and prominent civilians from all over the Northeast.[78]

Alarmed to discover that a few nonnaturalized Germans had frequented 329 Pacific, the BNI and FBI became concerned that naval forces were in danger of enemy infiltration. On March 14, 1942, after spying on the house for six weeks, the authorities had gathered enough evidence to spring from the shadows and arrest Beekman, along with several of his guests (both clients and hustlers). The nonnaturalized Germans were tracked down and imprisoned at Ellis Island without trial. Three military hustlers facing court-martial accepted plea bargains, and testified that Beekman had committed sodomy with them.[79] The operation shut down Beekman's peg-house permanently.

In a new twist on old biblical metaphors, the "unnatural," according to the government prosecutors, encompassed a queer combination of the "nonnaturalized" (the alleged German spies), and their crimes against nature. Swedish-born peg-house proprietor Gustave Beekman, though a naturalized United States citizen since 1918, was in his very essence "nonnaturalized," having committed sodomy with "normal" (or "natural") U.S. soldiers and sailors. Beekman was guilty of enticing these "natural" men to perform unnatural acts. The judge informed Beekman's lawyer that pleading guilty to sodomy would not lighten his client's sentence.[80]

In this Byzantine configuration of the natural and the unnatural, infiltration and espionage became synonymous with homosexual seduction by monetary persuasion. Beekman was prosecuted for perverting (or converting) Navy cadets, for confounding the natural and unnatural, and for turning patriots into the enemies of the state. Even *The Nation* editorialized in favor of the investigation, worrying that "the exploitation of sexual irregularities has been a favored Nazi method of gathering information."[81] This was precisely the kind of technique that intelligence agents in Roosevelt's administration had used, but the irony went unnoticed.

Madam Wilbur Fox, a frequent guest of Beekman's and a witness for the prosecution, had been operating peg-houses for years, first in Brooklyn and then in Manhattan.[82] Police regularly raided Fox's houses in the late 1930s and early 1940s. By March 1942, Fox had endured as much official harassment as she could stand. She cooperated fully with the Beekman investigation, talking her head off to keep out of jail.

"I am a patriotic American," Fox announced to the *New York Post*. "Believe me, if I had known that some of these fellows in Beekman's place were Nazi spies, I would have notified the authorities."[83] With this statement the clever Miss Fox slipped a stick into the wheel of Franklin Roosevelt's grinding prostitution prosecution machine. Though her peg-house network was dismantled, the madam skirted conviction.

Meanwhile, Gustave Beekman, attempting to shed his turncoat image, informed on William Elberfeld, one of his German clients. Beekman alleged in his testimony that Elberfeld "proclaimed Hitler as his God."[84] Investigators took this charge lightly, especially after discovering that Elberfeld operated a rival peg-house on Prospect Street. The court also learned that Beekman and Elberfeld had been fighting over the attention of a tall, slim, golden-haired sailor named Bob. Both pimps were soon in jail.[85]

In a desperate attempt to take some of his enemies down with him, Beekman named Massachusetts senator David Walsh as a Pacific Street habitué. This claim catapulted a covert operation into the national headlines: Walsh was the chairman of the Senate Naval Affairs Committee. On May 12, 1942, Beekman pled guilty to the charge of "maintaining a house for immoral purposes." Senator Walsh did not escape unscathed. The *New York Post* was very interested in this element of the story and interviewed numerous house hustlers. One Marine recalled "Senator X," as the *Post* would refer to Walsh, as having a "very red complexion," with "a good-sized jaw," an oversize belly, and "ripples of fat around his face," a dead-on description of Walsh. [86] Walsh's home life also made him an easy target for the tabloids: He had never been married, did not have a girlfriend, and retained a handsome house-boy, Ysidro Cariño. (Cariño, who knew a keeper when he saw one, lived with the Senator for more than 30 years.)[87] Gay historian C.A. Tripp claims that Walsh's visits to Pacific Street had ended abruptly the day before the BNI and FBI began their surveillance.[88]

FDR kept abreast of the Walsh gossip through *Post* lawyer

Morris Ernst, who sent the president weekly updates. Ernst eventually offered to "keep in daily touch with the situation," calling the scandal "a shocking story...which may be of great help to you." This ominous addendum suggests that Ernst was aware of the beating Roosevelt took from J.R. Rathom in 1919. If Ernst was goading Roosevelt into taking a hand in this case to boost sales of the *Post,* he succeeded on both counts. Roosevelt soon pressed Attorney General Francis Biddle into service, pleading for the latest information.[89]

"If the chairman of the Senate Naval Affairs Committee was a regular visitor to a house of prostitution used as a base of operation by enemy agents, then he is either a fool or a rogue," the *Post* editorialized. Was this state of affairs "a poisonous menace to our national safety, or merely nauseating in its effect on morale"?[90] Ultimately it was both, but for different reasons than the *Post* editorial suggested. No spies ever turned up, and Walsh was finally exonerated. According to the FBI, the Walsh affair had been a case of mistaken identity; there was no shortage of self-important, heavyset clients at 329 Pacific, and investigators soon found a Connecticut physician who fit the bill. The whole pointless affair was poisonous to the sexual economy, and nauseating to libertines.

About the only house open for business in Manhattan by the end of World War II was a government front:

> *During World War II, the Federal Bureau of Investigation set up a house of male prostitution (on MacDougal Street in Greenwich Village) and staffed it with homosexual agents for the explicit and...highly successful purpose of extracting shipping information from foreign sailors. The decision to undertake this venture is perhaps less surprising than the Bureau's ability to effectively deal with the...problems that are entailed in running such an establishment—not to mention the problems involved in coming up with a sizable group of young, handsome, multilingual, adequately trained homosexual agents who were willing and able to carry out their missions.[91]*

It is not surprising that the FBI undertook this mission, considering the Navy's mishandling of the Newport scheme during World War I. Nor is it surprising that the FBI was able to recruit suitable agents for the assignment: J. Edgar Hoover was running the bureau at the time.

The Ghost Goes West: The War Years, 1942-1945

By 1942, Dolores Costello had refashioned her antique shop—originally a peg-house front—into a full-time business. Her hand may have been forced: Painter notes that "the FBI closed him down...he was an Italian alien, and Leo, his assistant, a pro-Nazi German alien, which did not help much in the eyes of the FBI either."[92] Molly King joined the Navy, as a cook, in 1942. Though her husband tried to keep her house going for a few months, business was never the same. Madame Fox closed her doors in 1942 as well. Other proprietors enlisted to fight in the war; one was killed at Dunkirk. And, with its manager in federal prison, Beekman's was no more.[93] Painter himself was drafted and sent to Miami for training. This diaspora made New York a forlorn place for thousands of former clients.

Who was left to hustle? In the East 40s, an African-American tailor nicknamed Manchester was running a small operation, using "poor quality boys, just any hustler who turned 16."[94] Wartime police presence at Times Square popularized Columbus Circle as a venue for the young. After taking in a matinee with his mother, diarist Donald Vining met a young man named Wallace in the circle on the first day of summer, 1943:

> THE GHOST GOES WEST proved very funny. After putting Mother on the train I was of no mind to go back to a hot dark room so walked up Broadway to Columbus Circle and sat on the stone benches. A kid of 16 sat beside me, offered me first peanuts then a cigarette and told me the story of his life. He said he hadn't a cent but was happy and thought he'd sleep in the park. That was my cue to invite him to my place but I didn't because of his youth and possible innocence. He left and I somewhat regretted having passed him up. In about 15 minutes he was back, with two dollar bills in his hand, which someone had given him for a mere feel. "I never made so much money as easily in my life. I really didn't do a thing for it. Come on, I'll buy you some ice cream." His generosity with his ill-gotten money amused me. I invited him down and he paid our fare as I had no nickels. I never heard of such a thing. He, the younger and better-looking, paying my way and making most of the overtures. He liked the candlelight, saying he was a country boy. He came to bed and we had a fine time...saving any real activity until the morning. We both took baths and then he sat around nude reading the Reader's Digest. I thought he intended to stay forever. I had carefully guarded my valuables but he made no attempt to take anything or to shake me down. Even when the electrician came to finish working on the lights, I couldn't stir Wallace to get dressed. Clothes and time didn't bother him. He's a strange boy but a definite personality for 16.[95]

Wallace's story recalls that of Julius, the Battery Park hustler interviewed by the Committee of Fourteen in 1931. The boys' ingenuousness is astounding. Julius was more business-minded than was Wallace—but, in the depths of the Depression, Julius faced more desperate circumstances than Wallace, who was hustling during the booming World War II years.

In 1942, Painter arrived in Miami to commence basic training. He returned briefly to New York City in 1944 before shipping out to Amarillo, Tex. In a letter to Kinsey in January 1944, he observed that the hustling world had changed drastically in the war years. Forty hustlers might have been found on any night in Times Square before the war, but in 1944 only a handful were noticeable—usually local boys under military age. Most of the old crowd had been conscripted or were finding better job prospects in the bustling wartime economy.[96] This comports with Donald Vining's account of street trade in Columbus Circle. The old gang was serving Uncle Sam, making at least $160 a month ($1,560 a month today) in the bargain.

Supplanting trade hustlers during the war years were men who were either kicked out of the military, denied entry, or too young to enlist. In a 1944 letter, Painter complained that "Times Square and Rockefeller Plaza are swarming, infested, with a peculiarly repellent and numerous mass of obvious homosexuals—with marked lack of trade." The trade Painter saw was "about the most repulsive collection of the dregs of the young male humanity...and mostly very, very young." Police activity was minimal: "There is a policeman on each corner who tries to keep them bothered, but [they] obviously abandoned the thankless task early in the evening."[97]

In early 1945, Painter noted that

> Miami and Chicago in war time have undergone a similar metamorphosis as New York as far as the subject is concerned. The handsome kept boys and the others who would like to be kept, who hung around Miami in the winters, are no longer to be seen. There is a very slight prostitution of Service men, especially the sailors, but the eleven o'clock curfew for them effectively cramped most of this. All the old spots are gone and one has to look hard and long to see any signs of [male prostitution] at all about Miami.[98]

Obviously the military was taking drastic steps to curb male prostitution within its ranks during World War II.

Under FDR, military police and intelligence agencies established civilian curfews, worked with local police to close peg-houses and prosecute street prostitutes, and incarcerated servicemen caught engaging in sex together. Ironically, this crackdown helped Tom Painter land a plum assignment. With the help of letters of support from Harry Benjamin and Alfred C. Kinsey, Painter became an internal affairs operative in the last year of the war. His assignment was to catch homosexuals in the military and to prepare them for court-martial.[99] Moving from base to base, he was able to expand his knowledge of small-town male prostitution, as we will see in the next chapter.

In the Southwest, Painter pined for the Big Apple. He wrote his friend Bill Begg about a young man he had met on the train, and the New York memories their conversation stirred:

> I caught the 6:15 train to Amarillo...chatting with [a sailor] in the aisle...it developed that he had lived on 181st St., Manhattan. I took a flier: Did he, then, know Johnnie G. (a big, handsome boy who had hustled downtown—to earn a motorcycle)? Yes, he did, well. It seems Johnnie was quite a character. He and his gang

used to catch cats (when about 9-12 years old), go to the cellar of an apartment house and toss the cats into the furnace.... They would also catch pigeons and tie rocks to them, make them fly away carrying the rocks. The sailor granted this was all pretty deplorable, but said, "That's the way kids are." They used to swim in the Hudson. When they got out he said they had to take feces and condoms out of their hair—the Hudson being an open sewer. He was well acquainted with Johnnie's hustling activities (tho' apparently Johnnie had said he got the money from "rolling" people). Most of the gang had been drafted now, he said, but many of them had gotten out in one way or another—one, at least, by pretending, convincingly, to be queer.

I have dwelt on this partially as a side light on Johnny, partially as a striking account of gang life in New York among tough kids—and one of the most grisly bits of juvenile sadism I have ever heard.[100]

In this letter we get a sense of the accepted sexual roles played by New York City's juvenile gang hustlers. Johnnie understood it was considered acceptable to "roll," or rob, men who were interested in him. Painter further surmised that a young gangster like Johnnie would never have admitted to his peers that he got fucked for money. This casual hustling by scores of heterosexual, underclass young men attests to the persistent economic hardships they faced, and to the relative ease with which they could obtain paid sexual work (and a measure of satisfaction).

Sum of the Orgasms: Flotsam and Jetsam, 1945-1948

Nostalgic for halcyon hustling days, Painter reflected on the successes of his favorite hustlers, those former petty criminals now happily fashioning military careers for themselves. "Theirs has been a very splendid record, hasn't it?" he asked his old Yale friend Bill Begg, who had himself become a lieutenant. "I am sure the general public would have to radically alter its preconceptions to believe it."[101]

VJ Day was August 15, 1945, and by the end of October the old boys had begun to trickle back. Times Square was flocking with reunited personalities. Molly King was back after a three-year stint in the Pacific, but not for long. He had "re-assumed his natal appellation" and found work as a cook at a drag revue in Hollywood, Fla.[102] The war had provided many young men with new opportunities; their professional hustling days were, in many cases, coming to an end. This left the streets to a fresh batch of teenagers, whom Painter referred to as "the most unpleasant, shop-worn, rag-tag sort of youth" that he had ever encountered.[103]

We see further evidence of this shift in an article by Dr. William Butts, who conducted interviews in 1946 with 25 young men observed "soliciting in the square of a large city."[104] In the Butts study, 11 hustlers were 15 to 18 years old; only six were older than 20, and none was older than 24. Butts doesn't name the city where he conducted his interviews (he lived in Hartford, Conn.). His data suggest that former military hustlers were aging out of the profession or finding more lucrative and dependable work, or both.

Like Painter, Butts could not help noticing the preponderance of boys with "effeminate characteristics."

> There are many more effeminate boys and young men around the square than this study indicates. Most of these, however, do not do promiscuous soliciting but live together in groups, pairing off as "man" and "wife." They hold "shag parties" to which are invited a few outside wealthy "angels."[105]

What Butts called "shag parties" were also called "drag parties"—planned affairs, held regularly at a series of private homes. Admission was by invitation only. These parties provided a comfortable atmosphere and met a variety of social, emotional, and financial needs for the trannie girl.

Hustling was only one of a number of ways adolescent males were making money. One of Butts's hustlers juggled four jobs, including sex work and gigs as a busboy, dishwasher, and errand boy.[106] About half of the Butts boys were otherwise employed—his group included "two clerks, two musicians, one male nurse, a shipping clerk, an elevator operator, and a dishwasher"—and several of the rest were in high school or college.[107]

As the younger set supplanted older vets, the latter were driven to find keepers (both male and female) and to supplement their income by pimping and theft. Painter noted that some veteran hustlers had to develop new strategies or leave town altogether:

> Ran into Kentucky again. (Yes, he is still here. Reckons he may go to Detroit "next week.") He is making his living by what the newspapers call "mugging." He cases a bar, spots his mark flashing the stuff, tails him to a dark side street, asks for a match, and, as his hand goes down—and up—in striking it, the hand goes on and connects with the gentleman's jaw instead, knocking him out in one blow. Easy because so unexpected. Frisk him and scram.[108]

But his knowledge of the city's underworld kept Kentucky in New York. The old boy seamlessly integrated his competition (the rising generation) into his business by taking on the role of pimp.

Older hustlers were more likely to be involved in other sex industry roles. The oldest interviewee in Butts's article was 23, "dissipated in appearance and flashy in dress." "His greatest worry," Butts wrote, "is that he is getting too old to attract the best paying customers."[109] Not coincidentally, this ancient 23-year-old was the only subject working as a pimp. If those who entered sex work were trying to meet emotional and sexual needs, those who remained focused more keenly on the financial payoff.

Butts's case studies illustrate this point with raw and fragile clarity. His histories portray queer youth discovering their sexuality through hustling and cruising. For many, remuneration was a secondary, or even irrelevant, consideration. Two 18-year-old college boys were on the scene, but cruising for free. One "selects his customers on the basis of their attractiveness to him and not on what they will pay."[110] For the other collegiate, the square was his "only way of meeting men...[he] enjoys their companionship...and takes no money."[111]

One 16-year-old was propositioned in a movie house toilet, and soon began hustling because "he had often dreamed of homosexual relations and to be paid for it was beyond his wildest dreams."[112] Another ran away to the city, shattered after being caught having sex with another boy:

> Normal appearing, well built boy. Clothing clean but inexpensive. Both parents living. Glad to talk. Had been in city for about six weeks. His mother had discovered him and another boy of his own age exploring each other's bodies. She shamed him before the rest of the family. He says that sex relations are repulsive to him. Wherever possible avoids going to a room with a man, confining his activities to fondling in a movie. His self-respect is low. He is convinced that he is not a homosexual and talks with pride of a girl inviting him to her room where they had satisfactory intercourse.
>
> He is bitter against his mother but never the less homesick. He says he wants to "make good" and then return home. He seems to have no plans about how he shall "make good."[113]

Hustling was a way to fulfill emotional and sexual needs, and it also helped keep these needs subconscious. For the runaway who enjoyed other boys' bodies, the choice of sex work might both satisfy and justify his sexual desire. One 17-year-old, "effeminate in appearance" and with a "high voice and slight lisp," searched round the clock for affection, even hitting on Professor Butts:

> Talks freely. Submitted to various forms of sex play from a man boarder when about ten years old. Later, with older boys. He has never been accepted by the group in school. Makes fair grades but is unhappy because the boys in school make fun of his effeminate ways. He is not particular about his customers and says that he will cooperate in any form of homosexual act. It was impossible for him to understand why all that the interviewer required of him was conversation. He kept asking, "But don't you like me?"[114]

Alfred C. Kinsey, who benefited from the nonpareil recruitment skills of Thomas Painter, interviewed several hundred male prostitutes for *Sexual Behavior in the Human Male*. Kinsey and his coauthors, Wardell Pomeroy and Clyde Martin, noted high levels of "total sexual outlet" for this population. Total sexual outlet referred to the "sum of the orgasms" resulting from masturbation, wet dreams, animal sex, heterosexual petting and intercourse, and homosexual relations.[115] Historian Joanne Meyerowitz wrote that Kinsey's sound, but limited, conclusions regarding male prostitutes were evidence of his general obsession with sexual outlet.[116]

Kinsey noted that male prostitutes' ability to perform often limited their work—a problem unknown to female prostitutes. But, more than their female counterparts, they were drawn to prostitution because of the opportunities for sexual outlet. Kinsey wrote about his most prodigiously orgasmic male prostitute subjects with a sense of awe:

> Some male prostitutes ejaculate five, six, or more times per day with a regularity over long periods of years.... In a few cases, there are records made by persons who have observed the actual performance of particular male prostitutes from hour to hour, over periods of time, and there is no question that there is frequent arousal and actual ejaculation of semen five or more times per day in some of these cases. One such set of observations concerns a 39-year-old Negro male...[who] had averaged more than three [orgasms] per day from 13 to 39 years of age, and at the latter age was still capable of 6 to 8 ejaculations when the occasion demanded.[117]

Kinsey's simple, radical suggestion—that male prostitutes might experience (and learn to have) more orgasms than their non-sex-working peers—was never again mentioned in American hustler research.[118]

Hustling was an inextricable part of the social fabric of poor, runaway, gang-affiliated, and sexual minority youth of the 1940s. Was the ritual use of hustling as an initiation rite becoming more common, or were observers only just beginning to explore the phenomenon? It appears that male and trans *youth* sex work was becoming more common—more public—in the mid 1940s. We can attribute this surge in sex work among youth to the increasing population density in coastal cities, but it is certainly also a consequence of wartime conscription. When military prostitutes and other young adult hustlers left the square for the war, they left the hustling arena to the youngsters. This got the youth noticed, and not just by Painter, Henry, Butts, and Kinsey.

In the tradition of 19th-century pulp tabloids, *Salute* covered the re-emerging boy prostitution scene. "Nightmare Alley, U.S.A.," a 1948 article, used the same morbid imagery that the pulps had mastered by the mid 1850s in their reportage on male and transgendered sex workers. The title was a humorless Gothic inversion of a clever gay turn-of-phrase. The intersection of 42nd and Eighth Avenue was known as "Vaseline Alley" by those in the know.[119] *Salute* writer Selwyn James filed this report on the Times Square boys:

> The handsome, shabbily dressed youngster was about 14. He stood outside the crowded penny arcade, watching the faces of the Saturday-night funmakers. He was shivering.... He was one of the dozens of twisted, money-mad kids who daily offer themselves to homosexuals along New York's Nightmare Alley—a 200-yard block of once-glamorous 42nd Street, between Seventh and Eighth Avenues.

But of all the social tragedy and moral ruin to be found on this street, that of free-lance child prostitution is the most heart-breaking, the most urgent. These unfortunate kids can be seen plying their sordid trade in the nightmare alleys of every sizeable city in the U.S.

Their ages range from a pitiful ten to about 18. Most are victims of low-income homes... Many flock to 42nd Street from the appalling slum areas of Greater New York. Others are runaways from as far off as Montana and Texas. Still others are reform-school escapees—tough, wily boys to whom hustling is only a new twist in delinquency....

About 20% of them have no homes at all. In summer they sleep on rooftops or in Central Park. When cold weather strikes, they bunk down in hallways, flophouses, cheap hotels, and YMCAs, or at the homes of "clients." Or they hitchhike to Florida resort towns.

Possibly excepting a few older youths, none of the lads is homosexual. On the contrary, they openly express disgust for the grisly profession they have adopted. They are prostitutes because prostitution offers big monetary rewards. With clients paying from two to five dollars, a boy can net as much as $35 a week.

"Show me another way to make five bucks in an hour," comments a tow-headed 12-year-old from nearby New Jersey. "It's easy dough—I'd be crazy to go back to shining shoes," says a chubby 15-year-old Brooklynite.

...They may voluntarily give up their wretched Jekyll-and-Hyde existence because of a guilty conscience; or, if they are runaways, homesickness may draw them away.

Drives by the New York Police Department to clean up this blighted street take place about **twice a year.** Shoeshine boys and all other loitering youngsters are warned away. Truant officers pick up some of them. A few youths may be arrested for vagrancy. The effeminate, powder-and-lipstick type of homosexuals may spend an uncomfortable night in jail. But none of this has a lasting effect.

Johnny, a robust, flaxen-haired 13-year-old...was quick to discover that some of his playmates make pocket-money the same way. Last fall, when a friend told him about 42nd Street, Johnny made the trip and picked up two men the first day.

He appears on 42nd Street in the late afternoon, eats at an Automat, then just hangs around and waits. His waiting looks aimless, but it isn't. "You can spot them fairies every time," he says confidently. "They all give you that look."

Perhaps more distressing is the case of a tall, undernourished, sallow-faced youth of 16, whose total reliance on himself for food and shelter has given him deep, premature worry lines on his fore-

*fig. 3.1 "Salute Boys," Salute
magazine, March 1948.*

head. Paul escaped from an Ohio orphan asylum last September. The night he arrived in New York he met two boy harlots of his own age, who told him he was too young to get a job. They advised him to take up hustling. Paul did.[120]

James was careful not to describe his subjects as too monstrous (they were only boys, after all). Instead, monsters surrounded them, sucking out their strength over time. *Salute*'s tone was sanctimonious; the accompanying photographs were almost certainly staged. The subjects are everybody's children, the boys next door. One kid is "tow-headed," another is "chubby," one more is "robust." Save a passing reference to Jekyll and Hyde, these are not opiate-addicted specters haunting the American midnight. Still, these youngsters are clearly headed for sallow-faced trouble. James enjoined Americans to respond to their plight, lest their deepest nightmares come to life. Yet what James advocates—increased intervention from police—ignored the real problems of runaway teen hustlers: employment, education, and housing.[121]

In the late 1930s, Tom Painter's prototypical street hustler was between 18 and 24, a coal miner's son from Ohio, Pennsylvania, West Virginia, or upstate New York. He was affiliated with the armed services, or willing to enlist if necessary. Meanwhile, he was making ends meet with a variety of under-the-table jobs, including hustling, though he did not identify himself as queer. Moreover, Painter's hustlers were generally uneducated: Of the 67 men he interviewed, none was college-educated, "and few had had any opportunity of so

being."[122] By 1947, Butts had found most hustlers were between 15 and 20, many were in high school or college, and the majority identified themselves as (or were very worried about being) queer. By 1948, Selwyn James's hustlers were 10 to 18. To be sure, James's emphasis on youth, to the exclusion of older trade, was a blatant play for typical American sympathies. But the demographic shift in the average age of street hustlers was undeniable. By 1948, male and transgendered sex workers had discovered the fountain of youth in the city square: They were getting younger every day.

---

[1] Minton, Henry L. "On the Thomas Painter Papers: An Invitation to Tell the Life Story of a Gay Activist." Paper presented at the symposium "Uncovering the Interpersonal Context of Sex Research: Revelations from the Kinsey Archives." Chiron, 2001; p. 4. Minton's brief biography of Painter is enormously interesting and useful. Also see Minton, *Departing from Deviance*. University of Chicago Press, 2002.
[2] From Painter, "Autobiographical Sketches," Box 3, Series II D.2. Folder 1: "Biography," VIII, p. 7 (KIL).
[3] See Chauncey, *GNY*, p. 303 on the availability of housing in the Times Square area: "The district offered rooming houses, theatrical boardinghouses, and small residential and transient hotels...as well as most of the city's elegant bachelor apartments." For prices, see Doshay, pp. 21, 23. Doshay categorizes income levels of the families of the boy sex offenders whom he studied. Middle-class families were those who made $5-15 a week. Average rent was considered to be $5-10 a month per person between 1926 and 1934.
[4] Painter, "Autobiographical Sketches," p. 8. Painter here remarked on the naïveté of his early work: He later wrote about the 1930s, "I am afraid what I was doing was conning trusting and idealistic friends, such as Luther Tucker, to finance my having a ball—in the name of

'FIELD RESEARCH.' I DID OF COURSE LEARN A LOT, AND DID WRITE A BOOK OR TWO, BUT THEY CAME MUCH LATER."

[5] IBID., IDEM.

[6] IBID., IDEM. SEE PAINTER'S COMMENTS ABOUT THE UNLOVED "HEROIN ADDICT" WILLIE O'ROURKE.

[7] HENRY, GEORGE. *SEX VARIANTS*. PAUL B. HOEBER, INC. (NYC), 1941. HENRY DESCRIBED PAINTER AS "A TALL, THIN, ANGULAR MAN OF TWENTY-NINE, SOMEWHAT AWKWARD," WITH "LARGE, PROMINENT EARS, A LARGE NOSE, THIN LIPS AND A POINTED CHIN." IN A SUBTLE GOTHIC METAPHOR, HENRY WROTE THAT "THE SKIN OF HIS FACE IS REDDENED AS THOUGH FROM DISSIPATION." SEE P. 370 (UNDER "WILL G.").

[8] IBID. FOR DANIEL, SEE PP. 425-438; FOR VICTOR, PP. 438-450; FOR ANTONIO, PP. 414-425.

[9] PAINTER, *MHP*, P. 3 FOR "KEPT-BOYS," AND PAINTER, *MALE HOMOSEXUALS AND THEIR PROSTITUTES II*, 1941, P. 129.

[10] STANNING, HAROLD. "GALS NIP HARD NUTS." *BROADWAY BREVITIES*, VOL. IX, NO.1, DECEMBER 26, 1932, PP. 16, 14.

[11] SEE STANNING'S "WIVES FOR HIRE!" *BROADWAY BREVITIES*, VOL. VIII, NO. 6, NOVEMBER 21, 1932, WHICH "DOCUMENTS" THE DALLIANCE OF A PARK AVENUE MATRON AND HER UNLUCKY PARAMOUR.

[12] STRAIT, GUY. *DOM IN EXILE*. UNPUBLISHED MANUSCRIPT, 1980, REPRINTED BY PERMISSION OF THE KINSEY INSTITUTE FOR SEX, GENDER, AND REPRODUCTION (KIL); PP.11-12.

[13] PAINTER, *MHP*, P. 129.

[14] RAMSEY, LYNN. *GIGOLOS: THE WORLD'S BEST KEPT MEN*. PRENTICE-HALL; NEW YORK, 1978, P. 40.

[15] IBID., P. 38.

[16] IBID., P. 41.

[17] IBID., P .41.

[18] IN A LETTER TO KINSEY FROM PAINTER, MAY 15, 1946.

[19] PAINTER, *MHP*, P. 44.

[20] IBID., IDEM.

[21] *VANITY FAIR*, APRIL 2001.

[22] PAINTER, "HOMOSEXUALS IN THE U.S.," UNBOUND MS, CIRCA 1941. FOUND WITH ACCOMPANYING HANDWRITTEN NOTES—INCLUDING THIS ONE—DATED 7/73.

[23] SEE EHRENSTEIN, DAVID. *OPEN SECRET: GAY HOLLYWOOD, 1928-2000*. HARPERCOLLINS, 1998; PP. 27-28. ALSO SEE PAUL ALEXANDER'S *BOULEVARD OF BROKEN DREAMS*.

[24] PAINTER, *MHP*, P. 48.

[25] PLIMPTON, GEORGE. *TRUMAN CAPOTE*. DOUBLEDAY; NEW YORK: 1997, PP. 87-89.

[26] IN A LETTER FROM PAINTER TO CLOSE FRIEND BILL BEGG, DATED OCTOBER 15, 1945.

[27] VIDAL, GORE. *PALIMPEST*. PENGUIN; USA: 1995, P. 180.

[28] IN A LETTER FROM PAINTER TO KINSEY, SERIES II.C.1, VOLUME 3, DATED JULY 13, 1946.

[29] PLIMPTON, P. 87.

[30] VIDAL, P. 179.

[31] PLIMPTON, P. 89.

[32] SEE PLIMPTON, P. 89. VIDAL CLAIMS THAT FOUTS DIED OF A MALFORMED HEART; PAINTER ATTRIBUTES IT TO SUICIDE. KINSEY ONCE ATTEMPTED TO INTERVIEW THE LEGEND: "I TOOK YOU TO HIS HOTEL ROOM TO GET THE CASE, HE HADN'T GOTTEN UP YET," PAINTER WROTE KINSEY IN A LETTER DATED JANUARY 1, 1949. NED ROREM, THE COMPOSER, RETELLS ONE OF CAPOTE'S STORIES: "TRUMAN SAID IF FOUTS HAD SLEPT WITH HITLER, AS HITLER WISHED, HE COULD HAVE SAVED THE WORLD FROM THE SECOND WORLD WAR, AND THAT'S REALLY RATHER AMUSING." FROM PLIMPTON, P. 89.

[33] FROM A 1936 ARTICLE, "DEGENERATES OF GREENWICH VILLAGE," IN *CURRENT PSYCHOLOGY AND PSYCHOANALYSIS*, DECEMBER 1936. REPRINTED IN DUBERMAN, *ABOUT TIME*, PP. 132-134.

[34] PAINTER, *MHP*, P. 41.

[35] IBID., IDEM.

[36] IBID., P. 42.

[37] Ibid., p. 45.

[38] See Cole, Shawn. *Don We Now Our Gay Apparel*. Berg, Oxford: 2000; p. 53.

[39] Chauncey, *GNY,* p. 294.

[40] Ibid., p. 297.

[41] Ibid., p. 296.

[42] Ibid., p. 257.

[43] Ibid., starred page note, pp. 332-333.

[44] Ibid., p. 340.

[45] Jones, A.J. and Lee Janis. "Primary Syphilis of the Rectum and Gonorrhea of the Anus in a Male Homosexual Playing the Role of a Female Prostitute." *American Journal of Syphilis, Gonorrhea, and Venereal Diseases 28,* July 1944; pp. 453-457. This trans hustler had grown up on a farm, where she was raised with apparent tolerance, performing household tasks and growing her hair long. Under examination, the patient recalled that "people used to talk to each other and say, 'That isn't a boy, that isn't a boy.'"

[46] Like Jennie June's earlier usage of "androgyne," this subject used "hermaphrodite" to denote her mixture of masculine and feminine qualities, crossing the semantic chasm between tolerable transgender self-expression and modern medical terminology.

[47] Jones and Janus, pp. 453-457. There is no follow-up provided on the hapless johns.

[48] Hall, Bruce Edward. *Diamond Street.* Black Dome Press, 1994; p. 125.

[49] Benjamin, Harry and R.E.L. Masters. *Prostitution and Morality,* p. 297. These prices, however, also correlate to drag brothels run in the 1960s. It is difficult to pin the date down, as Benjamin prefaced it only as "some years ago."

[50] See Painter, *MHP,* p. 100.

[51] Ibid., p. 31.

[52] Waggoner, Raymond and Boyd, David. "Juvenile Aberrant Sexual Behavior." *American Journal of Orthopsychiatry,* 1941; pp. 276-277.

[53] Ibid., pp. 281-282. This client's street experiences do not seem to have offered any better security or affection than his home life.

[54] Ibid., pp. 287-291.

[55] Painter, *MHP,* p. 62

[56] Ibid., p. 61.

[57] In a letter from Edward Melcarth to Painter, received October 12, 1950 (KIL).

[58] From a 1975 report to Huckleberry House, Northern California Gay, Lesbian, Bisexual and Transgender Historical Society (NCGLBTHS); p. 26. (Unfortunately, this is an incomplete document, without relevant notes and bibliography.)

[59] Ibid., idem.

[60] Ibid. idem.

[61] Ibid., p. 28.

[62] Ibid., idem.

[63] Marotta, Toby, with Bruce Fisher and D. Kelly Weisberg. "URSA Report on Adolescent Male Prostitution," 1982. Interview with "Tom," p. 4. (See Chapter One in this book for another economic downturn faced by San Francisco street hustlers when horny, sex-working sailors invaded the Presidio during the Spanish-American War.)

[64] Interview with Susan Stryker, conducted by author.

[65] From "Where to Sin in San Francisco," printed between 1938 and 1944. Reprinted in Huckleberry House document, p. 29.

[66] Ibid., p. 30.

[67] Painter, *MHP,* p. 37.

[68] Ibid., p. 39.

[69] See *Broadway Brevities,* August 30, 1933. "Haulers Joints Oiled," by Q.N. Bush.

[70] Painter, *MHP,* p. 71.

[71] Ibid., idem.

[72] Ibid., p. 18.

[73] Ibid., p. 29.

[74] See Robert P. McNamara, *The Times Square Hustler*. Praeger (Westport, CT), 1994; p. 20.

[75] Painter, *MHP*, p. 26

[76] Ibid., p. 87.

[77] Ibid., p. 73; also see Painter's 1945 prefatory note to Kinsey, in manuscript folder.

[78] See Lawrence R. Murphy, "The House on Pacific Street: Homosexuality, Intrigue, and Politics During World War II." *Journal of Homosexuality*, Vol. 12 (1), Fall 1985; p. 29.

[79] Ibid., p. 31.

[80] Ibid., p. 29.

[81] *The Nation*, February 1942.

[82] Painter, prefatory note to Kinsey, in 1945, for *MHP2*.

[83] *New York Post*, May 4, 1942. See also Murphy, "Pacific Street," pp. 31 and 48 (note 18).

[84] Murphy, "Pacific Street," p. 30.

[85] Beekman was interned at Sing Sing for 21 years, from 1942 to 1963, when he was released at the age of 78. See Katz, *GLA*, p. 585.

[86] *New York Post*, May 2, 1942.

[87] See Murphy, "Pacific Street," p. 33.

[88] Tripp, C.A. *The Homosexual Matrix*. McGraw-Hill, 1975; p. 226. It is unclear where Tripp obtained this information.

[89] See Murphy, "Pacific Street," p. 34.

[90] *New York Post*, May 6, 1942.

[91] Tripp, p. 217. This claim is impossible to verify, as Tripp's footnotes refer only to his own direct observations and his personal communications with Alfred C. Kinsey.

[92] From Painter's Name Book, in the Painter Papers (KIL).

[93] Painter, 1945 prefatory letter to Kinsey.

[94] Ibid., idem.

[95] Vining, Donald. *A Gay Diary*. The Pepys Press (NYC), 1979; pp. 272-273.

[96] In a letter written by Painter to Kinsey, in manuscript folder, ca. 1944. In this (and other) letters, the code letter "y" has been substituted for "homosexual."

[97] In a letter written by Painter to Kinsey, dated August 1, 1944.

[98] In Painter's 1945 prefatory letter to Kinsey.

[99] In a recommendation letter dated August 16, 1944, an Army Air Corps intelligence officer wrote that Painter "has an educational and academic background which qualify him peculiarly well for his present duty assignment." In the Thomas Painter Papers (KIL).

[100] From a letter written by Painter to Bill Begg, April 1945. For the continuation of this tradition in the 1960s (minus the cats), see Jim Carroll's *The Basketball Diaries*. Bantam (NYC), 1980.

[101] In a letter from Painter to Bill Begg, dated August 1945/6.

[102] In a letter from Painter to Kinsey, dated October 4, 1945.

[103] Ibid., idem.

[104] Butts, William Marlin. "Boy Prostitutes of Metropolis." *Journal of Clinical Psychopathology*, April 1947 (Vol. 8, No. 4); p. 673.

[105] Ibid., p. 674.

[106] Ibid., p. 678.

[107] Ibid., p. 675.

[108] In a letter from Painter to Begg, dated October 10, 1945. In another letter from Painter to Begg, dated November 24, 1945, Kentucky drags a "Teutonic youth of some 17 summers" off the street and into "the malted-milk place" for the expectant Painter and Melcarth. The boy turns out to be a tough kid from the Bronx who nevertheless agrees to pose nude while the artists sketch him at a rate of $1.25 an hour. "I'd do anything for money," he tells Painter calmly.

[109] Butts, p. 680.

[110] Ibid., p. 677.

[111] Ibid., p. 679.

[112] Ibid., p. 679.

[113] Ibid., p. 680.

[114] Ibid., pp. 679-680.

[115] KINSEY, ALFRED, WITH WARDELL POMEROY AND CLYDE MARTIN. *SEXUAL BEHAVIOR IN THE HUMAN MALE*. W.B. SAUNDERS (PHILADELPHIA), 1948; P.193. FOR "SEVERAL HUNDREDS OF MALE PROSTITUTES" INTERVIEWED, SEE P. 216.

[116] PERSONAL COMMUNICATION, NOVEMBER 2001.

[117] KINSEY, ET. AL., PP. 216-217.

[118] ALBERT REISS, JR., COMES THE CLOSEST TO VERIFYING KINSEY'S CONCLUSIONS, IN HIS 1961 STUDY, THOUGH HE DOES NOT DISCUSS IT DIRECTLY. SEE CHAPTER FOUR IN THIS BOOK.

[119] VASELINE ALLEY, IN TURN, DERIVES FROM GASOLINE ALLEY, THE TRUCK-STOP CORRIDOR BETWEEN NEW YORK, NEW JERSEY, AND PENNSYLVANIA THAT HAD BECOME NOTORIOUS FOR FEMALE SEX WORK BY THE 1930S. (SEE CHAPTER TWO IN THIS BOOK.)

[120] JAMES, SELWYN. "NIGHTMARE ALLEY, U.S.A." *SALUTE,* MARCH 1948, PP. 4-5. (EMPHASIS MINE.) FOR A COMMENTARY LINKING THIS ARTICLE WITH THE JERRY FALWELL "SAVE THE CHILDREN" LITERATURE OF THE EARLY 1980S, SEE DUBERMAN, *ABOUT TIME*. THE SEA HORSE PRESS (NYC), 1986; PP. 135-139.

[121] FOR ANOTHER DISTURBING SOLUTION OFFERED FOR MALE SEX WORKERS' CONDITIONS, SEE ALSO FREYHAN, F.A. "HOMOSEXUAL PROSTITUTION: A CASE REPORT." *DELAWARE STATE MEDICAL JOURNAL,* MAY 1947; PP. 92-94. "I LIKE EASY MONEY AND I KNOW HOW TO GET IT," A SEX-WORKING MALE TOLD DR. FREYHAN. THE YOUTH HAD INTERNALIZED GOTHIC METAPHORS: "I KNOW THAT I AM NOT TOO GOOD LOOKING, BUT *I AM SURE THAT I HAVE SOME ATTRACTION OVER MEN BECAUSE OF THE CIRCLES AROUND MY EYES,* THE WAY I WALK AND THE WAY I LOOK AT THEM," HE CONTINUED (EMPHASIS MINE). "IT GIVES YOU A THRILL TO WALK AROUND TIMES SQUARE, WATCH THE CROWDS, TO PICK YOUR MAN AND MAKE HIM." FREYHAN DIAGNOSED THE PATIENT WITH SYPHILIS AND AN ANAL FISTULA, THEN CASUALLY SUGGESTED THAT THE BOY OUGHT EITHER TO UNDERGO LOBOTOMY OR LEARN A TRADE. *SALUTE'S* ESTIMATED WEEKLY RATE FOR HUSTLERS ($35) IS CONSISTENT WITH FREYHAN'S PATIENT, WHO AVERAGED $40 A WEEK IN 1947.

[122] PAINTER, *MHP,* P. 126. IT IS ALSO HIGHLY POSSIBLE THAT THESE CONCLUSIONS ARE WRONG, EXAMPLES ONLY OF SMALL, SPECIFIC SAMPLES ATTRACTED BY DIFFERENT RESEARCHERS.

four

Middle-American male and transgendered sex workers were more tightly constrained than their urban counterparts. There is no documentary evidence of male brothels in American small towns, but that lacuna is hardly surprising. Throughout the cities of the Midwest, brothels with male sex workers more easily avoided scrutiny from local authorities when women were the houses' main source of revenue. Rural male and transgender sex work thrived in an environment profoundly different from the American metropolis, and thus developed in profoundly different ways.

Trans girls in the sticks had to work with biological women to learn the ropes. In New York City, where there was a long tradition of transgender prostitution, street-based fairy sex workers often worked apart from hustlers and female prostitutes. But rural social structures prohibited this independence, compelling trans girls to click-clack the path blazed by biological women.

Civvies in Skivvies: Next Year's Jelly, 1938-1945

While street-based male sex work diminished during the war years, movie theaters, parks, rest stops, and other familiar venues with pretexts became places of introduction and negotiation. Rural boys naturally sought same-sex relations in similar venues in bigger cities.[1] For a few, Vaseline Alley provided their introduction to sex work. Others sought happier hustling grounds after having already developed an expertise both on the road and in their hometowns.

This expertise was not limited to servicing other men. Good-looking youngsters also sought remunerative sexual satisfaction with women. On base in San Antonio, Painter befriended a "very dark, Mexican-looking youth," 21, who had been a cowboy and a copper miner in Arizona. Upon hearing that the soldier had only 48 cents to his name, Painter invited him to share a hotel room during the young man's weekend furlough. The soldier asked whether Painter had anything "up" for that night, as the soldier knew some generous girls. "Some even pay me to go with them," he told Painter.[2] During the war, women paid servicemen for sex and cruised for them in many of same spots their male clients did. In early 1945, Painter's old hustler friend Fritz told him that "in three hours in [Central Park] 27 females accosted him (in his Merchant Marine hat and dungarees and civilian shirt)."[3]

Not long after Painter was shipped to the Southwest, his Kinsey-supported internal transfer went through, and he was sent to Wright Field, an Army Air Force base near Dayton, Ohio.[4]

Painter had trouble perfecting his double-agent role. He quickly discovered the town's gay bar, a place on Main Street called Lord Lansdowne's, "more overt and uninhibited...than any place now in New York."[5] The bar was packed with "60-year-old would-be wolves, and a gang of fairies (young)," who took up the end of the bar, while "the military [took] over the lion's share." Since "there [was] strictly no fraternization" between the three groups, there was little evidence of the kind of sex work Painter was used to, which would have involved lively fraternization between the military and the civilians—wolf, soldier, and fairy alike. That wolves were sexually employing the fairies had not yet occurred to Painter. He was perplexed by the military-civilian segregation in Lord Lansdowne's Bar. When it came to his military intelligence duties, he confessed to Kinsey that he was "not much of a menace."

Kinsey's boundless curiosity prompted Painter to befriend a fairy hustler in Liberty Park. Through this friendship, Painter gained some sense of transgender sex work in conservative Dayton:

> *Friday night I was accosted by a young faggot—a rather pleasant little boy—who was hustling. This was in the park—Liberty Park, which I had spotted as the likely place. From him I learned about the cliques of boys who regularly held "drag" parties (weekly, apparently) in private homes here and there about the city. One place was a rooming house, for men only, to which he took me—the landlady of which was the mother of a queer boy, and cooperated in the activities. Apparently this rooming house was not actually a peg-house. There seems to be no peg-house here...there are no, or few, "hustlers" (in my usual sense of the word) either resident or transient in Dayton. He is a regular commercial prostitute. He has been arrested for hustling in drag on the streets—and confined, as a result, for 6 months in an institution for the mentally deficient! This was in Cincinnati. He hails from Georgia, originally. He will be 18 in August. As all prostitutes he has also had his lovers—one of whom he calls "normal"—who is now in the Navy. The lover...was about his own age. Apropos your contention, I suggested that while he was walking with me he do so in as normal a manner as possible—which he did, saying this (the normal bearing) was natural to him, the other affected for business purposes—for cruising. He is a very decent, nice child—with all due allowances for his occupation.*
>
> *Is the aspect of male prostitution I have so elaborated upon, then, a phenomenon of the great cities? Does it not exist in Dayton? Or is it just nonextant now because of the war taking the potential hustlers away?[6]*

Painter followed Kinsey's intuitions and directions dutifully, and they served him well once again: This transgendered hustler used a high-drag stride more *for business purposes* than to satisfy emotional compulsion. Kinsey's theory about the distinction between commercially oriented drag and emotionally compelled transgenderism found proof in a real-life example. Precisely *because* Dayton was a conservative, Midwestern town, there was no distinct hustler scene. This young man from Georgia had no choice but to solicit in drag.

Emboldened by his diplomatic immunity, Painter pursued a boy named Lew in July 1945. Lew was a civilian: a "work horse type," with "dark wavy hair," and 22 years old. (Painter was 39.) Lew had a "large and heavy" penis, "legs very well muscled," and was "modest, amiable, friendly, obliging...and unspoiled."[7] He was also a casual hustler. Through his new friend, Painter began to understand small-town masculine sex work. Writing Bill Begg, Painter tested his theories and speculated that Dayton boys who liked getting head were just giving it away, expecting nothing in return. And he was amazed. "This," wrote Painter, "is the hustler before he hits Times Square or Michigan Boulevard or Hollywood.... This is also the youth who makes life tolerable for thousands of small city homosexuals over the country—because thousands of him never go to New York or San Francisco, but live in the Daytons and pass on to the rising generation their knowledge of Queers."[8]

Older youths, Painter found, made regular use of gay bars. Regarding Lord Lansdowne's, he wrote Kinsey that in Dayton, "the buying of 'trade,' while occasionally done, is done on the sly, as if shameful and humiliating—involving loss of face, indicative

that one is unable to get it without buying it."[9] Because of the silence enforced by the closet, clients preferred to use familiar trade to help them procure new boys. An Omaha boy named Stuart Loomis reported:

> *I came out in 1938, when I was 18. I was living in Omaha, Nebraska, and running with a bohemian crowd at the college I attended. I met other gay men in public places—parks, restrooms—but once you went with one of these older men, you'd get introduced around and invited to private parties.*
>
> *I quickly graduated from trade to procurer (**This year's jam is next year's jelly,** the saying went), introducing other curious and comely young men from my own growing circle of acquaintances to the weekly bacchanals. Certain traditions were instilled. I was taught how to mix a proper scotch and soda. I was never allowed to pay for a drink or dinner. "Oh **no,**" one of the older gentlemen would say, covering my hand as he reached for his wallet. "You'll do that **later.**"[10]*

Loomis's use of the colloquialism "jam" to denote "trade" indicates Midwestern queers were steadily appropriating metropolitan gay argot (we last heard such semantics in Greenwich Village in 1936, when a queen was "camping for jam"—see Chapter Three). In keeping with the sticky-sweet metaphor, "jelly" now took the place of "seasoned" trade, the man in the middle in a game of pickle.

Another striking respect of Loomis's remembrance is the absence of contempt among jam, jelly, and consumers. Loomis recalls that one friendly client, Smitty, could "talk the pants off of any young guy he wanted," using train stations and cafés to meet boys.

> He'd chat up a serviceman in the train station or a transient in a coffee shop, and invite him over for a drink and shower—and a blow job. They'd always pretend not to notice the last part—Smitty was so safe and friendly. Then when he'd had a drink and a hot shower, the young fellow would usually wander out with a towel around his waist and his dick poking up, mumbling "Did you mention something about a blow job?" and Smitty'd be on his knees and draining him in seconds.[11]

Duets like this easily became group parties in an environment that was half circus and half boxing ring. Why was this scene so well tolerated by trade and client alike? Neither clients nor hosts thrust newcomers into anything socially unusual. Instead, the scene was filled with "men's men," guys who talked sports, wrestled, drank, and smoked. For wayward soldiers, lonely hitchhikers, and homesick college boys, Omaha parties provided social, sexual, and economic support in a laid-back, non-threatening setting.

But trade and their clients did not always get along so well; perhaps Stuart Loomis's memories were rose-tinted. In Dayton, Tom Painter observed anxiety and condescension among customers, which mixed with trade boys' homophobia to create an "aura of guilt and mutual contempt."[12] The class tension was straight from Montague Glover's London in 1915. Young, poor trade boys in Dayton appeared to their seducers as "strange and rather frightening creature[s] from that foreign land on the other side of the railroad tracks," for whom "social communion is out of the question."[13] Because clientele had much to lose by procuring boys openly, and because boys could not risk public advertisement, middlemen kept the underground male sex work scene alive.

Aspiring sex workers in small Midwestern towns began to advertise themselves in the naturist fitness magazines that preceded gay porn. One anonymous boy from Ohio used a naked picture of himself and an association from the magazine *Strength & Health* to forge a connection with a New York queen. In the mid 1940s, Painter sent the Ohio youth's picture to Kinsey.

Responding to a question about its origins, Painter wrote:

> It was a small photograph given me by [Molly King] who had it in turn from a queen who had been in correspondence with the boy pictured in Ohio. The queen lived in New York. The back had written on it some sentiment like, "best to So and So from Jimmie" with four or five X's added. Seems the queen did not know the boy save by mail, either

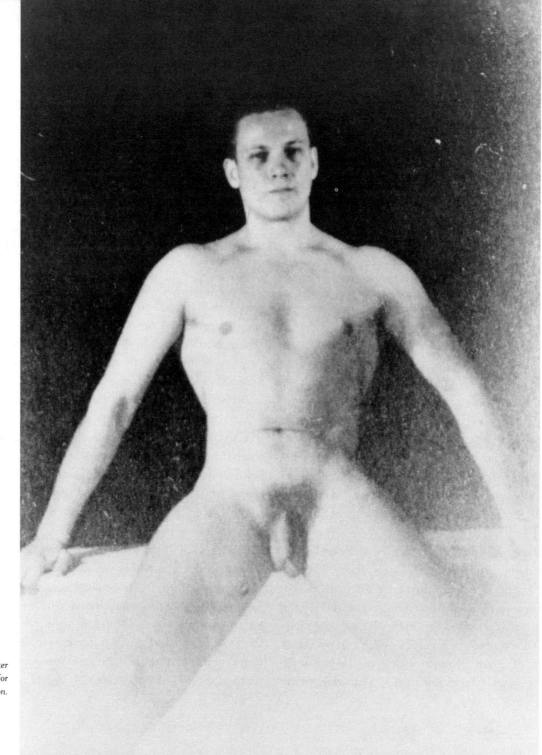

fig. 4.1 *"Seated Nude Man"* (ca. 1943) *from the Painter Papers, reproduced by permission of the Kinsey Institute for Research in Sex, Gender, and Reproduction.*

through S[trength] & H[ealth] League or a third party. The boy wanted to be invited to visit in New York. This picture and the inscription on the back were intended to encourage such an invitation, with perfectly obvious implications. The obscenity and looseness of thus peddling oneself naked through the mail for prostitutional purposes is to me extremely arousing, as is the grossness of the pose.[14]

In the early 1940s—and perhaps even earlier than that—male sex workers were learning to encrypt messages in media channels available to gay culture. If a young man found someone to photograph him nude, he could certainly find a way to disseminate those pictures for potential financial benefit. Bruce Bellas (later Bruce of Los Angeles) began his career by photographing the jam and the jelly at Omaha parties. While many of these photos were spontaneous, naturist shots, others have an intentional commercial quality to them, for the subjects were quite aware of the value of their bodies.[15]

In 1946, after the war, Painter returned to New York. He went straight to Diamond Jim's, a hustler bar in Times Square, where he met a boy whose description of informal male sex work in Fort Wayne, Ind., serves as a useful introduction to the rest of this chapter. This boy casually reported that before Fort Wayne's busy hustler scene was interrupted (by vigorous police actions culminating in the jailing of certain prominent citizens), he had developed a relationship with a local gay man. Their arrangement allowed for the boy to drive the man's car, and for the man to give the boy head.[16]

Innocent Delinquents: The Boys of Boise, 1955

Loomis and Painter reported that male and transgendered hustlers worked in small-town parks and squares during the war years, and that private parties were held as meeting grounds for clients, veteran hustlers, and fresh initiates. In Boise, Id., boys used similar venues shortly after World War II, and used the local YMCA to develop contacts. This "rambling brownstone building on Idaho Street, a few blocks from the capital" was conveniently located for transient boys and wealthy men alike. John Gerassi, an investigative reporter, interviewed chief of police Jim Brandon about the scandal that developed, in Newport fashion, around the beleaguered Y in 1955. Brandon blamed hobos for the hullabaloo, claiming that tramps would head to the Y as soon as they hit town. In an effort to herd them right back out, Boise police made Idaho Street a regular run, causing negative publicity for the YMCA, which reacted by hiring private investigator Howard Dice. Dice learned nothing about the tramps, but did discover, when talking to the Y's "juvenile delinquents," that a man named Joe Moore might have been paying the boys for sex. This news was leaked to a reactionary Mormon organization called the Allied Civic Group, who presented statements to district attorney Blaine Evans on behalf of the Y's private investigator.[17]

Even in isolated Boise, the YMCA had no monopoly on male

sex work, although it was a property on which sex-working boys landed with some frequency. Teenagers found out about these unorthodox opportunities for lucre through word of mouth. Gerassi reported that one 15-year-old and one 16-year-old learned of the YMCA's hidden scene from an older boy with whom they were masturbating freely:

> One day, one of the older boys told them that if they went to the YMCA and were willing to do that to some adult, they could get five dollars for it. Eventually, both did, though in one case it wasn't at the Y but in the public toilet of Julia Davis Park. Finally, these adventures led to oral-genital copulation [with the boys receiving the blow jobs].[18]

In Julia Davis Park, tearoom trade was booming. Brandon told Gerassi there was a regular Indy 500 circling this pit stop:

> "There are roads going through [Julia Davis Park], and the homos would cruise around waiting for a kid to go into or come out of the toilet. They'd stop him, start a conversation, offer to drive him home, then hand him a drink. In one toilet, which had no partitions between johns, we caught a guy sitting on one john reaching over for the genitals of a boy sitting on another. It wasn't very nice work, believe me."[19]

John Butler, a psychiatrist hired by the city of Boise to counsel the working boys, commented on the relationship between small-town conformity and the proliferation of glory holes. Discussing a client of the public library, who drilled glory holes so that he couldn't see who was getting him off, Butler philosophized, "Even when the moral code is completely broken down, indeed flouted in its most abhorrent manner, guilt remains in a perverted shape."[20] Boise's news organizations, and subsequently the national media, preyed on this sexual guilt and its distortions in various ways. The news hook was not the money or the homosexuality. Instead, the relative youth of the sex workers drew media ire and, thus, community attention.

On November 3, 1955, the *Idaho Daily Statesman* editorialized on the recent arrests of three working-class men charged with "lewd and lascivious conduct with minor children under the age of 16." The *Statesman* employed the traditional Gothic metaphors to engage community attention, likening the developing scandal to a monster that needed to be destroyed.

CRUSH THE MONSTER

*Disclosure that the evils of moral perversion prevail in Boise on an extensive scale must come as a distinct and intensely disagreeable shock to most Boiseans. It seems almost incredible that any such **cancerous growth** could have taken roots and developed in our midst....*

The situation might be dismissed with an expression of regret and a sigh of relief if only one could be quite sure that none other than these three men and *these 10 boys has been **infected by the monstrous evil here.** But the responsible court officer says that only the surface has been scratched and that "partial evidence has been gathered showing that several other adults and about 100 boys are involved."*

*Until the whole sordid situation is completely cleared up, and the premises thoroughly **cleaned and disinfected,** the job is one in which the full strength of county and city agencies should and must be enlisted.[21]*

Like Selwyn James's commentary in *Salute,* the *Statesman*'s verbiage echoed reports in the metropolitan sporting presses of the mid 1800s. The editorial caused an uproar in Boise and inspired a call to arms.

Blaine Evans, the prosecuting attorney, was the town's dragon-slayer. His first arrest—of shoe-repairman Ralph Cooper—made quite a statement. Cooper pled guilty to sex with Lee Gibson (a 15-year-old who also had sex with another man arrested during the sweep) and was sentenced to life in prison on November 10, 1955. As Gerassi astutely remarked, it was "strange that the young, innocent Lee Gibson should have been 'victimized' by two so different homosexuals. Could it not have been Lee Gibson who had made the advances?"[22] This was not a question the authorities were asking. Though the working boys were no doubt terrorized by the investigations, they were, by and large, let off the hook.

The fallout from the *Statesman*'s editorial proved toxic. Lifelong neighbors no longer trusted each other. "Anonymous calls kept pouring in," reported Gerassi, "as outraged mothers continued to demand blood."[23] *Time* magazine's December 12 issue gave Boise national media attention, stating that "Boiseans were shocked to learn that their city had sheltered a widespread homosexual underworld that involved some of Boise's most prominent men and had preyed on hundreds of teenage boys for the past decade."[24] Reporters for *Time* were clear on the economic incentive for the trysts:

> In the course of their investigation, police talked with 125 youths who had been involved. All were between the ages of 13 and 20. Usually, the motive—and the lure—was money. Many of the boys wanted money for maintenance of their automobiles (Idaho grants daylight driving permits to children of 14, regular licenses to 15-year-olds). The usual fees given to the boys were $5 to $10 per assignation.[25]

Most of these early articles grossly exaggerated the scale of the activity for dramatic effect. The number of Boise boys allegedly involved started at three, jumped to 100, spiked at 125, quickly dropped back to 100, then to 75, and finally landed at "60 or 65" (of whom 35 were Mormon).[26] And of these 60-odd boys, "only four or five youths were deeply involved," Gerassi reported.[27] During the media frenzy, hyperbolic estimates of the number of sex-working boys intensified Boise's righteous indignation.

The *Statesman* acknowledged the volatile situation and published an editorial to calm nerves. Suggesting an "objective approach and intelligent plan," the *Statesman* on November 20 argued for leniency. No longer was the scandal monstrous. Instead, it merely indicated sickness, contagious perversion to be isolated and treated:

> *Confessions by homosexuals invariably bring out the stark fact that these victims of a puzzling physical or mental quirk were themselves infected as young boys. Then the die was cast. They grew into manhood to infect other boys, who, in turn, unless effective intervention follows, will travel the same path and carry the identical threat to the next generation of youth. Tragically, the scourge multiplies since one adult homosexual usually infects several boys.[28]*

Sadly, there is no discernible difference between this rhetoric and Louis Dwight's beastly diatribes on incarcerated youth in 1824. To the *Statesman*'s credit, the newspaper acknowledged that "the proper correction is not an indefinite sentence to the state penitentiary," if only because there "the homosexual may do society more damage," infecting more prisoners with his perversion. The *Statesman*'s editors presented psychiatric treatment as a more reasonable alternative.

What about the boys? The *Statesman* called for "a public meeting of our courts, our law enforcement officers, members of the legal profession, the medical society, the agencies serving youth, the Parent-Teacher associations, the state pardon board and any and all interested and connected groups" to address the "young victims."[29] A youth rehabilitation program was established to help high-school age male youth access employment and mental health services. Unfortunately, the effort was hamstrung by a lack of funding. There was, however, plenty of money to support life sentences for the boys' clients.

The JDs: Toughs from the Sticks, 1955-1963

The handful of Boise boys deeply involved in sex work were teenage hoodlums whose sexual commerce was just another hustle in a string of petty thefts, blackmail, and assaults. Gerassi found "they knew who the homosexuals were, how to contact them, and how to profit from their contact. They were juvenile delinquents, not homosexuals, and one phase of their delinquency was male prostitution."[30] This finding parallels the sociological work of Albert Reiss, Jr., who studied boys in a Nashville reform school five years later. "The boys I studied," wrote Reiss, *"do not define themselves either as hustlers or as homosexual.* Most of these boys see themselves as 'getting a queer' only as a substitute activity or part of a versatile pattern of delinquent activity."[31] Because country hustlers participated in other more serious crimes in addition to hustling, they didn't see their sex work as part of their larger sexual identity.

Both Reiss and Jack Butler, the psychiatrist who treated the Boise boys, noticed that certain cultural norms served as helpful teaching and coping tools. In both Boise and Nashville, hard-core teenage hustlers were frequently gang members. In these small-city gangs, male sex work (or queer-baiting) served as an initiation rite, a bonding ritual, and a practical financial activity. "That hard core of kids supposedly seduced by homosexuals," Butler told Gerassi, "were actually made up of tough gang members. Technically, they were minors, and the law had to prosecute the adults as the responsible lawbreakers. As for the kids, they were fully aware of what they were doing. They may have been only 15, 16, and 17, but they were much too developed to be considered children. And, as it turned out, some of them became regular criminals. One of the boys later killed his father."[32]

Reiss, who collected sex histories from boys interned at the Tennessee State Training School for Boys, discovered that gang hustling was "almost exclusively limited to lower-class delinquent boys—particularly career-oriented delinquent boys."[33] He considered boys' sex work to be "institutionalized" within the delinquent framework. Experienced gang members (for Reiss, the "peer group") functioned as teachers in this "school of induction." After schooling initiates in the tricks of the trade, older, veteran boys accompanied new recruits and guided them through their indoctrination. Reiss uses this account from a boy named Doy L. as an example:

> I went along with these older boys down to the bus station, and they took me along and showed me how it was done...they'd go in, get a queer, get blowed and get paid...if it didn't work right, they'd knock him in the head and get their money...they showed me how to do it, so I went in too.[34]

Another Nashville boy, Jimmie M., learned about hustling from his brother, having already heard about it from "the other guys":

> Well, my younger brother came home and told me this gay'd blowed him and he told me where he lived.... And, I was scared to do it, but I figured I'd want to see what it was like since the other guys talked about it and my brother'd done it. So I went down there and he blowed me.[35]

We can reasonably infer that a similar socialization process developed in Boise, though the *Statesman* and the police regarded hustlers as innocent, exploited victims. Reiss argued that the gangsters' tight social structure made it "quite difficult to 'exploit' a lower-class boy who is socialized in a peer group. It is perhaps largely the very young boy...or those isolated...who are most vulnerable to solicitation *without previous preparation for it.*" These loners, Reiss mused, "usually form a strong dependency relationship with [one client] and are kept much as the cabin boys of old." [36]

The late artist David Wojnarowicz remembered that gang affiliation provided his introduction to gay sex, offering a prototype for his future hustling. Wojnarowicz grew up in a several small New Jersey towns. He remembered that, in 1961, when he was 7.

There was a gang of thugs in our neighborhood that we were warned to stay away from. The oldest was 19. They had bobby-pin guns and switchblade knives. The oldest one found me playing in a half-completed house and took me to the attic where he had me climb a ladder and tie his hands above a beam. Then he told me to take off his pants and take his dick in my hands and pull. I did for a while; he got red in the face. I got bored and grabbed a handful of insulation from a box and wrapped it around his dick and pulled. He screamed and I ran away.[37]

The next year, Wojnarowicz wrote, "another member of the gang took me in the woods and showed me how to put my dick in his mouth. Then he did the same to me. I asked him if we were allowed to do that; he said, yeah. Later I hit him in the head with a two-by-four and bloodied it."[38] The sexually charged, violent milieu of many American gangs set the tone for initiates' future prostitution.

These accounts ring truer than the statements offered by Lee Gibson and William Baker, two Boise boys who testified against their alleged former client, Joe Moore. We might expect these boys' sworn statements to differ from the sex histories recorded by an impartial sociologist. Still, we can discern the reality beneath Idaho's mirage of innocence. Gibson gave the following affidavit, in a tone more complaisant than delinquent.

My name is Lee Gibson. I am 15 years old. I was in Julia Davis Park next to the tennis courts. [Joe Moore] asked me where I was going when stopped [in] his 1954 Cadillac which was some shade of green, next to me. I told him I [was] going over to my girl-friends. He asked me to ride, which I did. He had Seagrams 7...he got it out and handed it to me. He asked me if I would rather get drunk than go over to my girl's. I said I guessed so. We drove around town, went to the show.... We got into [the] show and he started playing with me. Unbuttoned first top button. We got out of show around 6:00.... Asked me if I had even been blowed as we were driving around.... He parked on top of a hill and started playing with me. He put his mouth over my penis and worked it up and down until I come. I was feeling my liquor and after he got through going down on me he had me drink some more whiskey.... On the way home I passed out.... As we entered town he woke me up. Took me to Junction station café HiWay 14 and 44 and had me drink some coffee. He took me to [my home] and let me out. He said be quiet about this.[39]

Gibson's affidavit disturbed John Gerassi for several reasons. First, the name "Joe Moore" was hastily substituted for another, scratched-out name (perhaps someone wealthier than poor Mr. Moore). Gerassi objected that Gibson came off as a "very shy, or at least pliant, juvenile, when in fact Lee Gibson was a tough kid."[40] What went unmentioned was that Gibson was, by his own admission, no stranger to fellatio; Moore, in fact, was at the very least his second oral homosexual sex experience.

And William Baker, the boy who would later kill his father, mentioned that he and Lee partnered with Moore, just as the Nashville boys kept each other company during their adventures. Baker, then 16, had been at the roller rink until it closed. He missed the last bus and had been left behind by his friends. Like a knight in lime-green armor, Joe Moore happened by in his Cadillac and offered Baker a midnight ride. Baker declined, but met Moore again next Saturday night. Moore drove him around, played with his clothed penis until Baker told him to "cut it out," and dropped the boy off at home. The following Friday, Moore picked Baker up again, by the roller rink:

> He came out to the skating rink. He saw me there and asked me if I would like to go out with him and get a jug. This we did.... We drove around town and drank it until around one o'clock and he parked then we killed the rest of the bottle. Then he started playing around. He unbutt[o]ned my pants and played with my penis until it was hard then he put his mouth over my penis and worked it up and down until I came off. When we got ready to leave he put a $10 bill in my pocket and told me to keep still about it. I saw him again the following Wednesday. I was up to the Greyhound Bus station. He drove by slow and motioned me out. I got into the car and Joe Moore gave me several drinks while he was driving around. We saw Lee Gibson on the street. I yelled at him, we drove around the corner and stopped. Lee Gibson got into the front seat next to me. Lee was handed the bottle and he started to drink. Joe drove around town and got some more liquor.... We drove around about an hour and a half and then Joe drove out in the back of the Vets. Housing project. He parked and I got into the back seat with Joe Moore. He unbuttoned my pants and played with my penis until I was hard then he put his mouth over it and worked it up and down with my penis in his mouth. I went off. I put my penis back into my pants and he gave me a $10 bill. Lee Gibson was in the front seat and saw this.[41]

Whether Gibson was really just a witness during this escapade remains unclear.

These accounts illustrated a hustling milieu dominated by cars: the pickups were transportation offers, and the sex occurred on the way (or, more accurately, very much *out* of the way, but nevertheless in the vehicle). Also, Baker described a pattern of contact between himself and Moore. Fully aware of what he was getting into, Baker repeatedly accepted rides from Moore for beer, blow jobs, and money. Baker cruised the Greyhound station not to catch the bus to Spokane, but to get picked up by a client. Suspecting that Lee Gibson was also willing to hustle, Baker asked him to join the party. Gerassi shrewdly notes that these accounts were designed (either by the police department or by the boys, or through the collusion of both parties) to portray the youths as innocents. "Baker, like Gibson," wrote Gerassi, "is made to look like a stupid but innocent kid who at first doesn't like the idea of a man 'playing around' with him but eventually succumbs, when in fact he was a tough juvenile who knew the score."[42] The boys' street savvy is subtle but unmistakable in these accounts.

In Nashville, an extraordinarily similar scene unfolded. Reiss noted that boys would frequently "ride in the car with one of the gang's 'regular queens.'"[43] The relative familiarity and comfort with "queens," or clients, among the Nashville boys might indicate a greater acceptance of sex work among the city's adolescents. On the other hand, it might suggest that Mormon taboos against homosexuality isolated Boise's adolescents and prevented them from creating a vernacular for their sex work. Regardless, in Nashville as in Boise, gang boys were fellated for money, with little or no deviation from that norm. Reiss emphasized that "the sexual transaction must be limited to mouth-genital fellation. No other sexual acts are generally tolerated."[44] He reasoned that this boundary reinforced the boys' sense of masculinity. Because they didn't reciprocate, their straight identities weren't threatened.

Curiously, the Nashville boys played down the orgasmic elements of their sex work. Like the Boise boys who just *happened* to stiffen and come, the Nashville kids ignored the sexual gratification they experienced by defining their encounters as financial. One boy, Dolly L., played down the physical sensations he felt when men fellated him, and gave Reiss a summary of the sexual rules:

> (You like it?) It's OK. I don't mind it. It feels OK.
> (They ever try anything else on you?) They usually just blow and that's all. (Any ever try anything else on you?) Oh sure, but we really fix 'em. I just hit 'em on the head or roll 'em...throw 'em out of the car.... Once a gay tried that and we rolled him and threw him out of the car. Then we took the car and stripped it [**laughs with glee**].[45]

The Nashville hustlers acted violently toward their clients only when their clients humiliated them by violating established boundaries. Conversely, gang members referred to those Nashville hustlers who transgressed this sexual boundary using an old standby: "punks."[46] Power dynamics sanctioned the hustling activities of rural American youth; passivity, dependency, and relationship-building with clients were all severely derided. For their activities, punks relinquished any peer support. In this way, queer young townies were restricted in their sexual exploration.

Despite their hard-and-fast rules, the Nashville and Boise boys willfully underestimated the importance of getting "blowed." For the majority of them, this was the *only* sex they were getting, apart from mutual masturbation with other boys. A decade after the scandal, Gerassi gathered sexual histories from 12 ex-hustlers, and found that their average age was 16.7 in 1955, with a range from 14 to 17 years. In this Mormon town, *none* of the boys had had a heterosexual experience at the time of their hustling. All 12 knew classmates who were receiving blow jobs from adult homosexuals in 1955. In Nashville, of 87 boys whom Reiss regarded as lower-class delinquents, fully 47% were having sex with men; only 8% had sex exclusively with females. (Seventeen percent of this subsample also reported having sex with animals, a question Gerassi neglected to ask the boys in Boise.)[47]

Another similarity between the Nashville and Boise boys is their choice of pickup location. In both small cities, boys loitered in locales that provided a pretense for other activities, a degree of anonymity, and a quick escape route.[48] In Boise, as we have seen, these places included public rest rooms, the Greyhound station, the YMCA, the roller rink, and curbside venues where boys could hitchhike. In Nashville, boys were picked up in the bus station bathroom, on specified "queer-corners," and especially at the movies. Dolly describes the activity in the Greyhound rest room:

> Well, like at the bus station, you go to the bathroom and stand there pretendin' like...and they're standin' they're pretendin' like...and then they motions their head and walks out and you follow them, and you go some place. Either they's got a car, or you go to one of them hotels near the depot or some place like that.[49]

The movie theaters that Reiss discovered were used in the same way as the West Side Chicago theater made notorious by the Juvenile Protective Association's reports of the 1920s. Reiss noted that second- and third-run movie houses, "open around the clock and permitting sitting through shows," were popular sex work spots.[50] A youngster named Lester reported:

> I was down in the Empress Theatre and this gay came over and felt me up and asked me if I'd go out...I said I would if he'd give me the money, as I'd heard they did, and I was gettin' low on it...so he took me down by the river and blowed me.[51]

At age 11, another Tennessee boy named Dewey began working out of the Rex Theatre, where he was fondled by a guy who later invited Dewey to his house. Figuring it was "easy money," Dewey agreed, and made his $5. "I was a good boy before that," Dewey averred.[52]

Gang hustlers made one small exception to the code of masculinity governing their sex with men: They sometimes accepted liquor as payment. The Boise prosecutors alleged that defendant Ralph Cooper had "bought and provided liquor for himself and three other young boys." On one occasion, the court records state, Cooper "took the boys on a trip to Kuna Caves, during which trip they drank the liquor he had provided and during which trip he committed homosexual acts on their persons involving the use of his mouth."[53] In Nashville, a boy named Danny, the "leader of the Black Aces," admitted to his gang's involvement in a sex-for-alcohol scenario. Danny's history confirms that liquor could trump money as an incentive for going away with "a gay":

> There's this one gay who takes us to the Colonial Motel out on Dickerson Pike...usually it's a bunch of

us boys and we all get drunk and get blowed by this queer...we don't get any money then...it's more a drinking party.[54]

The substitution of liquor for money as sex work payment suggests that having sex with men for money was no more troubling to the young toughs than drinking alcohol underage—neither of which were as dangerous as attempting a heist.

Hustling's acceptance within the subculture of delinquent boys in the 1950s and 1960s was circuitously related to the criminal nature of prostitution. Because male prostitution was criminal, juvenile delinquents could configure same-sex activity as one of many petty crimes they committed. In other words, gang youths destigmatized their own prostitution by associating it with other forms of illegal and potentially violent activities.

This tricky balance engendered rules as elaborately structured as those of any brothel. Independent hustlers in New York City could slip in and out of the scene at will, but sex-working country boys necessarily formed small packs, using their collective identity as a shield against scorn.

[1] IN FACT, PAINTER OBSERVED THAT THE MAJORITY OF THE HUSTLERS HE KNEW FROM TIMES SQUARE WERE DISPLACED COUNTRY BOYS. OF THE 67 HUSTLERS HE INTERVIEWED BETWEEN 1935 AND 1940, MOST WERE STRAIGHT GUYS TRANSPLANTED FROM THE FARM OR THE FACTORY. SEE *MHP*, P. 126.

[2] IN A LETTER FROM PAINTER TO KINSEY, DATED MAY 27, 1945.

[3] IN A LETTER FROM PAINTER TO KINSEY, APRIL 1945.

[4] SEE CHAPTER THREE IN THIS BOOK.

[5] IN A LETTER FROM PAINTER TO KINSEY, DATED JUNE 21, 1945. THE FOLLOWING QUOTES IN THIS PARAGRAPH ARE EXCERPTED FROM THIS LETTER.

[6] IN A LETTER FROM PAINTER TO KINSEY, DATED JUNE 24, 1945.

[7] IN A LETTER FROM PAINTER TO KINSEY, AUGUST 15, 1945.

[8] IN A LETTER FROM PAINTER TO BILL BEGG, JULY 29, 1945. HUSTLERS PASSING INFORMATION TO THE "RISING GENERATION" RECALLS THE CASE OF NICHOLAS SENSION, GUILTY OF "INFECTING THE RISING GENERATION" WITH HIS USE OF SERVANTS FOR SEX. SEE CHAPTER ONE IN THIS BOOK.

[9] IN A LETTER FROM PAINTER TO KINSEY, AUGUST 15, 1945.

[10] FROM AN INTERVIEW WITH STUART LOOMIS, IN BELLAS, BRUCE. *THE NAKED HEARTLAND*. JANNSEN, SOUTH AFRICA; PP. 7-8.

[11] IBID., P. 7.

[12] IN A LETTER FROM PAINTER TO KINSEY, AUGUST 15, 1945.

[13] IBID., IDEM. FOR GLOVER'S PHOTOGRAPHS OF WORKING-CLASS HUSTLERS AND A COMMENTARY, SEE GARDINER, JAMES. *A CLASS APART*. SERPENT'S TAIL (LONDON), 1992.

[14] FROM A NOTE IN THE PAINTER PAPERS (BOX 10, SERIES A.IV.1C, BOX I, REGARDING PHOTO A-4). NOTE DATED SPRING 1949; BUT ANOTHER SIMILAR NOTE REGARDING THE SAME PICTURE WAS WRITTEN IN SEPTEMBER 1946. PROBABLY THE PICTURE WAS SENT—AFTER UNDERGOING NUMEROUS AMATEUR REPRODUCTIONS—TO KINSEY IN 1945, AND TAKEN IN THE EARLY TO MID 1940S.

[15] SEE BELLAS, *THE NAKED HEARTLAND*, FOR PRINTS.

[16] FROM A LETTER FROM PAINTER TO KINSEY, DATED JULY 13, 1946.

[17] GERASSI, JOHN. *THE BOYS OF BOISE*. COLLIER BOOKS, NYC, 1966; PP. 22-23.

[18] IBID., P. 33.

[19] IBID., P. 45.

[20] IBID., P. 32.

[21] *IDAHO DAILY STATESMAN*, NOV. 3, 1955 (EMPHASIS MINE). ALSO SEE GERASSI, PP. 4-8, FOR FURTHER ANALYSIS.

[22] GERASSI, P. 13.

[23] IBID., P. 15.

[24] *TIME*, DECEMBER 12, 1955.

[25] IBID., IDEM.

[26] GERASSI, P. 31.

[27] IBID., P. 35.

[28] *IDAHO DAILY STATESMAN,* NOV. 20, 1955

[29] IBID., IDEM.

[30] GERASSI, P. 37.

[31] REISS, ALBERT J., JR. "THE SOCIAL INTEGRATION OF QUEERS AND PEERS," IN *SOCIAL PROBLEMS,* VOL. 9, NO. 2, FALL 1961; P. 103.

[32] GERASSI, P. 38.

[33] REISS, P. 104. "CAREER-ORIENTED DELINQUENT BOYS" WAS MEANT TO SIGNIFY BOYS WHO PLANNED A CAREER OF DELINQUENCY AND CRIME.

[34] IBID., P. 109.

[35] IBID., P. 110.

[36] IBID., PP. 111, 116 (EMPHASIS MINE).

[37] WOJANOROWICZ, DAVID. "BIOGRAPHICAL DATELINE." IN *TONGUES OF FLAME.* UNIVERSITY GALLERIES OF ILLINOIS STATE UNIVERSITY, 1990; PP. 113-114.

[38] IBID., P. 114.

[39] FROM AFFIDAVIT SIGNED BY LEE GIBSON, IN *PEOPLE V. MOORE,* DATED NOVEMBER 3, 1955. REPRINTED IN GERASSI, PP. 54-55. (I HAVE CLEANED UP GRAMMATICAL ERRORS ATTRIBUTED TO THE ORIGINAL AFFIDAVIT.)

[40] GERASSI, P. 55.

[41] FROM AN UNDATED STATEMENT SIGNED BY WILLIAM BAKER, *PEOPLE VS. MOORE,* REPRINTED IN GERASSI, PP. 55-57.

[42] GERASSI, P. 58.

[43] REISS, P. 110.

[44] IBID., P. 114.

[45] IBID., P. 117. (REISS'S QUESTIONS IN PARENTHESES.) THESE BOYS' USE OF VIOLENCE CAN BE READ AS A SEXUALLY CHARGED PAYBACK UNDERTAKEN BY UNDERCLASS AND UNDERAGE BOYS. HERE, THE JOHN'S CAR IS "STRIPPED." IN BOISE, PSYCHIATRIST JACK BUTLER STATED: "SOME [HUSTLED] FOR MONEY. OTHERS DID IT FOR POWER. I REMEMBER VERY WELL ONE CHILD TELLING ME HOW IT MADE HIM FEEL IMPORTANT TO STAND THERE, WITH HIS ARMS CROSSED, WHILE AN 'OLD MAN,' AS HE CALLED HIM, GOT DOWN ON HIS KNEES IN ORDER TO—TO—AS THE BOYS PUT IT, 'TO BLOW ME.'" SEE GERASSI, P. 32.

[46] IBID., P. 115. "BOYS WHO ACCEPT THE FEMALE ROLE IN SEXUAL TRANSACTION OCCUPY THE LOWEST STATUS POSITION AMONG DELINQUENTS. THEY ARE 'PUNKS.'"

[47] STATISTICS INTERPOLATED FROM REISS, P. 105 (TABLE I).

[48] SEX RESEARCHERS WARDELL POMEROY AND R.E.L. MASTERS NOTED INFORMALLY THAT MALE PROSTITUTION WAS AS EASILY FOUND IN RURAL COMMUNITIES AS WAS FEMALE PROSTITUTION. "THERE ARE AS MANY HOMOSEXUAL AS HETEROSEXUAL PROSTITUTES," WROTE MASTERS, RECORDING POMEROY'S THEORY. "[POMEROY] FOUND THIS TO BE TRUE IN THE CITY OF ABOUT 30,000 WHERE THE [KINSEY] INSTITUTE IS LOCATED [BLOOMINGTON, IND.].... I'D SAY THAT IN SCHREVEPORT, LOUISIANA, THE CITY I'VE KNOWN BEST IN RECENT YEARS, THERE WERE AS MANY AND PROBABLY MORE MEN THAN WOMEN (OR BOYS AND MEN THAN WOMEN AND GIRLS) AVAILABLE." IN A LETTER FROM MASTERS TO BENJAMIN, DATED OCTOBER 21, 1962. HARRY BENJAMIN PAPERS (KIL), BOX ASSOCIATED WITH *PROSTITUTION AND MORALITY.*

[49] REISS, P. 107.

[50] IBID., P. 106.

[51] IBID., P. 110.

[52] IBID., P. 112.

[53] FROM A REPORT FILED IN THE PROSECUTING ATTORNEY'S OFFICE IN ADA COUNTY, NOV. 4, 1955. REPRINTED IN GERASSI, P.8.

[54] REISS, P. 113.

five

The period from 1950 to 1970 deserves its own slot on the hustler history shelf. Changing race relations, new definitions of sexuality, and countercultural politics dramatically influenced the sex work world. Our analysis of this era will rely on the usual sources from 1950 to 1962, drawing from the work of scientific observers. Thanks to the efflorescence of gay literature, from 1963 to 1970 there is a wide variety of source material from which to draw. The publication of John Rechy's *City of Night* brilliantly illuminated the shadowy world of male sex work. An emerging homophile movement was further inspired by street rebellions that male and transgendered hustlers instigated. Male brothels, which had been operating in samizdat mode since World War II, began to advertise their services in gay newspapers and periodicals whose authors were also willing to cover community prostitution.

We begin by returning from the heartland to examine shifts in gang hustler culture in the major cities during the 1950s and the early 1960s, when the streets offered a mix of cultural backgrounds and ethnicities and were split between gangsters and curious queer youth.

Gangsters and Curious Queers: Chicago, L.A., New York, Miami, 1950-1963

In the early 1950s, an English professor named Sam Steward became a tattoo artist. Steward had known Alfred C. Kinsey since the late 1940s, and his job switch piqued the sexologist's interest. In turn, Kinsey's probing was an incentive for Steward's philosophical research. The Sportland Arcade, in a black neighborhood on Chicago's South Side, accepted the new tattoo shop. It recalls Times Square: "There were arcades with tattoo joints in most of them, and burlesque shows, pawn shops, stores selling cheap clothing, and flophouses, one after the other," Steward wrote.[1]

Student researcher Harold Ross found that Chi-town sex workers operated out of seamy North Side bars. "In Chicago," Ross observed, "hustlers concentrate in that band of territory which serves to insulate the Gold Coast from the Slum, on the Near North Side."[2]

Chicago's Road Wolves, like the Nashville boys, were not above hustling outside the pack. Steward's account hints that Chicago's gang boys were as interested in battery and extortion as in fair business deals. "They talked a lot about homosexuality and about how they beat up 'the goddamned queers' after they jackrolled them," wrote the tattoo artist. A disenfranchised former gang member named Charlie, "one of the wildest young men in Chicago," drew Steward's attention. Charlie was "already smoking pot; it was only a step to bennies and goofballs, hustling the queers, and jackrolling the girls he went with."[3]

Steward's report illustrates how young men who were hard up might engage in remunerative relationships with women. While these were not always formal transactions—relying, as they did, on protracted relationships with a few select female partners, as opposed to quick, anonymous encounters with men—they nonetheless figured into the system of gangster commerce. Charlie told stories about wolves and pogeys (active and passive partners) in the state prisons and "was rolling his 'gurls,' smoking more marijuana than ever, and casing several apartments of the gays who picked him up, so that he could burglarize them later."[4]

John Rechy recalls that, in the 1950s, Pershing Square existed within similarly criminal surroundings:

> In Los Angeles, in the span of time that I experienced the scene, it was first of all downtown Los Angeles. Which then turned very rough, and a lot of ex-convicts, for example, would be at some of the places, and would hustle. So the scene moved gradually to Hollywood, because black people seemed to be moving into downtown. The scene moved...off of Hollywood Boulevard, and a couple of off-blocks, but it was a mixture of cruising and hustling. And then when that happened there was the ambiguity of whether somebody was hustling or cruising, and because the street was so busy, in fact it became increasing—this would be in the [19]50s—then the cars would drive around (it was a curious phenomenon how this occurred) and motion to a hustler to move to a side street. Eventually the side streets became the side of the hustling—that was Selma [Avenue].[5]

The geography of L.A.'s hustler economy shifted to relatively upscale West Hollywood for a few reasons. Increased use by African-American hustlers diverted racist clients and workers to mostly white WeHo. Another advantage to Hollywood Boulevard was that it was commercial, rather than municipal or strictly residential, reducing the chance that beat cops or neighborhood groups might persecute hustlers. And, as in Times Square, the sheer number of "innocent" consumers attracted by commercial strips meant that hustlers were less visible. As a coup de grace, West Hollywood was officially beyond city limits, and therefore outside the jurisdiction of the "faggot-busters," as Los Angeles vice squads were nicknamed.[6]

And in Times Square, the Port Authority bus terminal had opened in 1950, drawing vagrants, runaways, transients, and petty criminals.[7] Describing his growing disgust with the square, Painter complained to Kinsey that Diamond Jim's had been overhauled. The eatery had been torn out, and new management was unfriendly to hustlers and their clients. Sammy High Seas, a nearby alternative, was now packed with aging ne'er-do-wells and "juvenile delinquents of the most obviously criminal or depraved nature, who hustle." The streets, he added, were very much the same.[8] Where could polite trade be found? Hadn't Painter seen Rechy around?

fig. 5.1 "Hector, Victor, Bobby," from the
Painter Papers, reproduced by permission of
the Kinsey Institute for Research in Sex,
Gender, and Reproduction.

Sick of the dismal square, Painter began to explore the campier Village scene, on East 14th Street, and the upscale avenue of antiques, Third Avenue on Manhattan's Upper East Side. Fay Piston, who owned a pewter shop on Third and 54th from 1947 to 1960, remembered, "Third Avenue! From way down to maybe like where Bloomingdale's is now, *every* little place was some kind of an antique shop. For miles! People would come from all over the world to see the shops!"[9] Painter's window-shopping led to meetings with Puerto Rican hustlers, whose maschismo allowed for sex work as long as they were the active partners. He enjoyed this mindset and found it a throwback to the honest young sailors he met during the Depression and war years. Jay Roberts, a bar owner and hustler aficionado, wrote:

> The East Side was dominated by the greatest "Cruise-Hustler-Chick-Boy-Man-Girl-Woman Bar" to have ever been in existence, Shaw's at 50th Street and Third Avenue.... Bob's at 45th Street between Lexington and Third Avenues had the most beautiful gay hustlers of all—but they were expensive, $10 to $20, even $25; that was a lot in those days.... 42nd Street started changing. It became more a haven of heroin junkies and whores than gay guys and gay hustlers and the move was on.[10]

It's no wonder old clients were giving up on Times Square, with such a thriving crosstown alternative. Lexington had, in fact, supported male prostitution from the 1860s to the early 1930s, before Times Square's traffic intensified with the opening of the subway and the transformation of movie houses into porn dens.

Kinsey supported Painter's move wholeheartedly. "We have had some look-in on the Times Square area but a minimum [of] acquaintance with 14th Street and any other areas that you know," Kinsey wrote Painter. "You will realize that I have had quite a little contact with Latin Americans and know a good deal of the psychology of the group."[11] Kinsey's interest inspired Painter to take more pictures for the Institute.

Until 1953, Painter was primarily photographing white hustlers. After his rediscovery of 14th Street, he photographed Hector, Bobby, Victor, and many other young Puerto Ricans.

Painter was entranced and, beginning in 1956, traveled to Puerto Rico with a series of attractive young emigrés. Just before Painter's first trip, and shortly before Kinsey died, the doctor informed his protégé that in Latin America "homosexual relations are for free and for fun among children and older males when engaged with their peers." The bittersweet sexologist then qualified his idyll, writing that "American contacts have introduced the subject of pay and it will be interesting to know to what extent that is now the usual pattern."[12] True to form, Painter followed up, discovering that American tourism had spawned an active hustler culture in San Juan, Santo Domingo, and Havana.[13]

Although Painter had, after 20 years on the square, become

fig. 5.2 (left top and bottom) "42nd Street and 7th Ave., NW Corner" and "Diamond Jim's," from the Painter Papers, reproduced by permission of the Kinsey Institute for Research in Sex, Gender, and Reproduction.
fig. 5.3 (right top and bottom)"Around the Corner From Vaseline Alley" and "42nd Street and 8th Ave.," from the Painter Papers, reproduced by permission of the Kinsey Institute for Research in Sex, Gender, and Reproduction.

disenchanted, newcomers found it agreeably lively. "There was a thriving hustler scene on the streets surrounding Times Square in the fifties and early sixties," writes popular historian Charles Kaiser. One man whom Kaiser interviewed, the pseudonymous Sam Baron, began frequenting the square in the mid 1950s. Baron said,

> In those days it wasn't as scummy. There was a safer feeling about it. The boys were teenagers on into their 20s, a mix of whites and some Puerto Ricans. Not a lot of blacks. They cost $5; $10 was expensive. The thing that astonished me was I couldn't believe that these beautiful, magnificent specimens of manly beauty would be so pliable and agreeable in bed.[14]

John Rechy, who spent six months in Times Square in 1953 and most of the rest of the decade in Los Angeles, verifies these prices. "Oh, in the 50s, one could go for five dollars. I went for ten, but that was steep. That was really good.... By the time things shifted [for me] from New York onto here [Los Angeles], Main Street remained $10."[15] Jack Dowling told Kaiser that certain bars, especially the Astor, were known for high-end hustling, and had supplanted Marco's of the 1940s. Dowling said,

> The hustlers were mostly at the Silver Dollar bars. There was one on Sixth Avenue and 43rd Street that had a wonderful selection of hustlers and gay guys, gay older men looking for hustlers, whores, sailors.... It was also known that if you wanted to get picked up or pick somebody up and it involved money, you went to the Astor Bar, but you went in a suit and tie. If the hustler wanted some decent money and dinner, he went to the Astor Bar. On the street $10 was a lot, but not in a bar.[16]

Malcolm X steered Astor clients up to Harlem, to score black women, "the blacker the better," in the 1950s.[17] (Some historians have claimed that he traded sex as well, but that is disputed.) Malcolm also procured Harlem boys for wealthy women, through a messenger service run by someone he defined only as "the Lesbian." Malcolm said, "Some of her trade wanted the Negroes to come to their homes, at times carefully arranged by telephone. These women lived in neighborhoods of swank brownstones and exclusive apartment houses, with doormen dressed like admirals. But white society never thinks about challenging any Negro in a servant role. Doormen would telephone up and hear: 'Oh, yes, send him right up, James.' Service elevators would speed those neatly dressed elevator boys right up—so they could 'deliver' what had been ordered by some of the most privileged white women in Manhattan."[18]

Preferring the excitement of the streets to the rigidly stratified bar scene, Rechy observed the extensive criminal activities of some of his streetwise colleagues. "The dangers that are there are inescapable. Hustlers could take them—I would hear some of the things would happen [to clients]. And then of course the clients could also be very violent."[19] Reporting on a police sweep of Times Square in 1954, *The New York Times* quoted Deputy Chief Inspector James B. Leggett, who attributed heightened police activity to gang hustling. "The rise of organized young hoodlums," Leggett stated, "and the patent increase of homosexuals on the city's streets had brought a wave of rape, muggings, and other crimes of violence often culminating in murder."[20]

Leggett's statement was interesting spin, a plea to the homosexual community for support: We're not arresting you, we're keeping the streets safe from your attackers. Captain Louis Allen, of the Miami Police Juvenile Aid Bureau, must have been reading from the same public relations script. "Not more than 5 percent of homosexuals are psychotic or potential child molesters," Captain Allen pragmatically noted in 1954. "Parents must face [the] problem...of teenage boys going out looking for homosexuals, to roll them, or submit for money."[21]

The late John Preston submitted for fun rather than money. He recalled his 1958 cruising ground, a Greyhound bus station on St. James Street in Boston's Back Bay. Having read Rechy's earliest accounts in *The Evergreen Review,* the precocious 14-year-old was eager to test the waters. Preston soon met a salesman from Hartford, Conn., who took the boy back to his hotel room. He wrote:

> We had more orgasms than I could count....
> I truly hadn't been looking to do anything more than have sex, but when we were finally done...the salesman put a twenty-dollar bill in my pocket.... Twenty dollars was a lot of money for a kid in 1958....
> I went back long enough for a man to proposition me. Those men assumed that any adolescent they found in the area must be selling it....
> ...Money never became the reason I would go to Park Square. I kept on going back because it was the only way I knew to get sex.[22]

Richi McDougell's experiences, around the same time, confirm how neatly prostitution fit with gay boyhood desires. It was, he remembered, "the only way to get sex with men. I knew I was a homosexual at nine years old, I knew what I wanted, but the only way I knew how to get it was to go to the theater and ask for money. Maybe that's hustling, but it was very fulfilling—it served its purpose."[23]

Back in Miami, Bayfront Park had become an active hustling ground for young men by 1955. The following report managed to link a pastor, a teenage hustler, a spin-the-bottle game, a defensive mother, and evil plots against jungle-boy Sabu:

> While "Rev." Ed Wall, pastor of the First Church of Divine Science in Miami, was confined to an LA hospital—sleeping pill overdose—a warrant was issued. A 15-year-old boy...had Wall's address, and police got his confession to "unnatural relations." He testified that while on his way to Bayfront Park "to make some money from a sex pervert" as was his habit, he got a ride

fig. 5.4 "Dave 'Gyps'—A Tattooed Wonder," from the Painter Papers, reproduced by permission of the Kinsey Institute for Research in Sex, Gender, and Reproduction.

from a man who took him to Wall. He said he and Wall played "spin the bottle" each undressing as the bottle pointed to them, after which, sex. The boy received $10 and ride home, returned two later days for repeats and drinks with Wall and friend Andre Perez (both had checkered records—such as insurance-plot to burn jungle-boy Sabu's home).

According to the boy's mother:

"[He] didn't know what a homosexual was two years ago when we moved from California. Neither did I. Now his life is all messed up. He's scared somebody is going to kill him...I'm sick from worrying about my boy. It makes you want to fight somebody...."

The account ends with a "portrait of a mother unaware her son's a total stranger":

She quoted him telling a neighbor he expected to end up dead like Dillinger, and showed a letter written **before** his arrest saying he was leaving home to avoid testifying against Wall. (Police said they discovered his relationship with Wall only **after** the boy's arrest.) The **News** emphasized their choice angle: that homosexuals corrupt these boys. The story shows this boy corrupted willfully by another hustler. Lieutenant Earl Owens, police juvenile aid

bureau: "For every one of these boys we catch, there's at least a dozen get away."[24]

The really unfortunate party in this case was the unnamed young hustler, whose loyalty to his client was so great that he left home to avoid incriminating Reverend Wall. Hunted down and forced to testify, the kid was understandably afraid of the police. And all for $10 and a go at a seventh-grade parlor game. Given such intense official persecution, no wonder hustler strolls were a domain of young toughs used to harassment.

Painter wrote the following letter to Kinsey, documenting his introduction to a frequently incarcerated teenager named Dave, who embodied the young tough hustling for money:

I believe I mentioned in my last report that Edward [Melcarth] wanted me to meet a tattooed wonder which he had in stock. So...I did. It was not exactly as advertised, but outstanding in ways he forgot to mention. Dave is a great beauty—in face, especially, but also in his slender but beautifully formed tall body. He has a charming smile and a way with him. A psychopath, no doubt. He says...he was 3 years in Warwick [a juvenile penitentiary], has been in the Tombs [Riker's Island] since, tho he says he is only 16 now. Has no parents, but a delinquent younger brother... Dave's tattoos are the jail type mostly, and he still likes them—mostly on his arms. Says he has been going with a certain queer for three years—starting at

13? (If so when was he in Warwick?) Plans to spend the winter "in Florida or Puerto Rico" with one.[25]

As a member of the Diaper Bandits street gang on New York's Lower East Side in the early 1960s, Jim Carroll recalls "fag hustling" in the same vein as shooting heroin, screwing debutantes, and mugging old ladies. Times Square and Third Avenue were Carroll's prime spots. Like some Boise boys, Carroll enjoyed the power he derived from hustler sex, that "incredible rush of power [that] shook me with all those faces staring at my body fucking a mouth on its knees."[26] His recollections, which include fighting off at least one dangerous client, indicate that young hustlers were better off when they were streetwise. "What happened to the old fashioned homo who just wanted to suck your dick?" he asks in a diary entry. "You just don't know what the next trick you pick up is gonna whip out of his attache case these days. Handcuffs, masks, snakes, chains, whips, last week a guy had a pet parrot that [ate] grapes out of my pubic hair."[27]

Kinsey's colleagues Harry Benjamin and R.E.L. Masters identified a noticeable increase in gang prostitution. They envisioned a cooperative sex work atmosphere. "In "the girl gangs," wrote Benjamin and Masters, "members are required to prostitute themselves to finance activities of the gang, and sometimes those of friendly male gangs (whose school*boy* members may be required to engage in prostitution, also as a means of raising funds for the group)."[28] Ross similarly sketched a street culture wherein hustlers were as organized, as close-knit, and as self-protective as any successful gangs were, forming cliques of both sexes in Chicago bars.[29] Ross went on to depict a hustling hierarchy wherein elements of safety, price control, and vigilante justice developed seamlessly among bouncers, managers, and sex workers. These communal structures stemmed from—and closely simulated—gang rules, offering protections federally denied to American sex workers.[30]

Donald Webster Cory noted that hustler streetwear was, by 1963, indistinguishable from gang threads. "The hustler is not too difficult to recognize," said Cory. "He often wears garb usually identified with the juvenile delinquent, including a zippered jacket and tight jeans. It is complete, save for a switchblade, which he often feels might frighten the client or cause him to be apprehended for carrying a weapon."[31] The *Times* commented that in Times Square, "the hoodlums wore a kind of uniform to show they belonged." This consisted of "T-shirts, blue dungarees with leather motorcycle belts ornamented with artificial, glittering 'gems,'" as well as "short leather jackets and patent-leather peaked caps with white chin straps, and calf-high boots of the type worn by miners and engineers."[32]

Bill Regan remembers that John Rechy was completely attached to his hustling clothes in the late 1950s. "When things got so rough and he couldn't hustle, he used to go down to a lawyers' office on Wilshire Boulevard in a leather jacket, jeans and boots and prepare legal briefs," Regan told biographer Charles Casillo.[33] All across the country, hustlers were bringing *West Side Story* to 42nd Street.

fig. 5.5 Gang kid, provenance unknown

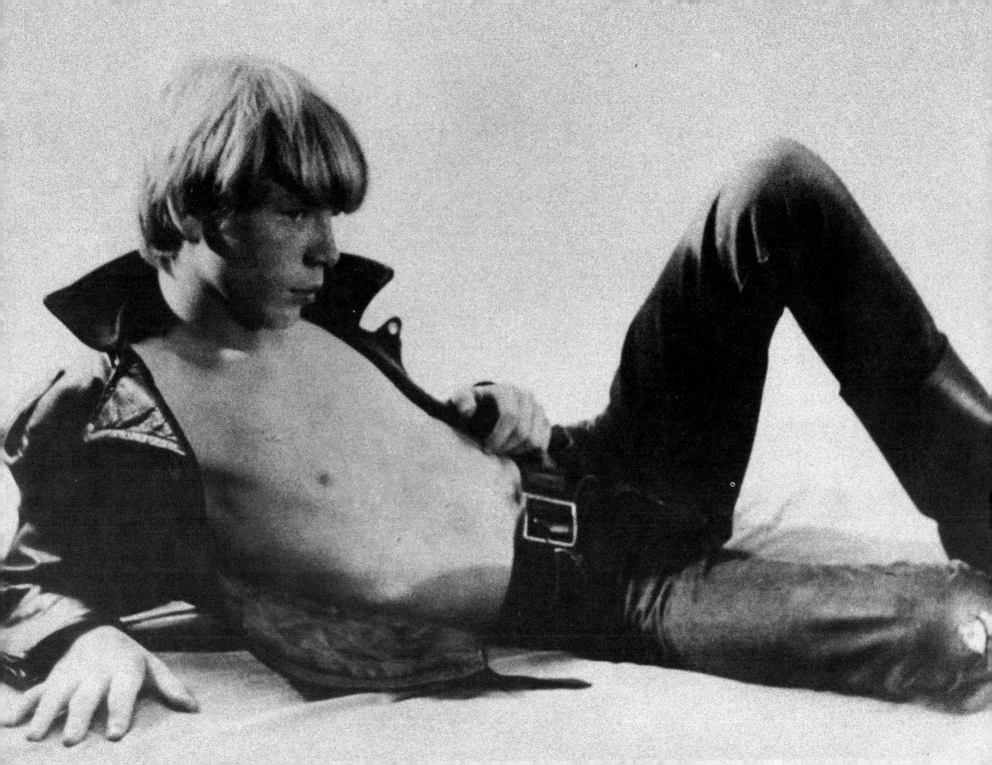

Levi's and leather evoked toughness, virility, and a working-class straight identity. Boots spoke to independence, freedom, alienation, and a willingness to kick the shit out of the wrong mark. You didn't have to be a gang member to fly those colors. The question, of course, is *why* hustler fashion changed from suits and ties in the 1930s to sailors' uniforms in World War II to the gang-themed style of the 1950s and early 1960s. The answer, quite simply, is that sex workers camouflaged themselves in whatever would both increase their allure and reduce their chances of encountering harassment. And the standard outfit by the 1960s—jeans rolled up three inches from the ankle—gave a sense of unity. "In the [19]50s, into the early [19]60s," Rechy says with nostalgia, "there was kind of a *pride* about being the hustler."[34]

Though the standard outfit was the height of machismo, it was by no means the only costume on the streets. This ultramasculine expression needed a feminine counterpart in the gay world, so hustlers and queens teamed up, as Rechy artfully puts, "in this grand charade of female and male."[35]

Stage Queens and Alleycats: Trannies, 1950-1965

Transgendered hustlers were in a tough spot. Working the streets alone was dangerous, and they operated from a far more socially marginal position than rough trade. Often transgendered sex workers began to hustle casually as queenie boys. As their gender expression became more feminine, many were forced to rely on prostitution as a means of income. It's not easy, even today, for a transgendered woman who doesn't seamlessly pass to gain even menial "legitimate" employment.

In the 1950s and 1960s, it was illegal for biological males to wear female clothing in public. Moreover, trans folk ran the risk of arrest for both masquerading and solicitation, even if they weren't hustling. Though it was terribly unsafe to dress in drag on most city streets, there were transgender-friendly zones in Los Angeles, New York, San Francisco, and New Orleans. These zones naturally flourished where social tolerance for sexual difference was high and police interference with neighborhood life was lax or nonexistent. These edgy, eclectic spaces were dangerous, but they also fostered a sense of community among many of America's dispossessed.

There was also an expanding national circuit of drag cabaret. If a gal was talented, she could make a living going from club to club, performing in the limelight, and turning tricks after-hours with patrons.

In Los Angeles, Pershing Square was relatively nondiscriminatory; in New York, Bryant Park was the designated spot; in New Orleans, the French Quarter let its hair down; and in San Francisco, the Tenderloin sheltered a funky urban family. Impersonator Kenneth Marlowe wrote that, in the 1950s, "the young queens around Pershing Square wore make-up, camped and swished all over the place." In this downtown park, they competed for tricks, banded together with other young hustlers, and went to Clifton's cafeteria after the day was done. "All they needed was $6 a week for a room," Marlowe wrote. "That was a necessity for keeping alive. The rest of the time they'd go to bed for a new shirt, a pair of trousers, or dinner."[36] Marlowe made friends with veterans Candy (who had a record of male prostitution a mile long) and the Duchess. Like novice gang hustlers, transgendered hustlers learned their trade from mentors in relatively safe public spaces. "I learned quickly to make dates," she wrote, "by watching the other young queens."[37]

After her parents caught her having sex with young men, transgendered Holly Woodlawn ran away, hitchhiking from Miami to Manhattan. She hustled Bryant Park in 1962, at the age of 16:

> One day I discovered Bryant Park, which was where all the queens and hustlers used to hang.... One afternoon, while sitting on a park bench, I met a Puerto Rican queen who empathized with my situation and took me under his wing.
>
> Then I met some queens from Miami who were living in a seedy hotel on 72nd Street and Broadway. They were all crammed into one room, and made their living on the street, hustling their young virile bodies for 20 dollars a pop. At the end of the day, they'd pool their funds to make ends meet.[38]

Woodlawn's newfound acquaintances suggested she move in and hustle for rent. Holly tried to hustle as a boy, haunting Bryant Park and Times Square alleyways. Even with her support network, she found it difficult. "I was a nervous wreck," she recalls. She would catch her breath in Bickford's cafeteria, then "go back out and hustle some more, hanging out in dark doorways or on street corners. I was so scared. I hated doing it, but I felt I had no other choice."[39] Woodlawn moved out of the hotel eventually, and shacked where she could. Like other homeless hustlers, she slept on the subway, in all-night movie houses, or on benches in Grand Central Station. She cleaned up in the men's restroom in Grand Central, "where there were shower stalls in the bathroom" that she could use for a quarter. Then she would make her way back to Bryant Park to hustle.

In Bryant Park, Woodlawn met another transgendered hustler who called herself the Duchess (not to be confused with the Duchess of L.A.), whose claim to fame was gumming: the toothless blow job. And she described a park scene as vivid as the eye makeup she applied in the Grand Central bathroom. She also told of an after-hours hustler bar on Eighth Avenue and 52nd Street that was ecstatic with Escatrols and sexy with Seconals. New York hustler culture in the 1960s prefigured the punk music scene of the 1970s (see Chapter Seven).

Male and transgendered hustlers developed systems of cooperative protection to shield one another from the more violent elements of New York's mean streets. Sylvia Rivera left her transphobic Lower East Side neighborhood at the age of 11 and began to hustle on 42nd Street using her boy name, Ray. She was quickly and fiercely protected by Gary, an 18-year-old hustler, and Marsha, a 17-year-old street queen who helped Sylvia find part-time jobs and taught her the rules of Bryant Park. "Marsha played the big-sister role, teaching Sylvia how to apply makeup skillfully (in those years full drag was only for special occasions, not for hustling)," writes Martin Duberman.[40]

In the same vicinity, Holly Woodlawn's friend Libra told Holly that "there was one golden rule to follow if you were a 'girl' (an effeminate boy) on the streets. You had to be nice to the male prostitutes.... The hustlers were the ones who looked after the 'girls' like me, buying us cigarettes, sodas, and candy. Also, they were usually of a rough breed, and if they became angered, they could pull a knife and kill you—or humiliate you to the point where you wished you were dead."[41] On the other hand, John Rechy (who worked in both Bryant Park and Pershing Square during the 1950s and 1960s) observed that the drag queens were the tough ones: "Even then...the roughest person knew not to tangle with a queen. Because they had nothing to lose."[42]

Trans sex workers encountered more violence from customers than they did when they hustled as boys. Johns had greater power over women than they did with trade, and could be especially rough when the women they tricked with turned out to have dicks. Writes Duberman, "After [Rivera] started to wear more drag, at about age fifteen, the odds got somewhat worse. People did pull guns on her several times and did try to rip her off."[43] In even the most regulated work environment, a good support system cannot save everyone. On the isolated and neglected streets, transgendered teens like Little Sheba, who met Woodlawn and Candy Darling in 1964, could meet terrible peril. Despite the veterans' efforts at initiation and intervention, Sheba came to an unfortunate end, stabbed and beaten to death by a trick in a hotel room.[44]

Certain zones in San Francisco fostered many of the opportunities (and dangers) transgendered sex workers found in Pershing Square and Bryant Park. In the 1950s, the Tenderloin, North Beach (home to the Beats), and the Embarcadero were all trans-friendly zones. The Embarcadero hosted Finocchio's, one of the most extravagant drag revues. All three areas featured drag-friendly bars and plentiful employment opportunities.

Dr. Harry Benjamin, who had established a summer office in San Francisco during the 1950s, dispensed estrogen hormones to prospective transsexuals. (His main office was in New York. In the early 1960s, Holly Woodlawn "went to see him for female hormone shots, and within a couple of months," she recalls, "I was looking damn good in a tight sweater!")[45] One of Benjamin's summer clients was a keen observer of Finocchio's sex work infrastructure. Benjamin related her story to Bob Masters:

> As to Prostitution, she says: "they [female impersonators] are all available or at least 95 percent." Since here at Finocchio's the performers are not allowed to mingle with guests, the dates are made thru the waiters. If a customer gives the waiter less than 2 dollars for delivering a note, this note is never delivered or remains unanswered. A 5 dollar tip to the waiter means the customer is willing to pay $50 or more for the date including sex of course.[46]

This arrangement, with waiters playing the middlemen, was somewhat unusual, but had its precedent in the messenger-boy culture in New York and Chicago during the early 1900s.

At $20 to $50, these "dates" were twice as expensive as a trick with a transgendered street hustler. Why the discrepancy? Most obviously, the environment of a bar tryst was usually safer than the setting of a street exchange. Another factor might have been the performers' appearances: Benjamin noticed that "the imperson-ator working in a club is typically much more attractive than the homosexual transvestite encountered soliciting on the streets. Some of the professional impersonators rival in appearance all but the most glamorous showgirls in the top-flight nightclubs."[47] Male-to-female (MTF) performers were considered exotic by clientele, who were willing to pay extra to fulfill their unorthodox fantasies. Finally, performers achieved a degree of underground celebrity that helped to inflate their sex work fees.

Ironically, the income enjoyed by transgendered workers appealed to young gay hustlers who ordinarily might not have cross-dressed. For this reason, Benjamin and Masters distin-guished between true transsexuals (who expressed themselves as females to fulfill a deep emotional and psychological need) and female impersonators (whose gender-bending was economically motivated). "The transsexuals," wrote Benjamin and Masters, "are very considerably outnumbered by the homosexual transvestite prostitutes, some of whom are streetwalkers and bar hustlers," as well as entertainers.[48] The pair in the next image was arrested on the East Coast, in the mid 1960s, for solicitation; we see that they (almost) passed beautifully as nontransgendered women.

Across the country, cabaret clubs instituted different rules for sex work. The Holiday Inn in Calumet City, Ill., was typical in encouraging its performers to hustle drinks; what they did with their bodies, after hours, was none of management's business. Club 52, in Indianapolis, prohibited performers from mingling with the customers until the performers were done for the night and had changed back into male attire. My-O-My, in New Orleans, not only encouraged entertainers to hustle drinks, but suggested that they also sell pictures of themselves in drag. Curiously, some of My-O-My's younger, wishful patrons turned the tables on the performers, offering *themselves* for money before the club opened:

> Boys who were too young to get into the club came very early each night before the first show to watch us dress. They'd say, "We'll show it to you for a quarter."
>
> "My God, what's that?!" I asked, the first time I heard them out there.
>
> One of the cast said, "Give them a quarter and see what happens." I took a quarter from my pocket and handed it to one of the boys. He smiled down at me.
>
> "Thanks," he said. "What's your name?"
>
> "Keni," I said.
>
> "Oh, you're new here." He dropped his pants and said, "Look!" I looked.
>
> "Go ahead and play with it, if you want to," he said. "You paid for it." He stuck it through the space between the bars.[49]

This inexpensive offering was more homage than hustling; but it does illustrate how thoroughly New Orleans's legendary sexual commerce had permeated the city's queer community.

In the 1950s and 1960s, some American cabaret clubs staffed only women, some employed only female impersonators, some mixed female impersonators and real women, and others included male strippers, drag queens, and women. No matter the mix, employees bonded like rock groups thrown together on a national tour. This national circuit was a floating playhouse as well as a traveling brothel; performers were reshuffled, but the game stayed pretty much the same. And it *had* to stay consistent; the scene's players could not have endured it, otherwise. Life on the road was sustainable only if there were a few stable elements to anchor a sense of home.

The Club My-O-My, located "on the East end of West End, in Jefferson Parish," was strictly drag.[50] "All the cast was really a club," Marlowe wrote. "We got thicker than thieves. We had potlucks together. We had orgies together. We went to the beach together. All of us were always together. I found that when you worked at the My-O-My you were part of the clique."[51] This intense camaraderie hid the sad truth that trans folk were not tolerated by the world outside the clubs; they were drawn together by shared oppression. Cabarets' privately commercial status not only eliminated the risk of police harassment, it often guaranteed police protection: The My-O-My was assigned a sheriff who stood "on duty at the front door during all performances to take care of any problems."[52]

fig. 5.6 Image KI-DC:69238 from the Documentary Collection of the Kinsey Institute for Research in Sex, Gender, and Reproduction. Reproduced by permission.

In New Orleans, the main trans-friendly zone was the French Quarter. Dusty Evening, a former MC at the My-O-My, owned a building "on Gravier Street in the Negro quarter." Marlowe wrote that "there were six apartments and every tenant in the place worked in the show at the Club My-O-My." Tenants ate together, hit certain trans-friendly bars, and cruised the Quarter, where "there were always tourists around, to be made."[53] Workers most often took their tricks back to their apartments. No discussion of New Orleans would be complete without a mention of whorehouses, which generally kept one boy in drag among a larger number of women. In a letter to Bob Masters, Benjamin wrote:

> That female impersonator I spoke to, worked as a "queen" some years ago in the plushest house in New Orleans. She was pointed out to the customers as a boy (in drag). She drew the biggest prices...$50-100. That may be exaggerated. Her customers were all homo- or bisexuals, she says, altho many of them claimed to be hetero. Some paid "just for talking."[54]

And Marlowe, after quitting the My-O-My, worked first as a hairdresser and then as a resident boy at a very similar New Orleans house. Marlowe claimed that prices were set by time ($20 for 15 minutes, $30 for 30 minutes, $100 for the night) and that the madam instructed workers to keep an eye out for sexually transmitted infections and to take their sweet time.[55] The circuit ended for Marlowe in San Francisco, where she auditioned for—and was rejected by—Mr. Finocchio himself.

By the mid 1960s a geographical shift in San Francisco had consolidated three previously trans-friendly zones into one. City planners decided that the bawdy Embarcadero was ripe for redevelopment, and by 1965, construction had begun south of Market Street. North Beach, meanwhile, was losing its countercultural appeal as the Haight-Ashbury began to beckon young drifters. A dispersed transgender population slowly resettled in the Tenderloin. This increased concentration of queer folk made the sex work scene increasingly visible, which attracted police attention. Susan Stryker, a Bay Area historian, tells the story of Carlos/Carla Lara, a Latin American immigrant who in the early 1960s ran a rooming house above the Checker Club, her coffee shop-cum-bar. When the San Francisco Police Department raided the Checker Club in 1962, they arrested dozens of denizens, mostly drag queens. Stryker recalled:

> Throughout the Sixties and Seventies there would be these periodic street sweeps where a lot of people would be arrested...46 people busted in one night! The second-largest police raid on a so-called "gay" bar happened on Turk Street in [19]62...at the Checker Club, it was a big trannie hang-out. Also known as a place where people could go to fence anything they'd stolen. The person who owned it (her legal name was Carlos Lara) was an immigrant from Central America who came here and opened the place first as a coffeehouse, it just had like folding tables and folding chairs

and a storefront. And Carla sold coffee and anybody
could just come in and stay there and sleep, it was a
place that catered to the street kids. And then as soon
as Carla had enough money to buy a liquor license,
she turned it into a bar, the Checker Club. It was
still...mostly transgender-oriented. And most of the
people arrested in the early [19]60s bar raid were
arrested for female impersonation.[56]

Another Tenderloin bust, in 1967, netted 33 streetwalkers, including a dozen in drag. (When asked why she was on the street, one trans girl said, "Not only do you get a chance to give a blow job and get paid for it, but you get a chance to handle a lot of different organs.")[57] While the police took names, transgendered sex workers took notice. They were increasingly unwilling to accept these routine arrests. It had been a long time coming, but the revolution was about to begin.

The Low Spark of High-Heeled Boys: Insurgence, 1966-1970

We know that the Tenderloin was a drag-friendly zone in the mid 1960s, and had been for at least 20 years before that. By 1966, the drag scene had exploded on Turk Street, home to various bars and clubs, including Sound of Music, Chukkers, the Camelot, and the Hilliard. El Rosa Hotel, at 166 Turk, offered its transgendered tenants affordable rooms and a convenient location. All you had to do was roll off the couch to start rolling johns. Significantly, El Rosa was incongruously named. The grammatically correct way to refer to "The Rose" in Spanish is *La Rosa*; *El* is a masculine article and *Rosa* is a feminine noun. This linguistic juxtaposition was intentional, a welcoming signal for the transgender community.[58]

El Rosa girls met their clients on the street or in hotel bars catering to tourists and conventioneers. Sex work occurred mainly in cars and in the safe space of the girls' rooms. When dealing with clients, they played it by ear, intuiting whether to disclose their biological gender. Some queens colloquially referred to themselves as *hair fairies,* and would "wear their hair long and tease it." According to researcher James Driscoll, trans girls in the Tenderloin hustled in "what seems to be almost a uniform. A little makeup, a bulky sweater, and tight trousers—as tight as possible."[59] Until they were able or ready to access hormones, they simulated voluptuousness using "girdles with built-in pads" and "padded towels around their hips and buttocks." A cradling device called a "gaff," made of denim or canvas, could be worn to "flatten the genitalia and even force it back into the body cavity." When they got together socially, they would share knowledge with newcomers, pluck one another's eyebrows, and trade gossip, clothing, wigs, stimulants, marijuana, glue, speed, and Seconals.[60] Social workers at the Tenderloin's Glide Urban Center listed Benzedrine, Nembutal, Methedrine (crystal), Doridan (goofballs), amyl nitrite (poppers), and LSD as easily available substances.[61]

Like the old native *mujerados,* 15 of 17 trannies Driscoll interviewed were "raised as girls," helping their mothers and sisters cook, clean, and tend to younger siblings.[62] All but one had grown up outside San Francisco. Of those raised in the South, many "were rousted by the police so often that they were in effect run out of town." For others, adolescence marked a time when their parents' tolerance reached its limit. One girl told Driscoll, "My mother wanted a little girl, but not a big one."[63] Prostitution was regarded ambivalently among El Rosa renters. They agreed that passing as a female with a trick made them feel feminine, but they abhorred the daily grind of sex work, which many experienced as a scary, dead-end road. "I'm not happy as a prostitute," said one. "I don't enjoy it and I'm scared all the time." Another said she hated the life, but "I have to have money to eat, and have a place to stay, and money for makeup and clothes."[64] Tellingly, when the San Francisco Economic Opportunity Council made clerical jobs available to street-based trans girls, all the vacancies were quickly filled, even though these legitimate jobs offered only $1.35 an hour. That came to $33.20 for a 32-hour week, less than gals could make "in one night of hustling."[65] Every one of them said that if given the choice they would have the sex conversion operation.[66] They just needed a chance.

By the latter half of the 1960s, the Tenderloin was a working-class, low-rent residential neighborhood with active commercial and vice districts and a thriving sexual economy. Of course, not all its residents were sexual minorities who had moved to the Tenderloin because of its higher tolerance; many were straight San Franciscans displaced by urban redevelopment. The diverse community included Japanese-Americans who had been removed from the newly gentrified Western Addition and interned during World War II, African-Americans from the Western Addition and the Fillmore, and folks displaced when developers razed boardinghouses along the waterfront. Poor, working-class citizens were left without affordable housing alternatives; this mix of reshuffled populations provided a pool of ready conscripts for resistance movements.[67]

The Tenderloin drew strength from its diversity. Compton's Cafeteria, on the corner of Turk and Taylor, was one community hub. During daytime hours, the cafeteria hosted a veritable game of musical chairs in which businessmen, curious tourists, sex workers out for lunch, and working-class folks could get a bite and make a friend. The conviviality of the place engendered in many customers a feeling of ownership. For regulars, Compton's was a second home; for the homeless drifters, it *was* home. Right above the café, the Hyland Hotel catered specifically to transgendered girls. According to Stryker:

> It was a place for youth—[Compton's] didn't sell liquor, so they could get in. The food was cheap, it was open all night, so people who—it's foggy and cold here most of the time, people who need a place to go at night go to hang out at those all-night coffeehouses and cafeterias. It was well known as a transgender-friendly place, 'cause it was in the neighborhood that trannies worked in. It was a place that chicken hawks would go cruising, it was a place where people would just camp and dish all night

long.... Between 2 and 6 [A.M.] it was almost entirely gay. Other working people would come in during the day, straights, you know, eat lunch, eat breakfast, it was more mixed. But the later it got, especially between 2 and 6, then it was just queer central.... It was really close to Market Street, you would just jump off the streetcar and walk that short block over to Compton's, and you would hang out and just wait for all your friends to show up. And you would go out bar-hopping, you would stay out drinking all night until it was 2:00, and then you would come back to Compton's and get some coffee and oatmeal and sober up, and camp and dish and cruise, and you'd go home and sleep it off.[68]

But the good times didn't last: Compton's instituted a 25-cent service charge on all orders. Mortally offended by this decision, a contingent of transsexuals, self-identified "hair-fairies," and hustlers picketed Compton's. The protesters were backed by Vanguard, a youth organization that had blossomed with the support of Glide Memorial Methodist Church. (Glide Memorial also facilitated early networking among the Gay Activist Alliance, the Society for Individual Rights, and the Council on Religion and the Homosexual, among others.) Cheap (and cheapskate) hustlers took to the streets to avoid paying the service charge.

The Compton's Cafeteria riot drew only passing attention. It was more important as an expression of pangender sex worker unity in the face of an affront. In "Young Homos Picket Compton's Restaurant," Guy Strait reported:

Gays rose up angry at the constant police harassment of the drag queens. It had to be first recorded violence by Gays against police anywhere. For on that evening, when the SFPD paddy wagon drove up to make their "usual" sweeps of the street, Gays this time did not go willingly. It began when police came into Compton's, to do their usual job of hassling the drag queens and hair fairies and hustlers sitting at the tables. This [the police harassment] was with the permission of the management, of course. But when the police grabbed the arm of one of the transvestites, he threw his cup of coffee in the cop's face, and with that, cups, saucers, and trays began flying around the place and all directed at the police. They retreated outside until reinforcements arrived, and the Compton's management ordered the doors closed. With that, the Gays began breaking every window in the place, and as they ran outside to escape the breaking glass, the police tried to grab them and throw them in the paddy wagon. They found this no easy task, for Gays began hitting them "below the belt" and drag queens smashing them in the face with their extremely heavy purses. A police car had every window broken, a newspaper shack outside the cafeteria was burned to the ground and general havoc raised that night in the Tenderloin. The next day drag queens, hair fairies, conservative Gays, and hustlers joined in a picket of the cafeteria, which would not allow the drags back in.[69]

Events of that night are preserved only in legend. Police called the riot "a minor disturbance," and mainstream homophile groups did not document the melee, staying out of the fray to avoid any association with prostitutes.[70] "While it is not yet possible to determine exactly what happened at Compton's in August 1966," wrote archivists for the Northern California Gay and Lesbian Historical Society, "the disturbance that erupted there achieved legendary stature within the early gay liberation movement in San Francisco."[71] More important for its precedent than for its actual accomplishments, the Compton's Cafeteria riot foreshadowed future street-based revolts.

The riot did not deter police, who continued to arrest hustlers en masse. It did, however, spark advocacy. It took less than a year for the police to establish a stronger Community Relations Division to focus on the transgender community. And local social service groups expanded to offer Tenderloin trans hustlers basic health care and other forms of support. Transsexual sex worker Louise Ergestrasse brought the police and Kinsey's Harry Benjamin to the same table, surely no small feat. Ergestrasse then started her own small trans advocacy organization, CATS.

Nascent organizations like Vanguard seized the riot as an opportunity to galvanize their members. As a stagy penitence for the riot, Vanguard organized a street-sweeping party, replete with this press release:

> *Tonight a "clean sweep" will be made on Market St.; not by the POLICE, but the street people who are often subject to police harassment. The drug addicts, pillheads, teenage hustlers, lesbians, and homosexuals who make San Francisco's MEAT RACK their home are tired of living in the midst of the filth thrown out onto the sidewalks and into the streets by nearby businessmen....*
>
> *This VANGUARD demonstration indicates the willingness of society's outcasts to work openly for an improvement in their own social-economic power. WE HAVE HEARD TOO MUCH ABOUT "WHITE POWER" and "BLACK POWER" SO GET READY TO HEAR ABOUT "STREET POWER."[72]*

The sweep was a success: Both the AP and UPI picked up the story. And the city had a part in it too, lending Vanguard 50 brooms, which may or may not have been suitable for short flights.

Vanguard's press release also coined the term "Meat Rack," referring to that choice strip in the Tenderloin: Market Street and two side streets, Turk and Powell, where hustlers were most available. The youth group's ostentatious act of virtue was pretty heartbreaking—We care just as much as you do what the streets look like! For all its showiness, the nonviolent action was as powerful a statement as the spontaneous chaos at Compton's. The teenage hustlers meant well and deserved respect—something social conservatives were loath to give them.

There were numerous small insurgencies at bars and clubs in the years between 1966 and 1969. But none has achieved the mythic status of Stonewall. If the East Village in 1969 was New York's equivalent to Haight-Ashbury, then Greenwich Village was its Tenderloin. John D'Emilio wrote that the Stonewall Inn "brought an 'unruly' element to Sheridan Square," with its steamy go-go boys and rumored Mafia connections. "Patrons of the Stonewall tended to be young and nonwhite. Many were drag queens, and many came from the burgeoning ghetto of runaways living across town in the East Village."[73] Duberman states that 53 Christopher St. was one of two trans-friendly downtown bars, known for its racial diversity and its tolerance of drag queens and hustlers, who "went there for relaxing nightcaps and gossip after a hard evening of hustling."[74]

When detectives raided the Stonewall in June 1969, they herded patrons into the street and began to arrest those flouting the masquerade law. Storme DeLarverie, a cross-dressing butch lesbian, punched a cop and incited the riot. "The cop hit me, and I hit him back," said DeLarverie simply.[75] In this star turn, DeLarverie combined elements of Joan of Arc and Calamity Jane. "Noses got broken, there were bruises and banged-up knuckles and things like that, but no one was seriously injured," DeLarverie recalled. "The police got the shock of their lives when those queens came out of that bar and pulled off their wigs and went after them."[76]

Sylvia Rivera screamed the name of a street queen being herded into a paddy wagon. Inside the van, a pantyhosed leg flexed to kick a cop in the chest, flinging him to the ground. The prisoner then helped her entourage to the cop's handcuff keys.[77] William Wynkoop eloquently recalls the street queens' part in inciting the old guard to fight:

> I stuck my head out and I saw a big crowd over on Christopher Street. It was two o'clock in the morning. I had to get out and see what was going on.... The more I heard about this, the more **exalted** I felt...it was amazing! And I think it's wonderful that the ones who started it were drag queens. Young, young, tender drag queens. Flaming faggot types... And I think maybe this is ordained because those who had been most oppressed were they.[78]

Certainly "mainstream," economically comfortable gay men and lesbians had a part in the Stonewall insurgency: They held their ground with everyone else and bravely joined the fray. But we must remember who started the riot: gender-queers and street hustlers with nothing to lose. To say that gay men co-opted Stonewall implies they were not part of the wreckage. A more apt conclusion is that gay men caught the riot's momentum and harnessed it for the purposes of political gain and liberation. Distressingly, the gay liberation movement would leave its most valiant instigators—street queens and teenage hustlers—at the side of the curb.

The gay community's neglect of its trench fighters is most apparent in the pattern of post-riot development in San Francisco's Castro district. In the early 1970s, gay men began moving en masse to the Castro. Old gay neighborhoods like the Tenderloin were disregarded by a newly liberated generation. In establishing the gay Castro, young middle-class baby boomers siphoned off the economic and social support networks that had sustained marginalized groups in the Tenderloin. The Castro of the early 1970s was homogenous: a primarily gay, white, male community that excluded poorer, non-gay-identified male hustlers and transgendered women of color. A microcosm of the gay liberation movement, the Castro community thrived by ignoring the plight of the politically cumbersome street community that had directly contributed to its success.

As support gravitated toward gay liberation in the Castro, Tenderloin street rats were left to fend for themselves. Developers began to transform Market Street into a tourist zone filled with high-class hotels, restaurants, and office space. Sex workers faced growing discrimination in the one neighborhood where they felt relatively safe, and the only one they could really afford.

During Driscoll's field research, "all of the girls involved" in his study "were engaged in prostitution."[79] Why was this? As previous research indicated, it was a question of proper documentation. "Prostitution is quite common in the lives of transsexuals," wrote Driscoll. "By their insistence on dressing as women they are denied many kinds of jobs. Identification, at least a Social Security card, is required for a job today." He observed that trans girls could only work in trans-friendly spaces, such as bars and coffee shops, where the pay was so low that "the major inducement is that girls are able to contact possible customers in their activities as prostitutes."[80] Glide Memorial's Urban Center cited similar difficulties among young male hustlers, who were marginalized by "lack of education and work experience."[81] A hustler could also face discrimination because of "his age, his sexual orientation, or in some cases, the years of his life spent in the Tenderloin area, for which he [couldn't] account on job application forms." He couldn't exactly enter "hustler" in the work experience box.[82]

In 1971, Compton's Cafeteria closed, supplanted by a peepshow club that catered to the straight population. Over the next three years, the Hyland, El Rosa, and several other trans-friendly hotels closed their doors to the transgender population. Displaced from their own ghetto, trans prostitutes went wherever they could, continuing to work and gather, if not live, in their historic haunts. Despite the energetic efforts of organizations like Louise Ergestrasse's, another transgender advocacy group named Conversion Our Goal (COG), and the Gay Activist Alliance (a radical outgrowth of Vanguard and a lesbian youth group called Street Orphans), the Tenderloin's vast drag network was completely disrupted.

The sorry ranks of homeless trans sex workers in the Tenderloin ghetto of the 1980s and 1990s were the legacy of the transphobia behind the city's redevelopment scheme, gay political backpedaling from sex worker issues, and the exclusionary attitude of Castro residents during the 1970s.

fig. 5.7 El Rosa Hotel, courtesy of Kate Friedman.

Cruisy Newsies: Hustlers in the Media, 1964-1969

In the early years of the liberation movement, the underground gay media system began to emerge from its foxholes. Mainstream newspapers and magazines closely followed the fortunes of its gay cousins. Together, mainstream newspapers and newly open gay media covered the politically charged street scene in San Francisco, Los Angeles, and New York City during the years of revolt.

Guy Strait's *Citizens News,* which he published from his apartment in San Francisco, first hit the streets in 1962. Strait's editorials were pro-prostitution and anti-vice. One 1964 article traced Pershing Square's notoriety for "undesirable elements" to the 1930s and warned that the Parks and Recreation Department of the City of Los Angeles was planning to remove interior walkways and eliminate benches. This would reduce the "seating capacity...from 550 to approximately 250" and appease those who believed "too many undesirables loiter in the park."[83] Three months later, Strait wrote that "Selma Boulevard has more police than hustlers," and in August he covered a Tenderloin "orgy raid" involving three "unemployed female impersonators" and "an 18-year-old who was in the act of taking an injection when the officers walked in."[84]

Strait wrote about varied topics, like Honolulu's Hotel Street, which had been popular among female prostitutes during World War II. Transgendered Hawaiians (*mahus*) were asserting their presence on Hotel Street, and getting arrested often enough for a judge to suggest they wear a pin stating their biological gender. This "ornamental brooch," which read, "I am a Boy," circumvented Hawaiian law prohibiting "dressing for the purpose of deception."[85] Strait also plugged "Syphilis A Go Go," the hip Bay Area STD clinic on Hunt Street. And his was the first gay newspaper to run advertisements for "models," which first appeared in the January 1966 classifieds. Nipping at Strait's heels, the *Los Angeles Advocate*'s inaugural issue extolled the 1967 federal court judgment legalizing mailed distribution of nude male images.[86] In Issue 2, Trader Dick's classified section advertised "Mexican Houseboys" for $24 a month, starting a long, grand tradition of *Advocate* hustler personals.[87] By 1969, the independent *Berkeley Barb* was known for its tolerance of massage advertisements, sometimes placed by transgendered practitioners.[88]

Both the *San Francisco Examiner* and *San Francisco Chronicle* reported on the plight of young hustlers in the Tenderloin as early as 1966. Citing statistics compiled by the Glide Foundation (which funded the hustler-friendly social services of Glide Urban Center), the *Chronicle* served as an intermediary among hustlers, social service agencies, and police. Staff writer Donovan Bess, in "The Cops Vs. City's Sin Jungle," reported:

> Police chief Thomas Cahill called yesterday for a program to help boys and girls who hustle adults in the neon glow of the Tenderloin district.
>
> But, he said, the police department is "really strapped" for personnel and cannot take the leader-

ship in any drive to relieve conditions that cause minors of both sexes to sell their bodies.

The shocking conditions in the district were revealed Wednesday in a report by three investigators for the Glide Foundation, a Methodist-sponsored social agency.

The report estimated that about 300 males of and from 12 to 25 years of age engage in prostitution in the area. The report also said females as young as 14 also offer sex to women as well as men.

At a press conference yesterday one of the Glide investigators, Mark Forrester, estimated that more than a thousand very young persons throng into the area each weekend.

"Sexual identification is a major problem for the youth of the Tenderloin," the report said. "Homosexual behavior is the most dominant"—but they "experiment with heterosexual relationships, sexual orgies, and all of the various types of physical relationships they can imagine."

Another investigator, the Rev. Edward Hansen, declared: "Even the businessmen of the area look down on them—nobody there affirms their importance, and this need we are trying to point up.

"We hope the Health Department, the United Community Fund and the entire city will relate themselves in every possible way to these young people's dire needs."[89]

Compared to the exposés in mid-century tabloids, this is an astonishingly balanced article. The *Examiner,* on the other hand, pitted the Glide investigators against the police chiefs. In "Police Minimize Tenderloin Sin," an article without a byline, the *Examiner* stated:

Depending on who you believe, San Francisco's Tenderloin District either is or is not a ghetto of vice peopled by hundreds of prostitutes of both sexes, some as young as 12 years old.

San Francisco police say the report is "ridiculous" and "grossly exaggerated."

According to the report, entitled "The Tenderloin Ghetto," youthful male prostitutes "sell their bodies to practically anyone who is in the market. We have met and talked with boys 12 and 13 who indulge in this activity after school and on weekends."

Police chief Thomas Cahill conceded that the Tenderloin is a major vice problem "and has been for a long time." But, he added:

"We have been criticized and criticized heavily for our arrests of homosexuals there. But there aren't any 12- and 13-year-old kids running wild there."

Captain Charles Barca, commander of Central Station, called the report a gross exaggeration. He said some homosexuals are arrested time and again in the Tenderloin but "the youngest are 17 and 18, we never see any 12- and 13-year-old kids."[90]

The available evidence does not suggest that any large number of 12-year-old hustlers were working the Tenderloin. Judging from their report, Glide workers met *some* younger hustlers and used them as a ploy for media attention and fund-raising.

This gambit may have been useful in the short term, but mainstream coverage continued to focus on the sensational aspects of hustling, still largely ignoring the problems faced by street youth: emotional troubles, malnutrition, venereal disease, long-term drug addiction, unemployment, poor housing, and lack of education. Glide ministers pushed for community-generated solutions: empowerment and advocacy groups, free counseling, educational and vocational training centers, legal aid, transitional housing, and interfaith street ministerial work.[91] Intentionally or not, the Glide Foundation had taken on a powerful American taboo by arguing for social outreach rather than scorn as the proper response to male sex work. Conservative reaction to the beginning of queer liberation prompted a swift rightward shift in media coverage. By the late 1970s and early 1980s, most mainstream reportage on queer life reappropriated the kind of Gothic sensibility that had typified the *Whip*, the *Rake*, and *Salute*. Attacks by the likes of Anita Bryant soon expanded the social divide between mainstream, relatively comfortable gay adults and disenfranchised street teens.

A hustler interviewed for a related KQED (San Francisco) documentary said, "The people who put me down in the daytime for being a male prostitute and a pill pusher are the same people who buy my drugs and go to bed with me at night."[92] This insult was directed primarily at closeted sexual tourists, but also makes a statement about gay organizations that excluded street youth from the scope of their concerns. As early as 1963, Hal Call, president of the Mattachine Society, observed a rift between hustlers and the more established gay activist groups. "Considered beyond the pale in many respects," Call wrote, "these organizations know that to maintain any ties with the hustlers would create a scandal that would immediately be their undoing."[93]

Marring an otherwise intriguing document, Call's statement was a slap in the face to young hustlers who railed against police harassment and to drag queens who supported the decriminalization of prostitution. No wonder Call noticed that "many of the hustlers themselves…would be loath to contact the recognized 'crusaders.' They are most likely to hold these groups in a not always quiet contempt." While the feeling was obviously mutual, Call was unwilling to consider that his own organization's establishmentarian politics caused street animosity. Instead, he suggested that hustlers' contempt for the "recognized crusaders" was in part a consequence of the hustlers' "outer expression of heterosexuality"—in other words, their sexual confusion. What was confusion, and what was performance dictated by the marketplace? Any conflicts in hustlers' sexual identities were certainly exacerbated by the throw-them-to-the-wolves-by-day, fuck-them-by-night behavior of certain "straight-laced" gay activists.

Other gay activists were supportive of prostitution, mainly because hustlers were important to their livelihood. In 1966, Guy Strait, then taking and selling nude photographs under the cognomen Dirty Old Man (DOM), editorialized in defense of prostitution:

> The writer has known thousands of whores of both sexes and has yet to find one that is a victim of 'white slavery.' We must dismiss this as merely Jedgarhoovergossip. And as good excuse for the enactment of the Mann Act which regulates the passage of persons from one state to another.
>
> We cannot find that prostitution is bad for the prostitute - in fact we must find that prostitution provides for the prostitute a source of income, a source of feeding of the ego, and a very definite step toward becoming a useful member of society. If it was not for the hard knocks in the life of a prostitute many of these people would be without any understanding of their own sexuality as well as a total misunderstanding of their potential in society. We are here speaking of the prostitute who has a certain amount of common sense and who does not look on prostitution as a permanent way of life.
>
> It has been said, probably in error, that all hustlers are homosexuals who are fighting their proclivities. This probably originated with the customer who would like to believe this. Some hustlers are homosexuals - some are not. Now if to commit a homosexual act makes one a homosexual forever then naturally they are homosexuals. However, we have found that a large number of hustlers do not continue their homosexual practices.
>
> They want to be wanted. They want to be appreciated. In America the greatest compliment that can be given is in cash.[94]

Customers *expected* hustlers to act the part. John Rechy remembers that hustlers' supposed sexual confusion was "a necessary subterfuge." Elaborating, Rechy discusses his clients' narrow vision of his sexual roles:

> For one thing, the clients would make it clear that they did not want you to be gay. And that was a whole milieu that was happening. And there would be a blunt-asked, "Now, you're not going to touch me?" And so the performance was required of survival, of the success. And we performed it. And we even believed it.[95]

Through his radical publications, Guy Strait advertised his photographic enterprise as well as his political views. He eventually renamed the paper *Cruise News & World Report* and devoted most of the back page to a section titled "Models Galore For Sketch Artists, Sculptors, and Others." Readers could order 8x10 photos of two dozen young men, all between the ages of 15 and 21. They were represented as rovers, sailors, effetes, and pretty-boys. They were well developed or of slight build, clean-cut or with unruly hair. Women—and probably trans girls—also found their way into Strait's portfolio. Sue was "a winsome type," Joyce was "blonde, busty, slender," and Miss Thing was 20, "blonde, slender, made up heavily."[96] Strait's most popular models were not necessarily indicative of the sexual economy's street scene, but they came from those corners and were textually marketable. They became icons for the era's male and trans sex workers and idols for their consumers.

With the exceptions of *City of Night* and *The Male Hustler,* accounts of hustling that were marketed to a gay audience rarely dwelled on the real-life struggles street youth faced. Instead, these stories portrayed the hustler experience in the most positive light possible. While not necessarily a bad thing, these stylized depictions of hustler life invariably came off as naively optimistic.

Pulp books of the late 1960s romanticized street hustlers' desperate circumstances. Floyd Carter's *One A Night* pictures a barely adolescent boy in a flimsy bikini halfheartedly hitching a ride from a shirtless hunk on a moped. Young Joe, the book's protagonist, has no second thoughts about his introduction to sex work, which takes place in a beach rest room; "I'll probably be in there, socking it to you everyday," Joe tells his first customer.[97] Jay Greene's *Rough Trade* pictures an oily, shirtless blond man, with the cover quote: "I know what you're looking for, Mister. If you think you can handle it...let's go."[98] Dennis Drew's *Boys for Sale* notes "a recent study of [the] Tenderloin district reported as many as 200 boy prostitutes operating there, some as young as nine."[99] If Drew was citing the 1966 Vanguard study, he had reduced the estimated age of the youngest prostitutes (12, which even the

police did not believe) by another three years! Drew also claimed that preteen boys routinely traveled from coast to coast for business purposes. "Recently," Drew wrote, "one of the authors talked with a 12-year-old boy prostitute in New York City. Two weeks later, in interviewing boy prostitutes in San Francisco, we met the same 12-year-old soliciting on Market Street. A man had picked him up in New York as a sexual traveling companion for an auto trip across the country and dropped him off in San Francisco."[100] While this is certainly possible—runaway youth could certainly hitchhike from one part of the country to another—it is inconceivable that droves of 12-year-olds were zooming across America in search of new strolls. Yet that was Drew's sensational implication.

Drew, who marketed his work to gay johns, had an interest in ignoring negative elements of juvenile male sex work. "Many of the boys to whom we talked," he wrote, "feel eternally grateful for the 'lift in life' that they received by engaging in high-level boy prostitution with influential customers."[101] Even when the boys reported being trapped and gang-raped, Drew spun their experience as educational and initiatory:

> When a boy gets into a car and goes off to another city—to a strange place where he is lost, he often finds himself trapped. A man may take him to a house where several other men are waiting to have the boy "participate" in a "gang rape." Once the boy is half-drunk, he offers little resistance. Usually, he

will have to go through a large variety of sexual acts. Thus, properly initiated, his head turned by the large amounts of money he can earn **so easily,** *a boy can develop an easy method for going on with prostitution.[102]*

Because his motives were so transparently mercenary, it is tempting to ignore an account like Drew's. But Drew had simultaneously pinpointed and blurred a fact of male sex work: There *were* youthful hitchhikers who populated hustling strips in the 1960s. Victor Banis interviewed a cruisy L.A. client named Lon, who said:

> *Los Angeles is heaven for the chicken queens.*
>
> *With the young stuff, I do most of my cruising in the car. There's a lot of hitchhiking, and the kids are pretty bold. They walk up to the car, give you a flirty grin, and ask for a lift. It's hard to refuse, even if I wanted to.*
>
> *There's one street, a major drive that runs from the beach through several of the suburban towns—one section of it is called "chicken row." There's always a number of guys hitchhiking along it, back and forth, anything from age 12 up. I'd say three-fourths of them can be had without any trouble. I've never been refused.*
>
> *A lot of them are prostitutes, and they make no bones about it. It's an easy way for them to make money—anything from two dollars up. They go to the coffeehouses in Hollywood, with their girls, and cruise the older guys. If they make contact, the girl waits there for the boy to come back. Then he has money to take her wherever she wants to go.[103]*

Again, it's tempting to write off Lon's relaxed description of adolescent male prostitution; it sounds impossibly open. Still, there are a few elements in his story to suggest these developments were natural.

Lon claimed that 75% of the boys he picked up "could be had," which indicates Lon's hitchhikers either offered sex freely, or in exchange for the ride and a few dollars. He also said he had never been refused, which says something about Lon's selectivity; surely, he didn't ask his most overtly homophobic young passengers if they would have sex with him. Lon comes across as fairly savvy—no doubt he was attuned to the boys' cues. We can also attribute Lon's success rate to his familiarity with L.A.'s liveliest cruising zones.

What's more, the boys and girls Lon described sitting around the coffee shop were following the arcane rules of gang prostitution. Suburban youth hustled in the late 1960s because sex work was easy, remunerative, edgy, sexy, and therefore cool. Male prostitution evoked old sailor tradition and a (recently refined) gang legacy, both powerfully masculine associations. For beautiful California boys, receiving money or a lift in exchange for getting head was a pretty irresistible proposition. Hal Call first remarked on this liberal attitude in 1963. "Some of the more 'resident' male hustlers of San Francisco claimed that competition from that year's high school graduating class was so fierce that many of them—as young as 18 or as old as 23—were having a hard time managing to score for more than a hamburger and a cup of coffee," wrote Call. "And it might take two or three forays a night on the street to wind up with a trick who would include a night's lodging after some food and drink."[104] Suburban samurai and weekend warriors were driving down prices for established urban hustlers; when the underground is co-opted by mainstream culture it is always altered.

Victor Banis hoped that more people would begin to identify themselves as homosexual, a possibility many gay activists inferred from America's thriving hustler culture. "It is not difficult to conceive," wrote Banis, "that a generation of homosexuals and pederasts are to inherit the nation, and that our society might become a homosexual society."[105] But Banis overlooked the fact that many hustlers had no interest in identifying themselves as homosexual.

On the East Coast, gay columnist Pat Conway was also beginning to take sex work seriously. He wrote "Advice to Hustlers" (perhaps the first American gay sex advice column) for the *NYRS,* a Manhattan monthly. As in *Cruise News & World Report,* trannies didn't get much play in the *New York Review of Sex.* Truth be told, even male hustlers didn't get that much attention—the column was really intended for johns. Conway did describe the shifting hustler strolls to one neophyte hustler, telling him that "Times Square is for creeps. You might make out at Port Authority Bus Terminal but there's lots of competi-tion. The Village is out as far as hustling goes. Third Avenue in the 50s is still OK but your best bet," Conway advised, "would be to try a couple of good hotel bars."[106]

Conway, however, was impatient with lower-class hustlers, and partial to the dial-a-model agencies that had surfaced on the scene. Still, he had established a distinctive public forum:

> *Q. I have recently started out hustling and have met some very important people. I would like to go to some of their parties, but every time I ask a john to invite me I get a half-ass answer and wind up being avoided. Any particular reason why? They like me sexually?*
> *A. DON'T PRESSURE. Remember, you are asked over for one reason, and one reason only. If they think you are acceptable to meet their "social" friends, they will ask YOU. (And don't get huffy, you ARE a hustler.) Bide your time. It will be well worth it.*
> *Q. Is there more money to be made in street hustling or by working for a madam?*
> *A. A madam is your best bet. It's reasonably safe and you meet a better class of people. It's also more profitable and, mentally, it keeps you in a better frame of mind.*[107]

Conway went on to suggest that a hustler should never make private arrangements with a client whom the madam procured. "It's not that much extra in your pocket," scolded Conway, sticking up for small, gay-owned businesses. "Besides, madam usually finds out and you would be cutting your own throat." By 1969, the boy-brothel dog days were over, and madams were spreading their wings.

I Only Look Expensive: Male Brothels, 1960-1970

As we've seen, benny houses—whorehouses that also offered boys to interested clients—had long been a feature of American life. "Scarcely a madam of a 'house' exists," wrote Hal Call in 1963, "who doesn't have a boy available of just about the right age, type, and proclivity the male customer might dare to designate."[108] After their World War II hiatus, houses devoted entirely to male sex work tentatively reemerged.

John Rechy recalls that a man named Patch, "a very successful hustler who had left the streets," was dispatched by "an actual house" to recruit hustlers from Los Angeles strolls by the early 1960s. "There were two [houses]," Rechy remembers. "One was strictly for hustlers to take their clients, but the other one was where hustlers could actually go, and clients could come."[109] Simply controlling a space where hustlers could take their johns was one thing, but operating a full-fledged business was another one entirely. Proprietors were responsible for recruiting both customers and employees, supplying space for in-calls, fending off or bribing law enforcement, providing social support, and ensuring the safety of both hustlers and johns. Previous experience was a big help—formerly street-based sex workers usually filled vacancies in brothel infrastructures.

In the early 1960s, few houses operated for very long without attracting police attention; two or three houses in any given city constituted an extensive network. In Los Angeles, Kenneth Marlowe competed with an established house run by a "Mr. Bean." One of Mr. Bean's hustlers, in the process of defecting, revealed how Marlowe set up shop:

> "We could advertise in the Hollywood Reporter, Daily Variety, and the Los Angeles Times...as young male masseurs. And we'd give our phone number and the number of the Answering Service. Didn't you notice all Mr. Bean's calls were from men?"[110]

Marlowe, as a new madam, established a standard protection: asking interested callers for their phone number and then calling them back, thereby verifying their authenticity. Marlowe also created a safe environment in her apartment, where her employees gathered communally:

> When tricks used the "studio," I camped in the kitchen with its desk and extension telephones. Several of the boys had been in the interior decoration field and were shopping in antique stores for me. They were forever buying more gilded mirrors and toss pillows for the place. It looked marvelous, with its Victorian touches.
> The boys all vied to stay in my good graces. They took turns at doing the marketing, the laundromat scene, and making spaghetti dinners for all of us.[111]

A little exaggerated, sure, but essentially credible: Camaraderie could make or break a call boy agency.

Newspaper advertising might have worked in Los Angeles, but elsewhere it was fraught with danger. "In San Francisco," wrote Call, "all freelance masseurs are checked out through the police department, and no one who has ever brushed the law with a 'morals offense' charge can be issued a permit."[112] Instead of providing massage, house-based sex workers in San Francisco offered themselves as "models." And it didn't take long for police to sniff out pseudo-massage enterprises in Los Angeles. "There were two other principal madams, in town, for call boys, who were being hit by the 'heat,'" Marlowe reported. "I wanted to get out of it." Kenneth Marlowe became a pedicurist, and that was that.

The house rules that Marlowe established are the earliest recorded example of the tightly structured Dial-A-Model services that grew, despite constant police pressure, throughout the 1960s and 1970s. Marlowe's pay scale ($15 per hour, per boy; boys kept $10, Marlowe pocketed $5) was in line with those of other madams'. And certain of Marlowe's rules were used to structure other agencies. In 1963, when porn producer Alan Stanford started

his Dial-A-Model service, he claimed it was "San Francisco's first all-male model agency." By 1970, Dial-A-Model's employees were charging $20 an hour for "studio" appointments (in-calls) and $25 for out-calls within San Francisco. (Rates were slightly higher beyond the city limits.) A 12-hour appointment was priced at $100; weekends (Friday evening through Sunday evening) cost the client $250; and a full week's service was $450.[113] Dial-A-Model's commission rate was 35% across the board, slightly exceeding Marlowe's 33%.

Dial-A-Model's house rules bespeak a tightly run organization, replete with a switchboard:

1. If you wish to make a telephone call, you will give the switchboard operator the number you are calling.

2. Any telephone call placed will cost you 15c per call plus any time and charges. NO CALLS unless you have the money!

3. DO NOT help yourself to whatever is in the kitchen without asking first. If anything in the office or throughout the building is missing, those models last known to be in the building at the time of its disappearance shall be contacted for

5.8 Dial-A-Model catalogue cover, courtesy of the Gay, Lesbian, Bisexual, and Transgender Historical Society of Northern California.

questioning. This does not mean you are considered guilty, but you may know of something to help solve the situation.

4. NO ONE will leave the building without first letting the switchboard operator know.

5. NO ONE will wait at the agency during SUNDAY or WEDNESDAY before 6pm. Telephones will be operative all day, but there comes a time when the place needs major cleaning not usually accomplished during each day.

6. The building is split into three sections. The office is one section and private living quarters are another. The other section will be for you to wait in...supplied with television, reading material, and home games for you to use. However, you DO NOT have full run of the premises. Stick to the front part of the second floor. Clean up your messes when they are made...do not leave books, magazines or ANY other items laying astrew for others to put away or you'll end up paying for maid service out of each of your calls. It is desired to keep you busy modeling, but there are times when business is slack, causing boredom and restlessness. You will be briefed about any other items as they come up from time to time.[114]

Stanford's rules maximized house profits and minimized personnel expenses. He was also concerned with security; although the rules make no reference to a guard, the switchboard operator functioned in this capacity.

Dial-A-Model claimed an affiliation with like agencies in New York and Los Angeles. Stanford also did some "modeling": He described himself in 1970 as "one of the five top professional male models in the San Francisco Bay Area." Appealing to passive queens and active tricks alike, he claimed to have both "a thoroughbred masculinity," and a "presence [that] conveys humility and a desire to serve." According to the catalogue, his models were white and Chicano, and all were 21 to 28 years old. "Eric" was a typical Dial-A-Model:

ERIC—0428

21 yrs., 5'11", 165#, 30" waist, 15" Neck, 42" smooth chest, short-curly blond hair and blue eyes. Between Eric's facial features, bone structure thickness and light complexion with medium tan, he appears to be a youthful Norseman. His collegiate-aggressive style is much sought after. His endowments are more than just physical.[115]

These models were also performers in the burgeoning gay porn industry, in which Stanford had a hand.[116]

[1] STEWARD, SAMUEL. *BAD BOYS AND TOUGH TATTOOS: A SOCIAL HISTORY OF THE TATTOO WITH GANGS, SAILORS, AND STREET-CORNER PUNKS, 1950-1965.* HARRINGTON PARK PRESS (NY), 1990; PP. 20-21.
[2] ROSS, HAROLD. "THE 'HUSTLER' IN CHICAGO." *JOURNAL OF STUDENT*

RESEARCH, FALL 1959; P. 14.

[3] STEWARD, P. 120.

[4] IBID., P. 121. "POGEY" IS AN AMERICAN DERIVATIVE OF "POGUE," AN IRISH SYNONYM FOR "PUNK."

[5] AUTHOR'S INTERVIEW WITH JOHN RECHY, CONDUCTED IN NOVEMBER 2001.

[6] SEE JOHNNY SHEARER, THE MALE HUSTLER. CENTURY BOOKS (CLEVELAND), 1966; P. 51.

[7] FOR AN EXCELLENT HISTORY OF TIMES SQUARE, AND THE ESTABLISHMENT OF THE PORT AUTHORITY, SEE KORNBLUTH, WILLIAM AND TERRY WILLIAMS. WEST FORTY-SECOND STREET: THE BRIGHT WHITE ZONE. BASIC BOOKS, 1994.

[8] IN A LETTER FROM PAINTER TO KINSEY, JANUARY 3, 1954.

[9] ORAL HISTORY WITH FAY PISTON, CONDUCTED BY AUTHOR IN FEBRUARY 2002. THE 93-YEAR-OLD FAY REMEMBERED THAT HER SHOP WAS FREQUENTED BY "HOMOS," FOR WHOM SHE HAD GREAT AFFECTION.

[10] ROBERTS, JAY. "JAY'S CORNER: THE HUSTLER—YESTERDAY AND TODAY." TOPMAN, SEPTEMBER 1980.

[11] IN A LETTER FROM KINSEY TO PAINTER, DATED NOVEMBER 10, 1954.

[12] IN A LETTER FROM KINSEY TO PAINTER, DATED FEBRUARY 25, 1956.

[13] IN A LETTER FROM PAINTER TO FRIEND NED JOHNSON, DATED AUGUST 20, 1956. FOR AN ELABORATION OF PAINTER'S TRIPS SOUTH OF THE BORDER, AND HIS RELATIONSHIPS WITH PUERTO RICANS LIVING BELOW 14TH STREET ON THE MANHATTAN'S LOWER EAST SIDE, SEE MINTON, DEPARTING FROM DEVIANCE, PP. 193-205.

[14] KAISER, CHARLES. THE GAY METROPOLIS, P. 83.

[15] AUTHOR'S INTERVIEW WITH RECHY. RECHY ALSO MENTIONS THAT NEW YORK CITY CALL BOYS CHARGED $15 IN THE EARLY 1950S (GIVING AT LEAST $5 TO THEIR PROCURER).

[16] KAISER, P. 83.

[17] X, MALCOLM AND ALEX HALEY. THE AUTOBIOGRAPHY OF MALCOLM X, PP. 130-131.

[18] IBID., PP. 132-133.

[19] AUTHOR'S INTERVIEW WITH RECHY. CRIMINOLOGIST DONALD MACNAMARA CLAIMS HIS 1960S RESEARCH WAS COMPELLED BY HIS REALIZATION THAT "THERE [WAS] AN INCREASING VOLUME OF CRIME COMMITTED BY OR COMMITTED AGAINST THESE PROSTITUTES." SEE MACNAMARA, "MALE PROSTITUTION IN AN AMERICAN CITY: A PATHOLOGICAL OR SOCIO-ECONOMIC PHENOMENON?" ARTICLE LATER PRESENTED AT THE 42ND MEETING OF THE AMERICAN ORTHOPSYCHIATRIC ASSOCIATION, NEW YORK CITY, 1965.

[20] "23 MORE UNDESIRABLES ARE SEIZED IN TIMES SQUARE AS ROUND-UP SPREADS." NEW YORK TIMES, AUGUST 1, 1954; PP. 1, 66. THIS ARTICLE FOLLOWS UP ON A JULY 31, 1954 TIMES PIECE LINKING THE SWEEP OF "HOODLUMS, JUVENILE DELINQUENTS, PROSTITUTES, SEX PERVERTS, AND OTHER[S]" TO THE UPCOMING NEW YORK STATE AMERICAN LEGION CONVENTION. SEE "125 SEIZED IN TIMES SQUARE IN A DRIVE ON UNDESIRABLES," PP. 1, 28. THIS ARTICLE MENTIONED THAT NUMEROUS ADMINISTRATIONS HAD PROMISED TO "RID THE DISTRICT OF ITS NEFARIOUS INFLUENCES," WITH LITTLE APPARENT SUCCESS. THE USE OF "UNDESIR-ABLES" TO DENOTE SEX WORKERS IS IRONIC, AS SEX WORKERS MAKE THEIR MONEY FROM THEIR DESIRABILITY.

[21] FROM A NEWS CLIPPING OF UNKNOWN ORIGIN, DATED NOVEMBER 1954, IN THE HOLDING OF THE ONE INSTITUTE; "MIAMI 1953-1954" FOLDER.

[22] PRESTON, JOHN. HUSTLING: A GENTLEMAN'S GUIDE TO THE FINE ART OF HOMOSEXUAL PROSTITUTION. MASQUERADE BOOKS (NYC), 1994; PP. 18-21.

[23] TSANG, DAN. "MEN AND BOYS." GAYSWEEK, VOL. 3, NO. 103, 1979, P. 8.

[24] FROM A NEWS CLIPPING OF UNKNOWN ORIGIN (PERHAPS A VERY EARLY GAY RAG), IN "MIAMI—1955" FOLDER, ONE INSTITUTE HOLDINGS.

[25] IN A LETTER FROM PAINTER TO KINSEY, DATED NOVEMBER 6, 1956.

[26] CARROLL, JIM. THE BASKETBALL DIARIES. PENGUIN, 1987; P. 188.

[27] IBID., PP. 104, 106.

[28] BENJAMIN AND MASTERS, P. 100. (ITALICS IN ORIGINAL.)

[29] ROSS, PP. 16-17.

[30] IBID., P. 18. ROSS ALSO NOTICED THAT CHICAGO HUSTLERS WERE ETHNICALLY INCLUSIVE: THEY ACCEPTED THE "NEGRO AND LATIN AMERICAN" INTO THEIR RANKS.

[31] CORY, DONALD WEBSTER AND LEROY, JOHN P. THE HOMOSEXUAL AND HIS

SOCIETY: A VIEW FROM WITHIN. CITADEL PRESS (NYC), 1963; P. 93. IN 1964, RESPONDING TO A WAVE OF CLIENT KILLINGS KNOWN POPULARLY AS THE FRUIT PLAYER MURDERS, THE SAN FRANCISCO POLICE DEPARTMENT CONFLATED THE POOL HUSTLER WITH THE STREET HUSTLER, NOTING THAT A "CUE STICK IS A WEAPON USED BY A FRUIT PLAYER IN MOST INSTANCES." SEE CASE #81779, MAY 20, 1964; HOMICIDE DETAIL, BUREAU OF INSPECTORS, SAN FRANCISCO POLICE DEPARTMENT. THE SFPD DESCRIBED A "FRUIT PLAYER" AS "A PERSON WHO KNOW-ING THE PROCLIVITIES OF HOMOSEXUALS, PREYS UPON A PERSON AND MAKES THE PRETENSE OF GOING ALONG WITH THE HOMOSEXUAL ACT FOR THE PURPOSE OF SOME OTHER CRIME, SUCH AS ROBBERY OR BLACKMAIL." ("FRUIT" WAS A RELATIVE-LY RECENT PEJORATIVE FOR GAY, FIRST CITED AS SUCH IN NOEL ERSINE'S DICTIONARY OF UNDERGROUND AND PRISON SLANG, 1938.)

[32] NEW YORK TIMES, AUGUST 1, 1954; P. 66.

[33] CASILLO, CHARLES. JOHN RECHY: A BIOGRAPHY. ALYSON PUBLICATIONS (LOS ANGELES), 2002; P. 114 IN DRAFT MANUSCRIPT.

[34] AUTHOR'S INTERVIEW WITH RECHY.

[35] IBID., IDEM.

[36] MARLOWE, P. 43.

[37] IBID., P. 42.

[38] WOODLAWN, HOLLY WITH JEFF COPELAND. A LOW LIFE IN HIGH HEELS. ST. MARTIN'S PRESS (NYC), 1991; P. 54.

[39] IBID., P. 55. BICKFORD'S CHAIN CAFETERIA WAS ALSO A POPULAR HANGOUT IN BALTIMORE: THE PHOTOGRAPHER AMOS BADERTSCHER WROTE THAT ONE OF HIS SUBJECTS, KENNY LEGS, "HIT THE STREETS OF BALTIMORE AT AGE 14, 1964. HE HUSTLED CITY HALL SQUARE, THE WHITE COFFEE POT AT HOWARD + FRANKLIN, BICKFORDS AT BALTIMORE + ST. PAUL, EDDIES BAR AT LIGHT AND WATER STS., THE CORNER OF PARK AND MONUMENT BY GRACE + ST. PETERS." SEE BADERTSCHER, BALTIMORE PORTRAITS. DUKE UNIVERSITY PRESS (NC), 1999; P. 5.

[40] DUBERMAN, MARTIN BAUML. STONEWALL. DUTTON, 1997; PP. 24, 68. ALSO SEE JOHANNA BREYER'S UNTITLED, UNDATED (POST-1994) PAPER IN THE VICTORIA C. ARCHIVE OF THE GAY AND LESBIAN HISTORICAL SOCIETY OF NORTHERN CALIFORNIA (GLHSNC), FOR A CASE STUDY OF A TRANSGENDERED YOUTH DIS-

COVERING HEROIN, SEX WORK, AND BRYANT PARK IN 1959.

[41] WOODLAWN, P. 66.

[42] AUTHOR'S INTERVIEW WITH RECHY.

[43] DUBERMAN, STONEWALL, P. 70.

[44] SEE WOODLAWN, P. 79.

[45] IBID., P. 73.

[46] IN A LETTER FROM BENJAMIN TO MASTERS, DATED JULY 27, 1963 (BOX 9, SERIES II, D.MS, FOLDER 2B OF BENJAMIN PAPERS, KIL).

[47] BENJAMIN AND MASTERS, P. 306.

[48] IBID., P. 305. (OF COURSE, THINGS ARE NOT QUITE SO SIMPLE. MEMBERS OF THE GAY AND LESBIAN HISTORICAL SOCIETY OF NORTHERN CALIFORNIA SIMPLY USE THE WORD "QUEENS." THEY DEFINE QUEENS AS "MTF TRANSGENDERED INDI-VIDUALS WHO TEND TO LIVE SOCIALLY AS WOMEN SOME OR ALL OF THE TIME, WHO MIGHT OR MIGHT NOT PASS AS NONTRANSGENDERED WOMEN, WHO TEND TO BE SEXUALLY INVOLVED WITH MEN, AND WHO MIGHT OR MIGHT NOT ENGAGE IN HORMONAL OR SURGICAL BODY ALTERATION TO HELP SUSTAIN THEIR GENDER PRESENTATION." THEY ALSO RECOGNIZE THAT "THE CATEGORY 'QUEEN' OVERLAPS AND INTERSECTS WITH POPULATIONS OF GAY MEN, MTF TRANSSEXUALS, AND NONTRANSSEXUAL WOMEN IN A COMPLEX MANNER THAT REVEALS THE BOUND-ARIES BETWEEN THOSE THREE GROUPS TO BE MORE POROUS THAN ONE MIGHT NAIVELY ASSUME THEM TO BE." FROM "MTF TRANSGENDER ACTIVISM," GLQ 4. DUKE UNIVERSITY PRESS (NC), 1998; P. 351.)

[49] MARLOWE, PP. 101-102.

[50] IBID., P. 93. REFERENCES TO FEMALE IMPERSONATION VENUES ACROSS THE UNITED STATES FROM 1950-1960 ARE REFERENCED THROUGHOUT MARLOWE'S CONFESSIONAL AUTOBIOGRAPHY.

[51] IBID., P. 98.

[52] IBID., P. 100.

[53] IBID., P. 100. FOR FURTHER DISCUSSION OF AMERICAN TRANSGENDER STREET SCENES IN THE 1960S, SEE CHARLES WINICK AND PAUL M. KINSIE, THIS LIVELY COMMERCE: PROSTITUTION IN THE UNITED STATES. QUADRANGLE BOOKS (CHICAGO), 1971. LIKE NEW ORLEANS, "LITTLE ROCK AND KANSAS CITY HAVE A

SUBSTANTIAL NUMBER OF MEN IN DRAG," THEY WROTE (SEE PAGE 93).

[54] IN A LETTER WRITTEN BY HARRY BENJAMIN TO BOB MASTERS, DATED JULY 27, 1963 (BOX 9, SERIES II, D.MS, FOLDER 2B OF BENJAMIN PAPERS, KIL).

[55] MARLOWE, P. 118.

[56] AUTHOR'S INTERVIEW WITH STRYKER.

[57] SEE WINICK AND KINSIE, P. 93.

[58] SEE "MTF TRANSGENDER ACTIVISM," P. 351. ALSO SEE DRISCOLL, JAMES PATRICK. "THE TRANSSEXUALS." MASTER'S THESIS, SAN FRANCISCO STATE COLLEGE. DRISCOLL WISELY KEPT THIS LINGUISTIC JUXTAPOSITION OF MASCULINE AND FEMININE IS HIS THOROUGH, THOUGHTFUL REPORT. "IT IS IMPOSSIBLE TO ASSOCIATE WITH THE TRANSSEXUALS FOR ANY LENGTH OF TIME, LET ALONE LIVE WITH THEM, WITHOUT THINKING OF THEM AS WOMEN," HE WROTE.

[59] DRISCOLL, PP. 41-42, 60.

[60] IBID., PP. 10, 60.

[61] HANSEN, REV. EDWARD WITH REV. FRED BIRD AND MARK FORRESTER. "THE TENDERLOIN GHETTO: THE YOUNG REJECT IN OUR SOCIETY." GLIDE URBAN CENTER, UNDATED (PUBLISHED BETWEEN 1966 AND 1969); P. 10.

[62] DRISCOLL, P. 31.

[63] IBID., P. 43.

[64] IBID., PP. 69-70.

[65] IBID., P. 74. FOR SOME DISCUSSION OF "UNFORTUNATELY SHORT-LIVED" EMPLOYMENT-RELATED INTERVENTIONS WITH SEATTLE-BASED MALE PROSTITUTES, SEE PATRICK GANDY'S "HAMBURGER HUSTLERS," A RESEARCH PAPER PRESENTED AT THE AMERICAN ANTHROPOLOGY ASSOCIATION MEETING, NOVEMBER 1971. FOR MORE RESEARCH ON THIS THEME, SEE ROBERT DEISHER'S "THE YOUNG MALE PROSTITUTE." *PEDIATRICS,* VOL. 42, NO. 6 (JUNE 1969); P. 940.

[66] IBID., P. 83.

[67] SEE AUTHOR'S INTERVIEW WITH STRYKER FOR GEOGRAPHICAL VERIFICATION.

[68] IBID., IDEM.

[69] STRAIT, GUY. *CRUISE NEWS AND WORLD REPORT 2,* AUGUST 1966. ALSO SEE "MTF TRANSGENDER ACTIVISM," PP. 355-358.

[70] FOR "A MINOR DISTURBANCE," SEE "MTF TRANSGENDER ACTIVISM," AN INTERVIEW WITH ELLIOT BLACKSTONE, P. 358. FOR THE SUGGESTION THAT HOMOPHILE GROUPS WERE ADVISED TO STEER CLEAR OF SEX WORKERS, SEE HAL CALL, "MALE PROSTITUTION ON THE WEST COAST," IN BENJAMIN AND MASTERS, PP. 320-321. HRC, ANYONE?

[71] "MTF TRANSGENDER ACTIVISM," P. 355.

[72] *VANGUARD* NEWSLETTER, VOL. 1, NO. 1; SEPTEMBER, 1966.

[73] D'EMILIO, JOHN. *SEXUAL POLITICS, SEXUAL COMMUNITIES.* UNIVERSITY OF CHICAGO, 1983; P. 231.

[74] DUBERMAN, *STONEWALL,* PP. 183, 189.

[75] KAISER, P. 198. THOUGH DELARVERIE DID NOT IDENTIFY HERSELF AS A FEMALE-TO-MALE SEX WORKER, THIS NICHE WAS SPORADICALLY OCCUPIED. MASTERS REPORTED TO BENJAMIN THAT HE WAS TOLD ABOUT A WOMAN WHO, WHEN EXPRESSING AS A MAN, WAS HER OWN PIMP. "A FRIEND OF MINE IS GOING TO TRY TO ARRANGE FOR ME TO MEET ONE PARTICULARLY INTERESTING GIRL WHO IS, IN HER WORDS, HER 'OWN PIMP.' THIS GIRL IS A KIND OF MALE IMPER-SONATOR, WHO GOES AROUND TO BARS LOOKING LIKE A MAN AND OFFERING TO 'GET A GOOD-LOOKING GIRL' FOR MEN WITH WHOM SHE STRIKES UP A CONVERSA-TION. SHE TELLS THE MAN TO WAIT IN THE BAR, AND THE CALL GIRL WILL TELE-PHONE HIM. THEN SHE GOES BACK TO HER APARTMENT, CHANGES INTO FEMALE CLOTHING, AND TELEPHONES HER CUSTOMER, INVITING HIM TO COME ON OVER, OR MEET HER SOMEPLACE. AS A GIRL, SHE IS, BY MY FRIEND'S REPORT, EXTREMELY ATTRACTIVE; AND SHE IS EQUALLY AS CONVINCING AS A MALE! THERE SEEMS TO BE NO END TO THE VARIETY OF THIS SUBJECT." MASTERS DOES NOT FOLLOW UP ON THIS, SO THERE IS NO EVIDENCE THAT THIS STORY IS ANYTHING MORE THAN URBAN MYTH. EITHER WAY, IT IS AN INTERESTING MODERN-DAY CALAMITY JANE STORY. IN A LETTER FROM MASTERS TO BENJAMIN, DATED JULY 14, 1963; BENJAMIN PAPERS (KIL), MATERIALS ASSOCIATED WITH *PROSTITUTION AND MORALITY.*

[76] KAISER, P. 200.

[77] DUBERMAN, *STONEWALL,* P. 198.

[78] KAISER, P. 200. (EMPHASIS IN ORIGINAL.)

[79] DRISCOLL, P. 6.

[80] IBID., P. 8.

[81] HANSEN, P. 15. ALSO SEE MACNAMARA, WHO FOUND THAT ONLY 14% OF MALE AND TRANSGENDERED STREET HUSTLERS HAD GRADUATED FROM HIGH SCHOOL OR EARNED AN EQUIVALENCY DEGREE; 43% OF STREET QUEENS IN HIS SAMPLE HAD SERVED TIME AS JUVENILES OR ADULTS. ALONG WITH THEIR POVERTY, LACK OF EDUCATION, AND GENDER CROSSINGS, THE QUEENS' EXPERIENCES WITH LAW ENFORCEMENT AND PENAL INSTITUTIONS MARGINALIZED THEM TREMEN-DOUSLY.

[82] SHEARER ALSO NOTED THIS DILEMMA, CONCERNED THAT THE STUD HUSTLER HAS "SOLD HIS MANHOOD FOR SEXMONEY AND HE IS SELDOM EQUIPPED FOR ANY OTHER OCCUPATION." SEE SHEARER, P. 25.

[83] *CITIZENS NEWS,* JANUARY 27, 1964.

[84] *CITIZENS NEWS,* MARCH 9, 1964 AND AUGUST 17, 1964.

[85] *CITIZENS NEWS,* FEBRUARY 16, 1965.

[86] *LOS ANGELES ADVOCATE,* SEPTEMBER 1967. "IN PASSING OUT CREDIT FOR ITS VICTORY, DSI GIVES A GENEROUS PORTION TO HAL CALL, PRESIDENT OF THE SAN FRANCISCO MATTACHINE SOCIETY, FOR SECURING THE HELP OF MANY OF THE PEOPLE THROUGHOUT THE COUNTRY WHO TOOK PART IN THE DEFENSE," THE *ADVOCATE* SUMMARIZED. CALL CONDONED AND DEFENDED THE USE OF MALE HUS-TLERS FOR PICTORIAL DISTRIBUTORS, IF FOR NO OTHER PURPOSE. DID DSI ALSO PLEDGE THE MATTACHINE SOCIETY A GENEROUS DONATION?

[87] *LOS ANGELES ADVOCATE,* OCTOBER 1967. MASSEUR ADS WERE PUBLISHED IN THE *LOS ANGELES ADVOCATE* BY AUGUST 1968.

[88] STRYKER CLAIMS THAT "THE FIRST TRANSGENDER PROSTITUTE TO DO OUT-CALL WORK IN THE BAY AREA STARTED [BY] ADVERTISING IN THE *BERKELEY BARB* IN [19]69 OR [19]70.... WHEN THEY OPENED UP THEIR CLASSIFIED ADVERTISING (THE UNCLASSIFIED CLASSIFIEDS, YOU KNOW, ADVERTISE ANYTHING)...THERE WAS A LOT OF MASSAGE AND OUT-CALL SEX WORK ADVERTISED THERE. SHE STARTED ADVERTISING, AND I KNOW SHE LIVED WITH ANOTHER MTF WHO WAS ALSO DOING OUT-CALL PROSTITUTION. EVENTUALLY THERE WERE THREE OR FOUR PEO-PLE WHO WERE [LIVING] TOGETHER WHO WERE ALL DOING THE SAME KIND OF WORK." AUTHOR'S INTERVIEW WITH STRYKER.

[89] *SAN FRANCISCO CHRONICLE,* FEBRUARY 25, 1966; PP. 1, 24. WAS HANSEN'S REF-ERENCE TO THE BUSINESSMEN OF THE AREA EUPHEMISTIC SHORTHAND FOR CON-TEMPTUOUS JOHNS?

[90] *SAN FRANCISCO EXAMINER,* FEBRUARY 25, 1966.

[91] SEE HANSEN, PP. 14-30.

[92] O'FLAHERTY, TERRENCE. "THE NOT-SO-TENDER TENDERLOIN." *SAN FRANCISCO CHRONICLE.* SEPTEMBER 12, 1966; P. 27. INTERVIEW EXCERPT FROM "YOUTH IN THE TENDERLOIN," THE KQED DOCUMENTARY.

[93] CALL, IN BENJAMIN AND MASTERS, P. 321. DONALD MACNAMARA VERIFIED THAT HE WAS "ASSURED BY THE OFFICERS OF" ECHO, THE MATTACHINE SOCIETY, AND THE COMMITTEE FOR SEXUAL EQUALITY "THAT NONE OF THEIR MEMBERS ASSOCIATES WITH MALE PROSTITUTES." SEE MACNAMARA, P. 4.

[94] *CRUISE NEWS & WORLD REPORT,* OCTOBER 1966; PP. 2-6.

[95] AUTHOR'S INTERVIEW WITH RECHY.

[96] *CRUISE NEWS & WORLD REPORT,* AUGUST AND NOVEMBER 1966.

[97] CARTER, FLOYD. *ONE A NIGHT.* ORIGINAL HOME LIBRARY, 1967; P. 49.

[98] GREENE, JAY. *ROUGH TRADE.* TOWER BOOKS, 1969.

[99] DREW, P. 144.

[100] IBID., PP. 144-145.

[101] IBID., P. 157.

[102] IBID., P. 146 (EMPHASIS MINE).

[103] BANIS, VICTOR. *MEN AND THEIR BOYS.* MEDCO BOOKS (LA), 1966; PP. 22-23. SEE CHAPTER SIX IN THIS BOOK FOR AN ACCOUNT OF THE GOLD CUP RESTAU-RANT, WHICH IN THE 1970S DREW HUSTLERS AND THEIR GIRLFRIENDS.

[104] CALL, IN BENJAMIN AND MASTERS, P. 321. ALSO SEE SHEARER, P. 69. SHEARER QUOTES A 22-YEAR-OLD JOURNEYMAN—WITH EIGHT YEARS OF SEX WORK EXPERIENCE—COMPLAINING ABOUT THIS PHENOMENON. "TAKE BROADWAY, HERE, AS AN EXAMPLE. WE HAVE KIDS WHO PLAY HOOKEY TO COME DOWN AND SCORE WITH THE CUSTOMERS. THAT'S PRETTY TOUGH COMPETITION. IT HAS GOT-TEN MUCH MORE COMPETITIVE AND—WHEREAS I COULD CHARGE $15 TO $20 FOR A SIMPLE BLOW JOB A FEW YEARS AGO—THE NUMBER OF GUYS IN THE BUSINESS HAS BROUGHT IT DOWN NOW TO AROUND TEN [DOLLARS]."

[105] BANIS, P. 27.

[106] *NEW YORK REVIEW OF SEX (NYRS),* AUGUST 1, 1969; P. 24.

[107] *NYRS,* JUNE 1969; P. 20.

[108] CALL, FROM BENJAMIN AND MASTERS, P. 320.

[109] AUTHOR'S INTERVIEW WITH RECHY. JOHNNY SHEARER'S INTERVIEWEES ALSO ELABORATE ON HOUSES OF ASSIGNATION, WHERE PROCURERS TOOK 40% AND CALL BOYS MADE $25 PER CALL. SEE SHEARER, PP. 19-22.

[110] MARLOWE, P. 200. (ITALICS IN ORIGINAL.)

[111] IBID., P. 220.

[112] CALL, FROM BENJAMIN AND MASTERS, P. 322. IT IS POSSIBLE THAT THE ENTIRE INDUSTRY OF MASSAGE CERTIFICATION AROSE DUE TO SEX WORKERS USING "MASSAGE" SERVICES AS A FRONT. IRONICALLY, SOME MASSAGE TRADITIONS, INCLUDING REIKI AND SOME FORMS OF SHIATSU, INCORPORATE GENITAL MANIPU-LATION INTO TYPICAL MASSAGES. SEE WINICK AND KINSIE.

[113] STANFORD, ALAN. "I ONLY LOOK EXPENSIVE." DAMI PRODUCTIONS, FEBRUARY 1970; P. 4.

[114] STANFORD, ALAN. "MODELING...MORE THAN MEETS THE EYE" (EMPLOYEE PACKET). SEPTEMBER 1971, PP. 13-14.

[115] FROM DIAL-A-MODEL CATALOG, 1972.

[116] FOR A DESCRIPTION OF DIAL-A-MODEL'S RULES GOVERNING THE NUDE POLAROIDS TAKEN OF EACH NEW MODEL HIRED, THE FURTHER PHOTOGRAPHIC PRINTS EXPECTED, AND THEIR DISSEMINATION, SEE STANFORD, "MORE THAN MEETS THE EYE," P. 23.

six

Beginning in the late 1800s, an underground market of erotic postcard photography thrived in Europe and, to a lesser extent, the United States. Baron Wilhelm von Gloeden was the first to use this market to disseminate pictures of sex-working young men. A German expatriate who moved to Italy in the 1880s, von Gloeden bridged artistic and erotic photography, employing teenage Italian models and framing their implicit sexual availability with exquisite interior and exterior panoramas.

In von Gloeden's photographs, a mythic, naturist context is conflated with sexually charged overtones. Von Gloeden's mixed imagery set the tone for hustler photography in the 20th century.[1]

Early American photographers of the male nude conformed to von Gloeden's aesthetic. Operating out of New England in the 1910s, Fred Holland Day took sultry pictures of adolescent youngsters posing in natural surroundings. While Day's photography incorporated religious folklore, he did not draw from the classic Greco-Roman pantheon. Instead, Day's homage to hustler imagery began where Michelangelo, Donatello, and Caravaggio left off. Day's 1910 print "Saint Sebastian" was an homage to the photographic work of von Gloeden and an evocation of the Renaissance master painters and sculptors.

Day was almost certainly familiar with von Gloeden's work—both held some affiliation with the Linked Ring, a secessionist photography movement. Ironically, in the fine art market, photographic nudes (or near-nudes) of men could feature sexual undertones only in the context of religious expression. "Saint Sebastian" is a distinctively American interpretation of an ancient hustler archetype, a result of the aesthetic progression from the passive Ganymede to a vigorous David. Day's "Saint Sebastian" is a teenager, shot through with arrows. His limbs are strapped to a tree. He is the censored American version of an old legend, a smooth-skinned martyr of lust held prostrate for plunder or rescue.

"Saint Sebastian" is not a hustler photograph; rather, among Day's influences were artists who routinely posed hustlers as religious icons. Day was also a passionate mentor who nurtured Kahlil Gibran and worked closely with underprivileged Boston children.[2] If the image of the American complaisant is implicit in this photograph, Day suggests he had been sexually restricted and unjustly condemned. This photograph is also a subtle rebuke to the prevailing taboos against sexual relationships, remunerative or not, between males. By composing a sultry, homoerotic image of a saint known for healing plague, Day reversed the metaphor of pestilence associated with sex (and sex work) between men.

fig. 6.1 Image KI-VG:43 from the Von Gloeden Collection, the Kinsey Institute for Research in Sex, Gender, and Reproduction.
fig. 6.2 Holland Day, Saint Sebastian, courtesy of the Library of Congress.

fig. 6.3 Man in suit, provenance unknown.

After Saint Sebastian, American erotic photographers moved beyond religious iconography to experiment with different veils. The simple naturism of Day's later photos (and the studied wholesomeness of Thomas Eakins's skinny-dipping college boys) is still used as a visual pretext in hustler photography. And photographers have used numerous other motifs in sexually subversive imagery over the last 90 years. We will consider, for example, hustlers posed as sailors and naturists posed as prostitutes. And we will meet the aesthetic successor to Saint Sebastian, the trans girl in underground porn, especially as she is depicted between 1930 and 1970. Finally, we will examine how hustlers have been erotically photographed *as* hustlers, with accompanying text. Simply posing for nude photographs does not constitute sex work. We can glean information about hustler culture from the signs, codes, and metaphors that have pervaded male erotic photography.

Nature Boys and Posing Straps: Dangerous Eros, 1930-1970

American nude male photography fit into three distinct genres in the early 1900s. Postcard photographs, supplied to the underground sexual economy, followed in the tradition of Italian and French work pioneered by von Gloeden and his imitators. Before 1920, few of these photographs were American-made. Here and there one comes across a bellboy, uniform around his ankles, showing off or performing for the fat tip; or a young man in a suit, his penis straining for contact. But these pictures are scarce, and it is often difficult to document their date and origin.

During the 1920s and 1930s, the artistic photography of George Platt Lynes recalled the pre-Raphaelite era, capturing the body as sculpture, muscle, and sinew. Lynes did not take up Day's religious motifs. He photographed European beach hunks, and his contemporary, Al Urban, concentrated on beefy American weightlifters. While either one of these men may have photographed hustlers here and there, they did not attempt to signal this. *Strength & Health* may have facilitated sex work connections through its correspondence leagues, but its content was strictly naturist. During this period, American artistic photography took its cue from the German FKK movement. Magazines such as *Strength & Health* in the 1930s and *Mr. Sun* in the 1960s emphasized muscled, virile men cavorting and posing in natural surroundings. They looked impassively at the scenery—primate adornments to the fluttering treetops.

This style was eventually co-opted by photographers with a keener interest in sexual imagery, such as Lon Hanagan. The work of these artists composed the third genre of male erotic photography. Thomas Painter and his friend Edward Melcarth took many casual snapshots, but they also took posed pictures that combined physique fans' affinity for musculature with their subjects' sexual availability. Habitual cruisers who looked for paid trade, Painter and Melcarth posed hustlers as sailors, but they also posed hustlers classically in the 1940s and 1950s, as "natural men." One Painter picture is, à la F. Holland Day, an odd admixture of ancient classicism and American bondage.

fig. 6.4 Image from *Mr. Sun* flyer, ca. 1964.

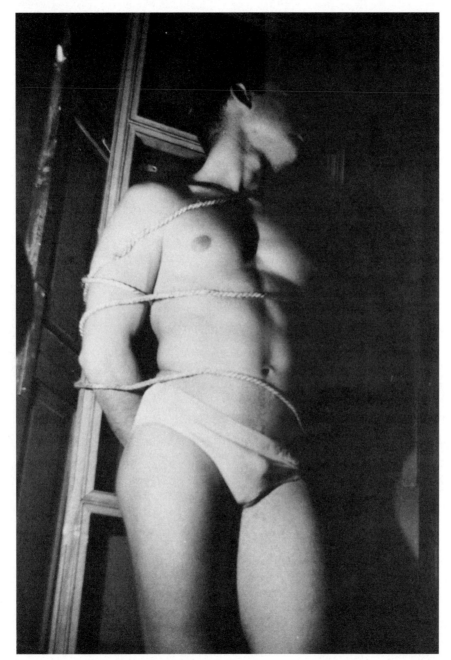

fig. 6.5 Image KI-DC:66251 from the Documentary Collection of the Kinsey Institute for Research in Sex, Gender, and Reproduction.

fig. 6.6 "Kentucky as a Farm Boy," from the Painter Papers, reproduced by permission of the Kinsey Institute for Research in Sex, Gender, and Reproduction.

Painter found his models through friends, on the streets, and in the bars. One of these models was hustler Cliff Ross, who had been "broken in" by Molly King before World War II. The protective hustler nicknamed Kentucky posed, as Painter would have it, "as a farm boy."[3] Figure 6.6 is the last in a striptease sequence evoking Kentucky's farming background:

Henry L. Minton writes, "Painter's photos reflected his sexual tastes," in that "he had somewhat of a fetish for well-defined torsos."[4] Indeed, Painter had hoped that the photographs he took could be fashioned into a book ("Muscles," he thought, would make a nice title). He never realized this ambition, though his work commands him as a worthy successor to von Gloeden and Day.

Lon had more commercial success, and his magazine photographs owed much to Al Urban's bodybuilding style. Lon, who recruited from Times Square and photographed John Rechy (as well as hundreds of other hustlers), was never comfortable with the classical and naturist props the physique magazine genre dictated, and his early magazine photographs are awkward. In 1945, Painter wrote of a visit to Lon's studio:

> Ed Melcarth and I dropped over to Lon's Second Avenue place (his big 45th St. studio is gone) where I gained an insight into his bad photography: he has bad taste. The decor, if you want to call it that, is what you would expect of a Lithuanian professional wrestler in 1880, who was also queer. Sort of Jumbo in lace panties....[5]

Painter's report, though a product of bitter rivalry and professional jealousy, conveys the difficulty inherent in posing sexually available men in a mode that hides their availability.

The photographer-model arrangement mirrored the hustler-john relationship. Many professional physique photographers, including Lon, sold their work in the same underground sex market in which they recruited models. This underground market benefited erotic photographers and their models alike. It was handy for hustlers to carry nude pictures of themselves, which gave them an advantage in their negotiations with prospective clients. Painter recalled that one of his models, Pat, "specially requested and posed this one—for a specific purpose, he said."[6] (See figure 6.7.)

Sam Steward reported that hustlers in Chicago tattooed their genitalia—one man had a tattoo of "69" on his penis, another one had "$10." Like their New York counterparts, they also carried pictures of themselves. One man named George, "on crutches with both legs paralyzed," panhandled and hustled his way through town. "He carried around with him a little 'advertising' booklet," Steward remembered, "Polaroid shots of his genitals. 'Saves time when you're hustling the queers,' he said."[7] Urbane male sex workers commissioned erotic pictures of themselves in the 1940s and 1950s, a mode of advertisement that bolstered their prices and helped them earn street credibility.

John Rechy says that his sessions with Lon helped to establish his reputation on Selma Avenue in Los Angeles. "On the streets, the thought that I had once been a famous male model

fig. 6.7 "Foto 11-17," from the Painter Papers, reproduced by permission of the Kinsey Institute for Research in Sex, Gender, and Reproduction.

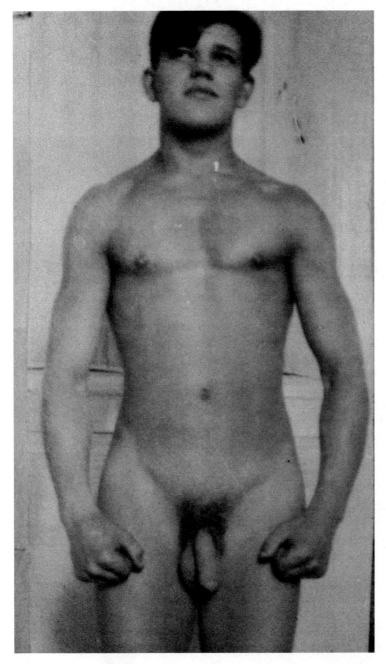

indicated the range of where [other hustlers] could conceive of (at least, *once*) success."[8] According to Rechy, physique photographers prowled the hustler strips in most large cities during the 1950s:

> But there were different photographers at the time. [Lon] was raided constantly, he was in and out of jail, constantly.... In Chicago, there was Kris. Kris of Chicago! And he recruited from Newberry Park [Bughouse Square]. And here the hustlers on Hollywood Boulevard. And there were a lot of clients in a kind of a circle where they exchanged hustlers and information.[9]

Douglas of Detroit, Bruce of Los Angeles, and countless gay artists and entrepreneurs hired hustlers to fill their lenses. Why hustlers? Quite simply, they were the men most likely to agree to have their photographs taken, nude or nearly nude, by relative strangers who would sell these pictures to magazines appearing in the gay marketplace.

Male nude photography was a dangerous business, due to some degree to its association with prostitution. Referring to the image in figure 6.8, Painter wrote, "[this] is a picture a queen took of a young hustler she picked up and took home (the original photograph indicates it was taken in a kitchen). He is very young and 'chicken'... a rather luscious looking little armful." Accompanying this anecdote is another annotation, handwritten: "Foto by fotog whom detectives

fig. 6.8 *"Standing Nude Man," from the Painter Papers, reproduced by permission of the Kinsey Institute for Research in Sex, Gender, and Reproduction.*

raided, fotogrphr jumpt out of window and commit suicide."[10]

"True" physique models, such as weightlifters and aspiring actors, were also hustling to get ahead. Steward wrote that one friend named Ralph was a "weightlifter and hustler" who refused a tattoo because he was afraid he'd lose points in body-building competitions.[11] Bob Mizer, who opened a studio in Los Angeles in 1945, drew his subjects from both the body-building and sex work realms. Many of Mizer's models, both in *Athletic Model Guild* and its successor, *Physique Pictorial,* were plucked from L.A.'s legendary street corners, though a stable of "legitimate" physique models kept Mizer out of jail for most of his career. Always wary of the authorities, Mizer obscured his models' genitalia until 1969.

Mizer worked with the popular props of the day and con-structed elaborate sets to frame a gallery of sailors, cowboys, beach boys, and bodybuilders. By the 1960s, Mizer was also run-ning a sex-for-pay service: He provided male prostitutes to an elite group of wealthy clients, allegedly including director George Kucor, among other Hollywood notables. Rechy, whom Mizer recruited from Pershing Square, states that "there were several other people" at Mizer's studio when he arrived. "He did have a kind of service," claims Rechy, "although he never considered him-self a pimp. He would put out magazines but also contact sheets that went out to several people, rich people, including a very rich director that I knew about."[12]

In February 1963, Mizer unveiled a technique to encode his *Physique Pictorial* photographs. Influenced by zodiac, hobo, and gender symbols, his codes constituted a "subjective personality analysis" that distinguished sex-working models from plain old beefcakes, and gay models from trade. Mizer provided definitions for his signs, yet even these were deliberately vague and open to interpretation. Not surprisingly, the dollar sign distinguished hus-tlers from bodybuilders. Mizer rotated it 45 degrees and inverted it—presenting it as if horizontal and mirrored.

Jerry Richards and actor Richard Harrison had the dubious honor of being awarded Mizer's first dollar signs. On one of two facing pages in the February 1963 issue, Richards was grinning in the shower, holding a spotty washcloth over his package (see figure 6.9).

According to the codes, Richards was a complaisant: an agree-able top who was receptive to suggestions and wanted to get ahead. Harrison, on the other hand, was self-controlled, open-minded, *doubly* enterprising (or expensive). While Mizer revealed no further information about Richards, he did say, "Dick [Harrison] had a very interesting life." We learn that he was "the co-pilot in the first scene of 'South Pacific'" and that he was a for-mer Mormon who, "when he first reached Los Angeles, was deter-mined to make it on his own without asking his family for help."

Physique Pictorial first took on hustler violence in 1965. In an odd business strategy, Mizer was happy to report how his subjects misled and even murdered their customers, though he seldom delved deeply into the hustler's experience. His compassion for hustlers was aroused when they were sweet, but he never record-ed occasions when they were beaten or robbed by clients. It is

fig. 6.9 "Jerry Richards," courtesy of the Athletic Model Guild and the Canadian Lesbian and Gay Archives.
fig. 6.10 "Richard Harrison," courtesy of the Athletic Model Guild and the Canadian Lesbian and Gay Archives.

thus ironic that chubby-cheeked John Davidson fronted this editorial: This proud, quick-to-erect hustler (whose genitals, apparent through his transparent posing strap, were inked black) looks like the last boy one would suspect capable of violence. (Indeed, when the Marine corps later took the boy for active duty, Mizer wrote a nostalgic blurb about Davidson's charm.) Perhaps that was Mizer's point, that even the sweetest-appearing stranger might turn sour. In his editorial, which centered on the gay-advance defense, Mizer reported:

> In Long Beach California recently there was a muscle-boy who was too lazy to work but kept up his high protein quota by dating and rolling "queens" (homosexuals). Soon he became increasingly bold and aggressive and would forgo the preliminaries and simply take his victim's money under simple threat of exposure.
>
> One day in a Long Beach public toilet, the muscle boy saw an old man whom he thought would be a profitable victim, threw a headlock on him and emptied out the man's wallet, threatening to "expose" him.
>
> But there was nothing for the old man to "expose." He had been in the toilet simply to relieve himself, and he quickly ran into the street, screaming "Stop! Thief!" The muscle boy almost ran into the arms of a policeman, who investigated the incident completely. The boy was charged with robbery.
>
> But at a jury trial the muscle boy contended that the old man had made "advances on him" and that in his manly self-righteousness he had hit the old man and run away because of the "repugnance" he felt. This asinine defense was swallowed by the jury and the muscle boy was released to victimize still others.[13]

Bob Mizer worked with numerous hustlers over a period of 40 years. In a typical *Physique Pictorial* from 1966 to 1989, a majority of models were marked with the inverted dollar sign. Mizer's periodic warnings helped protect customers from sex-working thieves. But Mizer was no psychic, and could not have predicted the murder of silent film star Ramon Novarro.

A Model Life: Paul Ferguson's Hustler Ethic, 1967-1970

On October 30, 1969, 22-year-old model-hustler Paul Ferguson asked his 17-year-old brother, Tom, to ride with him to the Hollywood Hills. The siblings had not had an easy life. Paul was the oldest of 13 kids, and Tom was the fourth oldest. They'd grown up in Florida. Paul reported that his "first homosexual act [was] in Brownsville, Florida, at 10. Father had a contact to build a radio tower in Mississippi, but left us while Mother was pregnant with [the] tenth kid. Me and brother Johnny made all the income (Grandma sent $5 a week) sweeping sidewalks and stuff for 5 cents for food. A gas station attendant gave me 50 cents, [and] food to mess around." When his dad returned, their home life worsened.

"Father was drunk every day," Paul remembered. "He died when I was 12...died from spinal meningitis—from booze."[14]

Paul ran away first when he was 12, because, according to a court psychiatrist, "he'd been hungry every day of his life." He left home permanently when he was 14 and hitchhiked aimlessly, working carnivals and eventually joining the Army at 15. Paul was honorably discharged for being underage when he was 16. He then moved to Alabama. Paul reports:

> Married Evelyn (age 42) in Alabama when I was 16. Annulled by her after nine months. J.M., who drove us up to Novarro's, introduced us. Knew J.M. was homosexual. Stayed with him couple months. Another marriage at 19. Divorce. Married Mary in July, 1968. Came back here [to Los Angeles] June 25.[15]

Paul, who had cared for Tom periodically over the years, rejoined his kid brother in Los Angeles after the latter was released from a Chicago mental institution (his fourth stay there). After his release, Tom had been staying with one of Paul's old Chi-town tricks, Bill S., who said that when he saw Paul in Dallas in 1967, they'd had an argument about Tom's unwillingness to have sex with Bill. According to reporter Jim Kepner, Tom himself had "lived partly with an aunt, but mostly on the streets since he was 12."[16]

Afraid that Chicago police were pursuing him, Tom wrangled a plane ticket from his grandmother and flew to see Paul in California. "Paul said he had work for me," Tom testified. They had heard from Pruitt, a mutual friend, that the aging film star Ramon Novarro was "a soft touch." Paul, who had just been laid off from his $6-an-hour job as a steeplejack and had "broken up" with his third wife, sought extra cash, and was pleased to include Tom in the scheme. Paul called Novarro and made the arrangements. "Come on up," Novarro told him. "We'll have a few drinks, and we'll see."[17]

There are conflicting accounts of what happened next. We know that J.M. drove the boys up to Novarro's, where they were served "more than a fifth of vodka" and chicken gizzards, an unfortunate combination. Novarro called his publicist and arranged an appointment for Paul. "While he was phoning Mrs. Shannon about making me a star," Paul testified, "he said Tommy could do his gardening." This innocuous insult may have been the last straw. Paul passed out; when he woke up, Tom led him to Novarro's bloody body.

The Los Angeles District Attorney argued that Paul thought Novarro had hidden $5,000 in his home and had beaten him to death when the gentleman did not produce the money. There was no evidence, however, that Paul and Tom had stolen anything but the contents of Novarro's wallet. Intriguingly, Paul cited his sex worker ethic in his defense. Though he was unhappy about it, he freely confessed to hustling. The following cross-examination revealed Paul's hustler pride:

> DA: What did you mean—you were going to hustle Mr. Novarro? Sell your body for money?

PF: Yes. Pruitt up there the night before said that guy [Novarro] had hustlers up every night and must have money, said Novarro paid even when he couldn't do nothing. Never discussed Novarro with Tom—just said we was going up.

DA: Don't hustlers discuss prices?

PF: No.

DA: What did you expect to get?

PF: $20, $25. Kinda cheap, really. We didn't expect to stay long because I was hungry. Strictly cash...I don't like checks. A hustler's a lot of things. A companion, mostly. Not just sex. That, I mean, is part of it.... Someone who hires out as a companion. Sex is expected, but not always.

DA: You hustled women, too?

PF: Yes, but chiefly men. A lot of homosexuals don't particularly care for being homosexual, but like the company of other men—and with sex. It was easy money. I did it between jobs.

DA: Why didn't you talk to Novarro about why you came there?

PF: I imagine you're straight. You don't make a big thing of it, man. You know why you're there, and they know why.

DA: Are there different types of hustlers? How do you classify yourself?

PF: A guy who don't beat up fags and take things.[18]

Paul Ferguson's hustler ethos excluded extortion and violence. The day after the murder, Tom said that Paul told him that Novarro "was a nice guy" who "just wanted to live his life and suck a few pricks."[19]

Tom threw the trial into chaos when he bragged to cellmates that he was responsible for bludgeoning Novarro while his "chicken-shit" brother was "pretending to sleep." Meanwhile, Paul claimed that Tom had confessed to the killing the next day, and that he, as Tom's older brother, had been sticking up for Tom all along. Gay journalist Jim Kepner wrote, "[Paul] spoke intensely, doggedly. I grew less certain of his guilt. He stuck to points that were unlikely to win the sympathy of jurors. Counsel and court castigated Novarro's sex habits. Only Paul defended the man he allegedly killed."[20] Novarro's gardening remark, followed by Paul passing out, left an angry Tom to deal with an expectant client. During Paul's sentencing, his little brother finally spoke up.

I didn't kill him. It was my fault he died. Mr. Novarro came up to me when Paul was asleep.... We had a sex act—oral copulation. He kept trying to put his fingers up my rectum...I started hitting him...I hit him again, and he hit the floor. I looked at him, and it made me sick...I was just mad, I tied him up...I got the glove and cane out of the closet, twirling [it] like a baton, then I hit him in the face and threw it on the floor. Just sickening, he was.... He was trying to force me. There's no way he could force me. He was like a sick punk![21]

Actually, poor Tom was the sick punk. For all his brother's experience, Tom was never really comfortable with hustling. Although he submitted to oral sex (and had, on a previous occasion, received a blow job for money), it was not really Tom's thing. Tom did not deny calling his brother a homosexual and a sissy because of his sex work. Novarro's probing fingers enraged the boy, and before Tom knew it, his client was dead. But the damage was done. Both Ferguson brothers received life sentences.

Kepner cited evidence that the prosecution, one defense attorney, and the judge had colluded to block Tom's confession from reaching the jury. "Tom said that he'd tried three times previously to change his verdict [to guilty]," Kepner reported. "The D.A. had stopped him." In his initial statement, Paul pleaded with the police to listen to him: "My brother's crazy, man.... *You* care to solve your case? Look, I don't know *what* happened, but Tommy is crazy!" Oddly, these sentences were omitted when the statement was made official. When Tom had first confessed in prison, during the trial, "two deputies refused to witness the statement." The judge, the jury, and the defense attorneys were all unable to distinguish between an honest hustler and a murderer. In this failure, they made clear their belief that no hustler was honest and that all hustlers were criminals.

When the trial ended, *Physique Pictorial* printed an old nude shower picture of Paul Ferguson, originally taken by Kris of Chicago in the early 1960s, when Paul was a teenager. This winsome, guileless portrait was, according to Mizer, the "portrait of a killer." Mizer bought into the scenario offered by the D.A., most likely because it proved his point about dangerous hustlers (and helped to sell magazines). Mizer wrote,

> How often do you brush shoulders with a psychopath willing and capable to snuff out your life? Do you avoid the conditions which would make you vulnerable? Can you always trust your judgment?[22]

Mizer encoded Ferguson as extra criminal-minded, a hustler, a top man, and a guy who didn't mind a blow job now and then. Mizer never bothered to defend his model or discover the real truth. But Paul, a poverty-stricken kid who'd been on his own since he was 14, was no different than most of Mizer's models, boys from destitute backgrounds just trying to scrounge a meal and a place to sleep.

Physique Pictorial emphasized its hustler-models' most macho occupations, playing up any double entendres with sex work connotations. In a questionnaire, Mizer asked his readers, "Should we occasionally include fellows dressed in Levis, Military uniforms and other garments often associated with intensely masculine type of men?"[23] His subscribers must have responded positively. Brian John Hunt "got his build from logging" and, in 1965, was "self-employed as a masseur at which he is most adept."[24] David O'Boyle "wrestled a shark in Miami" and "learned plumbing in college."[25] Mike Waschelkin was a "rugged but most congenial marine" who "got his build from farm work and logging." Mike was photographed upright and from the rear, a construction hat on his

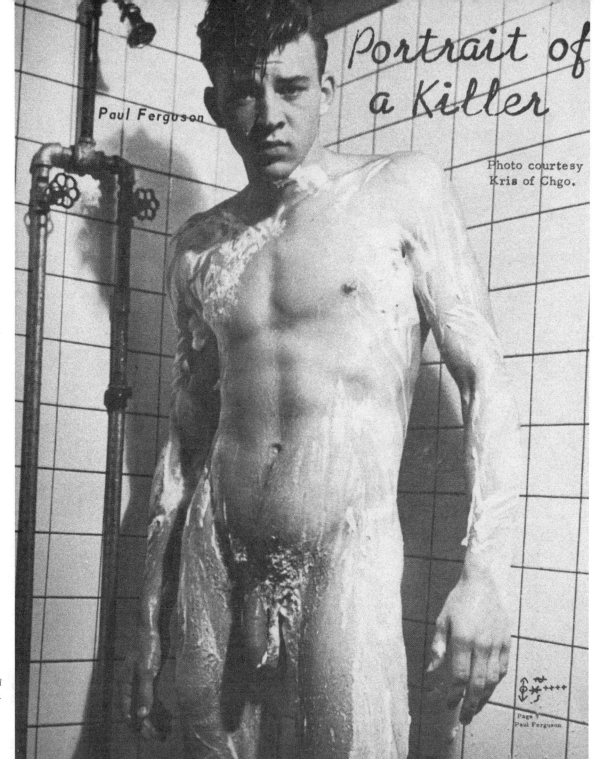

fig. 6.11 "Paul Ferguson," courtesy of the Athletic Model Guild and the Canadian Lesbian and Gay Archives.

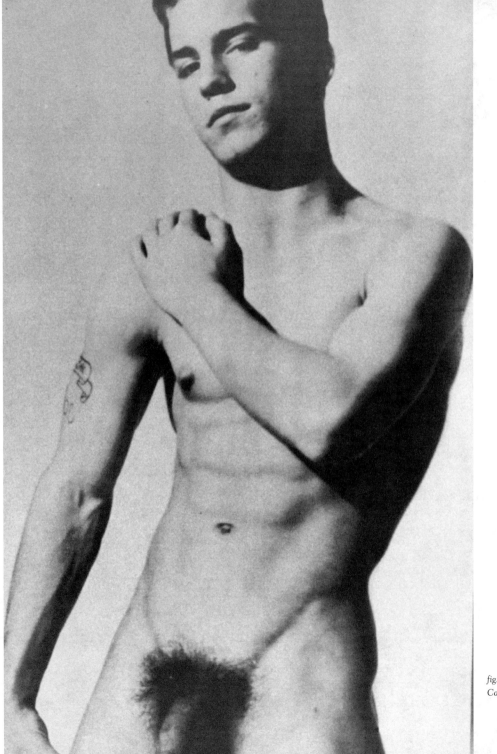

fig. 6.12 "Joe D.," courtesy of the Athletic Model Guild and the
Canadian Lesbian and Gay Archives.

head, boots on his feet, and a telephone belt around his waist.[26] And Joe D'Allesandro, soon to gain cult fame for his work with Holly Woodlawn in Andy Warhol's movie *Trash*, was one of Mizer's first full-frontal nudes. Little Joe, in 1969 a "short-order cook," had "also done hard construction work laying pipe."[27]

And Lou Reed had the beginning of the third verse of his most famous song. Little Joe was not the only model taking a walk on the wild side.

Latter-day Eromenos: Naked Teens, 1961-1975

Other magazines followed Mizer's example, further distorting the *Strength & Health* template. Witness the mission statement of the *Grecian Guild Pictorial:* "The Grecian Guild is a brotherhood of bodybuilders, artists, physique students and others dedicated to the radiant health of body, mind and spirit which frees man from the vulgar and the base and inspires him to noble ideas and endeavors."[28] Ironically, the *Grecian Guild* most often published images of slim adolescents who could never have been mistaken for bodybuilders. One series recalled the photos of Holland Day, picturing a teenage boy strapped to a pole. A bigger, older friend gives the younger boy a sideways wedgie, exposing nothing but emphasizing his genital bulge (see figure 6.13). The captive kid, meanwhile, gazes lustily at his tormentor.[29]

Here photographer Frank Borck reversed Day's tone, suggesting that this Saint Sebastian willingly accepted his punishment as a part of the game of seduction. Borck's photo advances the theory that if young hustlers are constrained in their role it is only because their bonds give them satisfaction.

By the mid 1960s, *Grecian Guild* was boldly publishing work by several photographers who had abandoned the pretext of health or art in their compositions. The fall 1965 issue featured a cast of characters from the modeling agency DB Associates, of Berkeley, Calif. DB's models ranged in age from 15 to 20 years of age, all uncomfortably posed in the same transparent bikini brief. Little textual information was provided about these boys, who uniformly eyed the camera with the gaze of hardened street hustlers.

On the inside cover, DB offered the only text: a listing of the models, their ages, and their page number. There was also a promotion for expanded photo series of each model, along with ordering information. Without any other textual interference, this bald advertisement method was the modern, mail-order version of the 19th-century peg-house.[30] DB's photographic composition reinforced the brothel feel. Each boy stood alone in the same spare room, lit only by light from an unseen window.

The fall 1966 *Grecian Guild Studio Quarterly* featured images from Lyric Studios. Lyric was financed by Billy Byars, heir to a Texas oil fortune. Guy Strait, Lyric's principal photographer, cared little for separating naturist/physique imagery from hustler expression. As prepubescent Armando grinned innocently from his clean sheets, Raol Cobar stared menacingly from a white bear rug (see figure 6.14).

fig.6.14 "Raol Cobar," from the *Grecian Guild Studio Quarterly*, Fall 1966 (#19). Reproduced by permission of the Kinsey Institute for Research in Sex, Gender, and Reproduction.

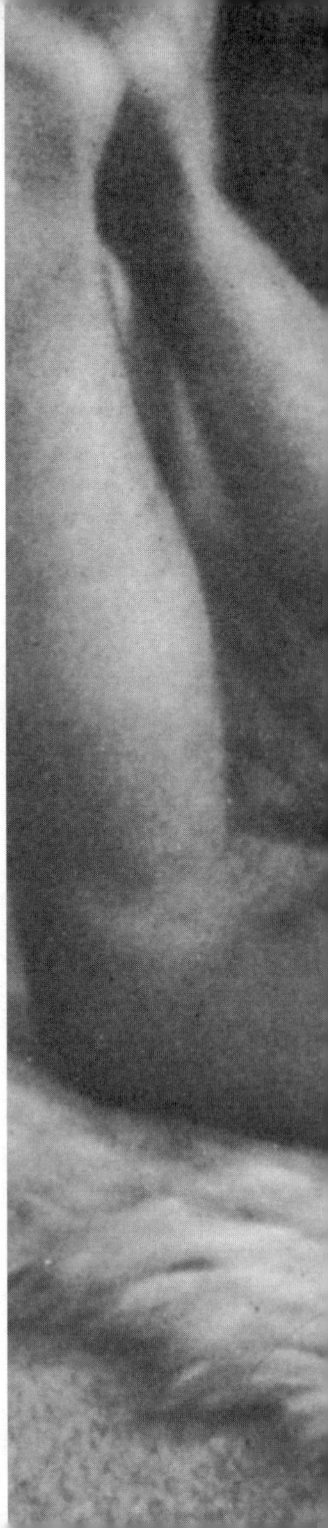

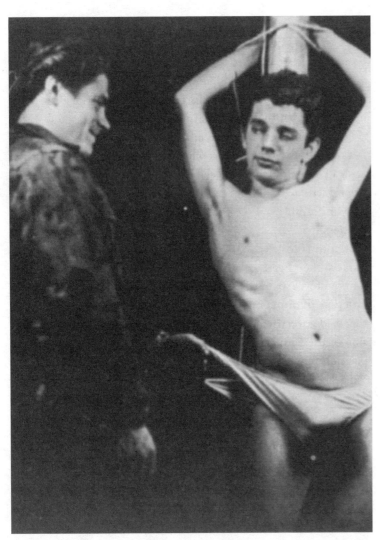

Armando was also featured in the November 1966 *Grecian Guild Pictorial* frolicking in the California hills with several other fancy-free teenagers supposedly "studying the geological formations of the rocks and dense foliage." In the inaugural 1967 issue of *Chico,* Armando sidles up to two older boys (see figure 6.15).

The Lyric enterprise churned out magazines under different names, including *Hombre, Naked Boyhood, Sun Children, DOM's Boys, American Boys,* and *Naked Teens.* Byars even wrote, directed, and produced a film, *The Genesis Children,* which enjoyed art-house popularity upon its 1975 release.

The studio enlisted boys through word of mouth. Billy Byars picked up Terry Stuart, of *Grecian Guild* fame, on the streets of San Francisco, and kept him in a Los Angeles apartment on Mulholland Drive. Stuart, in turn, kept the even younger Peter Glawson (second from right in the image below), who was reputedly his nephew, and who had moved from Texas to California.

Another boy, Billy Marshall, was recruited at the tender age of 10. Billy, claimed the makers of Lyric, jumped

in front of the nude camera just before his 10th birthday and has been there ever since. Most of the pictures were taken in the yacht of a friend and the color pictures were taken in the backyard of a relative. Billy is an accomplished drummer, guitarist and has more hobbies going on than Carter has little liver pills. A look around his room at home will

fig. 6.13 "Ray and Chuck," from the *Grecian Guild Studio Quarterly,* Fall 1965 (#15). Reproduced by permission of the Kinsey Institute for Research in Sex, Gender, and Reproduction.

RAOL COBAR

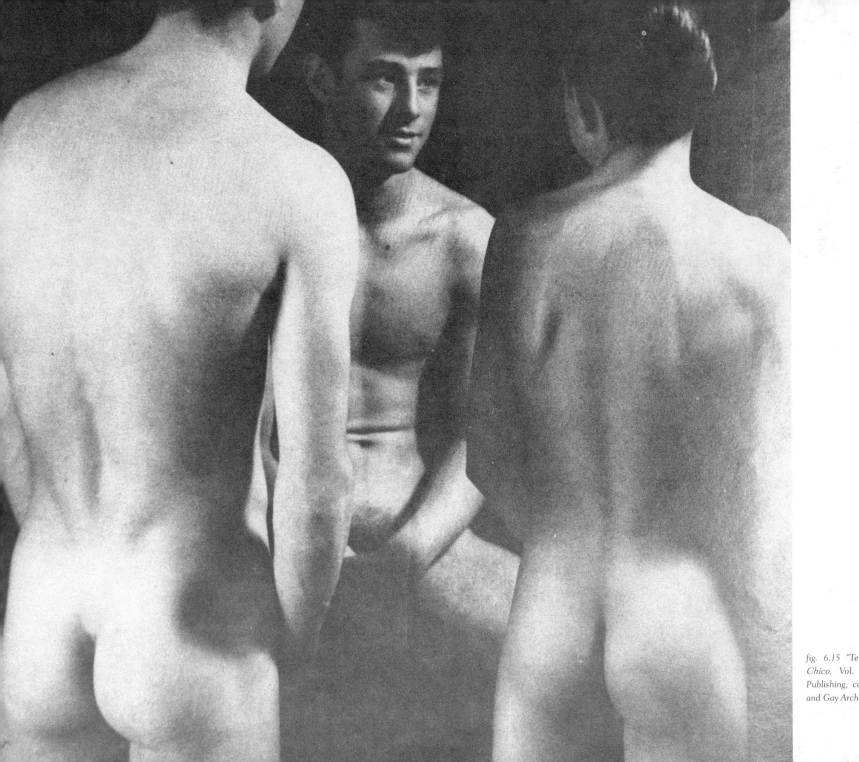

fig. 6.15 "Terry, Junior, and Armando" from *Chico*, Vol. 1, No. 1 (ca. 1967), DOM Publishing, courtesy of the Canadian Lesbian and Gay Archives.

fig. 6.16 Peter Glawson (second from right)
from *The Genesis Children* flyer, ca. 1975.

show psychedelic posters, tropical fish, drums, gui-tars, amps, a double closet full of clothes and so many other things that you know you are in the room of a real boy, full of pep, vinegar, and savvy.[31]

Billy looked baleful in those first photos. They were shower pictures, and they convey coercion: The child was plainly embarrassed, unsure of the appropriate expression. Billy seemed more comfortable a few years later, in the blush of puberty, sailing away on the yacht of his "friend," the Dirty Old Man.

Because their models were so young, Byars's publications did not dwell on their faults, as Mizer often had. Nor did Lyric chain, strap, or reign in their models. Though Lyric's captions hinted at their models' sexual availability, the boys' poses and gazes rarely made their status clear. The sheer number of boys who appeared in the studio's films and publications indicates that many young teenagers readily posed nude in the Haight during its countercultural heyday. Did they just as easily hustle? According to Clifford Linedecker, who interviewed Strait in prison, Strait claimed to have "helped educate them, showered them with gifts, and taught them that sexual activity is one of the most vivid, sincere, and appreciated forms of communication and physical expression between human beings."[32] Strait styled his commercial exploitation of children as a kind of surrogate parenthood:

I have seen thousands of kids who have left home. But very, very few of them were missed except in a legal way. The loss of a "possession" is about all that could be said. Kids that have been beaten by a drunken father are called "runaways" when the drunk no longer has any thing to beat on. Kids that have been told to "go away" are reported to the police when they do go away.

Haight-Ashbury was a haven for the runaways and throwaways....

I had set up a telephone strictly for the use of kids to call their parents. I had a system...first we would place a collect call, telling the operator who we wanted to speak to and who was calling. Ninety-five out of every 100 calls ended in, "I am not going to pay for a call to talk to that kid." And so then I would, in a few minutes, allow the kid to place a call and charge it to the phone. Most of them felt they had discharged their obligation [sic] to notify their parents when the collect call had been placed and most went out with tears in their eyes. So after a while we discontinued the collect call...not to save the parents...fuck them...but it was too damn rough on me to see the kids hurt that way.[33]

By the mid 1970s, Strait was also on the run—not from his parents, but from the LAPD. After a short stint in Illinois, he was finally arrested in Arizona in 1976, convicted for giving head to a 14-year-old Rockford boy whom he'd paid $200 to have sex on camera with two young friends. Strait died in 1997, a decade after his last release. Feeling the heat, Billy Byars moved permanently to Europe in the late 1970s, with photographer Slim Pfeiffer following behind.[34] When Pfeiffer died, he left model Peter Glawson his estate, including negatives, photographs, and film reels. Glawson eventually rereleased *The Genesis Children,* and is now purportedly married, with children, and living on a ranch in the Southwest.

Double Exposure:
Transgender Underground Porn, 1935-1969

If male hustler imagery could proliferate under the streetlight, images of trans sex workers were relegated to the shadows. The general public tolerated wrestling beach boys, but it could not accept mass-marketed transgender eroticism. Because of opprobrium, commerce in representations of trans people was never lucrative. Nevertheless, certain themes are apparent in the surviving photos. Without a need to cater to a public market, the makers of trans porn had a remarkable degree of creative freedom. Little documentation accompanied these images, and most of these photographs do not contain text. We can group American trans porn in three concentric circles: informal, candid snapshots; images that focus on exposure; and compositions involving bondage and discipline.

Some early donations to Alfred C. Kinsey function as documentaries of the street world, with fairies blowing boys in sock garters. The fairies are rouged and plucked; the boys remain (like most johns in hustler photography) faceless and anonymous, further exposing the fairies. They are engrossed in their activities, which gives the photographs a starkly voyeuristic quality.

Breaking the fourth wall served to connote availability. In this undated picture, probably from the early 1960s, a young trans girl and a boy sit on a couch and masturbate together (see figure 6.17).

The trans girl stares at the camera, unsmiling, while the boy grins off into space. This hard look, as we have seen in physique pictorials, distinguished the hustler from the model.

Underground trans porn from the 1950s and 1960s emphasized two-gendered exposure. But photographers denoted their trans subjects' femininity in torturous ways. Unlike male hustler porn, which derived from bodybuilder and nudist imagery, street queen porn was strongly influenced by femininity fetishes. Trans bodies were strapped in corsets and garters, as in female *Exotique* portfolios.

Transgendered women received (and arranged) savage treatment in early, underground American porn: They were fucked from behind, strapped into chairs, their genitals almost always on display.

The preponderance of bondage photographs in the surviving trans underground imagery heightens conflict: straps, bonds, and gags were extensions of a femininity fetish that Joanne Meyerowitz has called "Petticoat Discipline," a pattern likely appropriated here by cross-dressing, upper-class straight men who eroticized their gender-bending self-portraiture.[35] Did they also romanticize the life of their underclass compatriots, transgendered sex workers? Johns too

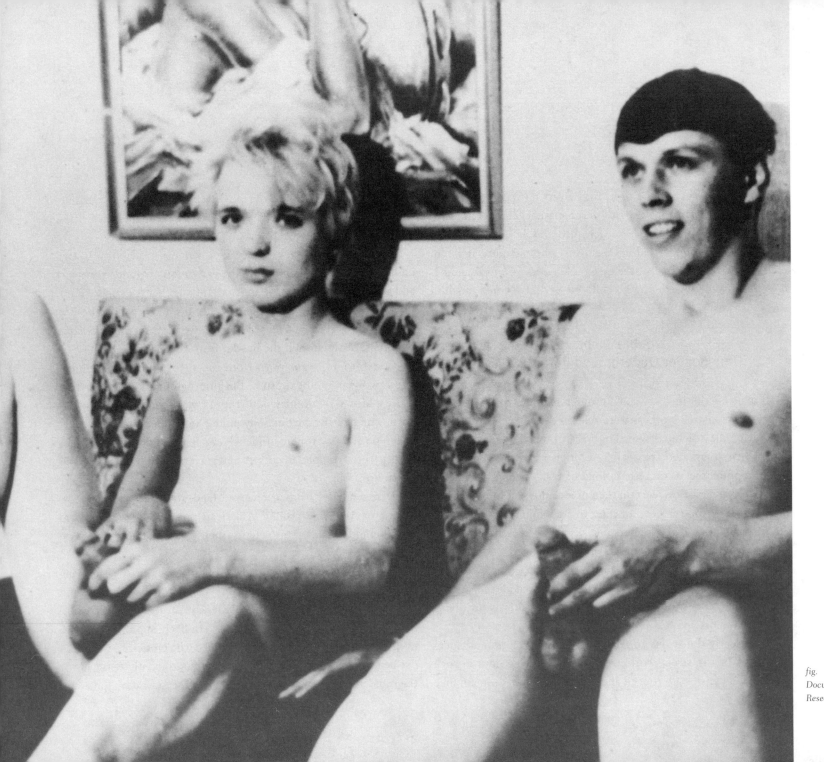

fig. 6.17 Image KI-DC:69014 from t
Documentary Collection of the Kinsey Institute
Research in Sex, Gender, and Reproduction.

were photographing street queens, following this theme with the rationale that if trans girls were going to whore, they were going to be treated like whores, and even worse. Who could blame trannie sex workers, financially lured into posing, for believing that if they wanted to be women so badly, they deserved to be tied down by an extension of the very clothing that expressed their innate femininity? We do not see this in the contemporaneous hustler porn sold aboveground, which was sarcastic at times but generally admiring.

Yet there were happier images that took von Gloeden's preceding work further. The Baron had occasionally pictured his young models in veils and long wigs, which conveyed femininity and passivity (see figure 6.19).

American underground trans porn exulted in the bait-and-switch, showing gender change occurring over a series of photos. One composition was arranged to draw the viewer's eyes from the model's hairy legs to her silky panties (see figure 6.20).

The image in figure 6.21, donated to Kinsey in 1959, pictures a trans girl with apparent breasts. Underground trans porn was a valuable marker for the street population's access to female hormones.

Work like this intersected with the medical photography of Harry Benjamin, who took portraits of nude patients for his book, *The Transsexual Phenomenon*. Benjamin covered his nude subjects' faces with gray boxes, whereas underground porn exposed trans girls entirely. Curiously, Benjamin's photos captured their subjects' personalities in a way underground porn photos rarely do. His before-and-after pictures are especially gracious.

In one case, Benjamin's gray box unintentionally paints kinkiness

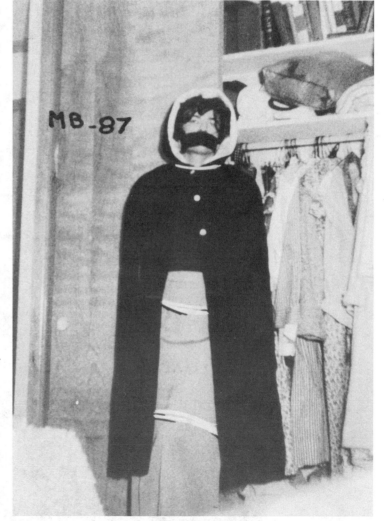

fig. 6.18 Image KI-DC:69645 from the Documentary Collection of the Kinsey Institute for Research in Sex, Gender, and Reproduction.

fig. 6.19 Image KI-VG:258 from the Von Gloeden Collection, the Kinsey Institute for Research in Sex, Gender, and Reproduction.

over his documentary surface: In figure 6.22 he seems to censor imminent popsicle sex. Indeed, this photo prefigures the black circles that blocked out blow jobs in hard-core adult magazines of the 1980s and 1990s, proving that Harry Benjamin was, in more ways than one, decades ahead of his time.

These darkly glamorous portraits confirm that by the late 1960s trans girls were passing readily, given good bones and the right female hormones. When a trans girl was able to arrange sex reassignment surgery, she transcended her previous exotic niche. Post-op porn would have been a redundant enterprise, as transsexual subjects appeared as biological women, with the attendant iconography.

Stool Pigeons: Hustlers Posed as Hustlers, 1968-1985

Harry Benjamin's privacy boxes had their precedent in the medical anthropometry conducted between 1932 and 1952. A small canon of American puberty studies was published during those two

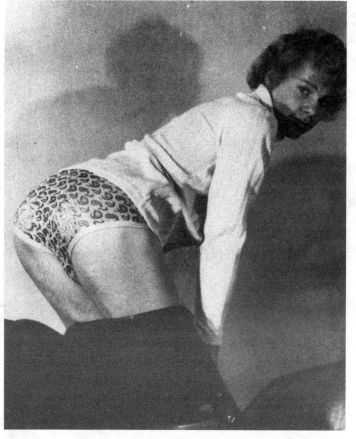

decades, and virtually all of them obscured their subjects' faces with black paint. One pose especially prized by later hustler pornographers was the boy on a stool. This technique was pioneered by William Greulich, who used the prop to accentuate the genital development of male teenagers.

The stool pose also evoked the peg-boy tradition—an aesthetic popular with mid-century hustler photographers. In this example, we see the contemplative "Dino," from *Portfolio #2*, distributed in the late 1960s by a Brooklyn-based press, Photographer's Choice.

This is a frank hustler-on-display pose. Its sexual current is heightened by Dino's relaxed masculinity and dark, averted gaze, conveying physical, but not emotional, availability.

Times Square Studio perfected this remote sensuality. *The*

fig. 6.20 Transsexual in panties, provenance unknown.

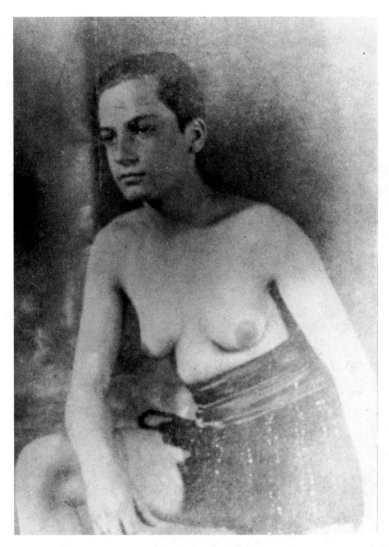

fig. 6.21 Image KI-DC:69104 from the Documentary Collection of the
Kinsey Institute for Research in Sex, Gender, and Reproduction.

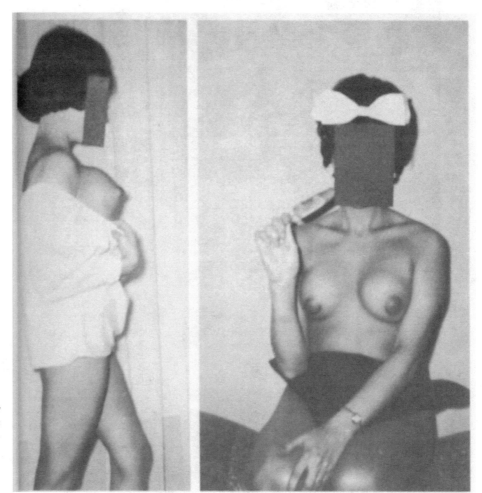

fig. 6.22 "Male Transsexual," from Harry Benjamin, The Transsexual Phenomenon; Julian Press (NYC), 1966.

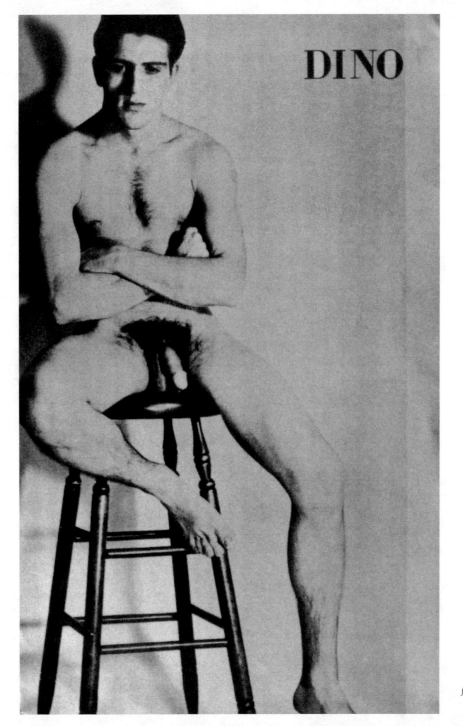

DINO

fig. 6.23 "Dino," from *Photographer's Choice, Portfolio 2*, ca. 1969.

Silent Men #1, from 1969, was multiethnic, showing Italian, Puerto Rican, Middle Eastern, and Jewish (but no black) models. They were all over 20 and stood next to windows or reclined on white bedspreads in black-and-white or three-color.

Lou (figure 6.26) has tears tattooed below his left eye, denoting his having killed men in jail. The meaning of the butterfly is a mystery.

The Silent Men has no photo credit, though the work is similar to that of a Toronto-based photographer whose pictures at the time bore only his initials: BDR. This BDR likely traveled south to do a lot of his work, and he sold photographs to American publishers for at least 20 years. (Various BDR photographs show youth wearing Oklahoma Sooners T-shirts, and most of his models were circumcised.)[36]

In figure 6.27 we see an example of his work, published in a treatise called "Why Teen-Age Boys Hustle."[37]

Tom Painter reported that the text (by "Dr. Jerome Rose") fell into pseudosociology. As photographers produced more honest hustler visuals, porn presses struggled to find a way to contextualize socially "inappropriate" images appropriately. They relied on pop psychology, faux ethnography, and other forms of questionable social science to frame erotic images. The result was science camp: often hilarious, sometimes horrifying, by turns frustrating and explosive.

Although he did not preserve the text, Painter did send his comments to Cornelia Christensen, his newest Kinsey Institute liaison. He was pointedly critical of "Why Teen-Age Boys Hustle"

and reacted sarcastically to its pseudoscientific premise. "The text comes to the sensational conclusion that they do it to make money," he wrote. Painter cynically denounced the magazine's pictorial of a young model's blatant, streetside crotch-grabbing: "Only once have I seen anything comparable to this display elsewhere—and I've been around some too." He was also puzzled by the boy's obvious excitement in a sexual spread within the magazine. Why was the boy performing fellatio on his supposed customer? Who was paying whom?[38]

Three weeks later, Painter had changed his mind. He began to worry about his attraction to the blond model, frightened of his pimply youth. He did not want to believe that the boy was a hustler, but he knew better.[39]

Tom Painter had trouble accepting the young, gay, sexually open hustlers who were becoming available in the 1970s. Perhaps the gay prophets and pornographers were right: Boys in the 1970s were more willing to experiment with dual roles in commercial sex, abandoning a longstanding trade tenet while refashioning masculinity. That was a sign of progress, another subtle revolt initiated by hustler youth against prevailing sexual codes.

Whether BDR's carefree subjects were aware of their radicalism, we may never know.

Some of the same farm boys who posed as hustlers were also pictured in pseudomedical texts. One was purportedly a study of the masturbatory practices of 200 teenaged boys. The photos are impossibly straightforward. Other magazines—like *Phallic Development of the Adolescent Male*, or *More Than Seven Inches*—went

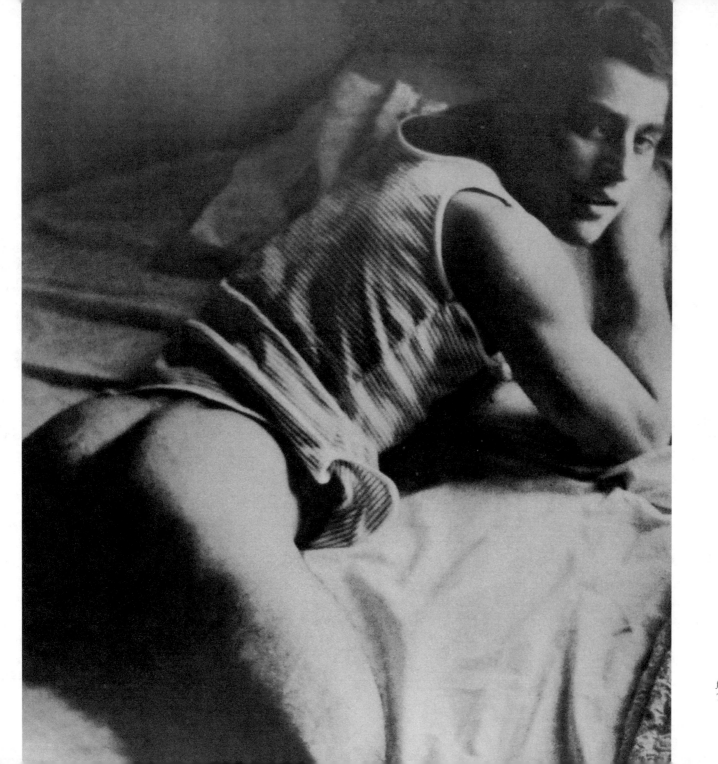

fig. 6.24 "Sal Rocco," from *The Silent Men*, Issue 1, Times Square Studio (NYC), ca. 1968.

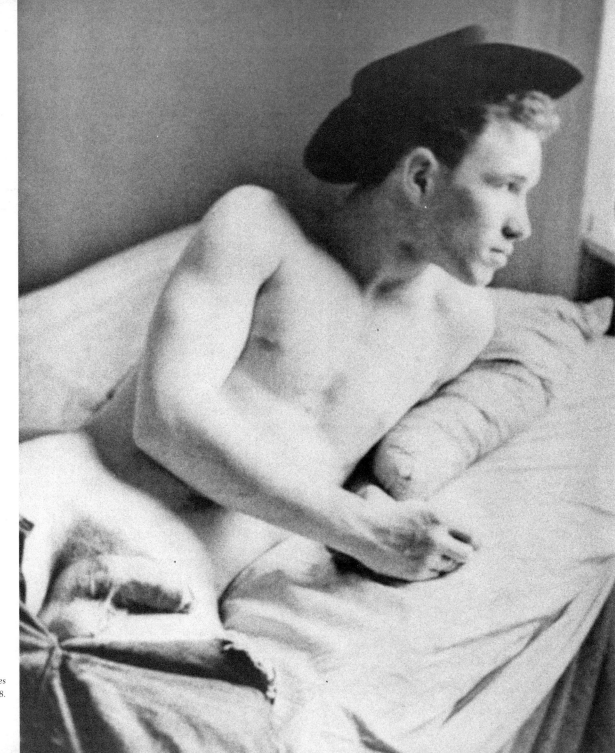

fig. 6.25 "Cowboy," from *The Silent Men,* Issue 1, Times
Square Studio (NYC), ca. 1968.

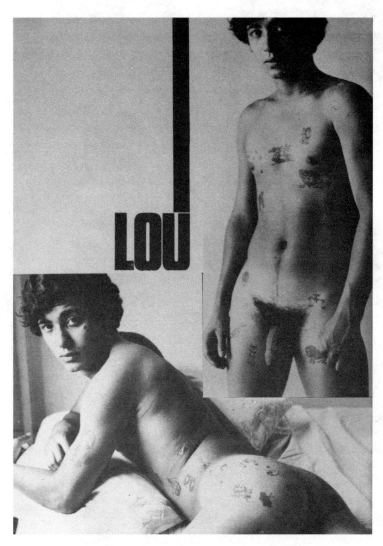

fig. 6.26 "Lou," from *The Silent Men*, Issue 1, Times Square Studio (NYC), ca. 1968.

where no medical journal had gone before. An apt homage to American porn's tradition of sleight-of-hand, quasimedical portfolios did not define their hustler subjects as hustlers, nor did they offer sound treatment options for the young, attractive patients who serially enrolled in anthropometric "studies." [40]

The realm of pseudosociology offered much more freedom. In the 1970s, gay pornographers refined the genre of unscientific ethnography that first appeared in "Why Teen-Age Boys Hustle." *Bus Stop,* for example, pictured a Texan in tight pants lounging near a sidewalk bus stop. The series indicates that he was easily induced to visit with a stranger and take off his clothes. And *Like, One* posed a kid named Cosmo hitchhiking in a shirt way too small for him. The caption reads:

> *The slim financial resources of most teenagers is reason enough for many a youth to hitch a ride. Though we would prefer that COSMO avoid riding with strangers (it's not the safe thing to do!) he was out on his usual Saturday afternoon rounds when the cameraman spotted him and gave COSMO a lift![41]*

These digest-sized magazines were equal parts far-out fashion, hustler pose, and cheeky pseudoscience.

The Burbank-based DSI magazines *Hustler's Night Off* and *Franky and Johnny* purported to document hustlers' activities during their leisure time. By the early 1970s, pornographers had begun to venture away from conventional "straight" hustler

fig. 6.27 "Why Boys Hustle," from Mutual Masturbation,
Trojan Book Service, ca. 1971.

imagery to explore different fantasies, among them the appealing notion that street boys screw one another whenever they have a spare moment. According to the flyer, hustlers "drop their hang-ups with their pants and really put out in ways their johns never dream of." To clear any confusion in the minds of readers, DSI's writers tell us:

> Dark haired Franky is a young country boy trying to get by in the big city by doing a little hustling. Blond boyish Johnny walks by and Franky realizes this is one he'll have to grab before he gets away. They go to Johnny's apartment and strip down. Once naked it's heavy sex all the way with one position after another until the ultimate climax.[42]

This open depiction of homosexual desire was completely novel. Though earlier publications like *Physique Pictorials* originated only because of the historical market for hustlers' services, the taboos against same-sex intercourse necessitated the kind of coded advertising that Mizer and others employed. As the sexual revolution progressed, gay hustler culture finally began to emerge from the closet.[43]

Other magazines, including *Hustling Dudes, Trade,* and *Times Square to Selma Avenue,* soon leapt onto the bandwagon. *Times Square to Selma Avenue* remarked on the proliferation of new species on the streets:

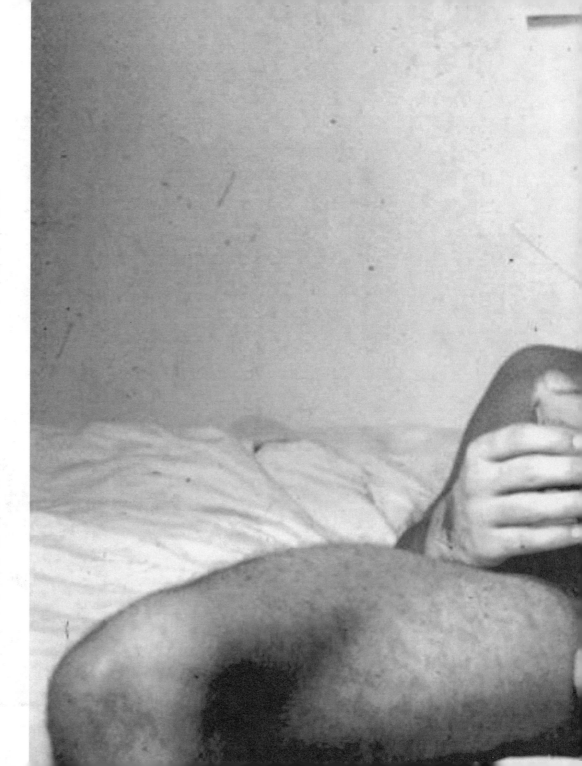

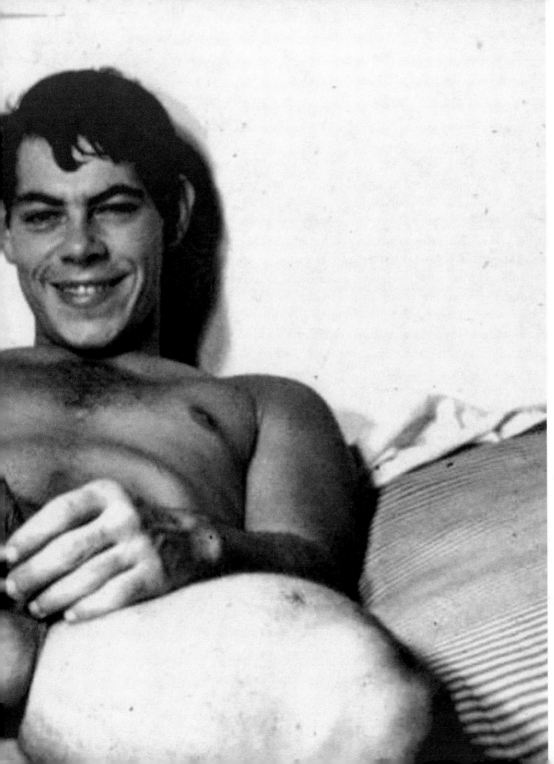

*In the last dozen years, the wide gap which formerly separated the drag hustlers from the butches, has been filled in, if not exactly bridged, by large numbers of hip, mod, willowy, androgynous, and often clearly gay types who are neither drag nor butch, and couldn't care less about muscle building. The old johns raised their eyebrows (so did the butch hustlers), asking, "Who on earth would pick **them** up?" But the newcomers did surprisingly well, and even some of the old johns found their taste changing slightly.... The old-type hustler, hard of face and muscle, had become a scarce commodity.[44]*

The same anonymous author (whose words accompany a picture of two young men having sex in a sun-dappled flat) suggested that traditional trade was best found in urban America's slums, where ghetto hustlers still played the macho hustler role:

Take a block of Polish occupied houses in New York or Chicago, New Haven or Detroit, or a Black ghetto anywhere. There are all those young studs lounging around the street-corners, hour after hour, apparently with nothing to do. Go up to a young man whose pose and appearance are identical to the boys' on Selma. Ask him what he's doing. Chances are slim that he'll say he's hustling. That would be an unlikely answer in your ethnic neighborhood. But ask, in the right way, if he'd like to earn $20.00 in a reasonably

fig. 6.28 BDR image, provenance unknown.

short time, and give him a fair idea what is expected, and chances are he'll go along.[45]

In the mid 1970s, American artistic photography finally caught up with commercial porn and tackled male and trans prostitutes. Nan Goldin and Mark Morrisroe, both educated in Boston at the School of the Museum of Fine Arts, began to document their lives on camera. Certain of Goldin's party photographs have a post-orgy feel—they are languid, candid images of her mod and willowy hustler friends, asleep in messy apartments, bathed in sunlight.[46] One of her favorite subjects, David Armstrong, is now a successful photographer in his own right. Armstrong, who lived with Goldin and several others in a railroad flat, remembers it as "just a really wonderful time. Nobody had any money. I was occasionally turning tricks. That summer of '72, Nan really started photographing a lot, and our lives revolved around that."[47]

Goldin's *Ballad of Sexual Dependency* pictured her friend, the late Mark Morrisroe, cradling a bottle of Jim Beam. Morrisroe, who had hustled on and off since he was 16, gloriously exploited himself in pursuit of fame and debauchery. He began shooting self-portraits in his late teens. According to his friend Ramsey McPhillips, by 1975 Morrisroe was still making his living as a prostitute, and had already suffered the gunshot wound that paralyzed his left leg.

The X-rays also showed the bullet that was lodged behind his heart. Mark was shot when he was sixteen

fig. 6.29 "Cosmo," from *Like, One: A Pictorial Study of the Male Teenager From the Private Collections of Amateur Photographers*, Guild Press (Washington, D.C.), ca. 1968.

by one of his "johns" while negotiating the payment for a twenty-dollar blow job. He had picked up a stranger off the street on Beacon Hill [in Boston] to get money to buy his mother a Christmas gift.[48]

Morrisroe personalized his autobiographical photography during the development process, when he added smudges, fingerprints, and blurring. His daring experimentation sometimes recalled F. Holland Day's artificially hazed prints. Morrisroe fiddled with Polaroid film prototypes donated to him by the company. McPhillips notes that "[Morrisroe's] relationship with Polaroid was really quite amazing considering that he was so open and cavalier about depicting his prostitution," and that his early work was that "of a promiscuous sensationalist (Dirty Old Man)."

During the 1970s, George Alpert also trained his eye on the transgender community. His work was intimate but less revealing than Morrisroe's porous self-portraiture. Alpert prefaced his photodocumentary, *The Queens,* by describing his subjects as professional female-impressionists. Though he made no textual references to their prostitution, Alpert posed two of his subjects on the stroll: One pretty gal wears a tight sweater and hip-hugging bellbottoms, the other sports a busty cowgirl vest and shiny boots, her open mouth an invitation. On the other hand, self-taught Baltimore photographer Amos Badertscher made sure to chronicle his subjects' gritty histories, which frame his photos in the awed shorthand scrawl of the documentarian (see figures 6.30 and 6.30a).

Larry Clark's 1971 photo-documentary, *Tulsa,* focused on young speed shooters in Clark's Oklahoma hometown. While Clark made no textual references to hustling in *Tulsa,* many of his images capture sexual situations involving injection drugs. Thomas Painter, who died in 1977, would have thoroughly enjoyed the last portion of Larry Clark's second book, 1983's *Teenage Lust,* which offers a candid portrait of 42nd Street. Clark was the first commercially successful artistic photographer to examine Times Square hustlers in an honest light. Painter showed us the beginnings, with 1950s boys like Little Chino; Clark brought us up to date.

In 1981, Clark described the winding road that led him into the Puerto Rican gang culture of the 42 Boys:

What I was finding on 42nd Street was not what I wanted to find. It was just a dead end. Everything gets old. But I think the kids don't know that. There's that innocence there. When I first met [some of the kids] and they were looking at me with those come-on looks, you know, the way they would look at the old men who would come and try to hustle them, the old homosexuals, just with their eyes. What would be the use of showing an old man picking up a young kid and maybe having sex with him? It's what the kid is offering, that's what I'm getting. The picture is of what the kid is offering. The kid is offering himself. He's selling something. It's more a look than anything. It's a look, right? It's an entire attitude. It's a way of seeing things, but it's all polished up. It's point of sale.[49]

fig. 6.30 "Todd" (1975), courtesy of Amos Badertscher and the Degen-Scharfman Gallery, NYC.

fig. 6.30a "Sandy" (1975), courtesy of Amos Badertscher and the Degen-Scharfman Gallery, NYC.

Sandy the mild prostitute – at eighteen. Her haunt was Eastern avenue supplying services all her life to men who needed people like Sandy. Initially, a sexually abused child from Armistead gardens in Baltimore City, uneducated, her only indulgences were a few beers, fun with her friends and later on in life, a little witchcraft. For this she earned a few years in prison for prostitution. Her last years were lived with drag queen Mary on Monument ST. and she died in September of 1993 of AIDS at age 32. Her real name: Steve Helmick.

Clark captured what hustler photographers had been after for years: the smoldering, uninhibited presentation of sexual possibility.

Boys, Drugs, Sex: Hustler Mania in Gay Porn, 1975-1985

As Goldin, Morrisroe, and Clark documented, street drugs remained an established aspect of hustler culture in the 1970s. Commercial gay porn could not help mining the erotic potential of the trend. The booklet *Boys, Drugs, and Sex,* photographed by David Hurles and with accompanying text by James J. Proferes, married highly charged imagery with gutter biography. The cover pictures a young man shooting up into his penis. Inside, we see another boy mainlining while masturbating. In the booklet's text, we learn the boy's sad story:

> My buddies felt sorry for me and gave me some customers' names again. I was able to support my habit that way, for a while; but when the boss found out what they were doing, he kicked them out as well.
>
> It's been almost a year since I got back. I'm still struggling to hustle. I dig drugs more now than I did then. The hustling is a necessity. I have to get my bread somewhere and that's the easiest place that I know to get it. That's what happens when you have a monkey to feed! The habit is expensive—damned expensive![50]

Because the hustling scene had become the primary subject matter of gay commercial pornographers, the spread of readily available drugs like heroin and methamphetamines was clearly apparent in the glassy eyes that graced the pages of many hardcore publications. Bob Mizer's continual recruitment at Pershing Square was unearthing a host of African-American hustlers whom he often stereotyped as enslaved drug-users, giving them such street names as "Cocaine" (see figure 6.34).

By 1980, much of the gay underground was as intricately interconnected as a subway system. As gay media spread across the country, escort agencies and private "masseurs" sprang out into the open, and the gay liberation movement hit its stride. But these new avenues of sexual advertisement excluded street-based hustlers who did not identify as gay.

Few gay pornographers understood this as well as David Hurles. Now calling himself Old Reliable, Hurles took advantage of the trade void and new VCR technology by marketing videocassettes with wrestling themes (à la Borck and Mizer). Old Reliable picked up L.A. street hustlers in pairs, spirited them back to his apartment, and took out his videocamera. The young men stripped down and oiled up, all the while engaged in extemporaneous conversation. They then wrestled on Hurles's two gymnastics mats, which floated like rafts over his living room carpet. Eventually Hurles would declare a winner, and jerk-off frenzies ensued, each athlete keeping his hands to himself.

There were still consumers of gay porn who longed for the old days when touching the other guy was OK only when the contact could be construed as roughhousing. Hurles refined this old trade dynamic by prompting his subjects to spit epithets at viewers. Old Reliable made money by catering to customers who eroticized their own denigration.

fig. 6.31 "Man With Unbuttoned Shirt," from the Painter Papers, reproduced by permission of the Kinsey Institute for Research in Sex, Gender, and Reproduction.

fig. 6.32 "Chuck With Basket," courtesy of Larry Clark and Luhring Augustine, NYC.

fig. 6.33 "42 Boy," courtesy of Larry Clark and Luhring Augustine, NYC.

Bobby GORDON (known on the street as "Cocaine"). Age 25 5'4 140, brown eyes and black hair, born March 21, 1953 in Monroe Louisiana. His hero is O.J. Simpson. Likes to jog, run, swim dance, have fun, and to "help people". Says his favorite reading is "law books" which is rather vital to his survival. Film G-94s $12. solo posing 150@ (solo colors done in June 1978, and 82@ solo colors done Oct of 79. Also 44@ (dual color solos done with Paul Tishler with chained SM theme.

About 200* (6cm bw). This is b&w photo 1-G and the shower shot on page 9 is 4-I. A beautiful color shot & 2 more bw shots of Bobby in AMG RAW #2 $10.

This is page 8 of # 33 Physique Pictorial

fig. 6.34 "Cocaine," courtesy of the Athletic Model Guild and the Canadian Lesbian and Gay Archives.

But some of his work is just plain fun, celebrating the sexual vigor of young men. His magazine *Street Hustlers,* from the early 1980s, showed mustachioed trade involved in reciprocal sex play. "These studs are from the streets of the big cities," Hurles editorialized. "Some did what came naturally just for kicks. Others did it for the bread."[51] Jack Nichols wrote in the May 1980 *Cruise* that "there are still many johns who are satisfied by the fantasy that they are paying for a stud who would not otherwise [engage in sex with him]." Yet the sexual revolution succeeded at least in broadening the scope of accepted sexual interaction between john and rough trade. "Part of the deliverance of the Seventies," writes Nichols, "has been the pose of the sensuous man, and both john and hustler know this. Sensuous means total body contact, and so even the straight-identified hustler disrobes."[52]

As Hurles's video enterprise took the nation by storm, transgender imagery achieved some mainstream success—although the bondage and discipline associations remained strong. By 1983, hard-core specialty magazines offered product lines featuring trans porn. One photograph, from a 1983 *Juggs,* advertised an offshoot with two naked transgendered women who still retained their male genitalia. Adolescent hustler porn was, by contrast, digging itself deeper underground. Law enforcement was cracking down in response to the concerns of parents agitated by mainstream media articles that drew links between male prostitution, child porn, sexual abuse, and homosexuality.

[1] THOMAS WAUGH WRITES, "THE CONNOTATION OF PRONE AND SUPINE POSES...MANY OF THEM QUITE EXPLICIT IN THEIR PASSIVITY, IS OF AVAILABILITY, ACCESS, VULNERABILITY. THESE 'SPREAD' POSES ARE INHERITED FROM HETEROSEXUAL EROTICISM OF THE HIGH OR LOW VARIETY AND ARE PRECURSORS OF THE POST-STONEWALL CENTERFOLD." SEE WAUGH, P. 99. MANY OF VON GLOEDEN'S BIOGRAPHERS, INCLUDING ROLAND BARTHES, ARGUED THAT HIS MODELS WERE *COMPLAISANTS,* SEXUALLY AGREEABLE FOR MONEY.

[2] SEE *INDEPTH ART NEWS,* "FRED HOLLAND DAY: SYMBOLIST PHOTOGRAPHER." VAN GOGH MUSEUM, AMSTERDAM. BRIEF FOR EXHIBITION, APRIL 2001.

[3] FROM PAINTER PAPERS (KIL): PHOTO BOX 6, PRINT 98, ACCOMPANYING TEXT DATED JUNE 1950.

[4] PERSONAL CORRESPONDENCE, DATED JANUARY 4, 2002.

[5] IN A LETTER FROM PAINTER TO BEGG, DATED APRIL 1945.

[6] NOTATION ON REVERSE OF FOTO 11-17; PAINTER PAPERS, KIL.

[7] STEWARD, P. 60.

[8] AUTHOR'S INTERVIEW WITH RECHY.

[9] IBID., IDEM. NEWBERRY PARK IS ACTUALLY WASHINGTON SQUARE PARK, KNOWN IN THE 1930S AS A GAY- AND HUSTLER-FRIENDLY PUBLIC SPACE. (SEE CHAPTER TWO.)

[10] FROM UNDATED NOTES ACCOMPANYING PHOTOGRAPH A2, IN BOX 10, SERIES A.IV.IC, BOX 1, PAINTER PAPERS (KIL).

[11] STEWARD, P. 11.

[12] AUTHOR'S INTERVIEW WITH RECHY.

[13] *PHYSIQUE PICTORIAL,* JUNE 1965, P. 5. "CAN WE AFFORD TO BE PREJUDICED?"

[14] COURT TESTIMONY, *PEOPLE V. PAUL FERGUSON.* REPRINTED IN AN ARTICLE BY JIM KEPNER, "PAUL FERGUSON'S STORY: 'TOM DID IT!'" FROM THE *LOS ANGELES ADVOCATE,* DECEMBER 1969; P. 36. KEPNER'S EXCELLENT TRIAL ANALYSIS DISTILLED 6,500-PLUS PAGES OF TESTIMONY INTO A CONCISE, UNDERSTANDING, DETAILED ACCOUNT OF THE NOVARRO MURDER.

[15] IBID., IDEM.

[16] KEPNER, "TOM FERGUSON BLAMES PAUL, THEN CONFESSES." *LOS ANGELES ADVOCATE,* JANUARY 1970; P. 5.

[17] KEPNER, *LOS ANGELES ADVOCATE,* DECEMBER 1969; P. 5.

[18] IBID., P. 37.

[19] KEPNER, *LOS ANGELES ADVOCATE,* JANUARY 1970; P. 6.

[20] KEPNER, *LOS ANGELES ADVOCATE,* DECEMBER 1969; P. 36.

[21] KEPNER, *LOS ANGELES ADVOCATE,* JANUARY 1970; P. 9.

[22] *PHYSIQUE PICTORIAL,* JANUARY 1970, P. 9.

[23] IBID., FALL 1958, P. 27.

[24] IBID., JUNE 1965, P. 8.

[25] IBID., APRIL 1967, P. 4.

[26] IBID., JUNE 1965, P.13.

[27] IBID., JANUARY 1969, P. 26. FOR STRONG CONTEMPORARY ANALYSES OF ANDY WARHOL'S FILMS AND THE 1969 FILM *MIDNIGHT COWBOY,* SEE MICHAEL MOON'S *SMALL BOY AND OTHERS* AND RICHARD MEYER'S *OUTLAW REPRESENTATION.*

[28] *GRECIAN GUILD PICTORIAL,* JUNE 1959.

[29] *GRECIAN GUILD STUDIO QUARTERLY,* FALL 1965, P. 2.

[30] IN *GOLDEN BOYS* #13 (1968). DB ASSOCIATES WERE FEATURED SHOWING NUDE MODELS.

[31] *SUN CHILDREN,* CIRCA 1969.

[32] LINEDECKER, CLIFFORD. *CHILDREN IN CHAINS.* OCTAVIO (NYC), 1981; P. 234. GIVING SOME CREDENCE TO THIS, ONE ANONYMOUS EX-MODEL RECALLED HIS CHILDHOOD EXPERIENCES: "IN 1966 I AND A FRIEND POSED FOR PNC STUDIOS IN WASHINGTON, DC. I WAS 16 AT THE TIME AND HE, 14. BASICALLY WE DID THIS FOR THE MONEY WHICH FOR THE RATE WAS MORE THAN MY DAD MADE FOR THE WEEK AT THAT TIME. OUR PICS WERE NOT PUBLISHED UNTIL THE [19]70S SOME TIME AS OURS WERE COMPLETE NUDITY WITH FULL ERECTIONS AND SOME LIGHT SEX ACTION. I BELIEVE FRONTAL MALE NUDITY COULD NOT BE PUBLISHED IN THE UNITED STATES UNTIL A FEW YEARS LATER, AROUND 1968. BOTH MY FRIEND AND I NEVER FELT THAT WE WERE ABUSED OR THAT ANYONE TOOK OUR CHILDHOOD AWAY FROM US.... FOR ME WHEN I WAS A CHILD I WAS SEXUALLY STIMULATED FROM MY EARLY DAYS OF GRAMMAR SCHOOL. THIS IS A NATURAL EVENT. I LOST MY "CHERRY" WHEN I WAS 11. CAN SOMEONE EXPLAIN TO ME WHY WITHIN THE LAST TWO DECADES THE UNITED STATES HAS ATTACKED THESE NATURAL PRESEN-TATIONS DURING BOYHOOD DEVELOPMENT? IN MY EARLY TEEN YEARS I DID HAVE TWO SEPARATE AND DIFFERENT RELATIONSHIPS WITH ADULT MALES THAT INVOLVED SEX ALSO. THEY NEVER HURT ME AND IN FACT TO THIS DAY I HAVE VERY FOND MEMORIES." PERSONAL CORRESPONDENCE, MAY 1999.

[33] STRAIT, 1980, P. 100.

[34] LORETTA YOUNG'S SON, CHRIS LEWIS, WAS IMPLICATED IN A BUST FOR HAV-ING SEX WITH THREE LYRIC MODELS. "WHEN THE HARD-CORE CAME IN," LEWIS SAID, "BYARS GOT OUT." LEWIS CLAIMED INNOCENCE, ARGUING THAT HIS ACCUS-ERS WERE "JUST HUSTLERS THE POLICE HAD DUG UP—I HARDLY EVEN KNEW THEM. THEY HAD WORKED FOR LYRIC A GOOD LITTLE WHILE AGO...THEY WERE WELL INTO THEIR TEENS, AND THEY SAID THEY WERE WILLING PARTICIPANTS." SEE JOHN MARVIN'S "PROFILE: CHRIS LEWIS TRIES TO UNDERSTAND," IN THE *ADVOCATE,* ISSUE 15 (NOVEMBER 1974); P. 14.

[35] PERSONAL COMMUNICATION. MEYEROWITZ ARGUES CONVINCINGLY THAT TGS IN UNDERGROUND PORN WERE OFTEN HETEROSEXUAL CROSS-DRESSERS WHO CONTROLLED TRANS IMAGERY MADE BY AND FOR THEIR COMMUNITY.

[36] IT HAS BEEN WIDELY RUMORED THAT BDR STANDS FOR BOB DAMRON, THE GAY GUIDEBOOK PIONEER, BUT I HAVE FOUND NO DOCUMENTATION TO WARRANT THIS NOTION.

[37] FROM THE MAGAZINE *MUTUAL MASTURBATION.* OVERSTOCK BOOKS, DEER PARK (NJ); CIRCA 1967.

[38] FROM PAINTER'S SCRAPBOOKS (KIL), SERIES II C.1., VOLUME 27B AND 28, DATED NOVEMBER 7, 1970.

[39] IBID., DATED NOVEMBER 11, 1970.

[40] SEE *MORE THAN SEVEN INCHES.* MORE, INC. (US), 1979. ALSO SEE *PHALLIC DEVELOPMENT OF THE ADOLESCENT MALE.* MEDIA ARTS/POTOMAC NEWS (NY), 1969.

[41] *LIKE, ONE: A PICTORIAL STUDY OF THE MALE TEENAGER FROM THE PRIVATE COLLECTIONS OF AMATEUR PHOTOGRAPHERS.* CIRCA 1968, GUILD PRESS; P. 6.

[42] FROM DSI SALES FLYER, *HUSTLER'S NIGHT OFF* AND *FRANKY AND JOHNNY.* UNDATED, BUT "OFFER" EXPIRES JULY 31, 1972.

[43] THE RESEARCH OF THE PERIOD ALSO CONTENDED THAT HUSTLERS HIT THE

BATHS ON OFF-NIGHTS: SEE NICOSIA AND RAFF, PP. 58-63.

[44] FROM UNATTRIBUTED TEXT IN *TIMES SQUARE TO SELMA AVENUE,* RDI. NO DATE GIVEN, MOST LIKELY 1971-1974.

[45] IBID., IDEM. SOCIOLOGIST ELIJAH ANDERSON'S WORK HINTS THAT SEX HUS-TLING WAS AN ESTABLISHED, MARGINALLY ACCEPTABLE ACTIVITY FOR YOUNG MEN FROM IMPOVERISHED NEIGHBORHOODS. IN 1976, ANDERSON WROTE OF RED MACK, A 33-YEAR-OLD, "LIGHT-COMPLEXIONED" CHICAGO HOODLUM: "MACK IS SINGLE BUT SOMETIMES LIVES WITH A SISTER IN THE NEIGHBORHOOD. WHEN SHE PUTS HIM OUT HE GOES TO LIVE WITH VARIOUS FRIENDS OR HOMOSEXUALS, WITH WHOM HE IS KNOWN TO EXCHANGE SEXUAL FAVORS FOR ROOM AND BOARD." SEE ANDERSON, *A PLACE ON THE CORNER.* UNIVERSITY OF CHICAGO, 1976; P. 122.

[46] GOLDIN'S *BALLAD OF SEXUAL DEPENDENCY* HERALDED THE "DAWN OF GLAM TO THE INCURSION OF PUNK," WRITES DENNIS COOPER. SEE COOPER, *ALL EARS.* SOFT SKULL PRESS (NYC), 1999; P. 68.

[47] SEE COOPER, P. 67.

[48] MCPHILLIPS, RAMSEY. "WHO TURNED OUT THE LIMELIGHT?" IN *LOSS WITHIN LOSS* (EDITED BY EDMUND WHITE), UNIVERSITY OF WISCONSIN PRESS, 2001; P. 109.

[49] CLARK, LARRY. *TEENAGE LUST.* 1983, NEW YORK CITY; UNPAGINATED: TEXT FROM PENULTIMATE AND LAST PAGE. FOR AN UPDATED SERIES ON CHRISTOPHER STREET AND OUTSIDE THE PORT AUTHORITY, SEE CLARK, *1992.* THEO WESFRIECH (NYC); 1992.

[50] PROFERES, JAMES J. *BOYS, DRUGS, AND SEX.* GP AWARD BOOK, UNDATED (PROBABLY 1973-1976); P. 79.

[51] OLD RELIABLE, *STREET HUSTLERS,* NUMBER 2. (UNDATED, PROBABLY 1980-1985.) HURLES'S SPONTANEOUS WRESTLING VIDEOS PREFIGURED THE AMATEUR WAVE OF NUDE MALE SELF-PORTRAITURE (AND HUSTLING ADVERTISEMENT) OF THE LATE-1990S INTERNET CRAZE.

[52] NICHOLS, JACK. "HUSTLING: NEW TRICKS IN AN OLD BUSINESS." *CRUISE,* NO. 48, MAY 1980; P. 85.

seven

As the American gay liberation movement gained momentum, writers contributing to rapidly proliferating gay publications began to report on the culture of prostitution that had facilitated sex between men for hundreds of years. By the late 1960s, as we have seen, mainstream newspapers were working with the gay community to understand the Tenderloin hustler scene. In the 1970s, mainstream news learned how many papers a good sex scandal could sell. Their coverage of male and trans sex work focused on sensational stories intended to attract the attentions of parents and children. This coverage, though biased and simplistic, was an important warning that hustlers faced grave dangers from their johns.

The Unholy Trio: Trade Reviled, 1971-1977

In Houston, Texas, in 1973, serial killer Dean Corll provided the apparent link between adolescent male hustling and certain doom that cultural conservatives had been waiting for since the *Whip* first cracked.

Houston had been notorious for its murder rate since the mid 1950s. "In 1957," wrote reporter Jack Olsen, "Houston had the highest per capita murder rate in the United States, earning the cognomen 'The Murder City,' and it has never been far out of contention."[1] Houston's gunslinger legacy, an understaffed police force, and the dramatic gap between rich and poor all contributed to this culture of mayhem.

The pressures were most active in the Heights, home to thousands of poor families in the early 1970s. It was the perfect area for Dean Corll to set up shop. During his late teens and early twenties, young Dean entertained schoolboys, managed the books, worked double shifts, and generally ran himself ragged at his mother's small candy factory. "I never saw anybody work like that man!" an unidentified "helper" told Olsen. "He was trying to build up business for himself and his mother."[2] In the meantime, the candy store was a place where Corll, given some function and authority, could interact with boys. After the sweets business folded, Corll found happier hunting grounds. The hustling scene in the Heights operated smoothly by hitchhiking and word-of-mouth.

Teenagers David Brooks and Wayne Henley became Corll's co-conspirators, recruiting boys to party at his apartment. Corll began to kill boys at random, and within three years dozens of local teenagers fell prey to him. Brooks elaborated:

Dean liked oral sex, and he'd pay boys to come over and let him do it to them. That was his sex life.

There was some boys that was involved with him for a long time; they kept coming back for more, and he kept paying 'em. But every once in awhile he'd take a kid by force, and then he'd do oral sex and rectal sex and all kind of other things, and he'd wind up killing 'em.[3]

This was how Brooks came to know Corll: He told police they'd met at the candy factory in 1967, when Brooks was in sixth grade. In the intervening years, Corll established an informal sex work relationship with Brooks, paying him $5-10 each time he gave the boy a blow job. "It was always Dean doing something to me," Brooks said, in keeping with the times, "never me doing nothing to Dean."[4]

Brooks eventually introduced Corll to Wayne Henley, a hardscrabble, fatherless youth. Henley soon became Corll's comrade-in-arms. This arrangement distanced Brooks from Corll. "One day Wayne slugged [David] when he walked into the apartment," wrote Olsen, "and then Dean strapped him on the bed and committed repeated acts of rectal sodomy." Detectives asked Brooks if this incident caused him to cut his ties with Corll. "'No, we stayed friends,'" replied Brooks. "'But after that I was always afraid of him, and we had a lot of fights.'"[5]

What was Henley's motivation for laying kids out? It was, apparently, financial: Brooks and Henley earned a small commission from pimping out their friends, but Corll had pledged hundreds of dollars for sacrificial lambs. Olsen transcribed a 1973 press conference held at one of Corll's burial sites. Henley was then 17:

> [A newsman asked:] *"How many people did Dean tell you that he killed?"*
> [Henley replied:] *"I cain't total it. 24, I believe."*
> *"Did he pay you to bring the boys over to his house?"*
> *"Suppose to have,"* Henley said disgustedly.
> *"Did he ever pay you?"*
> *"No."*
> *"200 dollars?"*
> *"That was the beginning price."*
> *"Did he pay you **any**?"*
> *"Some."*[6]

Henley later reported that, near the end, Corll had offered as much as a thousand dollars for boys brought for slaughter. But Dean didn't deal honestly: The IOUs piled up with the bodies. By August 8, 1973, Wayne Henley had had his fill of the scene.

On the night of August 7, Henley visited a despondent friend, Rhonda Williams, whose boyfriend had mysteriously disappeared a year ago. With a mutual friend, Timothy Kerley, they went to Dean Corll's new apartment in Pasadena, a Houston suburb. According to his visitors, Corll was angry because Henley had brought a girl over. Still, like a good host, he brought out the hors d'oeuvres: spray paint. The three kids huffed until they passed out. When Henley awoke, all three were bound or handcuffed.

Corll threatened to kill them. Henley talked Corll out of killing him, and offered Kerley to Corll in exchange for Williams's life. Corll suggested a compromise: Henley could have sex with the unconscious girl while he raped the unconscious boy. In the midst of these negotiations, Henley grabbed the .22 from Corll's night-stand and shot Corll when he charged. Then he called the police and confessed.[7]

Texas had a field day with Corll, Henley, and Brooks. "There was a new outspokenness against homosexuals," wrote Olsen, "as though homosexuality were an early phase of the dread disorder that consumed Dean Corll, and an impending epidemic of sex crimes could only be forestalled by harassing young men who wore eye shadow and tight pants."[8]

If Wayne Henley imagined that killing Corll and cooperating with the police would make him a hero, he was deluded. Henley and Brooks were, in the eyes of the police, "li'l snotty-nose punks." Prosecutors tried the pair as accomplices to murder.[9] Even Corll's victims got short shrift—their hustling made them unworthy of posthumous compassion. At a community meeting in a Baptist church, one local organizer railed against the press, the police, and outsiders. "They give people the idea that the people in the Heights are white trash, we raise punks, we don't [care] for our children!"[10] The assault on male sex workers spread throughout Texas. In the wake of Corll's serial killing, police as far away as Dallas took the opportunity to break up a brothel: "Dallas Police Probe Homosexual Call-Boys," crowed the *Houston Chronicle.*

Elsewhere in the country, alarmist reportage played to the fears of parents who knew little about casual prostitution and intergenerational male intimacies:

> It was the Houston story...that first screamed to the general public that there were adults using very young boys for sexual adventures. It was the Houston story that triggered a flurry of investigative activities by police departments across the country. And it was the Houston story that confirmed in many minds the often-suspected thought that "all queers fool around with kids"—an idea unsupported by fact.[11]

Bad press from the Houston mass murders further distanced the gay community from the plight of young male sex workers. The gay press approached the issue by differentiating between trade and gay hustlers, associating violent sex work transactions with trade while expressing sympathy for gay and trans hustlers.

In 1977, John Rowberry interviewed three Hollywood Boulevard hustlers for *Out.* Chance was gay. Warren was trade. Vanessa was a trannie. According to Rowberry, Chance had "the dark, mysterious look of a chance meeting: a stranger you come upon in an equally adventurous bar, where the overheard conversation somehow both intimidates and excites." He hailed from Oklahoma, and happened into sex work sometime after high school, on board a flight to Los Angeles. "The guy was perhaps 30, very well dressed, good looking, really cool. I'm sure he wanted me to notice where he was looking." Chance recalled:

We talked until the plane landed. I told him I was coming to Los Angeles to study acting. He asked if I knew anyone, had any friends, had a place to stay. Everything was progressing along so well, so predictably, it was like a B-grade movie. I could tell what would happen next. He knew I had limited cash and didn't know my way around. I knew this whole thing hinged on his having sex with me.[12]

Concluding that "the pleasant experience of his coming out was bought and paid for by the young doctor he met on the airplane," Rowberry turned Chance's first sex work experience into a gay initiation story. The reporter took great care to portray the gay hustler as honest, articulate, intelligent, ambitious, and of legal age.[13]

By contrast, Warren, the token trade hustler, got the short end of the stick. He was only 16, had been hustling for "over a year," and claimed "never to have engaged in a homosexual act himself, [only] submitting to oral copulation for money."[14] Warren came from a broken home: His father left when he was a baby, and his uneducated mother was a waitress. Rowberry found the boy hustling "the infamous Gold Cup restaurant in downtown Hollywood." Warren told Rowberry,

I've had this shirt for three years. I have to wear it to school. I have to wear it when I hustle. I don't have a lot of shirts, or pants, or anything.

I don't want my old lady to know I'm hustling. She thinks I have a part-time job with a gardener who pays me cash. I did, I had a job like that—$1.50 an hour on Saturdays and Sundays.

I can make three or four times that much hustling in one afternoon....

I turned my girlfriend on to grass one day and she dug it. I even brought her down here, where I was hustling. All the guys that have broads bring them around.

My girl thinks hustling's cool. She says that as long as I don't do anything to the dudes that I trick, I'm straight. I'm OK.[15]

"Gay hustlers hold their clients in higher esteem than Warren," crowed Rowberry, though nothing in Warren's interview gives the impression that he mistreated his customers. On the contrary, he comes across as guileless and honest. Rowberry made sure to classify him as underage (and therefore dangerous), and claimed: "Most [gay hustlers] say that many gays were victims of nongay hustlers." This generalization ignored the fact that all hustlers—gay and straight—were vulnerable to men like Dean Corll. Gay hustlers battling trade for customers had an obvious economic incentive to perpetuate this myth, and no trade press (so to speak) existed to refute their claims.

Vanessa was a glamour queen, dominatrix, porn star, and glittery piss-party doyenne. "I'm just doing this to save up for my operation," she began. "Now I know a lot of the girls say that, but I'm telling the truth, honey." In addition to remarking on Vanessa's "full and firm breasts," Rowberry described her as having "smooth black skin, huge doe-like eyes and long auburn hair" framing a "patrician face somewhat reminiscent of Egyptian queens and Hindu goddesses." Vanessa continued her story:

> I've made all the arrangements—the clinic, the doctor.... Now it's just a matter of money, another thousand dollars and I'm home free.
>
> ...I'm only doing this for the operation...I don't like being a whore. But I can't make this kind of money this fast at a regular job.
>
> And no one will ever know I was ever a man...or a whore.
>
> I became a whore because a friend of mine, a transsexual, was one. She told me how much money she was making...and the things she did! That was the hardest part, learning to do all those things like you knew what you was doing. Without messing it up for the john.
>
> I do golden showers, and spankings, and tie them up with rope and leather cord, and things like that. I make them clean my ass...sit on their faces and almost smother them.[16]

Vanessa earned Rowberry's sympathy because of her beauty, but also because she did not want to be hustling. Consumers of gay media in the mid 1970s were most comfortable when hustlers confided ambitions *beyond* sex work and when they could ascribe to hustlers a shared sense of discrimination. In a hierarchy befit-

ting Rowberry's own prejudices, Vanessa's "special services" fetched unspecified "higher rates" relative to Chance, who made $20 a trick, and Warren, who generally settled for $15. Rowberry portrayed Vanessa as the sexiest sex worker (Warren did not merit a physical description) and the most ambitious (she hoped to become a runway model).[17]

Naked Idealism: American Pederast Ethos, 1976

Investigating the experiences of teenage trade in Houston after the Corll fallout, NBC producer Robin Lloyd found that "following the murders, street hustling in Houston didn't diminish as one would imagine." According to Lloyd, one 13-year-old hustler named Larry "reported his business doubled overnight."[18]

From his schoolmates, Larry learned of the opportunities male prostitution offered. When he checked the scene out for himself, he was gratified by his take. After Larry "found out from his school friends that his body had marketable value," he "was picked up by a man and offered $15 to submit to oral copulation." Although Larry "disliked the man who performed the act...he liked the act itself—enough to repeat the performance four more times that night."[19] This account differs strikingly from most other reportage at the time in its emphasis on the sexual enjoyment boys could get from sex work. At the heart of the shifting taboo against queer sex lay old fears of conversion, that "normal" boys who experienced orgasm with males would then eschew straight sex altogether.[20]

In keeping with the adventurism of the 1970s, Larry was not shy about admitting that his sex role had evolved to where he could "play the receptor role in anal intercourse if that was demanded—and paid for." After the Houston mass murders, Larry realized "there was a new fear, a new element to contend with—the fear of violence." While his friends offered social support, he did not have much security. According to Lloyd, Larry formed a platonic, nonjudgmental relationship with Father Jack McGinnis, a local Catholic priest "who had a way with street kids."[21]

McGinnis, who ran a program called Project First-Step, theorized that fatherless adolescent boys were far more likely to enter prostitution than were other boys. "I think 100% of the boys I have talked to who have become involved in street hustling either had no father because of death, or because the father and mother were divorced," he told Lloyd.[22] McGinnis had already aired his theory when he was interviewed on NBC's "Tomorrow," shortly after the Houston murders. Unfortunately, the compassionate work of McGinnis and other grassroots activists (such as Sylvia Rivera, whose STAR program was trying to raise funds for a transgender youth shelter) was overshadowed by ongoing coverage of the Houston murders and the controversy that dogged the young gay liberation movement.[23]

In the tradition of the Glide Methodist Church in San Francisco, urban priests like McGinnis offered young male sex workers informal services that institutional social programs could not provide. Priests were, in turn, privy to the vulnerabilities hiding behind stereotypical hustler masquerades. McGinnis described his outreach approach:

> When I find a boy who's been hustling on the street I don't say, "Why are you hustling?" He can't answer that. Instead, I begin to look at his early life. I don't want to say, "Look, if you keep hustling, it's never gonna get you anywhere." Most of the kids find out it never ends up being worthwhile because it is very exploitative. I ask, "What's going on in your life? How are you feeling?" The direction I take is…toward finding a person to help reconcile the deep hurt this youngster has experienced through alienation; toward supplying the intimate relationship he needs in order to feel valuable and loved and, therefore, make him able to love. If we find that, if we supply that, then his behavior is going to change. And it's going to change without even talking about it.[24]

McGinnis believed that hustlers sought in their johns the absent father figures they desperately needed. He worked to give street youth a father substitute who would offer security and unconditional love. Sexual fulfillment and economic opportunity were harder to provide. Into this void stepped the boy-lovers, who summoned the tradition of the ancient Greeks to justify remunerative sexual relationships with street boys.

Boy-love activist D.W. Nichols distinguished between carefree adolescents and boys who were emotionally and eco-

Toward A Perspective

For

Boy-Lovers

By

D. W. NICHOLS

fig. 7.1 "D.W. Nichols Cover-boy," from Toward a Perspective for Boy-Lovers, Editorial Creative Products, 1977.

nomically deprived, as the Greeks separated *eromenos* from *porneia*. Nichols wrote:

> Like the poor, prostitution will always be with us and there is often a direct connection between the two. The majority of youngsters who "hustle," who "sell" themselves, do so out of dire **necessity** which may range from simply getting enough to eat to a need for affection and the assurance that someone—some **one**—likes and cares about them.... The important point in terms of the "rightness" or "wrongness" of hustling must be decided according to a young person's individual concept of the most rewarding way of life—does such an experience assist or obstruct him in his need-fulfillment and self-realization?[25]

Given the desperate circumstances of young hustlers, Nichols argued for the merits of making their experiences less exploitative. Society abandoned these children—are we to believe in the tenderness of the wolves that sniffed them out?

As part of a moral code for boy-lovers, Nichols considered the "relationship responsibilities" of the man who paid boys for sex:

> In any encounter he has with a hustler (boy-prostitute), it is one's responsibility to recognize him primarily as a human being. A man's obligation to such a lad are as they would be to any other boy he has a short-term intimacy with, for the hustler is as entitled as the rest of us to achieve his own state of self-realization. To regard him less than this is not only to insult his very being but also tends to discourage him from developing a healthy self-image and motivation to aim in a positive way toward worthy goals. Furthermore, this writing is opposed to any situation that encourages the casual, careless, often callous "renting" of the body which in effect equates it with being but a **commodity.** This is not to deny that a boy's need for monetary assistance is sometimes most urgent, just as is a man's need for an occasional one-time sexual experience which affords as well a temporary freedom from the burden of long-term responsibility.
>
> The above applies equally to contacts with lads who are "part-" or "full-time" hustlers. For the youngster who is a runaway in need of help and/or is already "ruined," one's responsibility may be even greater. To treat such a boy as a "rented" sexual object is condemnable. On the other hand, it must be realized that such a lad frequently has a very low threshold of tolerance for stress and frustration, in addition to other immature qualities, plus companions who are likely to reinforce his probably anti-social value-system. Therefore, any effort to help him over a period of time can be a very onerous and disappointing undertaking for the man.[26]

Nichols's advice bears a glint of compassion. Hustlers should, after all, be treated as human beings. But Nichols ultimately absolved boy-lovers of any responsibility to the boys who saw in their sexual interest the possibility of long-term adult commitment.[27]

Parker Rossman picked up where Nichols left off, reporting that "runaway boys told of being sent on a circuit which passed them from one man to another for six months, few of whom kept the boy for more than a few days."[28] He averred that 80% of runaways were sexually propositioned within their first 10 hours away from home. One runaway told him, "I said no to the first man, but a couple of days later I was cold and hungry, it was night and raining and a nice guy invited me to a motel, offering money and to drive me where I wanted to go the next day. He didn't want to do anything I hadn't already done with kids. I ended up going clear across the country with him."[29]

Gang hustlers were conspicuously absent from media portrayals of 1970s boy prostitution. But this facet of male prostitution did not escape Rossman, who found that adolescent gangs paralleled tribal societies. Those gangs that "organize[d] themselves for prostitution, blackmail, mugging, or exploitation of 'queers,'" Rossman noted, existed "well out of sight," having been effectively driven underground by police and sociosexual forces.[30]

Estimating that 15% of boys under 15 were engaging in sex play for money with men, Rossman could not overlook hitchhiking. "The happy hustler is not merely the poor boy who needs money," he asserted. "Often he is the middle-class hitchhiking adventurer or the upper-class runaway, one of the kids who are products of a commercial society where everything is for sale," as well as a sexual culture that prohibited childhood sexuality.[31] Rossman noted the "marvelous anonymity of hitchhiking which, from the boy's point of view, fits right in with his decision that he can explore sex, have fun, and earn some money while taking a spine-tingling step down that ladder which others have found so exciting."[32] The faint possibility of danger, reported one pederast interviewed by Rossman, was usually overwhelmed by the hitchhiker's excitement. Another interviewee verified what we have learned about the hustler-hitchhiker's evolution since the 1940s:

> I pick up nearly every boy I see hitchhiking and I ask them all if they would like to go to bed with me, just to see what the reaction will be. Twenty years ago, many boys were frightened, angry, or indignant—demanded that I let them out of the car immediately. Nowadays those who say they wouldn't be interested are more likely to be amused than frightened, annoyed rather than angry, and few are indignant enough to refuse my offer to take them to where they are going. Twenty years ago it was only boys who had been in reform schools, young delinquents, or desperate and hungry runaways who were immediately willing to go to bed with me. The average youngster today seems much more prepared to consider the possibility. He uses such limited negatives as: "Thanks, but not this time" or "If I did it someone might find out" or "I'd never do it for money, but maybe for fun." Is there a real change of attitude or merely of tolerance?[33]

This pederast's observations paralleled other accounts of the day, which revealed increased sexual availability among hitchhikers (in exchange for payment or *just for the ride*) as well as an increasingly casual attitude toward gay sex.

While Rossman did not acknowledge the degree to which adolescent rebellion factored into youngsters' decisions to hustle, he did offer an anecdote suggestive of this motive. One boy responded to a hustler-prevention speech by checking it out for himself:

> I had heard about getting blown, but it had never really interested me—I guess because I thought no one would really do it. Until one day a man came to our school with slides to lecture on the danger of getting into a car with a strange man. He showed slides of kids who had been beaten and killed, and he lied when we asked questions, although it was whispered all over the room that such men would blow you and give you money. He also warned us about the bad boys who hang around the fountain downtown and the bus station and the sort of men who pick them up. After the lecture some of the tougher boys teased the rest of us about being scared to try it, because we were sissies who couldn't fight and take care of ourselves. So of course we found it exciting to hang around the fountain some, just to show we weren't cowards. One of the big boys who had been to the state school said that being blown was just another way of jerking off, and that it was one way to prove you were a man. Being blown was a lot of fun, and there was nothing queer in letting a man do it to you. I'd never have been down there at the fountain if the man hadn't come to school to warn us.[34]

In this case, male adolescent peer pressure conspired to glorify street prostitution as an initiation into manhood, consistent with juvenile gang rites. By the mid 1970s, cutting-edge hustler chic had intensified through the success of such rock, glam, and punk bands as the Velvet Underground, the New York Dolls, T-Rex, and the Ramones.[35] Though rebellion did not fit into Rossman's perspective on hustlers, he understood that money, affection, friendship, adventure, and sexual desire were important motives, and that hustling increased during periods of economic depression.[36]

Rossman's research was the most comprehensive and detailed of the three pederast books published in 1976. Like Lloyd, Rossman did not claim to be a pederast, although his work reads sympathetically. Because he focused on the pederast underground, Rossman made little more than passing reference to political organizations. And he did not uncover a nationwide boy-lover mafia; instead, he found that "pederasts clustered in small groups, each heading in a different direction, as if struggling to find their way out of the darkness."[37] Much like the boys themselves.

The Dark Side: Hustling Mass-Marketed, 1977-1980

In 1977 the mainstream media truly began to pay attention to the gay sexual economy. We have already examined Rowberry's 1977 account for *Out* magazine. We will now attend to hustlers profiled in straight media channels and compare the treatment they received there.

National television had taken note of male sex workers in newsmagazine-style shows following the Houston murders. In 1976, a made-for-TV film starred Eve Plumb (who gained fame as Jan, the unlucky middle sister in "The Brady Bunch") as a teenage female prostitute. In 1977 NBC produced a sequel, costarring Plumb and her former on-screen boyfriend Leigh McCloskey. *Alexander: The Other Side of Dawn* promised to explore the male side of street-based sex work.

In this fictive docudrama, Alexander's parents have expelled him from their Oklahoma farm because his father believes he's too sensitive for farm work. Alex moves to Los Angeles, where he is too young to get a legitimate job. He finds a friend in a hustler who hooks him up with wealthy, horny women. But Alex can't keep business and pleasure separate and worries that he is falling in love with one of his female clients. To forestall this, he retreats to the streets and hustles men.

Soon Alex is entrapped and arrested by police, only to be saved by Ray, a sympathetic gay psychologist who miraculously appears on the scene just before Alex is booked. Ray escorts Alex to a gay community center. But troubled Alex knows deep down that he is different from the other boys: He's straight! Again he hits the streets, where a gay football champ named Chuck intercepts him and carries him to Malibu. Kindly Chuck employs Alex as a house-boy and lays no sexual expectations on the hapless Okie. After another run-in with the law, Alex retreats to Tucson with his gal to make a life far from L.A.'s sexual chaos. It is clear that he has barely averted certain doom.

For all its Hollywood hokiness, *Alexander* helped spark a national dialogue on the plight of hustlers.[38] "If kids are willing and able to work, and the laws of the land make it very difficult for them to do so, the laws should bloody well be changed," wrote Nancy Walker in a salient review for Boston's *Gay Community News*. "If hustling is your bag, that's fine, but you shouldn't be forced into that—or anything else."[39] Not long after *Alexander* aired, the *San Francisco Examiner & Chronicle* published an equally dramatic article titled "Hustlers in the Teenage Flesh Trade." Carol Pogash wrote:

> *If you're not looking for them, you probably wouldn't notice.*
>
> *If you are, they are available for a price.*
>
> *Child prostitutes, boys and girls under 18, hang out in laundromats, pinball parlors, on street corners and bus benches and up against store and hotel walls in the Tenderloin and along Polk Street waiting for pick ups.*
>
> *About 300 of them are hustling downtown, says Seth Stewart, communications director at Hospitality House, which provides help for those who want it.*[40]

Pogash reported that police had recently broken up a Visitacion Valley "childhood prostitution business," run by "a

360-pound convicted sex offender" who "gave boys, ages 12 to 15, skateboards and model airplanes in exchange for their bodies." The boys were then "transported in a red Cadillac to Polk Street customers."[41]

Pogash observed that this story was "unusual," remarking that boys didn't usually have pimps and that Polk Street kids were usually runaways instead of locals. Even so, she focused her report primarily on local youth, and only let one kid speak for himself. Pogash wrote:

> He's 16, a Galileo [High School] student with good grades. He's been hustling since he was 12. He says that he must have looked very innocent that first day, when a "rich dude" came up to him and offered $50 a trick. He had been minding his own business, eating a cheeseburger when it happened.
>
> By age 14 he was doing five and six tricks a week. "Now I do three or four a month," he said in an interview. He has slowed down "because I look older." No longer skinny, his body is filling out and he is losing his marketability.

The article provided equal amounts titillation and information, but Pogash had good intentions. Even as she exploited the theme that clients were only interested in children, she tried hard to direct parental anxieties in a useful way, to draw support for Hospitality House, Huckleberry House shelter (another offshoot of Glide), and Youth Advocates. Ultimately, Pogash repeated the message from primetime TV: Kids couldn't get jobs. "They've no legal status, no job skills," an activist told Pogash. "It is the only way to survive. [The] only thing[s] marketable are bodies."

It is so hard to separate fact from fiction in youth sex work exposés. Nicosia and Raff also reported on the phenomenon, claiming that in Chicago, "preteen or barely pubescent" Puerto Rican boys from impoverished families had become "a serious threat" to Bughouse Square hustlers in the mid 1970s, undercutting veterans' prices: "This constant surfeit of poor children and adolescents forces the established hustlers to keep themselves looking as young as possible."[42] Could it be that because gay bars (which had become the dominant gay social spaces) did not allow youth in their premises, men who were attracted to adolescent boys *had* to resort to the streets to find sexually available partners?

News of the Boston Sex Scandal broke a month after Pogash's article appeared in the *Examiner*. Revere, a Massachusetts beach town near Boston, had a long history of quiet toleration for intergenerational male intimacies. *Gaysweek* reporter John Mitzel wrote that "an Italian priest said that what people outside the Italian community in Revere don't understand is that teenaged boys going with men is part of the tradition in his community. Everybody knows about it and understands it."[43] *Village Voice* reporter Frank Rose termed Revere a "boy town" with a "boy culture" where hustling and sex play between boys and men was so common that 8-year-old boys would have oral sex with cabbies and policemen in exchange for rides.[44] Curiously, Rose found a link between the 1977 scandal and a Revere bar that had featured female impersonators in the 1930s and that had been closed by police in 1956. The bar, Mede's, was originally "opened by the father of one of the defendants in the current sex-ring case."[45]

In June of 1977, the Suffolk County sheriff quietly arrested Richard Peluso, who had been running a brothel offering teenage boys, and began the "Revere Sex Ring" investigation. By December 7, police had amassed enough evidence to indict Peluso and 24 other men on multiple charges involving 63 boys between 9 and 15. The *Boston Globe* falsely trumpeted the arrests as evidence of a "Child Porn Ring," although pornography charges were never brought. (In fact, police were the ones disseminating private pictures of involved teens. "Police showed nude pictures of [a 15-year-old gay boy named Gary] to neighborhood kids and encouraged them to badger him," writes Mitzel.)[46] Concerned local citizens teamed up to create the Boston-Boise Committee, which closely monitored the abuses of the investigation.

Events in Revere resembled the scandal in Boise, though the technical aspects of sex work (introductions and negotiations) were conducted differently in Massachusetts. Revere hustlers, emboldened by tacit social support for their activities, had lounged around Peluso's backyard pool and smoked his marijuana. At Peluso's, prices were set at $25, from which Peluso took an exorbitant 60 to 90% (leaving the boys with only $5 or $10). "You'd think the neighbor who said she saw all the boys in their swimsuits drinking beer on the back porch would have suspected something," wrote Rose, "but she didn't."

Mitzel argued that Revere's libertine culture was ripe for corruption: Intergenerational sex between males was so common that Suffolk County enlisted pro-police pedophiles as informants when District Attorney Garrett Byrne announced that the main focus of his reelection campaign would be based on the eradication of child molestation. Suspected hustlers were interrogated and threatened, even induced to fabricate depositions.[47] The Boston-Boise Committee polarized the straight and gay press and exposed the hypocrisy and incompetence of local politicians and law enforcement agencies. Byrne did not win reelection. Prosecutors eventually dropped many of the charges against alleged johns and reduced most sentences to probation with a guilty plea (although the men who fought their charges received three to five years in prison). Peluso was sentenced to three concurrent 25-year sentences, which amounted to life. The boys themselves were not arrested; many ran away—sometimes even running into former clients on the Boston strolls—or relocated, given their notoriety in a small town like Revere.[48]

Digging deeper into Revere's sex work culture, Mitzel and Rose unearthed an upscale organization called BUY-FUCK, which operated in Revere and Boston from 1977 to 1978.

BUY-FUCK provided teenage boys to male clients who, according to a boy who worked in the operation, paid up to $100—depending on the sex acts performed. Contacts for BUY-FUCK were made at several clubs in the downtown Boston area.

*During the panic and sensation over revelations about Richard Peluso and sex in his apartment, **not one mention** was made by police or local press about BUY-FUCK. No police investigation was ever made. Did police and the District Attorney of Suffolk County have the luxury of choosing which boy-sex-ring they would exploit?[49]*

Why did police arrest Peluso and not the owners of BUY-FUCK? The murder of 21-year-old Curtis Dale Barbre in February 1978 forced complacent authorities to act. Barbre, who had recently impregnated his girlfriend, spent the last night of his life at a gay bathhouse called the Regency Health Club, which BUY-FUCK used as an assignation site. In fact, BUY-FUCK had a history of violent clients: According to Mitzel, "another boy working for BUY-FUCK was stabbed by [a client] during a tryst arranged through BUY FUCK." Mitzel and other reporters learned that the owner of the Regency was politically connected, which partly explained why BUY-FUCK operated with impunity.[50]

A short time later, Bob Mizer's Athletic Model Guild studio was raided, after LAPD detective Lloyd Martin used "a fake complaint involving an unknown 14-year-old." Martin took the opportunity to seize $100,000 in cash and the customer mailing lists; Mizer was found guilty of not filing unemployment insurance for his models. In New York City's Chelsea neighborhood, just above the 14th Street cruising grounds, police busted a service known as the beeper boys, seizing 3,000 customer names (a virtual "Who's Who" list, according to police).[51]

Police had always been a presence on the streets, but they concentrated mainly on sex workers; their interventions with johns occurred as an infrequent result of brothel stings. By generally ignoring street-based sex clients and paying little attention to the disappearances of male and trans hustlers historically viewed as disposable, traditional police interventions only made America's streets more dangerous for sex workers. On December 22, 1978, Chicago police finally arrested John Wayne Gacy, who had been killing male and trans sex workers since 1973. It took the disappearance of nonhustler Robert Piest to prompt police to track down Gacy.[52] Events in Houston, Boston, and Chicago propelled America's adolescent sex work industry into the national spotlight.

Dissemination: Government Studies, 1980-1985

Alarmed by the murder of scores of young hustlers in the 1970s, the federal government established a committee on the exploitation of children. The Senate Committee on Juvenile Justice convened in November 1981 to conduct hearings on hustling. Senator Arlen Specter interrogated "David," a 17-year-old living in a Louisville group home, and attempted to link David's history of childhood sexual abuse with his subsequent career in prostitution. Academic studies established the validity of this correlation, which has shaped antiprostitution policy for the past 20 years.[53]

SENATOR SPECTER. David, what was your first introduction to the use of drugs?

DAVID. *When I ran away, the first time I ran away.*
SENATOR SPECTER. *And when was that, that you first ran away?*
DAVID. *I was 12 years old. And the guy I was staying with, who was a good friend of mine, had a party and I went to the party and I was introduced to alcohol and marihuana.*
SENATOR SPECTER. *At the age of 12?*
DAVID. *Yes, sir.*
SENATOR SPECTER. *Marihuana at the age of 12?*
DAVID. *Yes, sir.*
SENATOR SPECTER. *Any other drugs?*
DAVID. *Just alcohol and I did some speed, but that was about it. That was a little later when I was 12.*
SENATOR SPECTER. *You were exposed to speed also at the age of 12?*
DAVID. *Yes, sir.*
SENATOR SPECTER. *What caused you to run away from home at the age of 12, David?*
DAVID. *My mom found out I was smoking cigarettes and my mom and dad had just gotten separated and I was afraid she would tell my dad and my dad used to come down pretty hard on me, punishment-wise, so I got scared and left.*[54]

Arlen Specter may have been shocked by David's youthful drug use, but sharper observers of the scene were not surprised. David later described buying marijuana and reselling it to his peers in middle school for $1 a joint, netting him a profit of $25 per bag.

David fell in love with a 16-year-old runaway girl and hitch-hiked to California with her, but he was arrested for vagrancy and sent home shortly thereafter. Back in Louisville, David's alcoholic father "took a belt" to him; he had been throwing his son across rooms since the boy was 11. Specter then asked David about "some experiences [he] had at the age of seven" and "their influence on [his] later problems."

> *It really didn't have an influence on my life. It was something that happened when I was real young and I didn't know what was going on. There was a lot of resentfulness in it that carried through onto what happened in my later years....*
>
> *It was a baby-sitter, as a matter of fact, and it was just something that happened....*
>
> *I was resentful that someone had taken advantage of me like that and done to me what he did and had me do to him what I did. I'm not like that. I'm not the type of person that gets into things like that and I was really resentful that someone who knew what was going on and knew what they were doing would still go ahead with a little boy and do something like that, especially me. I'm not anybody special, but, you know, it's me.*[55]

After further questioning, David admitted that these experiences had caused him "personal problems that I deal with within myself," including "resentfulness toward people, my role, you know, my sexual role." Specter asked what David meant by this, and he replied:

> Well, OK, I'm straight. I'm not gay, but with things like that happening and then things that I did in the hustling, it just puts something in my mind like well, am I sure I am straight or I'm not sure. And it messes with my mind a whole lot...and then I get mad at myself for this...and it messes me up mentally....
>
> ...A lot of times I thought, a lot of people down-town told me, well, even if you are a hustler, you wouldn't hustle unless you had something in you that attracted you to men or some part that would let you do that. If you were totally straight and not gay at all you wouldn't be down here.[56]

The debasement and confusion David described would haunt many young trade hustlers whose heterosexuality had not tradi-tionally been questioned by society, and whose sex work already occurred under conditions of economic desperation and severe emotional turmoil.[57]

David told the committee that he began to hustle at 15, after he was expelled from a shelter for drinking and arguing. "I just walked over to a park a few blocks away," David said, "which I later found out was right on the hustling strip in Louisville." He ran into a former counselor hanging in the same park. In his late 20s or early 30s, the counselor was hustling after-hours and claimed to charge $50 to $60 a trick. David immediately began to hustle in the park, though he never made more than $45 a trick. He told Specter that he only hustled men; he was once proposi-tioned by a heterosexual couple, but "never went out with them. That only happened once and besides that it's always been men."

> SENATOR SPECTER. Going back into the earliest days of the origin of the problem, what got you start-ed on alcohol and drugs, which led you into hustling?
> DAVID. I got myself started—well, the friend I men-tioned earlier got me started by showing me where it was at. But I got myself started. And I kept into it because it made me happy, it made me feel good about myself. It made me feel like I was somebody and I fit in with somebody.[58]

David quit hustling after going through drug treatment in Minnesota, where he realized that his feelings of community in the sex world had been illusory, or short-lived: "The only thing hustling was doing was dragging me back down and making me feel like a nobody, a nothing." How had David been so deluded? Or, how did hustling get so old so fast? Was there a way to make the streets and parks more tolerable for young hustlers? There were many ways to do this, but the committee saw no reason, if they ever entertained the possibility.

Senators did not ask these questions, and subsequently stringent sex offender legislation reflects this decision. The Exploitation of

Children Committee's interest in adolescent sex work had nothing to do with improving sex work conditions. Instead it was a convenient launching pad for new anti-vice initiatives. Stepped-up law enforcement and declining social services made the streets more of a living hell than ever before.[59] David wished that the services he received had been less impersonal, arbitrary, and judgmental. "They did not even worry about what I thought I needed," he said. "If they had just taken more time. I think they need to take more time on each individual case." For that, social services needed more funding, but Reaganomics was taking hold.

These issues were raised back in the late 1960s, when reporters for the *San Francisco Chronicle* cooperated with their *Vanguard* colleagues to detail the plight of gay and trans youth. Throughout the 1970s, while gay media focused on queer hustlers and derided trade, mainstream media ignored gay sex-working adolescents and concentrated on their straight or sexually confused counterparts, who made more sympathetic victims. But in 1982 the publication of a Department of Housing and Human Services study conducted by Urban and Rural Systems Associates (URSA) changed the landscape entirely.

The URSA study, conducted by Toby Marotta, concluded that "adolescent male hustlers tend to be white, 17-year-old high school drop-outs" from the lower and middle classes who often endured family conflicts sparked by their increasing gay identification. But when asked their primary motivation for hustling, 69% of sampled hustlers reported sex-working mainly for the money. Marotta used these statistics to argue for expanded housing options, employment help, social support, and legal representation for this at-risk population.[60]

Reporters for mainstream media outlets used the URSA study to argue for better services and interventions for gay teenagers, a real triumph for gay activism.[61] Hilary Abramson, examining "boy prostitution" in 1984 for the *Sacramento Bee,* quoted activist Jerry Sloan, who sensed the need to do something, and not just for the boys who were hustling. "We need a place for all gay teenagers wrestling with their sexuality," said Sloan. Abramson found that some two dozen hustlers cruised in Plaza Park, directly across from City Hall. The scene was primarily a haunt for local boys, in contrast to the predominance of runaways along hustler strips in bigger cities. Although the accompanying picture was unremarkable, showing all-American boys in T-shirts and jeans, Abramson's prose depicted a gay bacchanalia:

> Until it's late, they all play their parts as if miming a 501 Jeans television commercial. One hand on the leather leash tied around his own neck, an 18-year-old sexual "slave" twirls under street lights like some kid Nureyev choreographing "Chorus Line." For a time, his comrades light each other's cigarettes—making one match do for 10. They jostle, joke, and pose.[62]

Abramson's gay activists come off as sensible father figures. According to the *Bee,* Sloan suggested "establishing a drop-in center with free food, clothing, and counseling so the boys wouldn't have to sell themselves for the basics." Sloan called for a new, safer, publicly subsidized alternative to the unregulated, underground sex work industry that had been swallowing marginalized American youth.

More than 200 years after the founding of the American democracy, moralizing about the evils of deviant sex finally began to give way to active concern for the welfare of young sex workers. Pragmatism—if not prosperity—had finally begun to trickle down from the highest echelons of power and social privilege. But this compassion would be severely tested by the AIDS and crack epidemics.

[1] OLSEN, JACK. THE MAN WITH THE CANDY. SIMON AND SHUSTER, NYC, 1974; P. 29.

[2] IBID., P. 213.

[3] DISTRICT ATTORNEY PAPERS, PEOPLE V. DAVID BROOKS. ALSO SEE OLSEN, P. 158.

[4] IBID., IDEM; ALSO SEE OLSEN, P.145.

[5] OLSEN, P. 145.

[6] IBID., P. 164.

[7] IBID., PP. 113-133 FOR A MORE DETAILED CHRONOLOGY OF THE EVENTS OF AUGUST 7-8, 1973. FOR AN ALLEGED ADMISSION BY HENLEY TO KILLING NINE OF THE BOYS HIMSELF, SEE "BODY HUNT MAY EXTEND OUT OF TEXAS." NEW YORK POST, AUGUST 9, 1973 (WEEKEND EDITION).

[8] IBID., P. 239.

[9] IBID., P. 189.

[10] IBID., PP. 243-244.

[11] LLOYD, ROBIN. FOR MONEY OR LOVE: BOY PROSTITUTION IN AMERICA. VANGUARD (NYC), 1976; P. 47.

[12] ROWBERRY, JOHN W. "ON THE BOULEVARD." OUT (LA): JULY 29, 1977; P. 17.

[13] FOR A SIMILARLY GLOWING PERIOD PIECE ABOUT A GAY HUSTLER, SEE AN INTERVIEW CONDUCTED BY WILLIAM J. LAMBERT, III. "MY PECKER MAY MAKE ME A MILLION!" GAY, OCTOBER 12, 1970; PP. 7, 8, 13.

[14] ROWBERRY, P. 18.

[15] IBID., IDEM. CAFETERIAS ALONGSIDE HUSTLING STRIPS HAVE ALWAYS PROVIDED SOCIAL SUPPORT, SUSTENANCE, AND SAFE ZONES FOR THEIR CUSTOMERS. THE GOLD CUP, AT 6700 HOLLYWOOD BOULEVARD, WAS RAIDED REPEATEDLY IN THE '70S. THE ADVOCATE'S JOEL TRUMLAK, PRAISING POLICE INTERVENTION, SAID, "TO MANY GAY PEOPLE...THE GOLD CUP BRINGS A SCORNFUL RESPONSE" AND THAT, WHEN THE CUP CLOSED AT 10PM EACH NIGHT, THE ENTRANCEWAY LOOKED "LIKE A HUSTLERS' CONVENTION." SEE TRUMLAK, "THE GOLD CUP RUNNETH OVER WITH HUSTLERS." ADVOCATE, NO. 139; JUNE 5, 1974. FOR LATER REPORTS ON A LOS ANGELES HUSTLER DISCO, THE ODYSSEY NIGHTCLUB, SEE DEBORAH HASTINGS'S ARTICLE, "POLICE SAY BOY, 14, KILLED BENEFACTOR." LOS ANGELES TIMES, JANUARY 20, 1984. AN UNSOURCED NOTE ASSOCIATED WITH THIS CLIPPING, IN L.A.-CRIME FOLDER AT THE ONE INSTITUTE, READS AS FOLLOWS: "THE USE OF 'BENEFACTOR' HERE IS ASTONISHING! ESPECIALLY CONSIDERING THE (ALL-GAY) REPUTATION OF THE ODYSSEY!!!" TOBY MAROTTA WROTE IN 1982 THAT "CERTAIN CAFES AND DISCOS...THAT CATER TO MINORS...BECOME PLACES FOR YOUTH TO MINGLE WITH YOUNG MEDIA PERSONALITIES AND POTENTIAL JOHNS, WHO GO TO DISCOS SUCH AS THE ODYSSEY TO MEET THE YOUTH WHO ATTRACT THEM." SEE MAROTTA, P. 52.

[16] IBID., PP. 18-19.

[17] ROWBERRY DID NOT CREATE THIS PRICE HIERARCHY; BUT WHILE REPORTING IT, HE ATTEMPTS TO JUSTIFY IT, AND THE PROBLEMS LIE WITH HIS JUDGMENTAL RATIONALIZATIONS. NICOSIA AND RAFF VERIFY THIS PRICING PATTERN WITH DATA FROM CHICAGO'S BUGHOUSE SQUARE FROM THE MID 1970S. "THERE IS NO BOY AT THE PARK WHO CANNOT BE HAD FOR $35, AND ONLY THE CLASSIEST TRANSSEXUAL IN NEARBY BARS CAN GET $50 ON A REGULAR BASIS." SEE NICOSIA AND RAFF, P. 7.

[18] LLOYD, P. 48.

[19] IBID., IDEM.

[20] This is, in fact, just an update on the old Gothic metaphor of infecting others with homosexual desire.

[21] Lloyd, p. 49.

[22] Ibid., p. 50.

[23] For a brief history of STAR's early struggles, see Duberman, Stonewall, pp. 251-255. When homophile organizations were giving STAR lip service, Rivera sent the youth back out to the streets in order to make money for her burgeoning organization.

[24] Lloyd, pp. 51-52.

[25] Nichols, D.W. Toward a Perspective for Boy-Lovers. Editorial Creative Products. Lansing (MI), 1976; p. 49. (Italics in original.)

[26] Ibid., p. 79. Nichols's text suffers from its flowery prose and its obsessions with the orgasmic process, the beauty of cutoff jeans, and the metaphysical differences between oral intercourse (which he abbreviates, due perhaps to its overuse, as OI) and anal intercourse (similarly abbreviated as AI).

[27] Joyce Hunter, a Manhattan-based social worker for sexual minority youth since 1978, recalls how terrible kids felt when johns rejected them. "I had to put a kid in the hospital once so that he wouldn't kill the john who got rid of him, who just told him he had to leave because he got too old. Since when are you so old at 15? And this kid loved him. Love is love at any age. And this kid, he was so stunned and traumatized by it." From an oral history with Joyce Hunter, conducted by author and P. Jayne Bopp, April 2002.

[28] Rossman, Parker. Sexual Experience Between Men and Boys: Exploring the Pederast Underground. Association Press (NYC), 1976; p. 41.

[29] Ibid., p. 149.

[30] Ibid., p. 80.

[31] Ibid., p. 84. Rossman also cites here the pulp autobiography of the pseudonymous Troy Saxon, The Happy Hustler (a male spin-off of Xaveria's Hollander's classic, The Happy Hooker).

[32] Ibid., p. 85.

[33] Ibid., p. 162.

[34] Ibid., pp. 149-150. Rossman did not specify the city where this boy was from, but it was likely Minneapolis, with its Loring Park fountain and Greyhound bus station in near proximity. (The late David Brudnoy recalled that Loring Park was a hustling and cruising zone already well established by the early 1960s. See Brudnoy, Life Is Not A Rehearsal. Doubleday, 1997; p. 87.) Minneapolis, it should also be noted, has been at the forefront of progressive sex education and prostitution-prevention workshops in classrooms.

[35] These bands gained initial success in the downtown Manhattan clubs Max's Kansas City and Mother's, which drew a diverse crowd of hustlers, street queens, artists, and fans. Viviane Namaste described the New York Dolls, a drag band, as "a dead-on-arrival disaster-area outfit who by 1975 had achieved the popularity of acne-blitzed transvestite hookers addicted to heroin." The Ramones recounted the hustler experience in "53rd and 3rd," released in 1976. See Namaste, Invisible Lives. University of Chicago Press, 2000; pp. 81-82.

[36] See Rossman, pp. 147-150.

[37] Ibid., p. 41.

[38] Alexander inspired other hustler docudramas, like "The Price of Love," which aired on CBS in October 1995.

[39] Walker, Nancy. "The TV Hustle: Alexander on 'The Meatrack.'" Gay Community News. May 28, 1977; p. 15. Walker's well-written, thoughtful review is indicative of GCN's progressive, contemporary coverage of American male sex work.

[40] San Francisco Sunday Examiner & Chronicle. November 20, 1977.

[41] This article is similar in tone to an Advocate piece written by Douglas Sarff in 1974. At the time he wrote "Hustlers—The Deadly Trap," Sarff mentioned that over several months 600 hustlers had been arrested on Selma Avenue. He also reported that a Hollywood hustler might well be "carrying a weapon," a "slave to drugs" (cocaine, speed, and heroin), and "involved with pimps" (who were "mulatto" and

"BLACK," DROVE CADILLACS, AND CONTROLLED "TRANSSEXUALS" DOWNTOWN, ALONG MAIN STREET AND EAST 7TH). SEE THE *ADVOCATE*, DECEMBER 18, 1974.

[42] SEE NICOSIA AND RAFF, PP. 73-74. FOR 1980S MEDIA REPORTS HYPING THE POPULARITY OF YOUTH AMONG STREET SEX CLIENTS, SEE PETE AXTHELM, "SOMEBODY ELSE'S KIDS." *NEWSWEEK*, APRIL 25, 1988; PP. 64-68. "BUSINESS DROPS SHARPLY AS THE AGE OF 18 APPROACHES," CLAIMS AXTHELM. ALSO SEE PETER FRIEBERG, "HELPING GAY STREET YOUTH IN NEW YORK." *ADVOCATE*, JANUARY 20, 1988. FRIEBERG INTERVIEWED STAFF FROM THE HETRICK-MARTIN INSTITUTE, INCLUDING JOYCE HUNTER, FOR THIS ARTICLE. IN PORT AUTHORITY, "OUTSIDE THE SECOND-FLOOR MEN'S ROOM, BOYS AS YOUNG AS 12 HUSTLE FOR TRICKS," HE CLAIMED. HUNTER REFUTES HIM. "THEY WERE ABOUT 16. THAT'S NOT TRUE," SHE SAYS. "I NEVER SAW THAT. MAYBE, IN A YEAR, YOU'D SEE ONE 12-YEAR-OLD OR 13-YEAR-OLD." SEE ORAL HISTORY WITH HUNTER. BUT THE PLOT THICKENS: LUIS MIGUEL FUENTES REPORTED THAT IN THE LATE 1980S, TIMES SQUARE'S PLAYLAND ARCADE WAS THE HAVEN FOR UNDERAGE, HUSTLING YOUTH.

[43] *GAYSWEEK*, FEBRUARY 27, 1978. "BOSTON/BOISE: PEDERASTY IN THE ATHENS OF AMERICA?" BY JOHN MITZEL, EDITED BY JAMES SASLOW; P. 13.

[44] A SIMILAR CLAIM WAS MADE ABOUT BALTIMORE IN 1978. SEE TOM REEVES, "OF BOYS AND BALTIMORE." *FAG RAG* (FEBRUARY/MARCH 1978, PP. 3-11). REEVES CLAIMED THAT IN CERTAIN SECTIONS OF BALTIMORE, 50 TO 70% OF MALE TEENAGERS HAD SEX WITH MEN FOR MONEY, A PHENOMENON THAT HAD PRE-VAILED FOR 75 TO 100 YEARS AND WAS SO CULTURALLY ABSORBED THAT POLICE-MEN WOULD, IN EXCHANGE FOR SEX, GIVE BOYS RIDES IN THEIR PATROL CARS. AMOS BADERTSCHER'S PHOTO-BIOGRAPHIES FURTHER VERIFY THIS CLAIM.

[45] ROSE, FRANK. "MEN & BOYS TOGETHER." *VILLAGE VOICE*, FEBRUARY 27, 1978; P. 19.

[46] MITZEL, *THE BOSTON SEX SCANDAL*. GLAD DAY BOOKS (MA), 1980; P. 43.

[47] SEE MITZEL, "THE BRILL FILES." *GAY COMMUNITY NEWS*, JANUARY 5, 1980.

[48] IN COURT, GARY (A RUNAWAY GAY TEEN) RECALLED BUMPING INTO A FORMER CLIENT ON "THE BLOCK," THE MEAT RACK IN BOSTON'S BACK BAY. THEY ALSO RAN INTO EACH OTHER ONCE IN A GAY DISCO, WHERE THE CLIENT GAVE GARY $100. THAT PARTICULAR CLIENT, A PSYCHIATRIST WHO TESTIFIED THAT HE HAD

ONLY BEEN CONDUCTING NECESSARY RESEARCH ON MALE SEX WORK, BENEFITED FROM SUPPORTIVE TESTIMONY OF HIS CHARACTER WITNESSES—ONE OF WHOM WAS THE KINSEY INSTITUTE'S OWN WARDELL POMEROY. PERHAPS WITH THOMAS PAINTER'S PARTICIPANT-OBSERVER RESEARCH ON HIS MIND, POMEROY "ESTAB-LISHED THAT THE KIND OF WORK [THE DEFENDANT] SAID HE WAS DOING—INTER-VIEWING MALE HUSTLERS AT PELUSO'S—WAS BOTH LEGITIMATE AND MUCH-NEED-ED." THE CLIENT RECEIVED FIVE YEARS PROBATION. SEE MITZEL, *BOSTON SEX SCANDAL*, PP. 94, 101, 104.

[49] MITZEL, "THE BRILL FILES."

[50] IBID., IDEM.

[51] SEE SELWYN RAAB, "3 ARRESTED IN RAID ON ALLEGED MALE PROSTITUTION RING." *NEW YORK TIMES*, DECEMBER 1, 1977. THIS "DIAL A MODEL" ORGANIZA-TION UNWITTINGLY SENT TWO SEX WORKERS TO AN UNDERCOVER OFFICER. (THE BOYS CHARGED $75 APIECE.) "LAW ENFORCEMENT OFFICIALS SAID THE HOMOSEXU-AL PROSTITUTION RING WAS BELIEVED TO BE THE FIRST ONE BROKEN UP BY POLICE IN THE CITY," WROTE RAAB. EITHER THEY HAD FORGOTTEN ALL ABOUT GEORGE BEEKMAN'S BROOKLYN HOUSE IN 1942, OR THEY LET THE FEDS TAKE CREDIT FOR IT. (SEE CHAPTER THREE IN THIS BOOK.)

[52] FOR A SYNOPSIS OF GACY'S KILLINGS, SEE *SERIAL KILLERS*. TIME-LIFE BOOKS (VA), 1992. BOTH GACY AND CORLL MAY HAVE BEEN MOTIVATED TO KILL HUS-TLERS BY AN INTENSE SELF-LOATHING BECAUSE OF THEIR DESIRE FOR THESE ADO-LESCENT BOYS, AS IF IT WERE THE FAULT OF THE HUSTLERS (WHOM THE KILLERS SAW AS EXCESSIVELY DESIRABLE, AVAILABLE, AND DISPOSABLE). SEE ROSSMAN, P. 73.

[53] FOR DATA LINKING ADOLESCENT MALE SEX WORK TO PREVIOUS CHILDHOOD SEXUAL ABUSE, SEE MAROTTA; NEIL COOMBS, "MALE PROSTITUTION: A PSYCHOSO-CIAL REVIEW OF BEHAVIOR," IN *AMERICAN JOURNAL OF ORTHOPSYCHIATRY* 44, PP. 782-789 (1974); AND JENNIFER JAMES, *ENTRANCE INTO JUVENILE PROSTITUTION*, FINAL REPORT TO THE NATIONAL INSTITUTES OF MENTAL HEALTH, GRANT NO. 29968 (1980).

[54] "EXPLOITATION OF CHILDREN," NOVEMBER 5, 1981. U.S. SENATE COMMITTEE ON THE JUDICIARY SUBCOMMITTEE ON JUVENILE JUSTICE; PP. 5-6.

[55] IBID., P. 10.

[56] Ibid., p. 11.

[57] Researcher Debra Boyer found that Seattle-based hustlers were experiencing the same confusion that David describes. "The heterosexual prostitutes in my study behaved according to the erroneous assumption that they must be homosexuals because of their homoerotic experience," she concluded. See Boyer, "Male Prostitution and Homosexual Identity." *Gay and Lesbian Youth.* The Haworth Press (NY), 1989; p. 181. Her interviews were conducted between 1980 and 1982.

[58] "Exploitation of Children," November 5, 1981. U.S. Senate Committee on the Judiciary Subcommittee on Juvenile Justice; p. 12.

[59] Joyce Hunter recalls the funding struggles during the lean years of the early 1980s. "During the 1970s, there were a lot of community-based residential programs for teenagers," she says. "In the early 1980s, those places really started to disappear.... The funding was reduced, and there were a lot of kids on the streets." That service gap inspired the creation of the Institute for the Protection of Lesbian and Gay Youth, which in turn led to the Harvey Milk School, Hetrick-Martin Institute, and Project First Step. See oral history with Hunter.

[60] Marotta found, curiously, that male and female teenage hustlers worked together only in Minneapolis (along Hennepin Avenue and Lake Street, leaving Loring Park only for guys) and Seattle (near Pike's Market). Secondary evidence for Seattle's multigendered street prostitution comes from the 1983 documentary movie, *Streetwise* (which avoids *directly* addressing male prostitution, unfortunately). Also see Boyer, pp. 151-183. Boyer found that Seattle-based male prostitutes averaged 16.2 years of age; 70% identified themselves as gay or bisexual, and many had their first gay experience on the streets. Boyer's interviewees reported a high incidence of homophobia, rape, physical abuse, previous sexual abuse, and single-parent family structures. "I was more worried about being found a homosexual than a prostitute," one said.

[61] For examples, see the *San Jose Mercury News,* February 11, 1982; p. 2. "Gay liberation has led to increase in male hustlers, study says." Also see the *Milwaukee Journal,* February 11, 1982. "More young male prostitutes found." These sensational titles belie the pragmatic content of the articles.

[62] *Sacramento Bee,* September 3, 1984.

eight

In the 1960s and 1970s, male and trans sex work thrived on streets that had tolerated sexual economies for decades. By the early 1980s, gay liberation had in many cities produced a two-zone phenomenon that separated hustlers by sexuality, race, and class. In San Francisco, trannies and lower-class trade worked Market Street, while middle-class, gay-identified youth staked out Polk. In Los Angeles, transgendered and African-American hustlers stuck to Main Street and East Seventh, while white males predominated on the Sunset Strip. In New York City, Times Square was more tolerant of nonwhite and visibly underclass hustlers than 53rd Street and Third Avenue. Surveying nationwide in 1980, Toby Marotta discovered that "hustling [was] apparently gayer, younger, and more street-focused" than ever before.[1] But as the 20th century drew to a close, these vibrant street scenes gradually vanished, leaving only echoes, footprints, and track marks.

What happened to street hustling? It fell victim to many occupational hazards. First, AIDS hit hustlers hard. From 1980 (the beginning of the American epidemic) until this writing, HIV has disproportionately afflicted street-based sex workers. Second, crack cocaine and crystal methamphetamine ravaged traditional sex zones, seeping into a street drug scene that had embraced opium in the 1900s, marijuana and cocaine in the 1920s, morphine

in the 1940s, pills and LSD in the 1960s, and speed, crystal, and heroin in the 1970s. Crack and AIDS were the primary reasons for the decline in street hustling during the 1980s and 1990s, but there were other factors as well.

In the 1980s, most local gay media outlets were advertising both individual sex workers and businesses in their classified columns. This trend increased the importance of sexuality and class: Straight-identified, underclass hustlers were less likely to pay to advertise in gay magazines than middle-class, gay-identified sex workers. Advertisements featuring transgendered sex workers were relatively rare, their existence varying widely from city to city. By the 1990s, entire publications were devoted to promoting escorts. Hustlers who could afford and operate the necessary equipment created sites to advertise themselves and their services on the Internet. Finally, urban redevelopment (euphemistic shorthand for cultural destruction) in the 1990s changed both the geography and the politics of indigenous sex zones.

Let us now examine the effects of AIDS, crack, the escort revival, and urban redevelopment on America's male and trans sexual economy during the last 20 years. We first turn to the mysterious case of a 16-year-old boy who died in 1969, a boy we know only as Robert R.

The Boy From St. Louis: The Case of Robert R., 1969-2000

"Boy Prostitute First U.S. AIDS case!" screamed the headlines from the 1999 International Congress of Virology.[2] Thirty years after his death, Robert R. achieved a measure of global notoriety he could scarcely have imagined. Researchers have concluded three things: He was a boy from St. Louis. He died of AIDS in 1969. He was a prostitute.

This conclusion spawns three questions: How do we know he had AIDS if he died 30 years ago? Who said he was a prostitute? And how have these separate claims converged in current media coverage?

The third question compels a look at hustler history. Male sex workers have often been cast as Patient Zeros in American public health research. As we've learned, this tendency has prevailed since the first Virginia colony. American medical literature and the Gothic undertones of 19th-century social reform crusades firmly established the adolescent male prostitute's status as a monster.

The Robert R. case amplified these themes, and the general public proved more than willing to believe that a boy prostitute was the first AIDS case in the United States. But there are problems with this hypothesis. First, Robert's family, friends, and many of his former doctors generally deny any supposed bisexuality on Robert's part.[3] Robert himself confessed to having sex; but only with one partner, an adolescent girl.[4] The qualitative evidence does not yield many risk factors.

Robert R. died on May 16, 1969. Officially, he died of bronchopneumonia.[5] Other contributing conditions, revealed during his autopsy, included disseminated chlamydia and Kaposi's sarcoma (KS), as well as a nephrotic condition: acute passive congestion of the kidney. For two years he had been suffering from lymphedema, a buildup of fluid in his legs and feet that eventually progressed to his genitals. Pathologist William Drake conducted the autopsy and found KS nodules on Robert R.'s thigh as well as around his anus.[6]

Two of Robert's attending physicians, Dr. Memory Elvin-Lewis and Dr. Marlys Witte, concluded that their teenage patient had been having anal sex regularly. They speculated that Robert R. had been gay. "It's just these intuitive feelings we ladies have," Elvin-Lewis would remark at a press coference 18 years later.[7] Following that, Witte conjectured that "he could have been a male prostitute."[8] And thus the legend was born.

Robert R.'s equivalent to a primary care physician, Dr. William Cole, "suspected that Robert *might* have been gay," according to researcher Edward Hooper.[9] Still, the evidence suggesting that Robert R. had AIDS was not unequivocal. He was infected with KS (a cancer linked to human herpes virus 8), which in America most often afflicts immunocompromised gay men. He had contracted chlamydia—perhaps heterosexually. Although it seems likely, there is no proof that Robert R. was having sex with men. There is no evidence whatsoever that Robert R. was a male prostitute, although that is also possible. He lived in a terribly impoverished neighborhood of East St. Louis; his desperate circumstances were undeniable.

Witte's theory about Robert's hustling was not mentioned in any medical journal articles to which she contributed. She omitted her hunch in her 1973 *Lymphology* article, her 1984 letter to the *Journal of the American Medical Association (JAMA)*, and her 1988 *JAMA* article.[10] Instead, she used more scientifically accurate phraseology. She referred to Robert as "this sexually active teenage boy" and admitted, "a homosexual history was not specifically elicited." Witte diplomatically stated:

> Involvement of the anorectum with obliterative lymphangitis, prominent hemorrhoids, and Kaposi's sarcoma raised the possibility that the patient, who admitted to being sexually active, engaged in anal intercourse.[11]

There is a marked difference between this restrained verbiage and the media reports leaked before the article's publication. A *US News & World Report* piece from November 9, 1987, is telling: "[Robert R.] was never asked about drug use or homosexuality, even though doctors found evidence that he may have been a male prostitute."[12] What was the evidence? The autopsy revealed no secret stash of crumpled bills tucked into a body cavity. Any suggestion that his anal engagements were remunerative made it only so far as one wire report—but that is all it took.

The implication is that Robert was infected with HIV during his prostitution. If he was 15 when he died of AIDS, chances are he contracted HIV as a preadolescent. This recalls Louis Dwight's observations in 1824: Isn't 7 (or 8, or 9) an awfully young age for a boy to be termed a *prostitute*? Preadolescent youth are considered unable to make consensual sexual decisions with adults. It would be more appropriate to say that if Robert R. was infected with HIV through sexual transmission, he had most likely been sexually abused.

But was he really infected with HIV at all? In 1987, Dr. Robert Garry used a primitive HIV test (a screening test called the ELISA, for enzyme-based immunosorbent assay) on Robert's serum. The results were consistently positive. Eighteen years after Robert's death, his confirmatory Western blot test also came up positive for HIV. All nine protein bands specific to HIV-antibodies were detected using a Biotech assay.[13] Robert's posthumous HIV results were published in the 1988 *JAMA* article, "Documentation of an AIDS Virus Infection in the United States in 1968," which was coauthored by Dr. Witte and Dr. Garry, among others. Although the HIV-antigen capture for Robert R.'s serum came back negative, Garry believed he had proof enough to declare, "There would be no question. He was infected with AIDS." Garry shared his thoughts with *Newsweek* a year before the results of his research were published.[14]

Other scientists were not as easily convinced. The CDC's own Harold Jaffe commented that "to find the virus in this particular patient is surprising. It's very puzzling that this would have appeared in a youth in middle America."[15] Polymerase chain reaction (PCR) testing was subsequently arranged, under the auspices of the Cetus Corporation's expert technician, John

Sninsky.[16] For the next *10 years,* not a word was heard, save Garry's preliminary claims that pro-viral HIV-DNA had been detected. Interviews Edward Hooper conducted with renowned AIDS researchers David Ho and Simon Wain-Hobson raised questions about this lengthy gap. Each scientist suggested that PCR tests repeatedly yielded *negative* results for HIV in samples of tissue from Robert's spleen, liver, lymph node, and brain.[17] In 1994, public health historian and Pulitzer Prize winner Laurie Garrett wrote, "The 'Robert R.' samples collected in 1968 in St. Louis did *not,* as it turned out, contain HIV."[18]

Finally, in apparent frustration, Garry retested the old tissue samples in 1997 and found that *all four samples* contained HIV-1-B (the strain predominant in the United States and Western Europe).[19] Despite Garry's claim that "it is unlikely that the results could be a laboratory contaminant," the viral sequences diverge by only 3% from standard lab clones isolated from HIV patients in the mid 1980s. The possibility of lab contamination might explain why these most recent findings have been published in newspapers rather than peer-reviewed medical journals.[20]

Certainly there is nothing wrong with historical curiosity: The more information we have about HIV's origins, the better our chances of predicting and managing its future evolution. But Garry was never interested in Robert R.'s behavioral history and made no attempt to research or re-create it. He instead relied on Witte's off-hand comments, even though she obtained virtually no information from the patient himself or his family. Plainly, Garry was interested only in proving that Robert R. was HIV-positive. The how was not

so important, and was easily imagined. And the journalists who encouraged his showmanship simply needed a story to sell.

In Garry's vision, perpetuated so enthusiastically by international media, the boy from St. Louis must have appeared a tight fit: a poor, black, gay prostitute, a diseased and deadly victim. The newspapers swallowed it whole. London's *Evening Standard* wrote about clues locked in "the frozen body of a 15-year-old rent boy."[21] *Agence France Press* wrote about "a male prostitute who died in 1969."[22] The *Sydney Morning Herald* summarized, "Unaware of HIV/AIDS at the time, doctors at St. Louis City Hospital froze tissue samples from a 15-year-old male prostitute from St. Louis, after his death from Kaposi's sarcoma, a cancer now linked to AIDS."[23]

Sensationalism aside, there is a sound reason that Robert R. got so much posthumous (if absurd) media play. American male and trans prostitutes *had* been infected with HIV at particularly high rates since the beginning of the epidemic. And this had not gone well reported at the time.[24]

In July 1981, Dr. Paul Volberding saw "a thin young man with pleading eyes" in the newly opened San Francisco General Hospital cancer clinic. The patient had the bluish-purple lesions associated with Kaposi's sarcoma, which baffled the attending physician. Volberding asked the patient what he did for a living. "I'm a hooker," the man answered. "Can you help me?"[25] Volberding remembers this as his first AIDS case, and the patient did not last long. "Homeless, moving from one San Francisco crash pad to another, the young prostitute would scrounge enough change every morning to buy a cup of coffee, a doughnut, and bus fare to the hospital," wrote Garrett. "In August, Volberding admitted him to the oncology ward: Soon, he was dead."[26]

Subsequent statistics are terrifying. Researchers studied HIV incidence among 235 street-based hustlers in Atlanta in 1987. They found that 29% were HIV-positive, and that a staggering 64% of transgendered sex workers had HIV. On one stroll 81% of transgender sex workers were infected with the virus.[27] In 1990, 37% of Atlanta-based clients of male prostitutes had HIV.[28] In 1988, scientists found that 53% of New York City male and trans hustlers harbored HIV.[29] Edward Morse's 1991 study found HIV infection in 17.5% of a group of 211 street-based adult male sex workers in New Orleans. Twenty percent of intravenous drug-using hustlers in this study were HIV-positive.[30] Morse concluded that his subjects were hopeless, isolated, and fatalistic: "Over two-thirds of the sample felt they had at least a 50% chance of getting AIDS."[31]

Paul Farmer, an anthropologist and medical doctor, argued that Haiti's AIDS epidemic likely resulted from sex tourism during the late 1970s and early 1980s, when American men traveled to Port-au-Prince to pay local boys, men, women, and girls for sex. "As Haiti became poorer," wrote Farmer, "both men's and women's bodies became cheaper. Although there have been no quantitative studies of Haitian urban prostitution, it was clear that a substantial sector of the trade catered to tourists, and especially North Americans."[32] Farmer saw causal similarities in other Caribbean islands, including Puerto Rico, the Dominican Republic, and Jamaica.

The bisexuality practiced by many male street hustlers in the 1980s was not as ritualized as it was in trade's heyday, the 1940s. Of the New Orleans sample, 81% identified themselves as heterosexual or bisexual, although almost half reported receiving anal sex. The great majority (79%) of gay-identified male sex workers had also done so. This gradual change in hustler sexual mores had lethal consequences.[33] Dennis Cooper, reporting in 1995 for *Spin* magazine, interviewed a young, homeless, HIV-positive hustler. When questioned about his acquisition of HIV, the young man replied:

> *Well, it was either from sharing needles with people I didn't know, or from letting guys fuck me without a condom, or from fucking girls I knew had AIDS without a condom. I could've been infected a hundred times, you know?*
>
> *I think, "Well, I could have gotten infected seven years ago, because I've been letting guys fuck me since I was 12." And I start to get really scared, and I think, "Fuck it, I'm going to kill myself now before I get sick." Because it's too much, you know?[34]*

This desolation pervaded the hustling community in the 1980s and 1990s. As sexual attitudes changed, clients came to expect more than they used to; fewer were satisfied with merely giving head to hustlers. Although any unprotected reciprocation could be sexually dangerous, protected sex was often a complete and drastic change in practice.

Joyce Hunter, founder and clinical supervisor of Project First

Step and the Harvey Milk School (a queer-friendly alternative high school) in Greenwich Village, recalls the issues that arose when talking with young hustlers about AIDS in the mid 1980s:

> *People were dying in that area, in Greenwich Village, a lot of the men. Looking out the window before school started one day, I caught one young person going into a limo. This kid got into this limo, we saw him coming, and we were watching, and our eyes went wide. He went into the car, because they motioned over to him. You know, we didn't intervene. And so when he comes back upstairs, I said something like, "I see you took a detour." "Oh, I didn't have sex," said the boy, "just gave him a blow job." So everybody's surprised that, you know, penetration is sex, a blow job is not sex. He had his breakfast and came to class, but you know, we said, "That's playing Russian roulette—did you use a condom?" He said, "No, that's safe." (I think it's Russian roulette, depending on what's going on in the mouth.)*
>
> *In any event, we got the young people to create comic books as a way of dealing with their stressful life events. And we taught HIV 101, what we knew at the time about AIDS and how it's transmitted. So they got a good sex education and an all-around kind of education on the street. Those kids were very bright. Sometimes you'd go out on the pier, and find one of those kids reading Walt Whitman. And at night, they'd be doing sex work.[35]*

Rock-Bottom Raspberries:
Crack and Sex Zones, 1986-2000

By 1986, crack cocaine was rife in American sex work zones. It quickly became the drug of choice among street-based hustlers because it was cheap ($5 per vial in 1989, $10 by 1995), easy to use (just toss it in the pipe and smoke it), and induced euphoria. Female prostitutes reported that the new breed of hooker, the "crack ho," was catastrophic for the dying street-sex economy, reducing prices during a period of national inflation. "Them chicken heads are bad for business," said one professional. "Them motherfuckers come from who knows where and start takin' dates."[36]

Crack-house ethnographers reported in 1993 that 12% of their male subjects (crack-house proprietors, dealers, drug runners, and customers) had, in the 30 days prior to interviewing, provided sex to others in exchange for money or drugs.[37] Male crack-users who hustled were most prevalent in Miami, where 41% reported exchanging sex for money. In New Orleans, researchers noted that 52% of street hustlers reported using crack or powder cocaine at least twice a week, with almost a third using cocaine daily.[38]

Sex-for-drugs exchanges increased with the national proliferation of crack, further straitening the economic circumstances of beleaguered sex workers.[39] "I want to tell you about something that we saw on the pier," said Hunter, referring to the old piers along the Harlem River from the West Village to Chelsea. "You could see kids go give somebody a blow job, get paid, go back, get some crack, and then run back to their stroll. And pick up somebody again, and then go back. It was back and forth for the drug."[40]

In Los Angeles, crack-using trannie sex workers felt ostracized by the gay community. "Society is willing to accept gay men, but not willing to accept transsexuals," one gal told an interviewer. "They [gays] don't want you around."[41] Denizens of L.A.'s crack scene distinguished by gender those who exchanged sex for crack: Women were known as *strawberries,* while men were called *raspberries.* (Trans street hustlers, depending on how well they passed, could fit into either category.) These sex-for-crack traders were "treated with scorn" by the crack-using community, including non-crack-using female prostitutes, who believed their competitors were "devaluing the profession."

Ironically, in Philadelphia, homophobia and sexism saved male prostitutes the humiliation that crack dealers laid on skeezers (women who had sex for crack). According to a male hustler named Lee:

> [A dealer] might get off on humiliating and having this girl give him a blow job in front of everybody, but he might feel a threat to his manhood to have a gay guy do that. That would be done [as] a more hush-hush sort of thing. And strictly kept between me and him. That's an unsaid, unwritten rule. It could be either for money or drugs.[42]

I know Lee's turf: In 1992 I spent seven months living in the crack and sex work zone of Center City Philadelphia, a grid between 12th and 16th Streets, from Lombard Avenue to Colfax. I observed that crack actually consolidated male, female, and trans hustling zones as it monopolized the street drug trade. Some hustlers settled for crack just because it was *available.* Mitch, a 21-year-old white male, tried to buy marijuana from a street dealer, but got something else instead:

> He said, "Look, if you really don't trust me, just take this shit, just take this." And he gives me this pack of Newports. And then he's off. And I look at his retreating form and wonder, What am I gonna do with a fucking pack of Newports? You know, you can always get Newports....
>
> Anyway, so he doesn't come back with the buds [marijuana]. He doesn't come back and he doesn't come back, and it's 15, 20 minutes later. Hos on every corner, I'm standing there, like, where the fuck is this man? 40 minutes go by, I said, "Fuck it...I'm not going to see him again," and flicked open his pack of Newports 'cause I thought, "Well at least I'll get something out of this." And all I found was a vial of crack.
>
> I took it out. I looked inside. It was full. I shook it back and forth.... I put a move on and jumped back to my apartment. And I called my girlfriend. I told her, "Yo, I just scored some crack by mistake." So she agreed to come down the next weekend to smoke it.[43]

By 1987, crack had taken over Times Square as well. Robert McNamara, an ethnographer, interviewed Port Authority hustlers in the late 1980s. By then, the boys were primarily nonwhite: 86% were Hispanic, 11% were African American, and 3% were Caucasian. They ranged in age from 14 to 35. Older hustlers were treated as respected elders and were likely to have links to community-based outreach programs. Seventy-seven percent of McNamara's hustlers identified themselves as heterosexual or bisexual, while 23% identified as gay and/or transgender.[44] While heroin, alcohol, and marijuana use had long been features of hustling communities, crack wreaked havoc.

McNamara interviewed a young hustler named Pretty Boy Tony, who remarked that crack had led both to an increase in extortion and to a decrease in the set rate:

> See, the hustlin' rate around here has dropped, OK? Because a lot of crackheads started robbing the tricks, all right? Instead of treating the guy right and doin' the right thing for the guy. But these motherfuckin' crackheads is makin' it harder on me to make a livin'. Say I normally charge $25 to $35, OK? And then some crackhead comes along, and he all fucked up, well maybe he say he go for $5 or even $3. Now you a trick, what you gonna do? You goin' with the $5 trick right? Well then how am I supposed to make a livin'? Some fuckin' crackhead come along and charge less than me, and then sometimes they do more than they should for that $5. It fucks it up for everybody else.[45]

In 1996, Samuel Delany, a participant-observer of the Times Square movie house scene from the 1960s through the 1990s, interviewed two hustlers in their 20s: an African-American man named Darrell and a Caucasian kid named Dave. Darrell said of his white friend, "Man, that nigger wants a hit of crack *so* bad...I stopped smoking it myself last week. But that nigger...will do *anything* for his hit!"[46] Canno, another hustler interviewed by McNamara, wailed, "You see these sorry-sorry-ass motherfuckers chasin' down a trick for a dollar, lettin' themselves get fucked in the ass or whipped and shit for a vial." As a vial of crack sold for as little as $3 in Times Square in the late 1980s, the price for sex dropped accordingly.[47]

Will, a veteran hustler I met in 1995 in Minneapolis, told me about his own experiences with hustling and crack:

> Man, I've wound up in bed with people just for crack. I've known other straight guys that come down here just for money to spend on crack. I mean, I'm bisexual, I guess, my lover is a drag queen, but I've been married, I have a daughter. You won't believe how much money's been through these hands in 15 years. Fifteen years of hustling and nothing to show for it. I've done tricks for $20 and I've done weekend getaways for $2,500. There's street prostitution, escort services, all kind of forms of prostitution, but it's all the same. It's fast money, so you don't appreciate it. And if you got a drug habit, forget about it, it's all going to the habit.[48]

When I met Will, I was working for StreetWorks, a consortium of social service agencies that enlisted outreach workers to concentrate on homeless and runaway youth in the Twin Cities. Loring Park, a tree-lined slope with a faulty fountain in a residential and fairly gay neighborhood, was the main hustler stroll.

Of 10 full-time Loring Park sex workers, eight smoked crack every day. Even in Minnesota, half of the regular hustlers were nonwhite. Crack dealers operated from quiet corners difficult to patrol by car, but easy to slink down to from Loring. The two youngest boys (Donahue, a 17-year-old estranged from his mother, and Newcomer, 15-year-old farm boy runaway) were the only ones who did not smoke crack daily. Because of their youth, whiteness, and chemical independence, Donahue and Newcomer were able to charge $40 to $50 per trick. This was twice as much as what clients would pay transgendered, African-American crack-users working the same stroll. One 19-year-old trans girl lived with her mother; her cash went to the household, and she shared her crack with her mom.[49]

Violence associated with the crack trade escalated in the 1980s and 1990s, making American sex work zones more physically dangerous than ever before. The great majority of Minneapolis hustlers had been stabbed, beaten, or raped during sexual exchanges. Mario, a 25-year-old Native American from Michigan, pulled up his shirt to reveal six pink slashes across his belly, scars he had sustained during a sex-for-crack date in Orlando. "He stabbed me six times and left me for dead," Mario said. "After I moved up here I heard one of my friends got killed down there."[50]

In Southern California, crack was just one of many easily obtained, comparatively cheap illegal drugs. G. Cajetan Luna's heartrending studies of runaway, sex-working, HIV-positive youth recall Cooper's *Spin* reportage. Jose, a runaway poster-boy, said he used "cocaine, crack, everything except heroin. Crystal meth, I shot up three times."[51] Crystal methamphetamine, the crack of the speed family, shared popularity with rock cocaine on West Coast strolls for the last 15 years. Crystal is more expensive than crack, but its effects last for hours rather than minutes. More significantly, crystal often heightens sexual arousal and response, whereas crack inhibits them. But crystal binges interfere with memory. One HIV-positive ex-hustler could not account for more than a few scattered days of his 16-month crystal habit. "When I think back on certain months, I just draw a blank. It's like it's just...all black," he said.[52]

The HIV-positive boys whom Luna interviewed were gay and bisexual runaways who engaged in sex work shortly after leaving home. (This is not surprising: In many cities, over 30% of homeless and runaway youth are assumed to be sexual minorities, and 85% of males began their sex work when broke, on the run, and in need of money, food, and shelter.[53]) Most of Luna's subjects had been multiple drug users during prostitution and developed friendships through such shared spaces as shelters, drop-in centers, and the streets. There was no one else left to protect them. With only a sprinkling of raggedy veterans left, young squatters and drifters had the sidewalks to themselves by the mid 1990s.

Hi, I'm Not From L.A.: Escort Revival, 1980-2000

In the 1930s, New York City male brothels stayed afloat by flitting from one location to another, only to be pinned down by the May Act of 1942. In the 1950s, a few brothels surfaced in major cities, drawing customers mainly by word of mouth. In the late 1960s, however, these small businesses began to use new gay media channels—mainly local newspapers—to advertise their services and attract employees. Dial-A-Model agencies in New York, Los Angeles, and San Francisco were successful in the early and middle 1970s, but eventually all of them had run-ins with the law. By the mid 1980s, however, brothels were back, taking advantage of a gay media network that was expanding with gay liberation and the need to provide AIDS information.

"Models," "masseurs," and "call boys" were the male brothel code words of the 1970s. By the 1980s, the term "escort" had been reappropriated from its gigolo history; it had already caught on as euphemism for female call girls. Its innocent evocation of dance halls and Latin lovers helped male and transgendered escorts envision themselves as an elite subcategory of sex workers, paid for their time as well as their sexual agreeableness. The phraseology emphasized professionalism, reliability, and companionship, freeing it from the mercenary, crack-addled, and homophobic connotations of the "hustler." ("Could it be that hustling is against all the new activism?" wrote Sam Steward in a letter to John Preston. "And therefore not approved of?")[54]

For two decades, the *Advocate* ran classified pages in which both individual entrepreneurs and escort agencies could advertise. In 1992, this section turned into *Advocate Classifieds,* where sex work advertisements shared space with the personals. Local gay newspapers quickly followed suit, printing "X-rated" pullout sections in the late 1980s and the 1990s. Many independent newspapers like the *Village Voice* also began to accept ads from individuals and agencies. And *Frontiers,* soon to become an escort-only ad magazine, began to disseminate personal advertisements in 1980.

But these windfalls of the liberation movement posed a new set of problems. On the streets, hustlers instinctively learned how to avoid violent dates and scamming clients by reading visual and verbal cues during initial negotiations and by heeding the advice of more experienced hustlers. The safety of agency work was solely the responsibility of the proprietor: If a madam discouraged an atmosphere of peer support and screened new clients poorly, the agency's sex workers were at the mercy of their tricks. My own experiences (detailed in the Introduction) are an example. For a new sex worker, established escort agencies have plenty to offer when they're properly run. When they aren't, sex work sinks into the same potholes associated with the street: fractious social support, problems negotiating sex acts and pricing, distrust and contempt between workers and clients, and high potential for violence and sexual danger.

Still, the financial rewards of escort work exceed those of street work. In his 1999 book *Hustlers, Escorts, and Porn Stars,* veteran sex worker Matt Adams wrote that although rates varied from market to market, "The predominant fee in the United States [was]

$150. The agency typically gets one third of the fee." Adams claimed that New York City escorts commanded $250 (or 10 times what street hustlers asked for), while Los Angeles escorts started at $50 (similar to street prices, after the agency cut). Adams offered these thoughts on the dramatic difference in pricing:

> Clients should not say they are from Los Angeles. Clients from Los Angeles are known as the worst possible clients and are rarely repeat clients. Clients from Los Angeles are accustomed to a broad assortment of available escorts and typically see someone new every time. Clients from Los Angeles are also accustomed to lower pricing than exists in much of the country since rates typically start at $50. Clients from Los Angeles who do not say they are from Los Angeles are generally exceptions to this rule.... Individuals who are dishonest give clues to their dishonesty. The phrase, "Hello, I'm visiting from Los Angeles," seems to be synonymous with the phrase "trust me."[55]

While filled with such unintended hilarities, Adams's book remains a good guide for escorts, their clients, and proprietors. It includes comprehensive listings of local and national advertising venues, a discussion of common sexually transmitted infections, and a chapter on the overlap between escorts and porn stars. But he does make some oddball recommendations. In a section about how an escort can maintain his personal appearance, Adams suggests exercise, hair and nail treatments, proper nutrition, Armani clothing, the use of tanning beds, and plastic surgery. "Fortunately," Adams wrote, "with the help of high quality plastic surgeons escorts can prolong their youth until after 40 years of age. The most common forms of plastic surgery are liposuction, chest implants, hair transplants, and facial surgery."[56]

America's escort market also embraced transgendered workers. Four trans gals I knew in Minneapolis started an agency that many street queens aspired to join. As was the case elsewhere, the rates were higher and the business more regular. Finding a boon in the racist appetites of some of their clients, two male-identified African-American Minneapolis teens worked as trans girls in both street and escort settings. One told me, "I don't even get hormones. I just grease my hair and smack my lip gloss. Tricks want the in-between—the *exotic*."[57] The other said, "I could hit the streets as a boy. But I wouldn't get picked up. Tricks won't pick me up as a black boy because they think I'm [going to] roll them. But at the agency, or on the streets, I can say, 'I'm Secret,' in my little high-pitch, and they say, 'Let's go girl.' My falsetto and my stilettos."[58]

As its popularity crested, the escort market even reenfranchised older male sex workers, who had been gradually edged out of the competition by teenage hustlers since the onset of World War II. In San Francisco in the early 1990s, Greg Roberts began escorting even though he was in his late 30s and had a successful career as a certified public accountant. He began his escort work more for pleasure than economic necessity.

For me, doing sex work was pure fun. There were no bad feelings surrounding what I was doing. I was providing a service that others wanted and were willing to pay $100 to have. My ads had this slogan: "Pleasure For All Ages," and were meant to attract older men, as well as younger ones. I think the oldest man I ever worked for must have been in his 70s, and showed up on crutches and a cast on his leg. We hugged and kissed for the entire hour. That was all he really wanted, just to be held and given some close attention. And I did that, and still do that, very well indeed.

I was thoroughly excited by this dual life I was leading, being the professional CPA by day and another type of "professional" at night! I never felt any fear about what I was doing and, fortunately, never did have any bad encounters. I found my sex clients basically friendly men who wanted some attention and closeness. Being the outgoing type I am, this work was easy and fun for me. I loved the attention too! Sure, there was always the minor concern that I'd be busted by the police, but it seemed like that was not something that was occurring with much frequency, at least not with the sex workers advertising out of the paper. I was never a street-walker type of prostitute, which I'm sure carries with it much more danger, both from bad johns and from the police. I also was clean and sober, and doing the work not only because I did need the money but also because I really enjoyed the work.[59]

Greg's account is representative of the experience of many older male escorts, who were comfortable with their sexuality and knew the gay scene well enough to avoid conflict, have fun, and make money. It is notably different from the ambivalent and often harrowing histories given by younger workers, whether street-based or house-based.

Roberts charged a basic rate of $100, much more than what street-based hustlers were making. Kirk Read, an essayist and activist, interviewed a Polk Street hustler in 1997: "It's $20 if they want a hand job, $40 if they want to blow you, $60 if you blow them," the man told Read.[60] In the economic boom times of the 1990s, market-savvy hustlers dropped off the streets and began to advertise. Read interviewed a female-to-male sex worker who found that escort arrangements were infinitely safer than street assignations. After advertising his services in a fetish publication, Terry concluded:

> *When johns find out you're not the kind of boy they thought you were, they freak out. I've been hit I don't know how many times. Who are we going to tell—the police? Nowadays my clients know exactly what they're getting, and with a phone I can make sure they're clear about who I am.[61]*

When *Advocate Classifieds* became *Unzipped* in 1996, personal advertising rates soared 40% (from $5 per line to $8 per line), causing many mainstream escorts to publish ads in local specialty magazines and, by the late 1990s, on the Internet.

When the World Wide Web became accessible to the masses, sex and porn were the commodities most often exchanged. Sex workers, procurers, and clients fashioned their own chat rooms, like America Online's EscortsM4M; created their own Web sites, like Rentboy.com and escorts4you.com; and used bulletin boards hosted by such reputable gay spaces as OnQ, PlanetOut, Gay.com, and Rainbow Classifieds. The Web allowed male and trans sex workers to reach a much larger pool of potential clients without exposing themselves to a hostile public or jeopardizing their anonymity. Through this targeted advertising, Internet escorts learned to circumvent a host of age-old dangers.

Of course, Internet sex workers must have access to a computer, the knowledge to work it, a picture of themselves in a readable format, a separate phone line, and money for an Internet service provider, all instruments indicative of social advantage. Whom does the Internet exclude? Runaways, throwaways, transients, the poor: 21st-century hobos. In short, the Internet excludes the underclass.

In particular, the Internet has left underage sex workers, whose advertisements are monitored and deleted by Webmasters, out in the sleet. Sex crimes units have shifted their focus in the last 50 years from adult male brothels to adult-adolescent sex. Denied admission to a safer environment, sex-working youths who can't pass for 18 (on the Internet) or 21 (in gay bars) are, by default, forced onto the streets, into a work environment far more threatening than cyberspace.

Like late imperial Rome, contemporary America has turned street hustling—a primal, recurring social behavior—into an endeavor practically guaranteed to dehumanize and degrade. The difference is that we have achieved this distortion more through restriction than through excess. Rather than attempt to improve the bleak social conditions of a marginalized population, we make those conditions even more desperate. And in doing so, we *create* the circumstances to affirm our belief that adolescent male and trans prostitutes are diseased, sex-obsessed, degenerate animals. Societies make their own monsters.

The Disney Zone: Urban Redevelopment, 1980-2000

AIDS, crack, and the escort revival had a partner in displacing street hustling: urban redevelopment. Facing the disturbing trend of white flight from core cities and the concomitant urban sprawl, city governments have lately allied themselves with developers and contractors tied to chain corporations intent on selling their merchandise on sterilized and tightly controlled street corners. Sadly, liberals and conservatives often cooperate in this movement toward a culturally homogenous corporate hegemony.[62] This section will explore the effects of such collusion on the street-based sexual economies of New York City, Minneapolis, Pittsburgh, and San Francisco.

City planners first proposed the present redevelopment of Times Square in the early 1980s, when the square had become so dangerous that tourists were afraid to change trains there. Of course, the square had been dangerous since the 1930s; its character had not drastically changed in 50 years. By the early 1980s, however, the face of danger—both perceived and actual—was no longer (only) white: The square's hustlers were just as likely to be Puerto Ricans and African-Americans whose neighborhoods were too impoverished to support their own sexual economies. The same eradication mentality that closed down the San Francisco bathhouses in 1985 helped demolish Times Square movie houses, live sex theaters, peep shows, and porn stores.[63] This combination of corporate deference, subtle racism, and AIDS panic made it easy for Mayor Ed Koch to create the 42nd Street Development Project.

This ambitious project will have cost the city over $3 billion by the time it is completed. Four massive office structures were proposed, and building has begun in earnest. The Port Authority transportation center has been wired for video surveillance; central command is located directly outside the second-floor tearooms. Arcades popular with street youth have been removed and replaced by coffee shops and magazine stores catering to tourists. The erotic movie houses, peep shows, and porn booths that lined the 42nd Street corridor are no more; a Disney store, a Loews multiplex, and new high-rises dominate a once-vibrant landscape. A new Gap has replaced an old residential Laundromat. Under scaffolding, police officers comb the curbs. Bryant Park has undergone landscaping; it is lit at night and closely monitored. There is no more hustling in Times Square.

Most sex-oriented businesses were closed from 1992 to 2000, during Mayor Rudy Giuliani's administration, which claimed to be "restoring the historic theater district." This verbiage masked a class war; for Times Square sex workers, the effects resembled Reconstruction more than restoration. The days of a chaste Times Square entertainment district were long gone by the 1930s, when movie houses turned to pornography to attract customers during an era of fierce competition and skyrocketing rents.[64] But did the restoration of the theater district have to mean a return to mid 1920s morality, shrink-wrapped and stamped with a corporate logo?

Street hustlers tried many strategies to adapt to the 42nd Street Development Project. They modified their geography: Some strolled down Eighth Avenue, away from the construction and police, and some moved southward to Chelsea and Greenwich Village. "Once they started gentrifying, those young people that were hanging out at Port Authority started coming south," recalls Joyce Hunter. "Drug users and sex workers were all being pushed to this area." Bruce Benderson, whose 1994 novel *User* follows a street boy named Apollo through Times Square's reconstruction, depicted this displacement. As his streets turn increasingly unfriendly, Apollo notices that:

> No one belonged to the old crowd. Those that
> were left...were all on Eighth or Ninth Avenue, with-
> out any bar to go to.... It was all part of a plan, he
> realized in his most lucid moments, to clean up
> Times Square. But who devised this plan, and how

had he enlisted so many supporters? Part of the plan had obviously been what turned 42nd Street, the main drag, into a ghost town.[65]

In real life, hustlers cited fears of keener competition, reduced peer support, and heightened violence. The diaries of teenager Luis Miguel Fuentes obsess over the shutdown of two video arcades called Playland, havens for underage hustlers on the north end of Times Square. "Damn, only two weeks left and they gonna close Playland. Playlands I should say because the death of one will bring the death of the next," he wrote in 1995. "I'll tell ya, it didn't take long for the deuce to become my home. Playland to be exact. The change attendants became my parents and the other kids became my brothers."[66] And a young hustler named Paco fretted,

> *Man, what we gonna do when they shut down all the shops and shit? How we gonna make a living? The peep shows is the way I make my money, you know what I'm sayin'? ...Like if I gotta do stickups, 'cause hustlin' has died around here, then that's what I'm gonna do. I don't want to do that 'cause if I get caught, I'm going upstate [prison]. I would rather hang out, chill, and hustle a few tricks, and everybody's happy. But if they cut that off from me, then [**pause**] man why do they gotta make it so hard for us? All we tryin' to do is survive, like everybody else.[67]*

Paco's braggadocio might sound menacing, but it reminds us that male prostitution is usually a misdemeanor offense. Because it is inapplicable to third-strike, mandatory-maximum felony sentences that propose to curb recidivism, it is not a crime that juveniles with criminal histories are concerned about committing.[68]

Redevelopment in Manhattan also exacerbated class tensions between different segments of the queer community. Former Times Square hustlers who tried to work in Greenwich Village watched the same thing happen. During the late 1990s, some waterfront piers were systematically demolished to widen biking trails, and others were leased to health clubs like Chelsea Piers, which rebuilt over abandoned warehouses that had long been ideal venues for public and commercial sex. Shira Hassan, a social worker concentrating on homeless queer youth, wrote:

> *Gentrification has really affected my work. The historic areas are Christopher and 10th Avenue and 14th Street—for queer kids—and 43rd between 9th and 10th Avenues. Almost all of these strolls have been shut down because of increased police presence and gentrification problems. In the Village, the middle class (HRC- Human Rights Campaign) "gays and lesbians"—the folks I call the "Will and Grace gays"— have pushed out the trans folks and the gay kids. Disney has all but taken over Times Square. Many [male and trans hustlers] are working sex stores and hanging out in clubs. But it's really, really bad here right now.[69]*

Hassan remarked that yuppie Village queers—terrified of non-white, sex-working youth—had conceived an organization called Residents in Distress (RID).[70]

RID colluded with police to disrupt 14th Street's transgender hustler culture, which had been active for at least 70 years. "We experience horrible classist, racist transphobia at every town meeting we go to," Shira said. "The gays are trying to get rid of the youth who they think are prostitutes whether they are or not. They are uninterested in the need for survival sex and the reasons why youth get involved."[71]

This shift away from street-based sex work was not confined to Manhattan. The same trend was apparent in hustler zones across the country. In Pittsburgh, traffic patterns along Dithridge Street changed in the mid 1980s, when city officials erected signs to prohibit cruising at night. Mellon Square, which had been a hustling zone since it was finished in 1960, saw heavy police intervention in the late 1990s, supported by 24-hour security guards employed by surrounding hotels and banks. In 1999, a nearby sex worker/crack bar, Sambino's, was closed in the interest of "preserving the historic theater district." In 2000, the square itself was flooded with light from the newly illuminated William Penn Hotel, and another sex work arena with a decades-long legacy was no more.

Trans sex workers who could pass as women continued to work Pittsburgh streets, while male sex workers who couldn't find johns through escort agencies, gay bars, or the Internet faced abject poverty. Younger male hustlers lost contact with more experienced hustlers and the sex work education and peer support they provided. An 11-year-old Pittsburgh boy named Scott Drake was found below a highway overpass in September 2000, murdered and mutilated by his client after engaging in remunerative oral sex. Would he have fared better in the Mellon Square of the 1980s, surrounded by veteran hustlers?

In Minneapolis, the south section of Hennepin Avenue, which had linked downtown hustling to Loring Park cruising in the 1970s and 1980s, was commercialized by the early 1990s, dotted with bright street lights and bagel shops. Hennepin's enormous porn warehouses, warm indoor spaces ideal for wintering hustlers, were empty by 1999. Their closure followed years of escalating rents and concerted antipornography protests initiated by the reactionary feminists Catherine MacKinnon, Andrea Dworkin, and Evelina Giobbe. Since 1996, Loring Park had witnessed unceasing road construction, intensified police patrols, and frequent protests by citizens' watch groups representing the predominatcly gay neighborhood.[72]

In San Francisco's Tenderloin, downtown redevelopment has scattered the indigenous population. Hustlers can no longer afford to live in the community where they work; the streets are left to the homeless. In Los Angeles, the aggressive police patrols that began in earnest in the 1970s coincided in the 1990s with a revitalization of West Hollywood by wealthy gay residents. Numbers, the once-notorious hustler bar, has moved to a busy, mainstream section of Sunset Boulevard, a sedate victim of its own hustler chic.[73] A trip to Selma Avenue is rewarded with manicured lawns and the faded echoes of a bygone era. Likewise in San Diego, "Cannibal Park," a popular public sex and hustling venue during the 1960s and 1970s, became the tony "Gaslight District" by the 1990s.[74] San Diego's steamy military trade scene was absorbed by a newly affluent gay community, which quickly established successful escort agencies and kept-boy networks.[75]

For these and other former street sex zones across the country, economic redevelopment was the last blow for a community already decimated by AIDS, crack, assimilationist queer politics, and America's historical lack of compassion, even in times of economic prosperity, for the underclass.

[1] MAROTTA, P. 46.

[2] XIITH INTERNATIONAL CONGRESS OF VIROLOGY: SYDNEY, AUSTRALIA, AUGUST 8-13, 1999.

[3] HOOPER, EDWARD. *THE RIVER.* LITTLE, BROWN & COMPANY: LONDON, 1999; PP. 133-137.

[4] SEE ROBERT R.'S AUTOPSY NOTES, REPRINTED IN HOOPER, P. 135.

[5] IBID., P. 134; ALSO SEE THE *TORONTO STAR,* OCTOBER 25, 1987; P. A20.

[6] WITTE, MARLYS ET AL. "AIDS IN 1968." *JOURNAL OF THE AMERICAN MEDICAL ASSOCIATION.* MAY 25, 1984; P. 2657.

[7] DODGE, LORI. "DOCTORS WONDERING WHETHER TEEN HAD AIDS IN 1969." *ASSOCIATED PRESS,* OCTOBER 27, 1987.

[8] "TEENAGER HAD AIDS 10 YEARS BEFORE FIRST CASE, MD SAYS." *TORONTO STAR.* OCTOBER 27, 1987; P. A20. [9] HOOPER, P. 135.

[10] ELVIN-LEWIS, MEMORY AND MARLYS WITTE, ET AL.: "SYSTEMIC CHLAMYDIAL INFECTION ASSOCIATED WITH GENERALIZED LYMPHEDEMA AND LYMPHANGIOSARCOMA." *LYMPHOLOGY* 6, 1973; PP. 113-121. ALSO SEE WITTE, *JAMA,* 1984; AND WITTE AND ROBERT GARRY ET AL., "DOCUMENTATION OF AN AIDS VIRUS INFECTION IN THE UNITED STATES." *JAMA,* 1988; 260 (14), PP. 2085-2087.

[11] ELVIN-LEWIS AND WITTE, ET AL., IN *LYMPHOLOGY,* 1973; WITTE ET AL., IN *JAMA,* 1984; WITTE AND GARRY, ET AL., IN *JAMA,* 1988.

[12] *U.S. NEWS & WORLD REPORT.* NOVEMBER 9, 1987; PG. 16. "THE SURPRISING DEATH OF ROBERT R."

[13] WITTE AND GARRY ET AL, *JAMA,* 1988. NOW NOTORIOUS FOR OVERSENSITIVITY, THE FIRST-GENERATION BIOTECH ASSAY WAS IMPLICATED FOR FALSE POSITIVE RESULTS IN ANOTHER RETROSPECTIVE TESTING CAMPAIGN, WHEREIN SERA EXTRACTED IN 1971 FROM INTRAVENOUS DRUG USERS WERE TESTED IN 1985 FOR HIV. ONE PERCENT OF THESE SAMPLES WAS FOUND TO BE POSITIVE ON THE BIOTECH WESTERN BLOTS. HOWEVER, FOLLOW-UP TRACKING AND TESTING INDICATED THAT NO ONE WAS ACTUALLY HIV-INFECTED. SEE MOORE, J.D. AND S.S. ALEXANDER, ET AL., "HTLV-III SEROPOSITIVITY IN 1971-1972 PARENTERAL DRUG ABUSERS—A CASE OF FALSE POSITIVES OR EVIDENCE OF VIRAL EXPOSURE?" *NEW ENGLAND JOURNAL OF MEDICINE,* 1986, 314 (21); P.P. 1387-1388.

[14] CLARK, MATT AND DANIEL SHAPIRO: "A NEW CLUE IN THE AIDS MYSTERY." *NEWSWEEK,* NOVEMBER 9, 1987; P. 62.

[15] TOUGHILL, KELLY: "EXPERTS WARY OF CLAIMS AIDS KILLED TEEN IN '69." *TORONTO STAR,* OCTOBER 15, 1988; P. A4.

[16] SEE HOOPER, P. 136.

[17] IBID., PP. 362-363, 496.

[18] GARRETT, LAURIE. *THE COMING PLAGUE.* PENGUIN (NYC), 1994; P. 380.

[19] GARRY, ET AL.: "THE EARLIEST KNOWN AIDS PATIENT IN THE UNITED STATES WAS INFECTED WITH AN HIV-1 STRAIN CLOSELY RELATED TO IIIB/LAI." PUBLISHED AS AN ABSTRACT FOR THE XIITH INTERNATIONAL CONGRESS OF VIROLOGY, 1999.

[20] HOOPER NOTES GENTLY THAT THIS DIVERGENCE IS A LITTLE "TOO CLOSE FOR COMFORT." (ON THE OTHER HAND, MICROBIOLOGIST ALAN BERKMAN WROTE, "A 3-5% VARIANCE IS JUST WHAT WE WOULD EXPECT." PERSONAL COMMUNICATION, SEPTEMBER 2000.)

[21] *EVENING STANDARD* (LONDON), AUGUST 11, 1999; P. 4. "BOY DIED IN 1969 OF AIDS."

[22] *AGENCE FRANCE PRESSE,* AUGUST 11, 1999. "FROZEN BODY PUTS BACK AIDS'

ENTRY TO U.S."

[23] SYDNEY MORNING HERALD. AUGUST 11, 1999. "AIDS CLUE FROM BODY FROZEN OVER 30 YEARS." THE ARTICLE'S LANGUAGE SUGGESTS THAT ST. LOUIS HOSPITALS ROUTINELY MADE POPSICLES OF DEAD BOY PROSTITUTES, IN SOME MEDICALLY SANCTIONED, DAHMERESQUE EXPERIMENT THAT HAD FINALLY BORE STRANGE FRUIT.

[24] WHEN THE MEDIA DID REPORT ON HIV RISKS FOR MALE SEX WORKERS, THEY SEEMED NOT TO COMPREHEND TRANSMISSION ROUTES. ED SAVITZ, AN HIV-POSITIVE FETISH CLIENT FROM PHILADELPHIA, WAS ARRESTED IN 1990 AFTER HAVING "SUPPORTED GENERATIONS OF PHILADELPHIA HIGH SCHOOLERS." HE WAS LABELED AN "AIDS/SEX OFFENDER." THOUGH SAVITZ DID NOT ENGAGE IN SEX WITH THESE YOUNGSTERS (HE BOUGHT THEIR UNDERWEAR, SOCKS, AND OTHER SOILED ITEMS) AND THUS DID NOT PRESENT ANY RISK OF TRANSMISSION, HE WAS VILIFIED, "TREATED LIKE A MONSTER, A LUNATIC, A MURDERER, A CRIMINAL" BY LOCAL AND NATIONAL PRESS. SEE ALEXANDRA JUHASZ. AIDS TV. DUKE UNIVERSITY PRESS (NC), 1995; PP. 177-178.

[25] GARRETT, P. 286.

[26] IBID., PP. 289-290.

[27] BOLES, JACQUELINE AND KIRK ELIFSON, "THE SOCIAL ORGANIZATION OF TRANSVESTITE PROSTITUTION AND AIDS." SOCIAL SCIENCE AND MEDICINE, JULY 1994, #39(1), PP. 85-93.

[28] SEE ELIFSON, KIRK WITH JACQUELINE BOLES, WILLIAM DARROW, AND CLAIRE STERK. "HIV SEROPREVALENCE AND RISK FACTORS AMONG CLIENTS OF FEMALE AND MALE PROSTITUTES." JOURNAL OF ACQUIRED IMMUNE DEFICIENCY SYNDROMES AND HUMAN RETROVIROLOGY, VOL. 20, NO. 2 (FEBRUARY 1999); PP. 195-200.

[29] CHIASSON, M.A. ET AL. "HIV-1 SEROPREVALENCE IN MALE AND FEMALE PROSTITUTES IN NEW YORK CITY." ABSTRACT FROM THE SIXTH INTERNATIONAL CONFERENCE ON AIDS (STOCKHOLM, SWEDEN, JUNE 1988).

[30] MORSE, E.V. ET AL. "THE MALE STREET PROSTITUTE: A VECTOR FOR TRANSMISSION OF HIV INFECTION INTO THE HETEROSEXUAL WORLD." SOCIAL SCIENCE AND MEDICINE, 32 (1991); PP. 535-539. INTRAVENOUS-DRUG-USING, WHITE MALE PROSTITUTES OVER 25 YEARS OF AGE HAD THE HIGHEST HIV INCIDENCE RATE: 25%. MALE HUSTLERS OF COLOR WHO DID NOT INJECT DRUGS AND WERE UNDER 25 HAD A PREVALENCE RATE OF 19%. BUT WHITE HUSTLERS UNDER 25 WHO DID NOT INJECT DRUGS HAD AN INCIDENCE RATE OF ONLY 8%. HETEROSEXUALLY-IDENTIFIED WORKERS (THE MAJORITY OF THEIR POPULATION) WERE MUCH LESS LIKELY TO HAVE HIV. THIS LAST FINDING IS ESPECIALLY IRONIC, IMPLYING AS IT DOES THAT THE SOCIOSEXUAL RESTRICTIONS OF "TRADE" COULD HAVE FUNCTIONED TO PROTECT THEM FROM HIV. THEY BELIEVED, ERRONEOUSLY, THAT THE RECEPTIVE PARTNER IN AN ACT OF FELLATIO COULDN'T CONTRACT THE DISEASE.

[31] SIMON, PATRICIA M., WITH EDWARD MORSE, HOWARD OSOFSKY, PAUL BALSON, AND H. RICHARD GAUMER. "PSYCHOLOGICAL CHARACTERISTICS OF A SAMPLE OF MALE STREET PROSTITUTES." ARCHIVES OF SEXUAL BEHAVIOR, VOL. 21, NO. 1, 1992; PP. 33-44.

[32] FARMER, PAUL. AIDS AND ACCUSATION: HAITI AND THE GEOGRAPHY OF BLAME. UNIVERSITY OF CALIFORNIA PRESS, 1992; PP. 146-147.

[33] A PERSONAL EXAMPLE: IN 1998 I TOOK THE TRAIN TO PROVIDENCE TO LOOK AT THE ARCHIVES OF WRITER AND HUSTLER JOHN PRESTON, WHO DIED FROM AIDS COMPLICATIONS IN 1996. I MADE A LIST OF 21 HUSTLERS WHO CORRESPONDED WITH PRESTON IN THE LATE 1980S AND EARLY 1990S. I WROTE LETTERS TO EACH ONE, ASKING WHETHER THEY WOULD LIKE TO SUBMIT HISTORIES FOR AN ONGOING PROJECT. OF THOSE 21 LETTERS, 17 WERE RETURNED TO ME WITH THE POST OFFICE STAMP "DECEASED." IN THE LAST YEAR ALONE, TWO HUSTLERS I KNEW DIED; THEY HAD BEEN INFECTED SINCE THEIR MID-TEENS.

[34] COOPER, DENNIS. "AIDS: WORDS FROM THE FRONT." SPIN, JULY 1995. ALSO SEE COOPER, ALL EARS: CULTURAL CRITICISM, ESSAYS AND OBITUARIES, SOFT SKULL PRESS (NYC), 1999, PP. 1-11; AND COOPER, GUIDE, GROVE PRESS, 1997, PP. 127-151.

[35] ORAL HISTORY WITH JOYCE HUNTER, CONDUCTED BY AUTHOR AND P. JAYNE BOPP.

[36] INCIARDI, JAMES. "THE MIAMI SEX-FOR-CRACK MARKET." IN MITCHELL RATNER, CRACK PIPE AS PIMP. LEXINGTON (MA), 1993; P. 62.

[37] RATNER, P. 11. AS A COMPARISON, 45% OF FEMALES IN THE CRACK PURLIEU HAD EXCHANGED SEX FOR MONEY OR DRUGS.

[38] Morse, Edward with Patricia Simon, Stephanie Baus, Paul Balson, and Howard Osofsky. "Cofactors of Substance Use Among Male Street Prostitutes." *Journal of Drug Issues,* 22 (4), 1992; p. 984.

[39] See Ratner, p. 91: "The major trends in [crack] cocaine-era prostitution appear to be a more monomaniacal fixation on procuring the drug of choice, an increase in the trading of sex for drugs, perhaps an increase in sexual activity in return for drugs or money for drugs, and a greater desperation that is reflected at the least in decreased prices for sex."

[40] Oral history with Joyce Hunter.

[41] Ratner, p. 174.

[42] French, John. "Crack and the Life in Philadelphia and Newark." In Ratner, pp. 225-226.

[43] Oral history with Mitch, June 1998.

[44] McNamara suggests that gay-identified hustlers were more common along Christopher Street, and on 53rd Street between First and Second Avenues, consistent with Marotta's 1982 assessment and Hunter's recollections.

[45] McNamara, *The Times Square Hustler: Male Prostitution in New York City.* Praeger (CT), 1994; p. 85. For demographic statistics, see pp. 36-38.

[46] Delany, Samuel. *Times Square Red, Times Square Blue.* New York University Press, 1999; p. 12.

[47] These dangerous liaisons contributed to a 28% HIV incidence rate among hustlers who smoked crack regularly in Miami, New York City, and San Francisco in the early 1990s. See Diana Jones, et al. "The High-Risk Sexual Practices of Crack-Smoking Sex Workers Recruited from the Streets of Three American Cities." *Sexually Transmitted Diseases,* April 1998; pp.187-193. For Canno's quote, see McNamara, p. 84.

[48] Oral history with Will, conducted by author, January 1996. "Ho money is no money," one transgendered ex-sex worker told HIV prevention worker P. Jayne Bopp. Personal communication, June 2002.

[49] Author's field notes, October 1995. For oral histories of five African-American, transgendered, crack-using sex workers in the 1985-1995 period, see Leon Pettiway's *Honey, Honey, Miss Thang: Being Black, Gay, and on the Streets.* Temple University Press, 1996.

[50] Author's case notes, September 1995.

[51] Luna, G. Cajetan. *Youths Living With HIV.* Harrington Park Press (NY), 1997; p. 7.

[52] Author's case notes, October 1995.

[53] See *Badgely Report,* 1987. Also see *F.I.E.R.C.E. Statement,* February 2002.

[54] In a letter from Samuel Steward to John Preston, dated March 5, 1991. Courtesy the Brown University Library, John Preston Papers.

[55] Adams, Matt. *Hustlers, Escorts, and Porn Stars.* Insider's Guide (NV), 1999; p. 168. For an equally ridiculous exchange, see Eric Konigsberg and Maer Roshan, "Boys on the Side." *New York,* August 18, 1997. Konigsberg and Roshan documented a conversation between media mogul David Geffen and a friend in Fire Island. "Your date is spectacular," Geffen's friend told him. "At these prices, he'd better be," Geffen responded.

[56] Adams, pp. 146-148.

[57] Author's field notes, July 1995.

[58] Field notes, October 1995. Joyce Hunter also recalls seeing "a lot of kids of color" who would cross-dress for economic (rather than emotional or sexual) purposes.

[59] Roberts, Greg. "Two Professions: CPA and Sex Worker." Unpublished account, 1998; pp. 5-7.

[60] Read, Kirk. "Working Boys." *QSF Magazine,* 1999. Manuscript copy, p. 2.

[61] Ibid., p. 5.

[62] If there is one way to see how the underclass is misrepresented in this democracy, look at the example set by street-based sex workers, whose political influence lasted only long enough to be co-opted by wealthier, and whiter, "sexual minorities."

[63] "The threat from AIDS produced a 1985 health ordinance that began the shutdown of the specifically gay sexual outlets in the

NEIGHBORHOOD: THE GAY MOVIE HOUSES AND THE STRAIGHT PORN THEATERS THAT ALLOWED OPEN MASTURBATION AND FELLATIO IN THE AUDIENCE." SEE DELANY, P. 15. ALSO SEE PRISCILLA ALEXANDER, "BATHHOUSES AND BROTHELS: SYMBOLIC SITES IN DISCOURSE AND PRACTICE." IN POLICING PUBLIC SEX (EDITED BY DANGEROUS BEDFELLOWS). SOUTH END PRESS (MA), 1996; PP. 221-249.

[64] SEE MCNAMARA, P. 20. DELANY TRACES THE NADIR OF SEXY MOVIE HOUSES IN TIMES SQUARE AND THE EFFECTS OF COMMERCIALIZED VIDEO PORN IN "TIMES SQUARE BLUE."

[65] BENDERSON, BRUCE. USER. PLUME, 1994; P. 223.

[66] FUENTES, LUIS MIGUEL. DIARY OF A DIRTY BOY. WALLACE HAMILTON PRESS (NYC), 1998; PP. 54 AND 112.

[67] MCNAMARA, P. 124.

[68] FOR A DISCUSSION OF HUSTLERS' QUASICRIMINAL PERCEPTION OF SEX WORK, SEE ELI COLEMAN, "THE DEVELOPMENT OF MALE PROSTITUTION ACTIVITY AMONG GAY AND BISEXUAL ADOLESCENTS." IN GAY AND LESBIAN YOUTH, P. 139. ANECDOTALLY, AS A MINNEAPOLIS GANG KID NAMED TONIO TOLD ME IN 1996, "IF I GET CAUGHT AGAIN, I'M GOING FOR FIVE [YEARS] AT LEAST. THAT'S WHY I'M IN THE PARK. THIS IS THE LAST HUSTLE I CAN DO." AUTHOR'S FIELD NOTES, SEPTEMBER 1995.

[69] PERSONAL COMMUNICATION, DECEMBER 2001.

[70] "THEY'RE IN DISTRESS?" ASKED JOYCE HUNTER. "THE KIDS ARE NOT IN DISTRESS? THIS IS ABOUT RACISM. THEY'RE PREDOMINATELY KIDS OF COLOR. THESE RESIDENTS ARE LITTLE WHITE YUPPIES. NEW GROUP WANTING TO GET RID OF THE KIDS, AND THEY'RE GAY. WHAT ELSE IS NEW?" SEE ORAL HISTORY WITH HUNTER.

[71] PERSONAL COMMUNICATION.

[72] LORING PARK WAS CONSIDERED A "PREDOMINATELY GAY NEIGHBORHOOD" BY MAROTTA IN 1982, AND IT RETAINS THIS DEMOGRAPHIC.

[73] "WHAT'S HAPPENED TO NUMBERS, BECOMING POPULAR WITH PEOPLE WHO AREN'T INTO THE HUSTLER SCENE, IS PART OF THE CHANGES THAT HAVE BEEN TAKING PLACE IN ALL OF GAY CULTURE," CLAIMED ACTOR MICKEY COTTRELL. FROM EHRENSTEIN, P. 54.

[74] HARDESTY, ROLF (PSEUDONYM). "HOLLYWOOD MARINES." FROM STEVEN ZEELAND, MILITARY TRADE. HARRINGTON PARK PRESS, 1999; P. 34.

[75] FOR AN ELABORATION OF SAN DIEGO'S CURRENT ESCORT/KEPT BOY SCENE, READ GARY INDIANA'S THREE MONTH FEVER: THE ANDREW CUNANAN STORY. HARPERCOLLINS, 1999.

nine

The first social service organizations to focus on male and transgendered sex workers were founded by former sex workers and others closely connected with local communities. Because of the funding problems and organizational difficulties that plague non-profits, most of these groups have not endured, and none has truly become national. In San Francisco, Glide Urban Center continues to work with sex workers. New York City's STAR, formed by Sylvia Rivera (of Stonewall fame) in the late 1970s, continues to be a strong and mobilizing force. But these are the exceptions. The Coalition Advocating Safer Hustling (CASH), a network facilitated by the Gay Men's Health Crisis from 1994 to 1996, made real progress in linking street-based social workers in major cities throughout the United States and Canada. But just as CASH was gaining momentum, it discovered that its grant would not be renewed, and GMHC was forced to discontinue the program.

Male and trans sex work activists have lately allied themselves with female sex workers in their fight for tolerance, understanding, and decriminalization. This has informed such street-smart, radical collaborations as the International Sex Worker Foundation for Artistic and Creative Expression (ISWFACE), WhoreNet, Prostitutes of New York (PONY), and Hook, all of which combine advocacy and social support. *Whorezine,* produced by Vic St.

Blaise, features multigender interviews and histories. Most of these can be found online.[1]

Local AIDS service organizations have also begun to work with sex workers. The best and most effective of these offer programs based on peer education and advocacy. Craig Seymour, when he was a D.C. strip-club dancer in the mid 1990s, established a novel escort support group at the Whitman-Walker Clinic. The New York Peer AIDS Education Coalition (NYPAEC) enrolls trannie sex workers to provide information to their clients and colleagues. And Honolulu's Life Foundation has established Chrysalis, an afterschool support group for budding *mahus,* which boasts consistently lower rates of prostitution among its attendees. Sexual minority youth groups such as San Francisco's LYRIC, New York City's Hetrick-Martin Institute, and Minneapolis's District 202 have also flourished.

Social conditions may change, but male and transgender sex work is too much in demand to ever disappear. Rather than attempt to eradicate hustling from our streets, we could use our energies to help today's hustlers. If we lobby long and hard enough, we can decriminalize prostitution between consenting adults.[2] If we advocate for better employment and housing opportunities, we can actually take care of homeless and disenfranchised young people.[3]

A LOT OF RESIDENTS, POLITICIANS, AND BUSINESSES WITHIN THE WEST VILLAGE ARE ORGANIZING FOR THEIR QUALITY OF LIFE BUT...

WHAT ABOUT OUR QUALITY OF LIFE?!

JOIN US FOR A VIGIL TO MOURN THE LOSS OF THE PIER AND THE VILLAGE AS A SAFE SPACE FOR LGBT YOUTH/ HOMELESS YOUTH!

RAISE YOUR VOICE TO SAVE OUR SPACE!

9.1 Promotional flyers reproduced courtesy of NYPAEC, WHIS-PER, and the Canadian Lesbian and Gay Archives.

If we continue to educate parents to embrace and support their GLBT children, fewer of them will wind up on the streets, hustling as a last resort.

We need to educate the general public in order to reduce the stigma associated with sex work. We should make comprehensive health care (including condoms, clean needles, and alternative treatment programs), mental health care, and public health information available to everyone. If we urge law enforcement to concentrate vice efforts on separating urban drug zones from sexual economy zones and remedying prostitution-related violence and theft, we might establish a more trusting street environment. Sex work should be an arena for folks who want to be involved, who derive enjoyment from its rewards, and who have been educated well enough to make informed choices.

Until we change our most fundamental approaches to hustling—which must include changing our approach to sexual difference, and might invite a reconsideration of public, intergenerational, interracial, and/or interclass sex—street-based sex work will only get riskier, lonelier, and more hurtful for its participants, clients and workers alike. It can always get worse. The problems contemporary hustlers face are deeply serious, but they are in many cases historical, since there have been so few real attempts to solve them. But can things get better?

The following oral histories, interviews, and written accounts present the experiences and suggestions of contemporary hustlers and social workers. They may not constitute the most representative sample, and they are more a result of serendipity than of extensive planning. Mostly, they're the voices of people I've known and respected. There are patterns in these histories that suggest what might be done to improve sex work conditions for once and for all.

My Grandmother's Stockings: Trans Histories, 1965-2000

Sinead is a transgendered ex-sex worker from Hawaii. We met in the offices of Life Foundation, a community-based AIDS service organization that provides education, support, and HIV prevention services to local *mahus*. She recalls the period from 1972 to the mid 1990s—the crest and ebb of Hotel Street's history as a sex trade zone.

The thing about it was I could always cross over, that was never a problem for me. Well, unfortunately, after a certain point, I couldn't go back to being just a guy, because I had the implants, there's no way I could get out there and look like a guy.

Back when I was younger I didn't cross over. I was 14 years old when I started out. My first trick was in a gay bar called the Gay 90s. It burnt down. And it just so happens that the owner of this bar and his lover offered me a hundred dollars to come back to their place. And these are millionaires, and I'm a 14-year-old boy, and they just wanted me. And that was my introduction into prostitution, and then I met TG people or transsexuals that were living as women and working downtown, and that's how I got downtown.

It was cool! I mean, it was money, and it was respect. You know, I put on a dress and got out there, that was the **most.** Because I'm kind of vain too, in my look, it was so exciting to be out there and have men hooting and hollering and wanting to pay me to have sex—that was the attraction, that was the addiction. That was what hooked everybody out there. And never mind, every time you get in a car, you're risking your life, you don't know if the guy's got a gun or a knife, or whether he's gonna throw you off a cliff.

And I've had, you know, some bad experiences. I was 16, a Marine took me to Makapu`u Beach. I was a fucking prostitute for two years and I knew better than to let anybody take me away from the strip, right? I mean, that's something you learn right off the top, get the money first and don't let them take you where they want to go. It's always where you want to go. But, you know, he was a Marine.

And these Marines, and these Navy guys, they're all freaks! And so he was doing me, he gave me $20 and he was giving me a blow job, and then he stopped, and we were talking, and then all of a sudden he says, "Oh, I'm getting discharged from the Marines." And he says it real spooky kind of, I'm getting kind of heebie-jeebies already, we're on Makapuu Beach, up on the overlook, and he grabs me around the throat and starts choking me, and he says, "This is why."

And he was gonna kill me! I had to get out of the car and jump over the rail, and go run and hide all night. And you know how dogs search for bodies? I hid in the bushes and watched him drive back and forth for like three hours, looking for me. And that didn't stop me. I was back out the next night.

It was just outrageous, you know. Never mind that every time you go somewhere you can get killed. You're putting your life at risk every minute that you're out there. It's just, the attraction was the glamour. You know, because it's about the nice clothes, the jewelry, and having anything you want, the pocket money. It was endless.

I was identifying as female. I was living as a woman. For a lot of transgendered people, they get into prostitution **to be validated as a woman.** But it was also the excitement. It was just exciting. If I had to do it again, I would just not do drugs [**laughs**]. But you know what? I know prostitutes that have been successful, are millionaires, owned homes, have businesses now, all from prostitution. It's what you put into it, and how you go into it, and what you do with it. You know, it really is. I wish I knew then what I know now. Oh, God! [The money all] went into drugs: drugs, clothes, jewelry, the material possessions that all are gone. You know?

But mostly drugs...cocaine. Injecting. Definitely injecting. That was the worst. But you know, I started doing drugs from 8 years old, smoking weed and then moving up to acid and marijuana and Valium and the Quaaludes, and reds, and Seconals, that was the big thing. And that's what made it so easy at 17 to step right into heroin, when I was working for a massage parlor in Waikiki as a real girl, nobody knew. And I was introduced to heroin by the prostitutes that were already working there.

So I did that for about two years. And then I woke up one day and I looked in the mirror and I had real black bags under my eyes, from the heroin, and the lifestyle, hell, any drug, even cocaine—and I looked in the mirror, and said, "Oh, God, what are you doing to yourself?" And that's what happened. I walked away from it. And I was sick for a week. Later on, maybe 10 years later, I would do it and know not to do it twice in a row. It was a still a drug that I used, but cocaine was the downfall. I was spending a thousand dollars a day at one point, for nine months.

And that's why, you know, I did what I did to go to prison, the robbery. After a while, flatbacking—even though I was making a thousand dollars a day flatbacking (turning tricks and stuff), it wasn't fast enough—after that, I started taking the money, you know. And that happens. Because you see other people, all the other junkies around you are doing the same thing. They network like that. God, what a culture.

Mostly, I was always by myself, from the very beginning, but Hotel Street back in those days, you know, a one-block radius, there had to be 50 to 75 **mahus** on any given night. It was wall-to-wall. They folded up the drug trade down there, and [police] closed down the Glades, which was a female impersonation showplace, it was right off Hotel Street.

Hotel Street was nothing but bars, the whole thing, there was no businesses, just bars and restaurants and things like that. It was where the sailors and everybody who visits Hawaii goes downtown, it was prostitution, gambling, and sex, and drinking, for many, many years. OK, it was like: What was it called in San Francisco, the North Shore? Or like Hollywood and Vine, or the Tenderloin. It was the same thing, it was famous all over the world. And like, New Orleans, or the French Quarter, or things like that. To have their own street! They have that in a couple of different countries, have their own street.[4]

Sinead was infected with HIV in 1985. She served 16 years in an all-male prison with a 36C bust size. When released, she tried to get a square job. "How is a 40-year-old transgender woman who's been a hooker for the first half of her life and a convict for the second half going to find a 'real' job?" asked one of her social workers.[5]

Melody was a female impersonator, drag queen, and trans sex worker whom I met in Loring Park in 1995. Mel came right up to me on a warm summer night and asked how I was doing. She submitted an oral history in January 1996, covering the period from 1979 (when she was 16) through 1995.

I grew up in Michigan. From three siblings, I'm the youngest—two girls. I guess I'm half of a girl, because I live as a woman. My mother was at one time a model. She had to offer her body up for access to drugs, as a form of prostitution, because she was so deeply involved in drugs, in heroin. My father was Air Force. We were split up at a very young age because my mother was a drug user and we all had different fathers. One thing I knew from a very young age was that I was gay.

I got a chance to live with my father because he had the income to support me. At that time my mother's career had went down, her life had went down due to drugs and prostitution and alcohol, so she was incapable of taking care of all three of us. I was raped at a young age by cousins when I had left my mom to go live with my father, in and out of school from one city to the next.

As a child molested, there's a pain and a hurt inside me that lingers on, and it's something I'm trying to cure myself of. As far as transgendered, I've always been dressing up as a woman. As a kid I used to take my grandmother's stockings, I used to put them eggshells under my shirt when my father wasn't home. In school they couldn't believe I was a boy. Even in high school I was known to wear makeup. My first trick I was 16 years old.

I didn't know it was a trick back then. My friend had told me about this old guy who liked young boys. And I was like 16, he wanted a boy 15 or 14 years old. So I found out what hotel room to go to, I went up to his hotel room, he offered me in, and he handed me $200. He was fat, nasty—I can still remember the smell—the smell was so fucking bad, he stank, he reeked. His breath stank, his body stank, and he wanted me to give him head. And I was like, give you head?

No, wait, first he asked me how old I was. I remember my friend had told me, "If this guy asks you how old you are, tell him that you're 15."

He asked me, and I said, "I'm 14." He asked me what my boy name was and I told him what my boy name was. He told me I looked too much like a girl and I said, "Well, I guess it's because I'm young and that's the reason, I haven't matured yet to a man's state." Then he wanted to get on top of me and I felt... I was smothered by the funk of his body 'cause he didn't take a bath and he smelled so awful. When I left the hotel, I remember walking out that door, and it seemed like, his smell was on me, his smell of his body was just reeking all over me and it smelled so fucking bad I threw up, I vomited. But I knew that I had $200 on me.

I was very fortunate, at a young age, to have a friend teach me about HIV and AIDS, and how to keep your risk to a minimum. I think he has prolonged my life. I've lost everything due to prostitution and drugs. I was homeless for a year, lost my job, my house, my car, everything. It'll get you killed. Education means everything. Get your education. Your mind's your power. Do what you can to keep yourself careful.

I've been in prostitution, on and off, for 10 years. I can show you the hurt. They can see that in your face, your eyes. Find another way to make ends meet. After a while, you're gonna find out you don't like it. In the long run it really affects your life. When you really want to be someone, your past is gonna haunt you when you try to move on.[6]

Pam is an intersexed person on female hormones. She lives in California. Adrienne Walnoha, a social worker and AIDS housing expert, conducted this interview, which covers 1963 to 1999.

AW: So how old were you when you started sex work? You were 16, right?

P: Yeah, 25 cent movie shop. Ever since then I was kind of hooked. I don't know, dude never gave me too much money, only gave me five, ten dollars, so hey, what the hell. If I can do this to a man, and you know, it feels good, make 50 bucks over it or maybe more, what the hell? I was impressionable at 16, you know?

AW: So you had other jobs.

P: Security guard, asphalt laying, grocery store, truck driving, deliveryman—delivery**person**—

AW: Films?

P: Porn films, prostitute [*laughs*]. Shoot, let's see, working temporary jobs, like dredging out the river, you know, after an oil spill. I had so many jobs, you could fill that whole damn paper up.

AW: So for the majority of your life, you were able to pay your own bills?

P: Yeah, well I had guys pay for me. I looked, I mean I still looked good when I was younger. I mean, even when I was young I was hot, you know, I didn't know exactly how to deal with myself and so on, you know? But I was kind of hot. I went back to Texas, I lived with three drag queens down there and they kind of showed me the ropes. And then, really told me what I was (which I didn't know) with having both [a penis and a vagina]. And they said, girl, do you know what a hermaphrodite is? That's what you are. Ah. They said, didn't you even know that? No! [*Laughs*] They started me into, you

know, the finer parts and stuff, you know?

AW: Right. Was that before you had the surgery?

P: Yeah, yeah, that was before. I had the surgery after my husband died.

AW: How did you have it?

P: Well, I started drugs, and that didn't help with matters none. [*Laughs*] I started drinking heavy and drugs, after my husband died, I was still messed up over that. Men started using me, abusing me, abusing what they could get off of me and everything else, the games they play.... And I ran into a plastic surgeon, and I started screwing around with him. I started using him like men used me. So, I had him give me the operation. You know, just pulled the testicles out from inside me, and seal the joint up, and make a sac, you know? I'm sorry I did that now, but...I'm gonna get reopened. Probably close to the end of this year. I can hardly wait.

AW: You have been homeless at times in the past, have you not?

P: Yeah [*sighs*]. One time I was in Pittsburgh, during a bad winter, something like now, but was mainly more snow, I lived on the North Side, when the North Side was still the old buildings, the old bars, and so on. It was a car lot there, right? It was an abandoned pickup truck. With a cab on it. I used to sleep in that thing. Me and the guys, they'd go steal food for me. I found this one girl at [the shelter], and so on. Which they didn't let her stay there, she was too late or something. So she stayed in the pickup truck with me, and the windows really got fogged up that night!

AW: Did you ever stay in shelters?

P: Well, the way I was when I came to Pittsburgh, I was, like, getting on my status, I was dressed like a male. So you could see, a person like I was, staying with men...at a shelter. Which I did it, a couple times, you know. You know, especially when I—when they wanted me to take a shower, and I wouldn't take it. You know, how would—*how could I?*—how could I tell them, they'd probably freak out, they'd see both equipment down there.

AW: I know you've had lots of experiences with the police.

P: I went downtown one day, got stone drunk, didn't feel like drunk driving and stuff like that. So I put on a dress and walked down Penn Avenue, this one guy came up to me and said, "Baby, I bet you get a hundred dollars a trick, how you look." I said, "That's good, if I wanted to." And he left, he said, "Get in contact with me when—before you go home." I said, "Whatever," you know? And then, all of a sudden, I start walking down Penn Avenue, just to walk the alcohol off, right? So I got, like, certain blood clots in my legs from too much walking and stuff, you know? So I stopped to rest, and...this one black guy came over and said, "C'mere." I said, "No, I'm leaving, I'm going home." You know? "Come here for a second!" I said, "OK, what the hell do you want?" So I started talking to him, and he started saying about doing this, doing that. I said, "Baby, I'm going home. I'm tired and stuff, OK?" So he said, "Well, you're limping, where's your car at?" And I told him. He said, "Why don't you let me drive you there, to your car?" I said, "It's not that far, I can walk it." He

says, "Baby, let me drive you there." I said, "OK," that's one word I said. 'Cause I think he worked that into entrapment. All of a sudden, I got into the car, and he took off like a bat outta hell, a van all smashed in the side of the car where I was. Drove into the next parking lot, and he said, "Well, that's the end of your ride, baby." I said, "Asshole, my car's over that way. Shithead." You know. And then all of a sudden, he says, pops out of the car and says, "Get out the car!" And these two guys walking from the other car, these two guys coming and I'm not knowing what they're doing, he's getting out of the car getting ready to walk on that side, these two guys flash a badge. Said, "Baby you're busted." I said, "For what?" Prostitution. I said, "I'm heading home, I wasn't doing a damn thing." They said, "Well, you propositioned." I say, "I didn't proposition nothing to you." And then all of a sudden they frisk me. The men frisk me. And, I mean, put the cuffs on me, threw me in the back of the paddy wagon, took me to jail. Two counts of prostitution. And I wasn't even doing a damn thing. That night. But the nights I'm doing something, they don't even—they don't even harass me, but the nights I'm not doing nothing, that's when they come get me. I was pissed off 'cause I wasn't doing nothing.

AW: But you have pretty good luck, actually, with the cops? They're pretty OK with you?

P: Well, see, the thing is that I was going with a police lieutenant, I was going with an assistant district attorney, and I was going with two narcotic officers, so.

AW: Well...

P: Like I say. And my sugar daddy, he took the car back off me 'cause he's pissed off I'm going back to California. So he took my car away from me. Not that it would stop me. Now he wants to give the car back and I don't want it. 'Cause, shoot, what I'm gonna do with a—it's a nice car, but what I'm gonna do with smoking [emissions] out in California, how strict they are about pollution laws. They'll pull me over in a second.[7]

Iris was in her early 30s when we met. She was a social worker and a female impersonator at clubs, and had been HIV-positive since her teens. She had been prostituting for 20 years, lately using the Internet to make connections. She was seeking a sponsor for sexual reassignment surgery and had received money for breast implants from another patron after copping street hormones for years. She has lived and prostituted in Denver, San Diego, and Chicago. In her oral history, submitted in 1999, she focused on her past and on her ideas for effective, trans-oriented social services.

When I was 13 I was homeless because my parents had kicked me out of the house 'cause I told them I was gay. Then, I was a boy. And then, when my parents gave up custody of me, I entered into a life of being a ward of the state. That means that I was in and out of group homes and halfway houses for boys. Some of them were coed. Let's see, when I was 17, and I had got kicked out of the Job Corps for being HIV-positive, I was homeless then and was staying in a shelter for a little while. Never actually sleeping there, just using it as a place to change clothes, take a shower. I didn't stay there long because I was always out at night and I never came in when I was supposed to. Then I stayed at an AIDS house. At that time, you know, people were dying left and right and they had AIDS housing for people with AIDS. And I stayed in the basement, and I was out all the time. So that's about the extent of that.

I dealt with the police on many, many, many occasions. And, when I was living back home in Denver, and I was prostituting as a boy, the police would just come by and pick me up. They'd see me, obviously they knew I was on the run, and they would just stop the car and say, "Come on, get in." They'd take me down, and the next thing I know I'd be in juvenile hall again. As a transsexual prostitute, I dealt with police on many, many, many occasions as well. Sometimes all I had to do was be walking down the street and they'd harass me or arrest me, whatever. And I've had a few other experiences—not here in Pittsburgh, or in Denver, but almost every other place I've ever lived. And it's basically been all negative experiences. Did my lawyer work for me? Well, I had a public defender. And you know how that goes: Public defenders just try to do the bare minimum, they don't try to fight your case or anything. They plea-bargain, and I've been on probation or parole quite a few times.

You know, when I was a boy I didn't even think about safety issues. I wasn't thinking that I was a tough guy or anything, but I could handle my own, and I never had any really violent kind of experiences as a male prostitute. As a female prostitute, I've been a little more worried, you know, keep my purse a little closer to me, and just keep an eye out, 'cause the tricks can be just as dangerous as anybody walking down the street or whatever, so I'm always on guard. I've had a couple bad experiences, but that was about it. And if I had to protect myself, I'd fight, or find anything I could grab, to hit them with, or throw at them, or whatever. I even had a stun gun at one point. I never actually had a pistol. I used to carry around knives. And also a—I don't know what they're called, but the case is leather, and it's got a hard ball on the end of it, and it, like, really hurts when you hit somebody upside the head with it.

When I was out there, I always had to have a drink, or two, or three, and a couple shots, just to get relaxed and comfortable, 'cause it was very hard for me to turn tricks sober. I needed something so I could be numb. I could never use and work—all I could do was drink and work. And it loosened me up, and it made me more relaxed and able to talk to the johns or tricks or whatever.

At the time I sought out treatment, as a transsexual, it's been very difficult, as far as like the housing issue was concerned. You know, what part do we put you in? 'Cause if I get arrested, I go straight to general population with the men. And when I go to the rehab, it's a big to-do. So they don't really know what to do with me. If I was in charge, or if I had enough money, I'd make my own treatment center for transgendered people. Or, you know, anybody, but I definitely would have better regulations and rules and options for transgendered people. And my staff would be very caring and sincere when they dealt with transgendered people.

All my tricks have used condoms, and I've always insisted on that. And there was a time where I didn't care: I didn't care about them getting anything, and I didn't care about them giving me anything.

When I was out there, I really didn't have that many people to talk to. Kinda just kept all my burdens...kind of buried. But at that time I was just numb, so I really didn't feel anything, so, you know, I didn't feel like I needed to talk to anybody about any deep, dark secrets, or any problems, or whatever.

I would like to learn how to write grants, so I could apply to get money to do different kinds of programs, especially transgendered programs. I believe [in] a drop-in center...there should be clean needles, bleach kits, condoms of course, lubrication, there should be testing available...I know there are girls who work during the day, but it's very few. Maybe open for a few hours during the day and then reopened at like 10 or 11 o'clock at night till about like 4 in the morning, 'cause I think that's when everybody is really out, then. And I think it should be directly on the stroll, where the girls are. So it's easy to walk to, or have a trick drop them off there or whatever. Also I believe it should be a safe place, so there shouldn't be any drugs or alcohol brought in. And you know, in case a girl got a bad trick or something, she needs to at least feel safe, you know she can come right in there (he or she or whatever). You know, maybe get a shower, have some coffee, a sandwich or something.[8]

Born in 1980, J.T. LeRoy is the author of *Sarah,* a cross between memoir and magic realism. *Sarah* details the adventures of a kid growing up in the truck stops of Appalachia, first in the care of his young, single, sex-working mom and then the charge of a succession of pimps. Calling himself by his mother's name, the novel's protagonist is revered by truckers for miles around. I talked to J.T. in May 2001, as his second book, *The Heart is Deceitful Above All Things,* hit the presses.

I was born in West Virginia. I lived with my grandparents over in West Virginia. But other than that I lived all over, wherever my mom wanted to be.

*My main goal (after I read [**Sarah**] and saw what I had, and I think one of the things it came from), was, like, my fantasy of a world where your sexuality isn't an automatic stumbling block for people. It's just like, "Oh, it is what it is," you know? Taken for granted. Where prostitutes are holy and transgendered prostitutes or transgendered people can be worshipped, you know what I mean? Where it's not something that needs to be hidden or [that you need to be] ashamed of. I think I wrote from my own issues around that, and my own fears, you know?*

I don't really know what I am yet, what gender. [Photographer] Mary Ellen Mark was like, you're the third gender. Mary Ellen Mark has deemed me the third gender.

I haven't been off drugs all that long, and off the street, and I think for me it's getting used to...I don't know, it kinda fucked with me in a way, because...it's kind of like coming in

from the jungle. You know, I was out there in the jungle using drugs and being somebody else and then, recovering from craziness, and then I get off drugs and then all of a sudden it's like, I have a book coming out, you know?

Drugs really interfered with my writing. Well, that's not true, because I would write, and be off drugs, and then I'd use drugs again, so. So, yeah, I finally—I mean, when I got my book deal, I was still using—but living with my family, they pretty much made it clear that if I use drugs, I'm out. And I don't want to end up living in SRO [single-room occupancy] hotels, you know? They're pretty disgusting, and they're a lot more expensive than they used to be. Little room, and you share a bathroom that you don't even want to walk on with fishing boots.

*[My therapist] told me to write.... He taught a class for people who wanted to be social workers, and he said, "Well, you can educate them." And that really appealed to me. That really, really appealed to me. So, you know, that's how I started, to be able to have a voice back to these people. Be like, "Fuck you, idiots, this is what you should do. What you don't do, what you should do." I mean, I think of lot of them don't have a clue. In **Sarah** there are no social workers, there are none of those things. The truth is there are places in the world where things are really horrible, and nobody comes and rescues the kid; or when they rescue the kid it doesn't necessarily make it better. I lived in areas where if you were being raped by your daddy or your stepdaddy, you stayed with it because if you got removed you got put into the boys' home,*

which was with all the juvenile delinquents. They were all in one place. You would get gang-raped by boys every night. It was like, what would you rather be, raped by your daddy or raped by an institution? So, it doesn't necessarily—I think those are real, what's the word, not misnomer, but misplaced idea.... Well, the idea is that the first step is getting a kid out from the abusive household, and once they do that, it's all OK. And the truth is, very often that's the first step in a nightmare. And a lot of times when a kid turns 18, they throw him out on the street and that's it, you know?

For me what worked in therapy was that the therapist just held his hand out, and he realized that I was a wild animal. You know, it's like, social services or shelters: The kids who are on the street, the hardened ones who've been there, they're like wild animals. So if you go to Africa [and work in the jungle], you don't say, "Here, eat out of my hand and jump through these hoops, jump through these hoops, otherwise we're not gonna feed you. And you gotta come eat out of my hand too." It's not gonna happen! So they [social workers] tend to focus only on the new kids, the kids on the street who haven't become hardened. They kind of triage and just do harm reduction with some of the other ones. And then they just kinda like write those people off. And they had written me off. You know, one woman wrote in a letter after an article came out with me, saying she knew me from the street. And they had done, I was one of the people that they just do triage with, that they just, they don't even bother, you know? "He's just too far gone. He'll be dead. Don't waste your time."

And my therapist basically didn't make me jump through hoops as he treated me. Slowly I was jumping through hoops before I even realized it. But he did it really slowly: For the first three years, we had a session every day...and then we went to six days a week, and that was seven years ago. Now I'm at three days a week. And so, you know what I mean, I just think that for people, you know, social workers need to be a little more, like, forgiving in their plan....

The thing that's funny is that...every area has their little den of iniquity or something. And I feel a lot calmer when I'm in a city.... They all have their games [in the country], and usually the sheriffs and everyone really knows. And you really have to work with a pimp because it's like a well-oiled machine. And if you're not with a pimp, they'll bust you, because they're paid off.... So they're just like, they're paid, everyone's paid, and it just kinda works like a little machine.... It's kinda like how the Starbucks are running out the little ma-and-pop coffee shops, it's almost like that. The TAs and the Loves are running out the little independent truck stops. So the truck stops that don't have all the amenities like movies and Jacuzzis and all that, that the newer truck stops have, they go the opposite way. They're just like, "All right, well, here you can get your pump shined. Go there and get your clothes pressed, you know, come here and get your dick pressed."

I think it's really hard to be different in an area where there aren't a lot of gays, you know, where there's not like—like in San Francisco or in New York, it's so part of the culture, you know what I mean, it's like, "Well, you're gay, big deal." You leave there, and it's really hard and it's dangerous, you know?[9]

Yet even in bigger cities, street hustlers are facing community expulsion by upwardly mobile gays, disrupting their contact with service providers. On a flyer for FIERCE! (an advocacy project combating RID and administered by the Ella Baker Center), a transgendered woman named Erykah pleaded for more neighborhood tolerance:

I am 19 and I live in New York City. Trans means that I am a woman who was born biologically male and now live my life as a female. I work at the New Neutral Zone, a drop in center for lesbian, gay, bisexual and transgendered young people. In many ways, I am just like you. I go to work. I cook, I clean, I bleed. Last November, I left home. I was sad to leave my mom's house, but I was 18. I thought it was the right thing to do. I left by choice. I got to pack up my stuff and take what I wanted. But that is much more than most of my peers. Everyday I talk to my mother, just like all my mother's daughters. These are things a lot of people take for granted, but to me they are blessings. Many young people are homeless because their parents didn't want gay kids around. Just like you don't want gay kids on your block. The fliers you are putting up are a big deal to me. Many of my friends are working the streets having to do what they have to do to survive. At my job, we call that "survival sex." It's hard to support yourself when you're

young, homeless, and queer. If you want these kids off your streets, please help us find them a place to go. If you put your energy into helping solve the problem of homelessness, and homophobia/transphobia, everyone will win.[10]

All of these stories highlight the need for vastly expanded social services and better understanding of transgendered sex workers among service providers. Shira Hassan writes:

Gentrification is the evil that makes our world stop. At this point in the movement, we are fighting gays and lesbians who achieved socioeconomic stability that allows them to pass in the straight community and take rights away from those of us who will never be middle-class (and who don't want to be). It is sad to say that the biggest enemy of trans people and sex workers and other folks not buying into the American way are actually gays and lesbians. The Human Rights Campaign has made a conscious decision to deny transgenders and any one else who is gender-queer (femme boys and butch grrls etc.) the same rights that they have. The right to marry has outweighed the right to sit on a stoop. It's ridiculous and terrifying at once. Housing and HIV prevention are just not important to these passing gays and they are literally kicking us (service providers) out of the Village because they say that we "attract youth" to the site. In fact, our outreach is determined by places that people are populating, not the other way around. Nonetheless, youth outreach workers and agency workers have all been removed *from the Village and the piers where most kids lived have been completely shut down. There is no excuse for this kind of behavior.[11]*

Every Ho Has His Day: Vic, Will, Roberto, Chris, Shorty

Vic St. Blaise, the San Franciscan who created *Whorezine* and collaborated with CASH, has long been a staunch advocate of sex workers' rights. He echoes Delany's acceptance, even celebration, of public sexuality, and Hassan's strenuous objections to corporate re-zoning. St. Blaise's testimony to the 1996 San Francisco Task Force on Prostitution illustrates his frustration in not being taken seriously as a sex-working man fighting for prostitutes' rights.

People talk about problems of prostitution, about drugs, miniskirts, and fishnets, and I don't embody any of that so people either don't take me seriously, because I don't fit into their expectations, that I am not worth being bothered with. Sometimes I feel that in some of the activist work that I do and sometimes on the task force as well, and that's too bad because a lot of the problems people complain about as far as prostitution are things that I have either avoided or overcome....

People don't get busted for having sex for money, but people get busted for agreeing to do it, and I think that is for a reason. Prostitution is very much something that deep down people don't want to get rid of. I mean everybody uses it, people who enforce the laws, people who preach sermons. People from all sorts of backgrounds use prostitution in one form or another, and I think if there was a sincere effort to crack down on it, it would have been done a long time ago. So the way it's set up now is that some things you are allowed to get away with but some things you are not allowed to get away with, it's definitely about control.

I do think that it's been for the control of women.... But the sad thing is, people don't understand, it's not just about controlling women, and it does affect every other facet of humanity because prostitution touches people everywhere. Women are being controlled by these laws, but they also affect the customers, they affect the families, they affect the relationships people want to have with friends and families and neighbors, and that's really sad....

Another part of it is the problem our society has with sex. Let's say that prostitution was decriminalized, there would still be a lot of stigmatization, judgment, and a lot of uncomfortable feelings about seeing someone dressed provocatively....

There will always be people, at least in the near future, who will be bothered by sexuality. Instead of asking themselves why they have a problem, they attack whoever. I think that's why I'm in this, not just about sex for money, but sex in general. I think we need to come a long way as far as this society.

The whole thing about disease and HIV, safer sex, and responsible activity is everyone's responsibility...it's for everybody. More than just singling out prostitution for health checks, it's not right. It doesn't reward good behavior, instead it punishes people for stuff that may or may not even happen.

The whole HIV testing law has nothing to do with actual physical acts. It has to do with agreeing to commit some nebulous act so it makes HIV a status crime for people in the sex industry and I think that's really wrong.

I don't like the idea of [sex] zoning, because it's us versus them. The whole county should be a tolerance zone in my opinion, the whole country, but I guess you have to start somewhere....[12]

Will was a veteran of Loring Park, popular with clients because he was always reliable and because he embodied trade—cowboy boots, a leather jacket, and torn jeans. He was homeless and involved with Melody. With emergency funds and Mel's informal connections, they secured housing before winter struck (not that it kept them from freezing their asses off in the park). Will was in his early 30s in 1995. He grew up in Los Angeles, and talked of the period from 1972 to 1995:

I was adopted when I was three weeks old. My mom thought she couldn't have kids, so they adopted me, and about nine months later she got pregnant with my brother. After that, he was their kid, and I was just a token, so to speak. I always had problems with my dad, as long as I can remember. My father would call me a bastard. You know, children believe what they're taught.

I started smoking weed when I was 10. My family was ultra-Christian, pro-white; I did everything they told me not to. My mom was a beautiful person—she loved everybody.

My dad, if you weren't white, you weren't right. Everything was run by his rules. I didn't go for it. I ran away from it. I had a pool, but I didn't have a dad. He was never around, and when he was there he was yelling or beating on me.

I ran away for the first time at the age of 11. I went to Hollywood, and that's when I started to prostitute. My first trick I turned was in my last year in Little League. I used to be a real good baseball player, football, you name it. He was an old pedophile. He gave me 100 bucks to—he got off 'cause I was just reaching puberty, I didn't have a whole lot of hair, I was 11 years old. That's what he wanted. He just rubbed my body while he got himself off.

I ran away again when I was 12 and got picked up in Hollywood by a man. Me and another kid, we were offered 50 bucks and candy or cookies or something and we went home with him. There was a party goin' on upstairs, and we were taken down into the basement. Whatever we were eating, the candy or whatever, it was drugged. We were tied up, molested, beat on, spit on, whipped—as far as penetration I don't really know, I passed out or overdosed or whatever. I think we were penetrated, I don't know with what. We came to about a day and a half later, blood all over us, I still got scars on my chest and back from the beatings.

They let us go.

There was a party goin' on upstairs, some sadomasochism thing, there were about 12 people participating down in the basement.

They dropped us off on Santa Monica Boulevard. That

kind of changed the way I thought about a lot of things.

I had a lot of problems being adopted, being told at such a young age "You're nothing" by my dad, I guess I took it to heart, got into drugs, not caring at all. I guess I never really had a sense of self-worth, of being loved.

Two drag queens took me in, in Hollywood. I lived in their apartment. There was no sex, they weren't coming onto me. They cleaned me up and I stayed with them on and off. I was like their son. I didn't have nobody and they didn't have nobody; we had each other. I went back home about a month later. I stayed a year. I ran into Trixie, one of my drag mothers, when I was about 14 or 15, and she gave me an envelope with about $500 cash. When I had come back to their place after being raped and molested by these men, Trixie and her lover had me take them back to that house—I remembered where it was—and they started writing down all the license numbers from the cars outside. I kind of forgot about it, I was sort of dazed and confused then. When I ran into them a couple of years later, I found out they had been blackmailing these men. Some of these men were married.

They had taken pictures of me when I got back to their motel room after it happened, dried blood running down my legs, blood on my chest, so they had proof this really did happen to me. They got a lot of money from these men for quite a few years. I thought it was pretty cool, actually, that somebody got something out of these men for what they did to us.

I never saw the other kid again. Maybe he learned from that. Maybe it steered him the other way. It didn't steer me

away. It pissed me off. It drove me deeper into prostitution and drugs....

We were a middle-class family. I had everything a kid could want except love. If you're young and you're looking for love, there are other places to go. You're young, you're high, that trick's gonna manipulate you. That's why they like youth, 'cause they think they don't know nothing, they're gonna make you do whatever they want. You're 13, 14 years old, you don't know. A trick's gonna use you. Insert penis in mouth, collect 30 bucks. That's all it is. They don't care about you.[13]

Roberto, like Will, did not identify as gay. He told wild stories about bank heists and prison escapes, priding himself on his heterosexual vigor. Roberto was 19 when we met, and he'd spent most of the last decade in juvenile correctional facilities. Last I heard from him, he had hit his three-strike deal and was serving five to 10 years. Roberto's oral history covers the period from 1985 to 1995.

I started gang-banging when I was about 9 years old...got affiliated with the Crips out in South Los Angeles and Watts, in the projects...I first got into the California system when I was 10 years old for a drive-by shooting on a bounty hunter for Watts Bloods, in the projects where they were from. I served a four and a half month sentence in Camp Kilpatrick, that's when I was like 10...I was living with my aunt...it was a little shaky—she was into dealing drugs herself, she was out there selling PCP; PCP and nitrodose.

You start high school when you're 12 or 13, right? Yeah...served time when I was 9, 10, 11, 12...it seemed like it was an everyday thang, gang fights, knife fights, shootings, on the East Side of L.A. and Watts.

My first sexual experience I was 13. I was staying with my aunt and she had her friend over to baby-sit me and she was about 35. My first sexual experience was with her. My baby-sitter. One day she looked at me and said, "What do you know about women?"

I said, "A lot."

She said, "What do you mean, a lot?"

I said, "You stick your thing in and you take it out."

She said, "No, that ain't all it is. One of these days I'll be your teacher."

So one day she had my aunt drop me off at her house. I was sitting on her couch and she came over and unzipped my pants. After that anytime I needed a place I'd go over, and...all that shit.

When I was 13 I got picked up, they sent me to a private facility, out there it was a hands-on program, which meant that the staff there, they can push you around...all the staff there are ex-wrestlers, ex-boxers. Every four months you get to go back to your home and stay for four days. On my first furlough I decided I wasn't going back. And so I got picked up again on two different drive-by shootings, they sent me to a juvenile prison in Colorado. The same thing happens in here as in a real prison: Don't nobody get kicked out of prison, if you mess up it gets worse.... Got into more trouble beating people, robbing people, selling drugs: I was out on the run....

The first time I did stuff for money—the first time I went down to the park—I just robbed these guys, stickups, one after another. I made one guy get naked, get out of the car, and I took his ride that night. Got into a chase, got picked up, booked. The next time I got in a car, I let the guy suck my dick for 40 bucks. He dropped me off. All I had to do was let them suck my dick.

I don't think no guy's attractive. I don't think I let any of them get me off. It's easy for me with a woman.

I started hustling because that was the last thing I could do. I couldn't get picked up again for sticking anyone up, otherwise I'd be serving five years. They let you out of jail with nothing but your name and your clothes, what am I supposed to do? You need money to get money.

I ain't been down that way for a while. I tore up all my regular customers' phone numbers. It was sick. Ain't enough money in it. Clothes, food, rent, drugs, either way it's gone. All the other hustlers I know just do it 'cause they smoke crack—that's all.

You gotta show respect for yourself. Have a little dignity, respect for yourself, respect for your body. You don't know where the next mouth's been. You don't know what that guy got from sucking up—I got herpes for the rest of my life now. You don't know where that asshole's been.[14]

Chris hustled alternatively as a young man and as a street queen. Because I mainly knew him as a boy, I will use masculine pronouns to describe him here. Chris was smart, funny, competitive, and addicted to crack. He was prematurely ejected from a (mainly white) gay treatment center south of Minneapolis for "inappropriate" behavior and returned to the streets. The last time I saw him was in June of 1996—he stared through me in a bleary crack daze, lying on a couch at a drop-in center. This oral history covers the time period from 1980 to 1995.

I'm currently unemployed, and I plan to leave for San Francisco this coming Monday. I was abused as a child. I can recall incidents back to age 5 where me and my mother were constantly physically abused by my stepfather, who legally adopted me because my real father did not want to acknowledge me as his real child. I was beat down practically every day, it went from marks on the body to busted heads to sprained ankles and black eyes, you know, the whole works....

I knew I was gay because in kindergarten me and the other little boys used to go down into the basement and kiss...I know that's normal...but by junior high I knew I was gay.

I got to high school and freshman year was hell, my rep followed me from junior high to high school, and they knew, they were always giving me hell about it. They would chase me down the halls as a freshman, and a bunch of them caught me one day and they threw me in a garbage can upside down, headfirst. I mean, it wasn't mean or whatever, it was kind of funny, they just like tortured me—take my candy, chase me down the hall, it was kind of fun. Tenth grade I started checking out the football players, you know,

thinking how can I get some? When they talked to me they'd say to me, "Little queer this, little queer that." Locker room talk was all about how they hurt these girls during sex. I didn't want it to hurt, I wanted it to feel good. I wanted to be penetrated but I didn't know how to go about it. Then I started lifting weights, looking at all them hunks in bicycle shorts, people were like, "Well, is he a fag or what? He's lifting weights, acting like a boy."

And then I transferred high schools, which were the best days of my life. My attitude was, if I was gonna talk the talk, I was gonna damn well walk the walk. I joined the soccer team, I was popular, everything was going great. I was 17 years old, and my dad started hitting me again. One time he took my head and knocked me into the TV. But it didn't faze me at all, I mean, because when I was younger, he would hit me so much upside the head, I was used to it. I went to school one day and never came back.

I went back to my mom's. One particular occasion I was walking down the street, [my dad] was, like, stalking me or something, he came out of nowhere and he slapped me. I said, "Don't hit me again, motherfucker." He, like, chased me down the street and he couldn't catch me, I, like, dropped my house keys, but he was a big man, he couldn't get me. I told my mother what happened, and she told me, she goes, "If he comes over trying it, we gonna kick his ass." So he came over, beat on the door, and she opens the door, and he tried to walk in, but she's got a big old broomstick. And he choked her but she started whacking him with it, and all I saw was his head, and I came over and whacked him across the head with the frying pan. He ran down the stairs, screaming, "I'm'a get you, I'm'a get you." She said, "If he hits you again, just turn his ass in." That next week he found me again and tried to slap me. I rounded him.

I said, "That's from the time I was small, all the beatings you gave me, all the time you beat on my mom, you caused five miscarriages." I could have had five other brothers and sisters. I even heard there could have been a twin, mysteriously, a twin of mine. Sometimes I think, "Another me, what would it have been like?"
Right now today this man is suffering.

The first time I had sex with a man I was 17, a senior in a new high school where they didn't know about me. One day after soccer practice I went down to a gay bar.... Even though I was 17, they let me in. It was like, I needed to see what it was like, to do it. I wound up losing my virginity to a 49-year-old man in the back of his car in the parking lot of this gay bar. It was that easy. I started going down there every night.

I dropped out of school, I moved out of my mom's 'cause she was smoking crack, and I shacked up with this girl. She got me started on smoking pot, we smoked like every day, all day, it was all I was doing. Then she started dating a coke dealer, and before I knew it I was hooked. She introduced me to my first boyfriend. My first boyfriend, who I was totally in love with, he got me into prostitution. He had me call an escort service. The funny thing was, when I called I recognized the voice, my friends that were running this place! They were like, "Hey girl, come on over." They loved them some smooth black skin. I was turning four tricks a night,

giving 15% to the house, making $400 a day. But by this time I was smoking crack, and I smoked like $300 of rock every few days.

I quit prostitution for two months, no drugs, no prostitution. And I couldn't wait to get back to the cities. I was involved in a credit card scam on the streets my first weekend back, and I was arrested. After they let me out of jail, I was right back out there prostituting. I [have been] involved in prostitution almost two years....

The consequences you will pay: STDs, serious drug problem, you will get beat up, you will get assaulted, you will get ripped off, you will perform acts and not get paid.... I've been through it and it's nothing nice. It costs you your friends, your self-esteem goes way down. People don't see you as nothing but a sex toy, that's all they look at you as, so stay away...that's all I have to say, stay away 'cause it is not worth it.[15]

On a few occasions, I'd smoked cigarettes with Shorty under the mossy awning in front of my workplace. He was bisexual, primarily dating tricks and teenage girls. He lived down the block from me in his first real apartment, a single-room occupancy unit whose centerpiece was a hospital bed with tricked-out machinery. Shorty had AIDS. He died in 2001, at the age of 26. He had been hustling, on and off, for 12 years. His oral history covers the period from 1988 to 2000.

I was living in Homestead. My friend stayed there. [I met him] through one of my girls. He was a runaway, I was a runaway. So we had to make money, and he came up with the idea of going downtown. I started hustling for money. He was 18, I was 14. So we just went from there. We went downtown, he introduced me to a couple people he was making money with...and it went from there. Make some loot, and everything's OK. Got high, chill, crash, the next day I went out and did it again. If they wanted a blow job, that's $25. If they wanted to do you, that's another $25. You know, it all depends on what they liked and what they wanted. Yeah, it's just going about business, you know. Like, I give you what you want, if you want to give me the right price, know what I mean? I'm never gonna give you anything unless you give me the right price for what I'm doing. You know, not none of that $10, either, 'cause you know, that's not me. I'm not a $10 ho. [*Laughs*]

There were like five of us, we all, like, had our spots. And it's like, no one leaves, no one—know what I'm saying—no one leaves to go home until we were all together. At the end of the day, it's like, we have our meeting place, and that's where we met. If you don't come back, then we knew something happened, and we never went in no one's house, you know, it was like in the parking lots, somewhere up by the garage, alley-cut. Stay in the car, you know, and ask him if he has any affiliations with the Pittsburgh police, stuff like that, and he's gonna have to answer. OK, now, if he don't answer, we don't get in.... I picked up on it because of my friend was telling me a little bit here and there, each time we went down, you know: Do this, never have them lock the door, you know,

see the money first, you know, things like that. I was thinking too, he probably already had the knowledge so that, with me, he was gonna hook me up with it. He knew what corners, you know, what alley-cuts they ride through, things like that. Actually, it hasn't changed, to be honest with you. 'Cause I feel like it's more from here up, know what I'm saying. Like, where you met me: from that corner [Penn and Ninth] all the way up to the other side.... I haven't seen anyone that I knew back in the day, though. I've been meeting—every time I went down there and met different people, like different guys, stuff like that. It's never the same. I don't stick with one client, you know, I get different men each time I go out.

It's kinda hard to know nowadays who's doing what down there. It's so different, 'cause you don't see them all in one spot, you know, you see them—they're spread out more, and stuff like that. You don't know if he's gay, or straight, or looking for a female or whatever.

If something comes by, you either have, like, a choice: to do this, or not. You know what I mean? And if you don't do it, then—if I don't do it, then I'll be thinking to my head, Man, I could've made some money—I could have made some loot before I went home. Get back to the crib and be happy, 'cause I did make the money, while I was there in town. Even if it's only $50, oh, well, that's $50 I ain't got. You know, go home and call it a day...$50 is hard to pick up any other day of the week, except for going downtown.

I basically do it every other week or something.... It's not hard. It's just, find a way to get down there, or walk down. If

I walk down, then I know I'm getting money to come back home with. And there's certain nights—you know, there's certain nights that are good nights. Wednesdays and Thursdays. You know, you go down at midnight, it's pretty packed down there. It's all right though. Maybe on weekends, but I don't know, I ain't never went down there on weekends. You know, the weekend thing's not for me...plus nowadays, it's hard to tell if you're a cop or you're not a cop, so that 'noids me out mostly, you know, and I'll just be like, No, fuck it, not today.

You bring home, like, I dunno, $200, $250. It depends on how many guys I get that night.

MF: *Whatever happened to the boy that you were with?*

S: *He died, he had AIDS, and like that.*

MF: *How long ago?*

S: *Like, couple years ago.*

MF: *Were you close with him?*

Yeah, I grew up with him, he was my lover.... Yeah, and that's how I got it. That's how I contracted that. I don't hate him for it though, you know, but what can you do? Rob. Called him L.A. Yeah. L.A. That's where he went, he went to L.A.

We just needed money, because we had lived together for a year and couldn't pay the rent, and stuff like that, so we just started hustling, just for the hell of it. We started doing credit bills and stuff like that, and get high, things like that.

[When] I was 11, my dad started smoking pot with me. I didn't know what it was, I just thought it was a cigarette. You know, I used to smoke at 10, and I thought it was one of his

roll-up cigarettes 'cause he used to roll cigarettes, so I started smoking on that, about 10 years old, 10 or 11, I started doing that with my dad....

This one [street] group was real heavy into acid, I ain't know what that was, so I took that, I tried that, that was pretty good, I liked that.... I don't know, I guess I was 18, all this experimenting going on, and I just experimented. Hung out with different people, kept asking me if I did this, or, "Hey you wanna try it?" "All right, well, I ain't got no money." "Well, here it is, try it." And just started liking it from there, you know. That's how it was, you know, my life's like. I like 'em all. You know what I mean? LSD, that's great, Ketamine, Ketamine's great, Ketamine's bomb, just don't take too much or you'll be in a K-hole, coke's all right, I snorted coke, and heroin's all right, I like heroin, you know. I don't know about no pills. And weed's all right. I guess I'm not really picky. I like them all.... [L.A.] used to get acid a lot. We used to just trip our ass off, you know, when we go home, laugh about how our day went, "Oh, we made this, cool...."

I was—what?—14. Yeah, I was out there for a while there, for a minute. Then things started to slow down, and I was arrested, and now I'm starting to do it again. Which I have no idea why. It's the money. You know it's there. And you know you can always go back to it.... I kinda like the nightlife. And it's like, well, sometimes I don't even have to go anywhere sometimes. I have people call me. And [they] say, "Well, I need this, and I got this much." "All right, well, come over. You want me to come over there?" Things like that. You know, so it's like—I really ain't got to go any-where, except stay home, still making business...it's not as risky, because you know the guys ain't affiliated with the police. And I even feel safe with them. So it's OK. 'Cause even like my wife—I don't wanna bring that up—but she used to do that too.... You know what I'm saying? So. We **both** was doing it! [**Laughs**] We both did it. I didn't know for a while, you know. Yeah, when she went down to hus-tle, I'd call my girls, and they'd come down, yeah, 'cause I knew that she was gonna do it. I said hell, if she can do it, I can do it!

Me and my Ma was having problems, and she told me to get the hell out, and I said, "All right, whatever." So I rolled. You know, and then after like two months I was living in the streets and stuff like that, you know, end up getting picked up because I run away, which I didn't know and I tried telling them, the cops told me, my mom called the cops on me.... I told the cops that she kicked me out, and they didn't care, I was a minor. I don't know where I was, I was back out on the streets though I don't know where.

Yeah, my Ma ended up putting me in [a youth shelter], for a few. I ended up running from there all the time. And they kept placing me in more secure places and I couldn't stay there, couldn't take the rules, and running from there. It was just the rush of being wanted. It was like, "Yeah, police are gonna chase me." It was a rush. Got that blood pumping.

Yeah, so back then I didn't care. Now it's like, I like it at home. Like, all this. I am so happy right now 'cause I ain't never had all this and kept it as long as I did like this. I'm doing good. I'm doing good. I don't really need nothing except me.... That, and drugs. You know, little things like that. I don't know the good life. Well, I do, but I don't know the good part of me. You know, like the being—to be good.

Just I wanna do something different with my life instead of prostituting and doing drugs and—just something better, you know. Something different. Enjoy the finer things in life, you know. Being a good guy at work—you know, everyone comes over, "Shorty's a real nice man." I don't see it yet. I ain't seen it in me. You know, I'd have to do something to see that. Getting into all these bad influences in my life and, you know, but I can't quit. That's all I know is bad people and things like that....

I'm not really a bad person. I wouldn't do nothing wrong. But I had my times where, you know, I used to. I used to mug people, you know, rob houses, steal cars, do all that dumb shit. I'm kinda glad I'm done with them stages in my life. I'm an adult, so...being in jail ain't—ain't gonna work.... I've been there before. Two days, four days.

It was all right. I mean that's the environment I'm used to: the jail and all that, institutions and hospitals. This is the first time I've been managing on my own like this, you know, without being in jail. So it's kinda like, sometimes freaks me out 'cause I feel like dropping myself up at the hospital some-time, 'cause it's like, I can't handle this, being hungry like this, plus I'm afraid, so who knows, who knows.

[I'm afraid of] just failing. Failing. Losing everything that I've accomplished. It'll be all right. It's like, I gained so much, and so fast. And then, when you rebuild, it's like, "Oh, I've got to start over." When I first moved here, I went two, three months without my furniture. You know, nothing. Not even a TV. Not even a phone. Yeah, that was my zero point right there. I didn't even actually want to move in until I had everything, but I was happy, got my own place, couldn't wait to get in, so. I been here for almost a year. Almost. I'm happy. I'm just afraid all this is just like—be a dream. Like I'm dreaming this. I feel like I'm dreaming all this, and I'm afraid to wake up one day and everything's gonna be gone. Like my life, you know. It'll be all right. It'll be all right. Wake up the next day and...

MF: When you were out there, were you thinking about HIV?

S: No. I wasn't ever thinking about it.

MF: Do your tricks ask you to use condoms? Do you ask them to?

S: Some of them want you to use condoms. I always just tell them, "I don't care." I **don't** care, 'cause I'm already fucked up right now! [**Laughs**] You know what I'm saying? And I don't have any intention to give them anything, it's just, I don't care—it's a risk that they're willing to take. So, if they're gonna risk coming up and finding someone to work with, they're gonna risk getting a disease. And I'm not trying to do it on purpose, but that's their choice. And I found out the hard way, so.

[I got tested at] a couple places. One in [a suburb], and I did-n't believe them. Then I went to the Health Department...and they come back with the same thing. So I said, "Oh fuck it, I got it," you know, "What am I gonna do?" And so I didn't know where to go, and who to turn to. I think I just, after a while, I just lived with it.

I feel like I had it since I was 14. 'Cause that dude Rob. And just didn't actually know until I got sick—I started getting sick too. It'll be all right.

Yeah, it's like, I'm already done going to the hospital. I don't even go anymore to get checked. You know how you go every month? I don't even go every month to get checked up, just to see how I'm doing. I mean [**laughs**]. I mean, I'm not—I'm not being a government punk. This is what it is. People with AIDS, they government-experienced. So it's kinda like, fuck it, I don't want—don't need no part of the government. I'm gonna live my life the way I want to live it, not worry about if I get sick or die. I just, when I die, I die. I mean, we all dying soon. Can't put a time limit on it. You know, I most definitely ain't taking no messed-up drugs to try to—"Oh, we're gonna save you for 20 years." What am I gonna do with my life for the next 20 years? The same shit, sit around and do nothing, right? That's how I feel about that.

Sex. Sex ain't everything. I'm starting to die from that—like, die out from it. You know what I mean, I don't even think about it. I don't.

It's getting cold and wet, don't need no sick ho's. Don't need no sick ho's. Every ho has his day. You know?[16]

Conclusion: Improved Working Conditions—*Now*

If sex work sucks, then we need to examine the working conditions. The oral histories above reveal an impoverished, unregulated world of police harassment, social stigma, child abuse, domestic violence, homelessness, substance use, and client assault.

How can America improve these appalling conditions? First, dedicated social service: harm reduction calls for nonjudgmental interventions, preferably peer-based. We need funded programs for indigenous outreach work, Internet support sites, street-based employment and education counselors, nontraditional shelters and devoted drop-in centers, and mental and physical health clinics. We need viable adoptive and mentoring networks and affordable housing. We need participant-observer research and ongoing needs assessments. We need more support from the mainstream GLBT community. We need to enact antidiscrimination employment laws on behalf of transgendered people, and to enforce them as vigorously as police have enforced our misguided solicitation and masquerade laws.

We must recognize and address the fundamental reasons for adolescent hustling. Homeless and runaway youth need money, food, and shelter; but they also seek affection, intimacy, compassion, and a safe environment in which to explore sex and sexuality.[17] "Many sex workers report that they have found individual clients and 'sugar daddies' to be more helpful and supportive in the long run than social services or agency interventions," noted G. Cajetan Luna.[18] If we sever the traditional social network of sex work, can we expect those needs to be met elsewhere?

Finally, we must forge tolerance and understanding beyond simplistic hustler chic. Recent books by sex-working authors Gavin Dillard, Aaron Lawrence, J.T. LeRoy, Craig Seymour, Matt Bernstein Sycamore, and Rick Whitaker challenge the prevailing view that hustlers are either unsavory delinquents or pitiful victims. Contemporary American notions of hustling are as unhelpful as the 19th century medical metaphors that linked male and trans sex work to monstrous pathologies. Prostitution is not deviance, nor is it an epidemic. It is a social behavior (adapted, for capitalism, from barter) that has been tinged with shame in Western societies for more than 2,000 years—since the Greeks first used the term *porneia* to convey condemnation. Because of its puritanical fears of expressed sexuality, American society has perpetuated this social neurosis for the last 400 years.

We must not be ashamed of our history, for there is much good to preserve. Our street culture's legacy of rebellion against orthodoxy endures. But it is time to move on. The time has come to fight shamelessly for new traditions: for freedom and respect, for self-determination, for unity.

[1] SEE WWW.ISWFACE.ORG, WWW.PENET.ORG, AND WWW.HOOKONLINE.ORG. HOOK'S ADVICE FOR NEW ESCORTS SHOULD BE READ BY ANYONE CONSIDERING SEX WORK.
[2] THE ORGANIZATIONS CALL OFF YOUR OLD TIRED ETHICS (COYOTE) AND ARRESTING PROSTITUTES IS LEGAL EXPLOITATION (APLE) ARE WORKING TOWARD DECRIMINALIZATION, AND VALUE NEW IDEAS AND ENERGY.
[3] ONE EFFECTIVE TRANSITIONAL LIVING PROGRAM, OFFERED BY MINNEAPOLIS'S PROJECT FOUNDATION, PAID HALF OF TENANTS' RENT. THE ENTIRE RENT WAS

THEN PLACED INTO A FUND THAT GATHERED INTEREST UNTIL YOUTH WERE READY TO USE IT TO GAIN AN APARTMENT OF THEIR OWN.

[4] ORAL HISTORY WITH SINEAD, CONDUCTED BY AUTHOR IN MAY 1999. THANKS TO P. JAYNE BOPP FOR HER INTRODUCTION.

[5] PERSONAL CORRESPONDENCE WITH P. JAYNE BOPP, JUNE 2002.

[6] ORAL HISTORY WITH MELODY, CONDUCTED BY AUTHOR IN JANUARY 1996.

[7] ORAL HISTORY WITH PAM, CONDUCTED FOR THIS PROJECT BY ADRIENNE WALNOHA IN JULY 2000.

[8] ORAL HISTORY WITH IRIS, SUBMITTED IN OCTOBER 2000.

[9] INTERVIEW WITH J.T. LEROY, CONDUCTED BY AUTHOR, MAY 2001.

[10] FROM "FIERCE! INFO ABOUT LGBT YOUTH FROM LGBT YOUTH," A FLYER PRODUCED FOR THE ELLA BAKER CENTER (NYC), SPRING 2002.

[11] PERSONAL COMMUNICATION, APRIL 2002.

[12] ST. BLAISE, VIC. TESTIMONY TO THE SAN FRANCISCO TASK FORCE ON PROSTITUTION, 1996.

[13] ORAL HISTORY WITH WILL, CONDUCTED BY AUTHOR, JANUARY 1996.

[14] ORAL HISTORY WITH ROBERTO, CONDUCTED BY AUTHOR, DECEMBER 1995.

[15] ORAL HISTORY WITH CHRIS, CONDUCTED BY AUTHOR, JANUARY 1996.

[16] ORAL HISTORY WITH SHORTY, CONDUCTED BY AUTHOR, OCTOBER 2001.

[17] IN A REVIEW OF JOHN PRESTON'S *HUSTLING: A GENTLEMAN'S GUIDE TO THE FINE ART OF HOMOSEXUAL PROSTITUTION*, G. CAJETAN LUNA WRITES: "THE REASONS YOUTH BEGIN AND/OR CONTINUE IN SEX WORK MUST BE DISENTANGLED FROM THE REASONS WHICH ADULTS GIVE FOR INVOLVEMENT. THE SITUATION OF ADOLESCENTS ENGAGED IN SEX WORK SHOULD NOT BE CONFUSED WITH ADULTS WHO ARE OFTEN IN BETTER POSITIONS TO EXERCISE CHOICE." *CASH NEWSLETTER*, VOL. 1, NO. 4 (AUGUST 1994); P. 11.

[18] LUNA, FROM "WORKING THE JOHN/SERVICING THE CLIENT: RESEARCH AND OUTREACH ON THE 'DEMAND SIDE' OF MALE SEX WORK." *CASH NEWSLETTER*, VOL. 1, NO. 1 (MARCH 1994); P. 9.

APPENDIX 1

AVERAGE STREET PRICES
AND BROTHEL RATES IN
VARIOUS CITIES BY YEAR

Base and Adjusted Street Prices, Various American Cities: 1921-2000

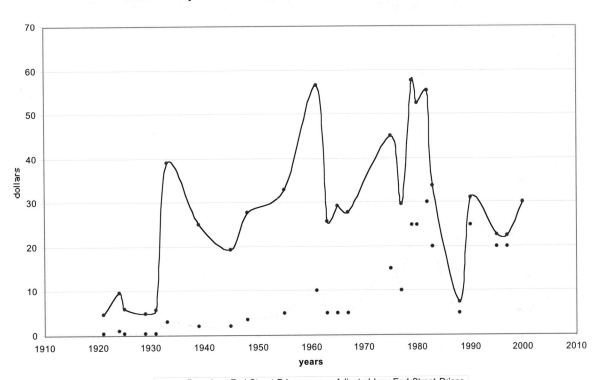

Base Low-End Street Prices ——Adjusted Low-End Street Prices

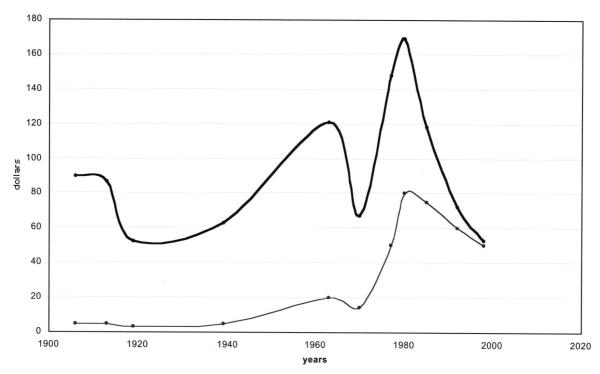

Low-End Brothel Wages, 1906-2000, Various Cities

APPENDIX 2

LOW-END STREET PRICES
AND BROTHEL RATES,
1906-2000, BY CITY

	Base Price ($)	Adjusted for Inflation ($)
1921, Ogden (Utah). Andersen.	0.5	4.81
1924, Omaha (Nebraska). Miller.	1	9.76
1925, San Francisco. SF Chronicle.	0.5	5.97
1929, Los Angeles. Waugh/Wade.	0.5	4.96
1931, NYC. Committee of Fourteen.	0.5	5.67
1933, Texas. Strait.	3	39.2
1939, NYC. Painter.	2	25.17
1945, NYC. Painter.	2	19.31
1948, NYC. Salute.	3.5	27.87
1955, Boise. Newsweek.	5	32.9
1961, Los Angeles. Rechy.	10	56.63
1963, Pittsburgh. Gary Black.	5	25.74
1965, San Francisco. Call.	5	29.25
1967, San Francisco. Vanguard.	5	27.72
1975, Houston. Lloyd.	15	45
1977, Chicago. Nicosia and Raff.	10	29.56
1979, Louisville. Senate Committee Report.	25	57.73
1980, Seattle. Boyer.	25	52.46
1982, San Francisco (Polk Street). URSA.	30	55.39
1983, Minneapolis. Twin Cities Reader, 9/7/83.	20	33.69
1988, NYC. McNamara.	5	7.38
1990, Pittsburgh. Shawn D.	25	31.1
1995, Minneapolis. Field notes.	20	22.68
1997, San Francisco. Read.	20	22.47
2000, NYC. Kristen A.	30	30

Average low-end **street rate**, adjusted for inflation: **$28.10.**
(Using the Cost-of-Living calculator on www.newsengin.com).

1906, Pittsburgh. Harrington.	5	90
1913, Philadelphia. Philadelphia Vice Commission.	5	86.52
1919, Newport. Murphy.	3	52.46
1939, NYC. Painter.	5	62.93
1963, San Francisco. Benjamin.	20	120.94
1970, San Francisco. Dial-a-Model.	14	66.92
1977, Chicago. Nicosia and Raff.	50	147.79
1980, Chicago. Graczkowski.	80	169.15
1985, Milwaukee. Graczkowski.	75	118.19
1992, Philadelphia.	60	72.24
1998, Los Angeles. Adams.	50	52.87

Average low-end **brothel rate** (amount given to the worker): **$94.55.**
(Adjusted for inflation using Cost-of-Living calculator on www.newsengin.com.)

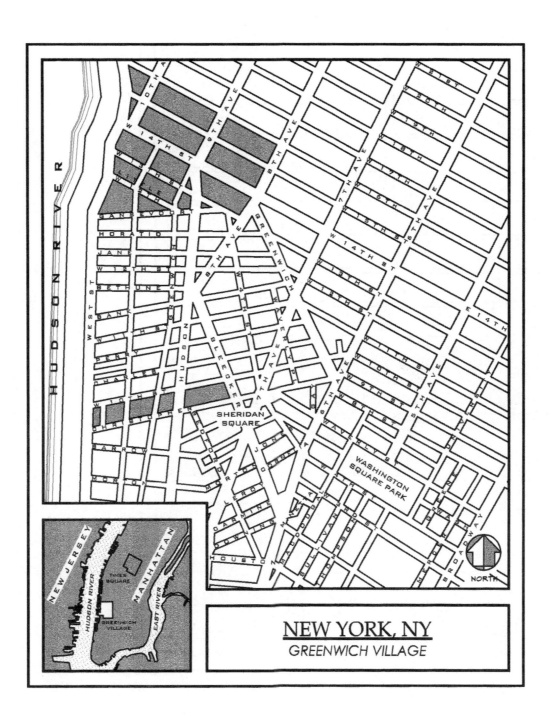

NEW YORK, NY
GREENWICH VILLAGE

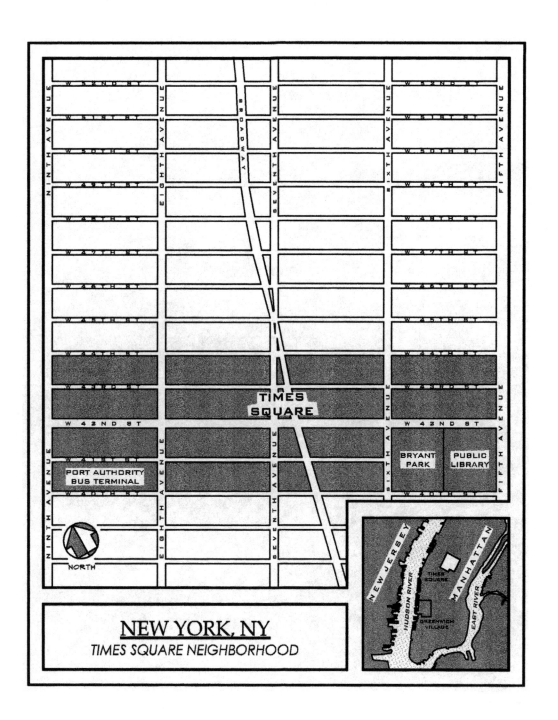

NEW YORK, NY
TIMES SQUARE NEIGHBORHOOD

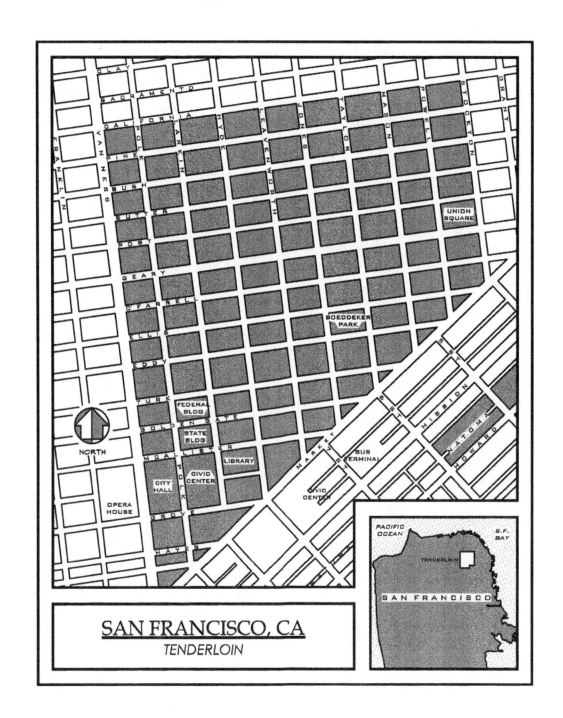

SAN FRANCISCO, CA

TENDERLOIN

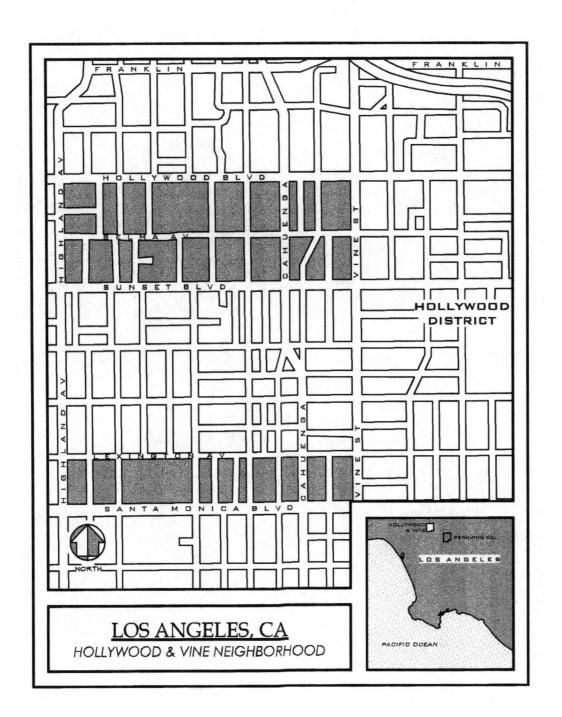

LOS ANGELES, CA
HOLLYWOOD & VINE NEIGHBORHOOD

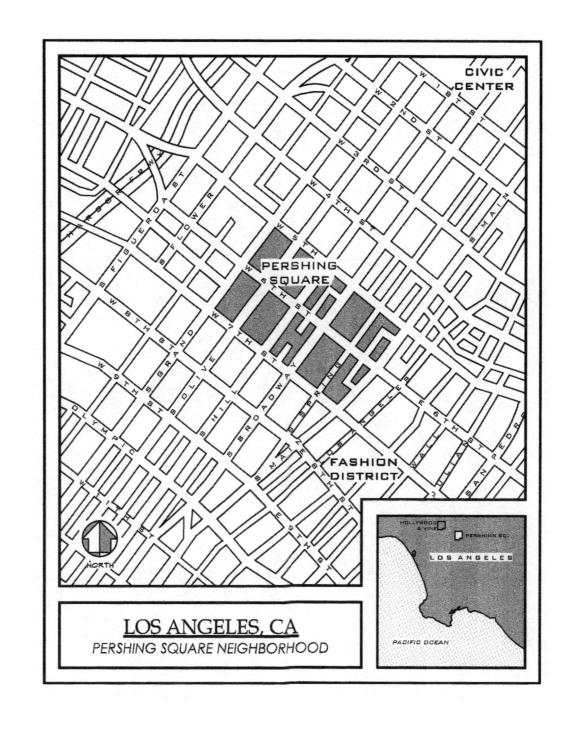

LOS ANGELES, CA
PERSHING SQUARE NEIGHBORHOOD

The author has made every reasonable effort to research the provenance of the images reproduced in *Strapped for Cash* and to secure permission for their use. The author and publisher will include any additional information, as it becomes available, in subsequent editions of this book.

Chapter One

1.1 "The Man Monster—Peter Sewally, Alias Mary Jones," Collection of the New-York Historical Society, negative #40697.

Chapter Two

2.1 "Powder Monkey," courtesy of the Library of Congress.

2.2 "Jennie June," reprinted from *The Autobiography of Jennie June*.

2.3 "Loop-the-loop," reprinted from *The American Journal of Sexology and Urology*, 1919.

2.4 "For Your Boy," YMCA Committee of Public Information, Division of Pictorial Publicity, ca. 1918.

2.5 "Newsboys," courtesy of the Library of Congress.

2.6 Paul Cadmus, *The Fleet's In!*, 1934; oil on canvas, 30 x 60 inches; from the collection of the Navy Museum, Washington, D.C.

2.7 Paul Cadmus, *Shore Leave*, 1935; etching, original edition of 50, 10 3/8 x 11 1/2 inches; courtesy of the DC Moore Gallery, NYC.

2.8 Paul Cadmus, *YMCA Locker Room*, 1934; etching, original edition of 50, 6 1/2 x 12 5/8 inches; courtesy of the DC Moore Gallery, NYC.

Chapter Three

3.1 "Salute Boys," *Salute* magazine, March 1948.

Chapter Four

4.1 "Seated Nude Man," from the Thomas Painter Papers, reproduced by permission of the Kinsey Institute for Research in Sex, Gender, and Reproduction.

Chapter Five

5.1 "Hector, Victor, Bobby," from the Painter Papers, reproduced by permission of the Kinsey Institute for Research in Sex, Gender, and Reproduction.

5.2 "42nd Street and Seventh Avenue, NW Corner" and "Diamond Jim's," from the Painter Papers, reproduced by permission of the Kinsey Institute for Research in Sex, Gender, and Reproduction.

5.3 "Around the Corner From Vaseline Alley" and "42nd Street and Eighth Avenue," from the Painter Papers, reproduced by permission of the Kinsey Institute for Research in Sex, Gender, and Reproduction.

5.4 "Dave 'Gyps'—A Tattooed Wonder," from the Painter Papers, reproduced by permission of the Kinsey Institute for Research in Sex, Gender, and Reproduction.

5.5 Gang kid, provenance unknown.

5.6 Image KI-DC:69238 from the Documentary Collection of the Kinsey Institute for Research in Sex, Gender, and Reproduction. Reproduced by permission.

5.7 El Rosa Hotel, courtesy of Kate Friedman.

5.8 Dial-A-Model catalogue cover, courtesy of the Gay, Lesbian, Bisexual, and Transgender Historical Society of Northern California.

Chapter Six

6.1 Image KI-VG:43 from the Von Gloeden Collection, the Kinsey Institute for Research in Sex, Gender, and Reproduction.

6.2 F. Holland Day, *Saint Sebastian,* courtesy of the Library of Congress.

6.3 Man in suit, provenance unknown.

6.4 Image from *Mr. Sun* flyer, ca. 1964.

6.5 Image KI-DC:66251 from the Documentary Collection of the Kinsey Institute for Research in Sex, Gender, and Reproduction.

6.6 "Kentucky as a Farm Boy," from the Painter Papers, reproduced by permission of the Kinsey Institute for Research in Sex, Gender, and Reproduction.

6.7 "Foto 11-17," from the Painter Papers, reproduced by permission of the Kinsey Institute for Research in Sex, Gender, and Reproduction.

6.8 "Standing Nude Man," from the Painter Papers, reproduced by permission of the Kinsey Institute for Research in Sex, Gender, and Reproduction.

6.9 "Jerry Richards," courtesy of the Athletic Model Guild and the Canadian Lesbian and Gay Archives.

6.10 "Richard Harrison," courtesy of the Athletic Model Guild and the Canadian Lesbian and Gay Archives.

6.11 "Paul Ferguson," courtesy of the Athletic Model Guild and the Canadian Lesbian and Gay Archives.

6.12 "Joe D.," courtesy of the Athletic Model Guild and the Canadian Lesbian and Gay Archives.

6.13 "Ray and Chuck," from the *Grecian Guild Studio Quarterly,* Fall 1965 (#15). Reproduced courtesy of the Kinsey Institute for Research in Sex, Gender, and Reproduction.

6.14 "Raol Cobar," from the *Grecian Guild Studio Quarterly,* Fall 1966 (#19). Reproduced courtesy of the Kinsey Institute for Research in Sex, Gender, and Reproduction.

6.15 "Terry, Junior, and Armando" from *Chico,* Vol. 1, No. 1 (ca. 1967), DOM Publishing, courtesy of the Canadian Lesbian and Gay Archives.

6.16 Peter Glawson from *The Genesis Children* flyer, ca. 1975.

6.17 Image KI-DC:69014 from the Documentary Collection of the Kinsey Institute for Research in Sex, Gender, and Reproduction.

6.18 Image KI-DC:69645 from the Documentary Collection of the Kinsey Institute for Research in Sex, Gender, and Reproduction.

6.19 Image KI-VG:258 from the Von Gloeden Collection, the Kinsey Institute for Research in Sex, Gender, and Reproduction.

6.20 Transsexual in panties, provenance unknown.

6.21 Image KI-DC:69104 from the Documentary Collection of the Kinsey Institute for Research in Sex, Gender, and Reproduction.

6.22 "Male Transsexual," reprinted from Harry Benjamin's *The Transsexual Phenomenon*; Julian Press (NYC), 1966.

6.23 "Dino," from *Photographer's Choice, Portfolio 2,* ca. 1969.

6.24 "Sal Rocco," from *The Silent Men,* Issue 1, Times Square Studio (NYC), ca. 1968.

6.25 "Cowboy," from *The Silent Men,* Issue 1, Times Square Studio (NYC), ca. 1968.

6.26 "Lou," from *The Silent Men,* Issue 1, Times Square Studio (NYC), ca. 1968.

6.27 "Why Boys Hustle," from *Mutual Masturbation,* Trojan Book Service, ca. 1971.

6.28 BDR image, provenance unknown.

6.29 "Cosmo," from *Like, One: A Pictorial Study of the Male Teenager From the Private Collections of Amateur Photographers,* Guild Press (Washington, D.C.), ca. 1968.

6.30 "Todd" (1975), courtesy of Amos Badertscher and the Degen-Scharfman Gallery, NYC.

6.30a "Sandy" (1975), courtesy of Amos Badertscher and the Degen-Scharfman Gallery, NYC.

6.31 "Man With Unbuttoned Shirt," from the Painter Papers, reproduced by permission of the Kinsey Institute for Research in Sex, Gender, and Reproduction.

6.32 "Chuck With Basket," courtesy of Larry Clark and Luhring Augustine, NYC.

6.33 "42 Boy," courtesy of Larry Clark and Luhring Augustine, NYC.

6.34 "Cocaine," courtesy of the Athletic Model Guild.

Chapter Seven

7.1 "D.W. Nichols Cover-boy," from *Toward a Perspective for Boy-Lovers,* Editorial Creative Products, 1977.

Chapter Nine

9.1 Promotional flyers reproduced courtesy of NYPAEC, WHISPER, and the Canadian Lesbian and Gay Archives.

INDEX